# Twisted Cross

The
University
of North
Carolina
Press
Chapel Hill
and
London

DORIS L. BERGEN

The German Christian Movement in the Third Reich

Twisted

**CROSS**

*Frontispiece*:
Photomontage by
John Heartfield, Berlin,
June 1933. From the
*Arbeiter-Illustrierten Zeitung*,
no. 23. Heartfield, a communist,
attacked the fusion of Nazism
and Christianity. The caption
above the image reads: "On the
Founding of the German State
Church: The Catholic Adolf
Hitler organizes the Protestant
German state church and names
a Reich bishop." In heavy print
below: "The Cross Was Not Yet
Heavy Enough." Facing the
cross is Ludwig Müller.
(Copyright Gertrud Heartfield,
Berlin)

Manufactured in the United States of America
The paper in this book meets the guidelines for
permanence and durability of the Committee on
Production Guidelines for Book Longevity of the
Council on Library Resources.
Library of Congress Cataloging-in-Publication Data
Bergen, Doris L.
Twisted cross : the German Christian movement in the
Third Reich /
by Doris L. Bergen.
p. cm.
Includes bibliographical references and index.
ISBN 0-8078-2253-1 (alk. paper). —
ISBN 0-8078-4560-4 (pbk. : alk. paper)
1. German Christian movement—History.
2. Germany—Church history—1933–1945. I. Title.
BR856.B398   1996
261.7′0943′09043—dc20      95-17954
                          CIP

00  99  98  97       5  4  3  2

TO MY FAMILY

Contents

# Illustrations

# Preface

Why write a book about the "German Christians" (Deutsche Christen), a group of pro-Nazi Protestants in the Third Reich? While working in the Community Archive in Minden, I came across some correspondence that led me to contemplate my motives. In 1960, two former adherents of the German Christian cause exchanged letters. How, they asked each other, could they promote new approaches to the history of the church under National Socialism? Despite the neutral language, their intentions were clear: they wanted someone to write a positive account that would help rehabilitate their movement. A doctoral student might assume the task, one of the men suggested. His friend was dubious. A student might be found, he responded, but who would supervise such a work? Those letters were written the year I was born, and both men have since died. In a sense, the line of inquiry that brought me to this study was the opposite of theirs. To me, the German Christian movement embodies a moral and spiritual dilemma I associate with my own religious questions: What is the value of religion, and in particular of Christianity, if it provides no defense against brutality and can even become a willing participant in genocide?

Perhaps my background in a family of ethnic German Mennonites from Ukraine has made me sensitive to and wary of certain connections between religious and ethnic identities. In my initial reading about Protestants in Nazi Germany, I was struck by what seemed contorted efforts to fuse Christianity with Germanness and purge it of Jewish influence. I wanted to explore how members of the German Christian movement synthesized Christianity and National Socialism, two systems of belief most people would regard as fundamentally irreconcilable. This book is the result.

Many people shared in this project at every stage. It is a great pleasure to thank at least some of those whose financial backing, guidance, and encouragement made its completion possible. A fellowship from the Social Sciences and Humanities Research Council of Canada and a Sir James Lougheed Award from the Alberta Heritage Foundation allowed me to conduct extensive research in Germany in 1988–89. Additional funding from the German Academic Exchange Service and the University of Vermont's Committee on Research and Scholarship enabled subsequent shorter research trips.

Staff at the many archives I visited in Germany were consistently helpful and accommodating. Encounters with archivists Bernd Hey in Bielefeld, Dietrich Meyer in Düsseldorf, Helmut Baier in Nuremberg, and Walter Fleischmann-Bisten in Bensheim helped keep my work on track. Professor Kurt Meier of Leipzig met with me and offered useful suggestions. Head archivist Hans-Eberhard Brandhorst in Minden kindly allowed access to the uncataloged collection of the Kirchengeschichtliche Arbeitsgemeinschaft (Working Group for Church History) there. Eberhard Bethge encouraged me and granted permission to use the Bonhoeffer papers; Herta Staedel and Annie Hauer allowed me to consult the papers of their late husbands. Retired pastor Herward Reiser in Augsburg put me in touch with Mrs. Staedel and offered his own insights. Professor Rudolf Fischer of the University of Bielefeld generously shared his collection of pamphlets and clippings from the National Socialist period, and Marlies Ostendorf and Dietrich Becker provided hospitality, ideas, and contacts. Conversations with Victoria Barnett and Anja Baumhof in Bielefeld and Nina Lübbren in Berlin helped clarify some key ideas.

Mentors, colleagues, and friends in Canada, the United States, and Germany have been enormously helpful. Annelise Thimme has inspired me since she supervised my master's thesis at the University of Alberta. Gerhard L. Weinberg of the University of North Carolina at Chapel Hill remains an unparalleled source of frank, insightful guidance. Daniel S. Mattern, Michaela Hönicke, and Cindy Hahamovitch read drafts and offered incisive suggestions. Boris Ruge sent me a copy of the John Heartfield photomontage. John S. Conway of the University of British Columbia and Rainer Hering at the Staatsarchiv in Hamburg provided stimulating and thoughtful criticisms of earlier versions of the work. Colleagues at the University of Vermont, in particular Patrick Hutton, James Overfield, and David Scrase, have given me advice, encouragement, and much more than simply a place to do my work. Lewis Bateman at the University of North Carolina Press has been unfailingly supportive. Two readers for the press made detailed, helpful comments that improved the work significantly. As managing editor and copyeditor, Ron Maner and Trudie Calvert have been wonderful. My friends Glenn Sharfman and Susannah Heschel listened to my ideas and generously shared their views and expertise; Linda H. Pardo helped me motivate and organize myself. And Arthur Kuflik brought his unerring judgment and ethical sense to the project at some critical junctures. I am deeply grateful to all these and many other people. Of course, any shortcomings and mistakes remain my own responsibility.

CHAPTER 1

One Reich, One People,
One Church!
The German Christians

*Those who claim to be building the church are, without a*
*doubt, already at work on its destruction; unintentionally*
*and unknowingly, they will construct a temple to idols.*
*—Dietrich Bonhoeffer*

National Socialism, the theologian Dietrich Bonhoeffer once remarked, "brought an end to the church in Germany."[1] For Bonhoeffer, one
of the few Protestant clergymen who took an active role in plans to over-
throw the Nazi regime, National Socialist ideology and Christianity were
profoundly incompatible. Most Christians in Germany did not share Bonhoeffer's conviction about the fundamental opposition between those two
worldviews, but hard-core Nazi leaders did. Martin Bormann and Heinrich
Himmler, as well as Adolf Hitler himself, considered Nazism and Christianity irreconcilable antagonists.

This book is about a group of people who disagreed with both Bonhoeffer and Hitler. Adherents of the German Christian movement (*Glaubensbewegung "Deutsche Christen"*), most of them Protestant lay people
and clergy, regarded the Nazi revolution that began in 1933 as a golden
opportunity for Christianity. National Socialism and Christianity, the German Christian movement preached, were not only reconcilable but mutually reinforcing. Along with other Protestants, members of the group expected the National Socialist regime to inspire spiritual awakening and

bring the church to what they considered its rightful place at the heart of German society and culture.

Certainly the German Christians, as adherents of the movement called themselves in the 1930s and 1940s, were not unique in their willingness to combine Christianity with other beliefs and traditions. The history of Christianity could be seen as a series of such accommodations and mergers, involving groups as divergent as the Roman imperial elites and the indigenous peoples of the Americas. But the Nazis' unconcealed, murderous schemes and antagonism toward Christianity might make the attempt to fuse Christian tradition with National Socialism the most improbable combination of all, producing a refiguration barely recognizable as Christian. Advocates of the cause called that outcome German Christianity.

Given the logical and theological contradictions that made up the German Christian movement, it is easy to conclude that it had little influence. Indeed, much of the standard literature on the churches in the Third Reich discounts the German Christians as marginal, soaring to prominence for a brief moment in the wake of Nazi ascension in 1933 but fizzling into obscurity within months.[2] The evidence, however, tells a different story. Despite their precarious location between the disapproval of some fellow Protestants on the one hand and the annoyance of the Nazi leadership on the other, the German Christians maintained a significant presence throughout the years of National Socialist rule. For more than a decade, they sustained a mass movement of over half a million members with branches in all parts of Germany. Adherents held important positions within Protestant church governments at every level and occupied influential posts in theological faculties and religious training institutes. From those offices, they controlled many of the decisions and much of the revenue of the Protestant church. The movement's quest to fuse Christianity and National Socialism reflected the desire of many Germans to retain their religious traditions while supporting the Nazi fatherland. Throughout the 1930s and during the war years, German Christian women and men held rallies, attended church services, and published newspapers, books, and tracts. They sang hymns to Jesus but also to Hitler. They denounced their rivals as disloyal and un-German; they fought for control of local church facilities. Through sermons, speeches, and songs they propagated anti-Jewish Christianity and boosted Nazi racial policy. After the Third Reich collapsed in 1945, instead of being ostracized in their congregations and shut out of ecclesiastical posts, German Christians, lay and clergy, found it relatively easy to reintegrate into Protestant church life.

What beliefs bound the German Christian movement together? How did adherents act out their synthesis of Nazism and Christianity and deal with the glaring contradictions within it? This book explores those questions and offers answers that challenge some standard interpretations. Many scholars dismiss the German Christian movement as merely a Nazi creation. But the German Christians built on theological as well as political foundations, drawing on a legacy of Christian antisemitism and a proclivity to disregard Scripture. Moreover, their fawning enthusiasm for National Socialism notwithstanding, the German Christians did not find themselves consistently within Nazi good graces. Instead, Nazi leaders frequently denounced the movement and resented its attempt to complete National Socialism by combining it with Christianity.

It is also tempting to disregard the German Christians as opportunists, interested in transforming Christianity only to curry favor with Nazi authorities. Evidence of opportunism exists, but it alone does not explain the German Christian movement or account for its tenacity. If the German Christians were opportunists, they were not very shrewd ones. Participation in the movement netted none of its adherents substantial rewards from the hands of top Nazis. After the early days of 1933, it could even have adverse effects. Those whose only interest was to gain the favor of the Nazi leadership generally found it more expeditious to ignore or leave the church rather than try to change it from within.

Finally, one might interpret the German Christian movement as a sincere but misguided mission to rescue Christianity from Nazi assault.[3] Many former members took such a stance after the war, arguing that they had wanted only to make Christianity acceptable in National Socialist society. This line of thought might appear to have some credibility in that the German Christians concentrated their energies on the same aspects of Christianity that were most severely attacked by the religion's Nazi denigrators. Nazi and neopagan critics in Germany reviled Christianity for its Jewish roots, doctrinal rigidity, and enervating, womanish qualities. The German Christians, in turn, focused their efforts on proclaiming an anti-Jewish, antidoctrinal, manly Christianity.

But correlation does not equal causation. Often two phenomena that appear linked as cause and effect are in fact both effects of a common cause. This book will suggest that such was the case with German Christianity and National Socialism. The German Christian movement was not just a product of Nazi orders or a response to neopagan charges against Christianity. Rather, parallels between German Christian thought and Nazi criticisms of it reflect the fact that both grew out of German culture of the post–World War I period. Shared ideas and obsessions about religion, race, and gender linked German Christianity and National Socialism and connected both to broader trends in the society.

If the German Christians were not pawns of National Socialism, craven opportunists, or would-be saviors of Christianity, what were they? I will argue that they were above all church people with their own agenda for transforming Christianity. Although twisted and offensive, German Christian teachings reflected a fairly stable set of beliefs built around a specific understanding of the church. The German Christians intended to build a church that would exclude all those deemed impure and embrace all "true Germans" in a spiritual homeland for the Third Reich. Proponents of the cause called that ecclesiological vision the "people's church" (*Volkskirche*), not an assembly of the baptized but an association of "blood" and "race." In the context of Nazi Germany, that goal had radically destructive implications. And the chauvinistic, antisemitic impulses behind it were anything but marginal.

## Definitions and Background

Labels are always tricky, but students of Nazi Germany face particular challenges. To describe National Socialism we depend on the same words and phrases that Nazi propaganda appropriated and infused with particular meanings: words like *race, blood, Aryan, German*, and *Jew*. Often authors resort to quotation marks to distance themselves from overtones and associations that they recognize but do not share. I will limit such use of punctuation while maintaining that this entire discussion belongs in quotation marks. We cannot talk about the world of the German Christians without borrowing their vocabulary. But we can keep in mind that use of those terms does not imply validation of that thought.

The problem of labels crops up as soon as we ask, Who were the German Christians? In this book, the phrase *German Christians* refers only to adherents of the German Christian movement in the 1930s and 1940s, not to any German nationals who professed Christianity. The group's organizers deliberately chose that name to produce confusion, to force anyone else who claimed both Germanness and Christianity to qualify that identity or risk association with their cause. Members of the group thus used their name to enforce the contention that they represented the only authentic fusion of German ethnicity and Christian faith.

Special problems of terminology arise in dealing with the group of people German Christians described either as "non-Aryan Christians," "Jewish Christians," or "baptized Jews." All three terms referred to converts from Judaism to Christianity or the children, and in some cases grand-children, of such converts. None of these labels makes any sense outside the context of a social order based on distinctions of blood. I will use the phrase *non-Aryan Christian* to describe people who, in Nazi Germany, might also have been called Jewish Christians or baptized Jews. The non-Aryan label is humanistically and theologically nonsensical, but histor-ically it is precise enough to be useful because it reflects a category defined by Nazi law with very real consequences for those who fell within it.

Finally, my use of the word *Protestant* requires clarification. In Ger-man, *evangelisch* is a general label that includes the Lutheran, Reformed, and united churches. Because the English *evangelical* has very different connotations from the German *evangelisch*, I have translated *evangelisch* in its broad usage as Protestant.[4]

Three main impulses converged to produce the German Christian move-ment in the early 1930s. Since the late 1920s, two energetic young pastors in Thuringia, Siegfried Leffler and Julius Leutheuser, had been preaching religious renewal along nationalist, *völkisch* lines.[5] Both members of the Nazi party, they called themselves and their followers German Christians. In the summer of 1932, a second group, consisting of politicians, pastors, and lay people, met in Berlin to discuss how to capture the energies of Germany's Protestant churches for the National Socialist cause. Wilhelm Kube, Gauleiter of Brandenburg and chairman of the National Socialist group in the Prussian Landtag, initiated this effort. Kube's circle planned to call themselves the Protestant National Socialists, but according to insiders' accounts, Hitler vetoed that label and suggested "German Chris-tians" instead.[6] Followers of Leffler and Leutheuser claimed he had pro-posed that name to them three years earlier.[7] Despite such rivalries, the Thuringian and Berlin groups soon began to cooperate.

A third set of developments fed into the German Christian movement as well. In the 1920s numerous Protestant associations has arisen, dedi-cated to reviving church life through increased emphasis on German cul-ture and ethnicity. Some of those groups merged with the German Chris-tians; others remained separate but lost members to the new movement or cooperated with it on specific projects.[8] That the German Christians did not break away from the established Protestant church eased such interchange.

In July 1933 Protestant church elections across Germany filled a range of positions from parish representatives to senior consistory councillors.[9] Representatives of the German Christian movement won two-thirds of the votes cast. Hitler himself had urged election of German Christians,

*Campaigning for the church elections, July 1933, in front of a Berlin church. On the left, the German Christian representative with his sign: "Vote for the German Christian List!" On the right, his opponent from the Gospel and Church group with the placard: "Church Must Remain Church! Vote for the List: Gospel and Church." The elections were a triumph for the German Christian movement. (Landesbildstelle, Berlin)*

who, he claimed in a radio address, represented the "new" in the church.[10] Affirmed by the biggest voter turnout ever in a Protestant church election and soon ensconced in the bishops' seats of all but three of Germany's Protestant regional churches, in mid-1933 the movement seemed unstoppable.

For the next twelve years, despite endemic factionalism, vociferous opposition at home and abroad, and an ambivalent reception from the National Socialist state, the self-styled "storm troopers of Christ" continued to seek a synthesis of Nazi ideology and Protestant tradition and to agitate for a people's church based on blood. The German Christians represented a cross section of society from every region of the country: women and men, old people and young, pastors, teachers, dentists, railroad workers, housewives, and farmers, even some Catholics. Some occupied powerful positions in the church hierarchy though most were lay members. A few, like Gauleiter Kube, later generalkommissar in White Ruthenia, were prominent in Nazi affairs. Others agitated against certain manifestations of Nazism; Professor Heinrich Odenwald from Heidelberg, for example, was banned from public appearances in 1934 after calling the church to battle against National Socialist excesses.[11] All supported National Socialism in some form, however, and many belonged to the Nazi party.

Fragmentation within the movement and the lack of full membership files make it impossible to gauge exact numbers of German Christians at any given time. Adherents of the movement, their opponents in the church, and Nazi authorities generally accepted the figure of six hundred thousand as a reasonable estimate of the group's numerical strength in the mid-1930s, arguably its weakest phase.[12] Despite their diversity, those more than half a million German Christians demonstrated allegiance to a common cause. They endorsed Nazi ideology. They favored German Christian domination of institutionalized Protestantism. Above all, they stood for a people's church as a community of race and blood. Other Protestants might share these traits, but their conjunction and institutionalization created the German Christian movement.

The German Christians were not unified organizationally throughout much of the Third Reich. Internal disputes produced a bewildering array of splinter groups that divided and coalesced in countless constellations. Nevertheless, various authorities treated German Christianity as a recognizable whole. Reports from the SS and its Security Service used the general label "Deutsche Christen" to encompass the movement's various strands.[13] The denazification questionnaire devised by the U.S. Forces of Occupation in Germany in 1945 listed German Christians as a single organization.[14] I too focus on the movement as a whole, emphasizing the shared identity that led people to describe themselves as German Christians, regardless of the subgroups to which they belonged at various times.

How much influence did the approximately six hundred thousand German Christians exercise? The question is difficult to answer with precision. Yet the group's tremendous impact is evident. Not only did German Christians dominate Protestant church governments from the Rhine to East Prussia, they also seized the initiative in religious affairs. They unleashed the "church struggle" in 1933, the battle between Protestant factions for control of church authority, and they pushed through the reorganization of German Protestantism under a Reich bishop, ending centuries of decentralized development in an effort to implement an ecclesiastical *Führerprinzip*. Many local pastors remained opposed to the movement, but none could refuse to address its charge that the church risked oblivion if it turned its back on the Nazi revolution. By the mid-1930s, German Christians controlled a network of women's groups and dominated most university faculties of theology; during World War II, they infiltrated the military chaplaincy. The "Protestant Soldier's Songbook," distributed by the millions to members of the *Wehrmacht*, even followed the German Christian lead in purging "Jewish elements" from church music.[15]

German Christian influence involved more than institutional domination. In fact, the movement was most significant in the intangible sphere of ideas. The German Christian vision of the church as the spiritual homeland of the racially pure "Volk" found resonance far beyond the circle of members. The movement's quest for a soldierly, hard Christianity reflected the ideals of many fellow Germans. And efforts to free Christianity from the confines of doctrine and Scripture gave voice to the yearning of many Germans for the comfort of familiar religious ritual and custom without the demands of ethical standards. For these reasons, the German Christian movement constituted much more than a marginalized minority. In significant ways, the strident extremism of the German Christians amplified and echoed tendencies in German society as a whole.

## The Centrality of Religion and the People's Church

The German Christians remind us of an often overlooked point: the centrality of religion in National Socialist society. Scholars such as James M. Rhodes and Robert A. Pois have analyzed Nazism itself as a religion;[16] others such as Richard L. Rubenstein have pointed to the intimate connections between National Socialism and Christianity. "The culture that made the death camps possible," Rubenstein insists, "was not only indigenous to the West but was an outcome, albeit unforeseen and unintended, of its fundamental religious traditions."[17] Much more common than either Pois's or Rubenstein's positions, however, are tendencies to present Nazism as a thoroughly secular phenomenon.[18] As the Holocaust scholar Steven T. Katz remarked, "The Jews survived 1,600 years of Christianity. . . . They almost didn't survive four years of World War II. Something different must have happened."[19]

Something different did indeed happen, but it built on and perpetuated existing tendencies in European Christianity. The Christian legacy of hostility toward Judaism and Jews, though not a sufficient cause for Nazi genocide, played a critical role. Christian antisemitism did not motivate the top decision makers, but it helped make their commands comprehensible to the rank and file who carried out measures against Jews as well as those who passively condoned them. In his analysis of German antisemitism before Hitler, Donald Niewyk concludes: "The old antisemitism had created a climate in which the 'new' antisemitism was, at the very least, acceptable to millions of Germans."[20] That insight can be applied to Christian attitudes toward Jews. As Gregory Baum has pointed out, "The Church's teaching of contempt for Jews and Jewish religion did produce a hostile imagination and symbols of negation which in our century helped Nazi policy gain approval by so many in so short a time."[21] When Christians in Germany encountered Jews, their perceptions were shaped by images and associations acquired through formal and informal religious education.[22] Even Nazi law, with all its claims about scientific racism, distinguished between so-called Aryans and Jews on the basis of religion, not biology.

Christianity permeated Nazi society. Nazi iconography is replete with Christian notions of sacrifice and redemption. Even committed National Socialists like the members of the German Christian movement clung fiercely to cultural manifestations of their religious tradition—the celebration of Christmas, favorite hymns, the symbol of the cross. If we take seriously the German Christian phenomenon, we can begin to grasp how even secularized Germans who rarely if ever attended church might imagine the war on the eastern front to be a holy crusade and condemn Jews as the killers of Christ.

Secular approaches to the study of fascism, as Jonathan Steinberg has observed, show the churches at most as reacting, not as acting. The Croatian Ustasa movement, Steinberg argues, defies such comfortable categories with its combination of "Catholic piety, Croatian nationalism, and extreme violence." For the Croats, he concludes, "religion, nation and self merged into an explosive, unstable mixture."[23] Steinberg's observation bears relevance to the German case as well. The history of the German Christian movement serves to remind us that for many Germans religious, national, and personal identities reinforced each other in deadly ways. The "ordinary men" whose transformation into mass killers Christopher Browning describes so powerfully were not just ordinary men or even ordinary Germans: they were also ordinary Christians.[24] Few were pious, many were not observant, and some opted to abandon the Christian churches in favor of neopagan groups. But all of them were born into a predominantly Christian society and participated in its culture. Viewed in this light, German Christian efforts represent an explicit attempt to accomplish what most Germans did implicitly: reconcile their Christian tradition with National Socialist ideology.

The German Christian movement is particularly instructive because it reveals which aspects of Christianity even ardent pro-Nazis held dear. One such element was the church. Indeed, a focus on German Christian ecclesiology reveals significant unity within the group. For all the German Christians, the ideal of the people's church represented the greatest gift they could offer to the Third Reich.

The notion of a people's church was no German Christian invention. Since the Reformation, regional Protestant churches (*Landeskirchen*) in the German territories had constituted themselves as organizations bound to a geographic region, its secular ruler, and its baptized population.[25] From Friedrich Schleiermacher on, German churchmen used the term *Volkskirche* to describe that form of church.[26] Defeat and revolution in 1918 challenged the *Volkskirche*. Abdication of the kaiser and removal of the regional princes who had served as *summi episcopi*—heads of the church—led many Protestants to fear complete separation of church and state.[27] Such anxiety and their own efforts to distance themselves and their church organization from the democratic state led them to define the people's church in new ways, often emphasizing ties to German culture and ethnicity.

The German Christians appropriated the notion of the people's church but gave it a twist by using racial categories to define the *Volk*. For German Christians, race was the fundamental principle of human life, and they interpreted and effected that notion in religious terms. German Christianity emphasized the distinction between the visible and invisible church. For the German Christians, the church on earth was not the fellowship of the holy spirit described in the New Testament[28] but a contrast to it, a vehicle for the expression of race and ethnicity. By stressing that distinction, they could claim allegiance to the ideal of a universal church of all believers in some otherworldly realm, while working to create its polar opposite on earth.

The German Christians believed that God revealed himself to humanity not only in Scripture and through Jesus but in nature and history. Together the German Christian view of race, the visible versus invisible church, and revelation formed a mutually reinforcing system. By separating the earthly church from the universal community of believers, German Christians freed that church from any obligation to universality. By allowing for God's revelation through nature, they could claim race was sanctified, part of a divine plan for human life. Accordingly, they saw establishment of a purely "Aryan" people's church as a God-given task to be completed while the historical, political climate was favorable and before the supposed degeneration of the German race had progressed to the point of no return. None of those ideas was new. What was new was their fusion in a setting that seemed to make their realization a distinct possibility.

The German Christian understanding of the people's church implied both exclusive and inclusive dimensions. German Christians envisaged the people's church as a closed entity. If the church was to be a people's church and the people was defined by blood, then, according to German Christian logic, anyone outside the racial group not only could but must be excluded in the interest of purity. So their rejection of non-Aryan Christians was not simply an awkward compromise to make Christianity palatable to Nazi power but a fundamental part of their vision of the church as the spiritual expression of the racially pure *Volk*.

At the same time, the German Christians maintained, the people's church was to be bound to the state with an organic tie to ethnic and racial Germanness; its membership was to be based on infant baptism, and it would have a claim to totality, a right and a responsibility to address all members of the *Volk*. To effect that inclusivity, German Christians defined the people's church as explicitly antidoctrinal. Considerations of orthodoxy, dogma, or confession, they argued, must not interfere with the spiritual communion of all Germans. Within the people's church itself, the German Christians foresaw a hierarchy based, among other things, on gender. The true people's church would be a "manly church" in which the storm trooper and the soldier felt at home. Yet the movement welcomed and relied on women. German Christians might idealize the people's church as a manly entity, but they by no means desired a church of men only.

## Christianity in Nazi Germany

For the German Christians, the Protestant church was a battleground. Through their bid to control and revamp it, they unleashed what came to be known as the "church struggle" (*Kirchenkampf*). The origin of that term, which "suddenly appeared" in the summer of 1933, is uncertain.[29] Yet it has shaped discussion of Protestantism in Nazi Germany.[30] Like many powerful labels, its meaning is contested. Some accounts use it to imply head-on confrontation between National Socialism and German Protestantism. That usage, however, is misleading. In his 1959 book, the Erlangen theologian Friedrich Baumgärtel dubbed notions of an all-out conflict between Christianity and National Socialism the "myths of the church struggle" (*Kirchenkampf-Legenden*).[31] In his 1968 study, John S. Conway cautioned against "hagiographical" accounts of the church struggle that demonstrate Protestant resistance, even if it means "suppressing certain facts."[32] Rather than dividing along clearly political lines, Protestants were confused in 1933. Church people struggled to comprehend the significance of National Socialism for their faith and hesitated to respond to its encroachment into church life. The so-called church struggle was less an expression of political opposition to Nazism than a competition for control within the Protestant church.

In addition to profound theological issues, the struggle for mastery of Germany's Protestant church raised practical concerns. The Protestant church received tax revenue collected for it by the state from every baptized member. It trained its clergy in faculties of theology at public universities and exercised the right to offer religious instruction in schools. Hence each taxation region could recognize only one legitimate Protestant church organization.

The German Christians' main rival in the church struggle was the Confessing Church (*Bekennende Kirche*), a network of Protestants loosely organized under the slogan "church must remain church." Many commentators equate the Confessing Church with Protestant resistance to Nazism. It did count among its members the theologian Dietrich Bonhoeffer, executed for his connection to the assassination plot against Hitler on 20 July 1944.[33] More numerous in its ranks than resistance figures, however, were professed apoliticals, supporters of the National Socialist regime, and party members. The Confessing Church rallied less against National Socialism than against German Christian domination of institutionalized Protestantism.

Like the German Christian movement, the Confessing Church never broke completely with the established Protestant church. In that regard,

Confessing "Church" was somewhat of a misnomer. But like the German Christians' name, that label served an important function: it expressed a claim to represent the true church of Christ. German Christians generally refused to grant the legitimacy the name implied and referred to their opponents as the Confessing Front. Both sides insisted they were the real Protestant church; they coexisted uneasily within the confines of state-recognized institutions.

The Confessing Church did assert independence from the official Protestant church in some important ways. It held its own national synods in 1934, 1935, and 1936 and set up a provisional church leadership (*vorläufige Kirchenleitung*) in Prussia. Eventually it trained some of its own clergy in illegal seminaries. Many of those clergymen were influenced by the Reformed theologian Karl Barth, who emphasized scriptural authority and God as the "wholly other."[34] They and their lay supporters stressed loyalty to the confessions of faith.

But the lines of battle in the church struggle were more fluid than a simple polarization of resistance versus collaboration. Most Protestant clergy and lay people remained neutral in the conflict between German Christians and the Confessing Church, although as Robert P. Ericksen has shown, neutrality often implied sympathy for German Christian views.[35] Even the space between the fronts was not always unbridgeable. Some German Christians later joined the Confessing Church; other people moved in the opposite direction.

A striking example of such mobility appears in the case of Wilhelm Niemöller, a pastor in Bielefeld, and his colleague in the same city, Friedrich Buschtöns. Early 1933 found Niemöller, a member of the Nazi party since the 1920s, among the ranks of German Christian sympathizers. In July, he informed his parishioners, "As to my position regarding the 'German Christians,' I am a member of the movement and will remain so." He went on to specify, however, that the destructive church politics of the movement's leadership made it impossible for him to acknowledge its authority.[36] By the end of the summer, Niemöller had broken with the German Christians. Alongside his brother Martin, he assumed a leading role in the Confessing Church, serving as its primary chronicler and an important spokesman, not only during the 1930s and 1940s but for decades after the war as well.[37] Buschtöns took the opposite path. A fiercely independent and outspoken individual, he moved from initial opposition to the German Christians to become an influential figure in the movement. Like Niemöller, his engagement in the cause extended past Bielefeld and beyond the Nazi years. In the late 1940s and 1950s, Buschtöns tried to reestablish ties among former German Christians; he became an active member of the revisionist Kirchengeschichtliche Arbeitsgemeinschaft (Working Group for Church History) in Minden.[38]

Antagonism was intense, division bitter, but as Dietrich Bonhoeffer pointed out in 1934, the factions in the church struggle did not correspond neatly to political categories. "Dreamers and the naive like [Martin] Niemöller still believe they are the true National Socialists," Bonhoeffer wrote, "and maybe it is kindly Providence that preserves them in this illusion." In his view, however, "the lines of battle are drawn in an altogether different place." He would continue to work with all his strength in the church struggle, Bonhoeffer pledged, but it was clear to him that such opposition was "only a temporary phase on the way to a completely different kind of resistance." Equally clear, he continued, was that "only a very few of the men of this preliminary skirmish will be involved in that second battle."[39]

The German Christians also faced opposition from neopagan groups. The 1920s and 1930s spawned many such associations in Germany, from that around the World War I hero Erich Ludendorff and his wife, Mathilde, to the "spiritualistic Christian" Artur Dinter, and the German Faith Movement (Deutsche Glaubensbewegung).[40] The latter, until 1936 under the leadership of the Tübingen professor Jakob Wilhelm Hauer, posed a special threat. Hauer, trained as a Protestant pastor, had spent time in India with the Basel Mission. His efforts to create a new German faith alongside the Protestant and Catholic confessions blended biological-racial notions with images and symbols from Nordic and Indian traditions and texts.[41]

The German Faith Movement never rivaled the German Christians in size. In 1937, a representative reported to the Ministry of Church Affairs that the group included "40,000 full members who have left the church, and about another 30,000 sympathizers who have not yet done so."[42] Nevertheless, it maintained the largest and most active membership of any of the neopagan groups throughout the Nazi period, and its beliefs were closer to those of Hitler and his inner circle than were German Christian ideas. Moreover, the organization's name—the German Faith Movement (Deutsche Glaubensbewegung)—was so similar to that used by German Christians throughout 1933—German Christian Faith Movement (Glaubensbewegung Deutsche Christen)—that people frequently confused the two organizations, often blaming the German Christians for their enemy's excesses.[43] In this way, German Christians reaped the disadvantages of having chosen a name that laid claim to a broad range of loyalties.

## Stages of German Christianity

This book is organized along thematic lines. The goal is to present the major ideas and consequences of the German Christian movement rather than to detail the group's organizational evolution. Kurt Meier did some of that work more than thirty years ago; German church historians who focus on local and regional developments continue to fill in the picture.[44] My own study links national and local developments by bringing the voices of prominent German Christians together with other participants who might be considered obscure. Such "marginal" figures are key to understanding German Christian influence. The movement had a national profile and spread its views via widely circulated newspapers and well-known theologians, yet its persistence depended on local bases of support. Protestant church members in a Westphalian village may never have attended one of the movement's mass rallies or read its publications, but they may have listened to German Christian ideas from the mouth of their pastor every Sunday.

In order to capture local German Christian voices, I use sources from isolated congregations and unknown individuals as well as more widely disseminated materials. Because German law protects the privacy of individuals, I have not identified most German Christians discussed in this book. Only published authors and well-known figures appear by name.

Whether local or national, German Christian developments took place in the context of broader political and ecclesiastical changes. The conjunction of external pressures and internal dynamics produced five distinct stages of German Christian history between 1932 and 1945: ascendancy, fragmentation, regrouping, ambiguous success, and postwar reintegration.

Ascendancy characterizes the movement's trajectory from its inception in 1932 to the Sports Palace affair in November 1933.[45] During that time, German Christians enjoyed open support from Nazi party and state organs. In the summer of 1933, they dominated the process that unified Germany's twenty-nine regional Protestant churches into the Protestant Reich church; they imposed one of their own, former naval chaplain Ludwig Müller, as Germany's first and last Protestant Reich bishop. German Christians gained control of ecclesiastical government in all but three regions—Bavaria, Hanover, and Württemberg. They rode the crest of a wave of religious-nationalist fervor that saw mass church weddings uniting storm troopers and SS-men with their brides and celebrated the opening of the new Reichstag session in the garrison church at Potsdam.

During this heady phase, several individuals who would remain central in the movement rose to prominence. One was Ludwig Müller, born in

*Branch office of the German Christian movement in Dortmund. The sign
at the top of the building reads: "German Christians: Regional Press Office
for Westphalia. District Business Office, Dortmund." In the window: "Land,
land, hear the Word of the Lord!" Much of the movement's activity occurred
at the local and regional level. (Kommunalarchiv Minden)*

1883, the son of a railroad official. Müller served as a naval chaplain during
World War I and decades later still displayed his decorations with pride. In
1933, his military background, early membership in the Nazi party, and
rumors of a close relationship with Hitler combined to make him a suitable
German Christian candidate for the new position of Reich bishop. By the
end of September, Müller had achieved that title, though not without
struggle; despite challenges, he continued to use it until 1945.[46] Often
mockingly called the "Reibi," Müller demonstrated in speeches and writ-

ings that his was a modest intellect. His coarse, earthy manner and conspicuous enthusiasm for the Nazi cause typified the German Christian leadership style.

For members of the movement, the euphoria of ascent proved short-lived. Withdrawal of party support, symbolized in the declaration of neutrality in church affairs by Hitler's deputy Rudolf Hess on 13 October 1933, engendered a crisis of identity within German Christian ranks.[47] Tensions between those who sought only an adjustment of Christianity and others who urged its complete overhaul exploded in the Sports Palace rally on 13 November 1933, an event that ushered in the second phase of the movement's development: fragmentation.

Sometimes in the history of an organization, one incident brings to a head existing concerns and anticipates future directions in uncanny ways. For the German Christians, the Sports Palace rally was such a milestone. Until that time, the movement's successes had concealed internal differences and masked uncertainties about its mission. At the Sports Palace rally, the key speaker, Reinhold Krause, blasted those issues into the open. Krause, a high school teacher and leader of German Christians in Berlin, had not enjoyed a particularly high profile in the movement, but his 13 November performance catapulted him into the spotlight. Before an audience of twenty thousand people in Berlin's massive Sports Palace, the forty-year-old Nazi party member presented a stark and shocking picture of what some German Christians thought of their religion. In crude, abusive language, he attacked the fundaments of Christianity as unacceptable marks of Jewish influence. Krause lambasted the Old Testament, the Apostle Paul, and the symbol of the cross as ridiculous, debilitating remnants of Judaism, unacceptable to National Socialists.[48]

Krause's speech attracted tremendous attention. In addition to the twenty thousand eyewitnesses, millions of Germans read detailed reports of the event in their newspapers. It sparked a wave of departures from German Christian ranks, although contemporary accounts differ as to the total number who quit the movement in its wake.[49] What is clear, however, is that the Sports Palace event precipitated a shake-up of the group's leadership. Krause lost his post; Reich Bishop Ludwig Müller withdrew his membership and publicly guaranteed the inviolability of Scripture and the confession.[50] Neither Müller's dissociation from the German Christian movement nor his pledge to preserve orthodoxy proved of durable significance. By the late 1930s, Krause's ideas had become common currency in German Christian circles. Still, in November 1933, observers both outside and inside German Christian ranks interpreted the Sports Palace scandal as a turning point and a signal for individual members to take more control of their movement's teachings.

Throughout 1934 and 1935, the German Christians' organization lay in shambles. Vicious personal rivalries, disagreements about tactics, and inertia paralyzed the central offices in Berlin. The Sports Palace affair left men like Joachim Hossenfelder, the thirty-three-year-old pastor and Reich leader of the movement, vulnerable to attack from other ambitious churchmen. Hossenfelder, an ardent Nazi, prided himself on his participation in the Kapp Putsch. Since 1925, he had ministered to an Upper Silesian parish that included three villages in Poland.[51] He brought that fighting spirit to the German Christian movement. In late 1933, his main rival was Christian Kinder, a party member, veteran, and lawyer from Schleswig-Holstein. Kinder, also in his mid-thirties, cultivated a more moderate image and played up Hossenfelder's recklessness. By the end of the year, Kinder had ousted his opponent and assumed leadership of the movement.[52]

According to the postwar recollections of one former member, the mid-1930s were the most bitter period of the church struggle.[53] Both Krause and Hossenfelder formed new German Christian circles; splinter groups proliferated all over the country. Many of them bore familiar names—for example, the Reich Movement of German Christians, the German Christians–National Church Union, the Church Movement of German Christians (Reichsbewegung Deutsche Christen, Deutsche Christen–Nationalkirchliche Einung, Kirchenbewegung "Deutsche Christen").[54] Yet the movement persisted. German Christian pastors went on preaching in pulpits across the country; parish representatives, synodal officers, and regional bishops, elected or appointed in 1933, remained in office and continued to propagate the cause. Indeed, the frenetic production of spin-off organizations throughout 1934 and 1935 indicates the intense energies generated by German Christianity. It is not surprising that fragmentation gave way to a third stage: regrouping.

In July 1935, Hitler created the new Ministry for Church Affairs under Hanns Kerrl. Unintentionally, that attempt by Nazi authorities to increase their control of church issues signaled the onset of German Christian efforts to regroup. Kerrl, an "old fighter" who held party membership number 8651, had occupied a variety of positions including Reich commissioner for the Prussian Ministry of Justice and president of the Prussian Landtag.[55] He remained minister of church affairs until his death in Paris in 1941. Kerrl's interest in Christianity seems to have stemmed from his devotion to Nazism. When he first experienced National Socialism, he once commented, he understood how "faith makes someone into a new person."[56]

Initially, Kerrl's personal proclivities and his ministry's efforts favored the German Christians, who exploited the new conditions to expand their activities. Subgroups of the movement came together, beginning with the creation of the League of German Christians (Bund der Deutschen Christen) in 1936.[57] Often such efforts to consolidate occurred under the leadership of German Christians in Thuringia, the so-called National Church Union (Nationalkirchliche Einung).[58] Pastors Leffler and Leutheuser, both born in 1900 and married to sisters, had been active in their adjoining Thuringian pastorates since the late 1920s. By the mid-1930s, they had not only secured their local and regional power bases but expanded their efforts to the national arena. They were characterized at the time as the most radical of German Christians; their open willingness to defy Protestant orthodoxy, emphasis on grass-roots organization, and commitment to the quest for unity between German Protestants and Catholics gave their branch of the movement a cohesiveness many others lacked.[59]

In an attempt to effect a truce in the church struggle, Kerrl's ministry created church committees led by neutrals but including representatives from the various camps. In 1937, Hitler called for new church elections. Both of those developments enhanced German Christian legitimacy by recognizing the movement as an established interest group. Although the 1937 church elections were never held, their prospect spurred German Christians to continue regrouping. Events outside Germany as Hitler prepared for war sparked further cooperation. In April 1939, representatives of the range of German Christian groups and some individuals of non–German Christian orientation pledged solidarity in the Godesberg Declaration (Godesberger Erklärung). The Godesberg Declaration, a response to the archbishop of Canterbury's condemnation of National Socialist aggression against Czechoslovakia, repudiated ecumenism and "World Protestantism" and presented Christianity as the irreconcilable religious foe of Judaism.[60] By the time Germany invaded Poland in September 1939, almost the entire spectrum of German Christian splinter groups had reestablished ties. Relations with purportedly neutral elements within German Protestantism had improved as well.

The war triggered the fourth phase of German Christian evolution, a period I call ambiguous success. Literature on the German church in wartime is scarcer than on the other periods of the Third Reich,[61] in part because the Propaganda Ministry almost completely stopped religious publications in 1941. Still, enough material exists to ascertain that war brought fulfillment of many German Christian goals. The movement demanded an aggressive Christianity that united the nation against its foes.

Its members claimed to find that spiritual solidarity in the Third Reich under arms. German Christians had insisted on exclusion of non-Aryans and Jewish influences from the German religious community. That goal would be realized by default, through the deportation and murder of those defined as Jews. Yet defeat tainted the German Christian movement's wartime successes. National Socialist authorities demonstrated increasingly open hostility toward Christianity, including its pro-Nazi variants. Even as German Christians proclaimed their devotion to Nazism, their publications were terminated, their spokespeople muzzled. The German Christians discovered that they belonged both to the beneficiaries and the targets of National Socialist war aims.

The final phase of the German Christian odyssey—postwar reintegration—began when the Third Reich crumbled in the spring of 1945. Their movement discredited, German Christians faced the task of justifying their involvement over the past years to occupation authorities, denazification boards, fellow Germans, and even to themselves.[62] They used different strategies to try to salvage legitimacy in the absence of the regime on which they had based their hopes. Many of their efforts pointed to their ideal of the people's church as evidence of genuine spiritual motivations. In that way, the ecclesiology that had unified the movement throughout the Nazi years proved to be an effective tool for reintegrating individual members into the postwar church.

Having glimpsed something of the end of their story, we can now begin to investigate in detail the German Christian movement and its quest for a people's church. What beliefs unified the German Christians? Chapters 2, 3, and 4 explore the bases of the German Christian view of the people's church as anti-Jewish, antidoctrinal, and manly. How did members of the movement deal with Germans whose very existence countered their vision of a people's church? Chapters 5, 6, and 7 examine that question by focusing on converts from Judaism to Christianity, Catholics, and women. How could German Christianity, a form of religion rife with contradictions, persist throughout the Nazi era? Those tensions and their resolutions are the topics of Chapters 8, 9, and 10, which look at efforts to dejudaize Christianity, effect a church without rules, and reconcile the manly ideal with a feminine image of the church. Finally, what became of the German Christians and their ideas after collapse of the Third Reich? Answers to that question make up Chapter 11.

*We must emphasize with all decisiveness that* Christianity did not grow out of Judaism but developed in opposition to Judaism. *When we speak of Christianity and Judaism today, the two in their most fundamental essence stand in glaring contrast to one another. There is no bond between them, rather the sharpest opposition.*
—*Reich Bishop Ludwig Müller, 1934*

*Protest against the German Christian* heresy *cannot simply begin with the Aryan Paragraph, nor with their rejection of the Old Testament, the Arianism of their Christology, the naturalism and pelagianism of their teachings of justification and sanctification, nor the idolization of the state that characterizes German Christian ethics. Rather our protest must be directed fundamentally at the source of all those individual heresies: at the fact that, next to the holy scripture as the sole revelation of God, the German Christians claim German* Volkstum, *its past and its political present, as a second revelation. We thereby recognize them as believers in "another God."*
—*Karl Barth, 1933*

To the theologian Karl Barth, the essence of the German Christian heresy was obvious. By elevating *Volkstum*—race—to the level of God's revelation, German Christians opened the floodgates to a torrent of non-Christian and anti-Christian beliefs, attitudes, and activities. Armed with a notion of race as an expression of sacred truth, they embarked on a path that led further and further away from recognizably Christian teachings. But Barth failed to mention the crucial factor that linked and motivated the German Christian abuses he cataloged: anti-Jewishness. Barth, like many theologians associated with the Confessing Church, recognized the German Christian racial heresy without acknowledging that it was rooted in hatred toward Judaism and Jews. On this point, Reich Bishop Müller's description of German Christianity proved more accurate. Blurring racial and religious categories, the German Christians defined their people's church as essentially and primarily anti-Jewish; their identity depended on the contrasts they established between themselves and Jews. In the context of Nazi Germany, that stance had consequences that surpassed even the theological aberrations Barth deplored.

Commitment to ethnic chauvinism and antisemitism united German Christians and linked them to Nazi ideology. And like their counterparts in the party and among the storm troopers, they made no attempt to hide their hatred. In February 1934, an agent of the Berlin Gestapo reported to his superiors on a German Christian meeting he had attended. The two-hour event in a Kreuzberg auditorium attracted nine hundred people, almost two-thirds of them men. Swastikas and black, white, and red flags adorned the space. Three Berlin clergymen, one a member of the Nazi party, addressed the crowd. "The Pastors' Emergency League wants to reinstate the democratic system," one of the speakers warned. "They say that everyone is equal before God. But baptism never made a Jew into a German, nor did it ever straighten a crooked, hook-nose." That pastor's message demonstrated how the exclusive and inclusive facets of the German Christian agenda were linked. "The Jew has no scruples," he claimed. "Even now he would manage to let himself be baptized outwardly in order to get into the top positions. We want a Christianity that is true to our race."[1]

The German Christian theory of race depended on a particular vocabulary. German Christians made heavy use of the words *Volk*, *Volkstum*, and *völkisch*. These terms are difficult to translate into English because they combine aspects of ethnicity, race, and culture. Accordingly, throughout this book, I have often left them in German. In cases where the implication seemed clear, I have translated *Volk* variably as "people," "race," or "ethnic group." The adjective *völkisch* is more difficult because there really is no English equivalent. *Völkisch* is an historically bound word; it reflects a way of thinking that emphasizes the ethnic, racial group—the *Volk*—and is obsessed with its preservation and advancement. German Christians also used the words *Rasse* (race) and *Blut* (blood). Various forms of the German *Art* (nature, type, or breed) appear as well. The problem of translating these terms highlights the alien nature of German Christian thought outside the context of Nazi Germany. We cannot recapture in another language, another time, and another setting all of the messages intrinsic in German Christian utterances on race. Still, we can learn a great deal about the movement by using the language of race as a window on the group's beliefs.

Ideas about race gave focus to German Christian pronouncements and projects. Theories about Jews and Germans linked the movement to legitimizing authorities and precursors—God, Martin Luther, *völkisch* Protestant groups, overseas missionaries. Moreover, German Christians used notions of race to define their identity, contrasting themselves with Jews and distinguishing their movement from other Christians and neopagans. Finally, attention to German Christians' racial notions about Jews and the handicapped sheds light on the movement's relationship to the Nazi state and on the question of opportunism.

## Race as the German Christians' Organizing Principle

The notion of race as the fundamental truth of human life played a role for German Christians comparable to that of the Bible in traditional Christian teaching. Ideas about race provided a fixed point around which spokesmen of the movement structured and organized their shifting views. This role remained constant at every stage of the group's development.

In 1932, the German Christian Faith Movement published its ten guidelines. Those principles illustrate how German Christians extrapolated an anti-Jewish platform from their view of race as God's revelation. Point seven read as follows: "We see in race, *Volkstum*, and nation laws of life that God has bequeathed and entrusted to us. It is God's law that we concern ourselves with their preservation. Mixing of the races, therefore, is to be opposed." Point nine elaborated: "In the mission to the Jews we see a serious threat to our *Volkstum*. That mission is the entryway for foreign blood into the body of our *Volk*. . . . We reject missions to the Jews in Germany as long as Jews possess the right of citizenship and hence the danger of racial fraud and bastardization exists. . . . Marriage between Germans and Jews particularly is to be forbidden."[2] Even before the Nazis took power, the German Christians had concretized their views of race and its place in the church.

In May 1933, near the peak of their period of ascendancy, the German

Christians issued revised guidelines. The language was muted, and the words *Jew, Jewish,* and *Judaism* did not appear. Euphemism, however, did not conceal their continued preoccupation with race. The guidelines described "recognition of the differences among peoples and races" as "an order willed by God for the world" and committed the German Protestant church to providing "weapons for the struggle against everything un-Christian and damaging to the nature of the *Volk*."[3]

German Christians adapted in various ways to a growing realization of the implications of their racial theory. The membership coupon attached to the guidelines of 1932 included no racial stipulations.[4] The 1934 application for membership in the Westphalian German Christian organization required a pledge of Aryan descent.[5] One year later, the newly restructured Combat and Faith Movement of "German Christians" included a more detailed clause: "I declare that I am of Aryan blood, as well as that both of my parents and my grandparents are of pure Aryan blood."[6]

As fragmentation set in among the German Christian ranks, many members saw attention to race as a way to halt disintegration and consolidate the core. In 1935, immediately after the Nuremberg Laws deprived German Jews of citizenship, a prominent German Christian from Silesia urged institution of separate congregations for "baptized Jews" in the Protestant church.[7] The following spring, a group of Westphalian German Christians reached the same conclusion. The time had come, they argued, to draw the boundaries: "Here a German people's church, there a Jewish people's church, both specially suited to the members of their *Volk*." The people's church, German Christians contended, must understand the racial imperative that governed the life of its *Volk*. Accordingly, they urged church people to support all state measures against Jews.[8]

When the German Christians regrouped and gathered force in the late 1930s, it was on the common ground of shared views of race. That race continued to function as a central organizing principle of the German Christian program is evident in the Godesberg Declaration. Signed in April 1939 by the German Christian leaders of eleven regional churches, that proclamation aimed to transform the Protestant church into a tool of racial policy. It included four main points; three of them addressed race. The declaration rejected universal, international Christianity, contending that "true Christian faith unfolds itself productively only within the given order of creation." It labeled Christianity "the irreconcilable religious opposite of Judaism," and it announced the establishment of a new institute: the Institute for Research into and Elimination of Jewish Influence in German Church Life (Institut zur Erforschung und Beseitigung des jüdischen Einflusses im deutschen kirchlichen Leben).[9]

In the wake of Godesberg, non–German Christian and moderate German Christian leaders drew up their own document on the relationship between the Protestant church and the Nazi state. It was signed in May 1939 by representatives of the Protestant churches in Kurhessen-Waldeck, Hanover, Braunschweig, and Aurich. In contrast to Godesberg, that statement acknowledged the validity of the gospel for all people. But it too affirmed race as the only principle around which Christianity in Germany could be organized. The Protestant church, it claimed, "has learned from Martin Luther that true Christian faith can only unfold in all its power within the *Volk* as created by God." While the National Socialist state strove to restore racial order, it went on, "the Protestant church affirms its responsibility for maintaining the purity of our *Volk*." Like the Godesberg Declaration, the minority statement posited a fundamental antagonism between Christianity and Judaism. "In the sphere of faith," it insisted, "there is no sharper opposition than that between the message of Jesus Christ and the Jewish religion of legality with its hope for a political Messiah."[10] This purported alternative to the Godesberg Declaration reveals the extent to which German Christian thinking about race had permeated Protestant circles and reflected mainstream concerns.

During the war, as the National Socialist regime systematically implemented its genocidal policy toward the Jews, German Christians were able to effect their racial ideas. Indeed, in the phase of ambiguous success, German Christians came closest to realizing their goals precisely with regard to issues of race. In September 1941, new regulations in Germany required all those defined as Jews to wear an identifying star.[11] Christians of Jewish background numbered among that group as well. In December, after mass deportations of Jews to the east had already begun, the German Christian–dominated church government in Saxony passed a "law to exclude racially Jewish Christians from the church." It stipulated that "people who fall under the conditions of clauses one and two of the Police Regulation on the Identification of the Jews of 1 Sept. 1941—RGB I S. 547— together with their offspring in the territory of the Protestant-Lutheran Church of Saxony, are excluded from any ecclesiastical community."[12]

Earlier that same month, leaders of church government in Saxony, Nassau-Hesse, Schleswig-Holstein, Thuringia, Mecklenburg, Anhalt, and Lübeck had issued a more detailed "announcement" on the position of "Protestant Jews." That statement blamed the Jews for the war and affirmed the necessity of all measures the Nazi state had taken against them. It denied that Christian baptism could change anything "about the racial essence of Jews" and stressed that "racially Jewish Christians" had no place in a church devoted to the German *Volk*. In conclusion, the signatories pledged to tolerate "absolutely no influence of the Jewish spirit on German religious and ecclesiastical life" and to "suspend all relations with Jewish Christians."[13]

Other German Christian proclamations during the war made no secret of the movement's endorsement of Nazi mass murder. In early 1942, Heinz Weidemann, the Protestant bishop of Bremen, declared his church "officially anti-Jewish." Weidemann's action fit the thrust of his involvement in the German Christian movement. Born in 1895, he joined both the German Christians and the Nazi party in 1933. A passionate opponent of Jewish influence within Christianity, Weidemann spent much of the 1930s generating "dejudaized" versions of the Gospels and hymnals purged of Old Testament terms. He also embroiled himself in scandals involving financial, sexual, and even ideological improprieties.[14] Nevertheless, his aggressive anti-Jewish stance found support far beyond Bremen. German Christians in twenty-six Franconian congregations adopted his 1942 declaration.[15]

Through their anti-Jewish people's church, the German Christians endorsed the crimes of the thousand-year Reich. In 1933, while German Christian pastors fought to eject non-Aryans from the Protestant clergy, Jewish civil servants lost their jobs. In 1935, when German Christian parishioners rejected use of Old Testament texts in their worship services, the Nuremberg Laws deprived German Jews of citizenship. By 1939, when German Christians consolidated the foundations of their dejudaized Christianity in the Institute for Research into and Elimination of Jewish Influence in German Church Life, Germans had already torched synagogues all over the country, destroyed Jewish homes and property, and incarcerated thousands of Jewish men. During the war, as German Christian church councillors vowed to expel non-Aryans from their congregations, German soldiers, SS men, and their accomplices murdered Jews by the millions. The quest for an anti-Jewish church was not just an ecclesiological whim; it was part of a brutal reality.

A 1944 proclamation in a German Christian newsletter indicated how thoroughly members identified their anti-Jewish people's church with the genocidal German nation: "There is no other solution to the Jewish problem than this: that one day the whole world will rise up and decide either for or against Judaism, and will keep on struggling with each other until the world is totally judaized or completely purged of Judaism. We can say with an honest, pure conscience that we did not want this war and did not start this war. But we can proudly profess before all the world—the world of today as well as of tomorrow—that we took up the gauntlet with the firm resolve to solve the Jewish question for ever."[16] With that declaration, German Christians echoed the threat Hitler had voiced in January 1939. Hitler had claimed to be a "prophet" in predicting that the next war would bring the "annihilation of the Jewish race in Europe."[17] German Christians phrased their affirmation of that goal and their recognition of its impending realization in the language of the apocalypse.

## Legitimizing Precursors

The German Christians did not merely parrot Nazi racial ideology. They recognized their own theory of race as a legacy that bound them to traditions in the church and to intellectual and spiritual antecedents in the distant and not so distant past. For German Christians, race was a divine command that sanctified their cause. In April 1933, German Christian leaders in the Saar professed their faith in a God who "decreed the principles of all life": marriage, the family, race, and "relationships of blood." To preserve those principles, they concluded, was "an inviolable duty of all Christians."[18] Other German Christians concurred.

In 1934, Guida Diehl and her nationalist New Land League in Eisenach pledged commitment to a "renewal of faith" based on the German Christian view that race, together with "the family, *Volk*, and fatherland," was the first revelation of God.[19] Diehl, born in 1868 in Odessa, had started the New Land League (Neuland-Bund) in 1914, in the interest of mobilizing Christian energies for the war effort. She joined the Nazi party in 1930, throwing her weight as an influential Protestant women's leader behind its cause. Outspoken, independent, and committed to revival of the Protestant church, she considered herself the mother of her New Land followers. When she endorsed the German Christian movement in the early 1930s and echoed its stance on race, people listened.[20]

By 1939, a German Christian confirmation examination asked candidates, "Who is the new temple of the Holy Spirit?" The ritual response placed race squarely in the midst of the articles of faith: "The *Volk* is the temple of the Holy Spirit. Sanctification takes place in the communal life of the *Volk*."[21] That July, a publication of the National Church wing of German Christians declared recognition of the sacred meaning of race to be Germany's gift to the twentieth century. Through the National Socialist revolution, that author claimed, God had revealed the secret of the racial aspect of true Christianity first to Germans. They could no more keep it to themselves than the "discovery of the Copernican universe" could have remained "restricted to one country." Germany, the author rejoiced, was called to be a "pathbreaker" to a new age when every race would recognize that it could accept Christianity only "in a way true to its nature."[22] For German Christians, the establishment of an anti-Jewish church was a sacred task.

Adherents of the movement also found authorities in this world to legitimize their cause. They especially liked to cite Martin Luther as a precursor of their attitudes toward Jews and Judaism. With glee they quoted his essay "Against the Jews and Their Lies" and presented him as a champion of antisemitism. A religious instruction book of 1940 quoted Luther's instructions to "set their synagogues and schools on fire, and whatever will not burn, heap dirt upon and cover so that no human ever again will see a stone or a cinder of it."[23] A German Christian publication from 1943 urged its readers to be hard like Luther in their attitudes toward the Jews.[24]

German Christians found forerunners in more recent German history, too. *Völkisch* enthusiasts had abounded in the Weimar period, and the Protestant church spawned more than its fair share of them. Throughout the 1920s and 1930s, individuals and groups agitated within Protestant communities to abolish collections for missions to the Jews, remove Old Testament sayings and stories from religious instruction and the worship service, and purge hebraisms such as Jehovah, Hallelujah, and Hosanna from the hymnbook. In bodies of ecclesiastical governance, *völkisch* Christians advanced motions on the subject of eugenics and made proposals to prohibit "baptized Jews" from church offices.[25] By 1931, reports noted that some schoolteachers were incorporating *völkisch* ideas into their lessons, and at least one physician in Speyer persuaded some parents not to give their children names from the Hebrew Bible.[26]

One of the most active of the *völkisch* Protestant groups was the German Church League (Bund für deutsche Kirche or Deutschkirche). Founded in 1921, the league existed in some areas alongside the German Christians until at least 1936.[27] Many of its ideas and more than a few of its adherents resurfaced in the German Christian movement. For example, a German Church League publication of 1927 described Jesus as "the transfiguration of the Siegfried idea," who could "break the neck of the Jewish-Satanic snake with his iron fist."[28] In 1933, the German Christian chronicler Friedrich Wieneke identified the league as a precursor of the German Christians and credited it with exposing "the dangerous impulses of the Jewish Old Testament." Wieneke conceded that the German Church group had strayed "too far" from the Bible but insisted that it was "truly the vanguard of fighters for a Christian way of life based on a German consciousness of race."[29] Wieneke had firsthand experience with the developments he described. A party member since 1929 and cathedral pastor in Soldin, he had been active with the German Christian movement since its inception in 1932.[30]

Some striking impulses in the German Christian theory of race hearkened back to a more respectable source: German Protestant overseas missions. German Christians claimed to have inherited the mantle of race consciousness from missionaries. Since the late nineteenth century, German missionaries had stressed the need to adapt the Christian message and its presentation to each *Volk*. The German Christians took that liberal impulse and developed its separatist potential into a justification of a racially exclusive church. "Just as the missionary to the heathens goes to the black or brown people to preach something entirely new to a foreign *Volk*," claimed one German Christian clergyman, "so must the pastor in the Third Reich set forth into a completely new land of Germanness (*Deutschheit*) with a completely new message of Christ." That message, he continued, needed to be presented in such a way as to resonate with the soul of the *Volk*, free of foreign, "Jewish-Christian dogmatics."[31] Overseas missions, suggested another German Christian in 1933, had taught that "according to the order of God's creation, there is no 'humanity,' rather only German Christians, English Christians, Chinese Christians, and so on."[32]

In addition to legitimizing the racially exclusive church, overseas missions offered a model of racist thinking that could be transferred to the Jews. Most German Christians, like most Germans at the time, had little or no contact with people of color. As a result, to them the missionary experience represented above all German interaction with people of different races. To make concrete their view of Jewishness as a racial category, they compared Jews to the African and Asian subjects of German missionary efforts and thus transferred the feelings of distance, superiority, and even loathing that they experienced toward the foreign "heathens" onto Jews both foreign and German.

In October 1932, the official German Christian weekly, *Evangelium im Dritten Reich* (The gospel in the Third Reich), provided a striking example of how racist models from the mission field helped shape the German Christian theory of race. A German Christian mission superintendent recounted the controversy surrounding a black pastor from Togo named Kwami and his speaking tour through Germany. Kwami was slated to speak in Oldenburg, but a group of people protested. They claimed it would be "cultural infamy" (*Kulturschande*) for him to lead the worship service; they called it a "provocation" that anyone would allow "a Negro, of all people, to preach salvation to the splendid, blond farmers of east Friesland." As a German Christian, the author of the article felt obliged to explain the group's stance on the affair. Attacks against Kwami, he contended, would have been understandable if the man were presented for a position in a German parish: "That would be just as unbearable as when Jewish pastors work in German congregations." Kwami, however, was merely planning to report on the fruits of German mission work.[33] From the German Christian perspective, his appearance would not challenge but reinforce the notion of the racially defined people's church.

Other models of racism also formed part of the legacy reflected in the German Christian movement. The panicked response of many Germans to black French troops during the occupation after World War I is well known.[34] In 1923, Wolf Meyer-Erlach, later a leading German Christian, wrote a play that took place in the occupied Ruhr. *Das deutsche Leid* (The German sorrow) was a Freudian nightmare of sexual antifantasies and racist clichés involving lecherous black soldiers ravishing German maidens.[35] It was performed almost one hundred times.[36] In his subsequent activities as a German Christian publicist, speaker, and rector of the University in Jena, Meyer-Erlach continued to deal in the stereotypes he used against Africans in the 1920s. But in the 1930s and 1940s, Meyer-Erlach's targets were Jews.

To boost their theory of race, German Christians deliberately manipulated the antipathy of many Germans toward people of visibly different races. From its inception, the movement rejected missions to the Jews. The same German Christian paper that carried the Kwami letter explained that stance with an analogy to race relations in overseas missions:

> Through baptism, a Negro who lived in Germany would by no means become a German. It is the same for a Jew. Missions—and that is the advance made by the *völkisch* way of thinking—do not eradicate differences among the races. For this reason, the current way of missionizing the Jews must be changed, so that just as a baptized Negro becomes a Negro Christian, in the same way the Jew will remain racially a Jew; "only" from the religious point of view will he become a Jewish Christian.... The mission to the Jews has no business existing separate from the overseas missions, rather it should be one of its branches, just like the mission to India and so on.[37]

That statement reflected the first guidelines of the German Christian movement, issued in 1932. Point nine had rejected the mission to the Jews as the "gateway for foreign blood into the body of our *Volk*," although it did suggest that the mission to the Jews might be incorporated into the overseas missions program.[38] Similarly, the first Reich Conference of the Student Combat League of German Christians (Studentenkampfbund Deutsche Christen) in August 1933 included a presentation on overseas missions and mission to the Jews.[39] By linking the two themes, organizers conveyed the message that Jews were as racially "other" as Africans or Asians.

Some missionaries helped legitimize the German Christian legacy of race by getting involved in the movement. A newspaper account from early 1933 described mission superintendent Siegfried Knak, director of the Berlin Missions Society, as a German Christian sympathizer. Knak addressed a large German Christian rally in Berlin; Gauleiter Kube shared the stage.[40] Knak subsequently joined the Confessing Church, but his rejection of German Christianity was as much despite the movement's theory of race as because of it. He continued to hold the view of race he had constructed on the mission field, advocating a clear separation between the Christianity of Germans and that, for example, of Africans. In Knak's words, "What God has put asunder let no man join together."[41]

By late 1934, most missionary organizations had followed Knak to the Confessing Church side of the church struggle. Few missionaries could have failed to see that the inner logic of German Christianity doomed the overseas missions endeavor. In the German Christian view, Christians of different "races" ultimately had nothing to say to each other. Over time, references to overseas missions disappeared from German Christian publications. No doubt it was an embarrassment that the movement had failed to attract missionaries. Moreover, as the National Socialist regime became entrenched and many Germans internalized the idea of Jewishness as a race, it became less necessary to produce racist models from the missionary experience. Nevertheless, German Protestant missionaries did contribute to the German Christian theory of race, linking it to familiar stereotypes and giving legitimacy to the acceptance and promotion of racial distinctions within the community of faith. Recognition of the German Christian debt to missionaries' thinking about race highlights the connections between the movement and more respectable voices in the church.

## The Quest for Identity: Race as Antithesis and Boundary

The German Christians used notions of "Jewishness" as the antithesis of their own purported "Aryanism." With the words *Jew, Jewish,* or *Judaism* they referred to diverse and contradictory qualities, but in every case,

Jewishness represented the foil to their concept of Germanness. Although Nazi legislation eventually provided legal contours to the category of Jew, the opposing construct of Aryan remained undefined. The function of Jewishness as an antithesis therefore was crucial to the identity of German Christians.

If race, as German Christians believed, was the fundamental principle of human life, then racial slurs provided the most effective form of derision possible. German Christians tarred all opponents with the brush of Jewishness. They used Jewish as synonymous with secular, atheist, and Marxist. In February 1933, a pastor concluded a diatribe against socialism at a German Christian rally with the observation that "the godless movement in Russia and in Germany is mostly propagated by Jews."[42] A German Christian woman even criticized Berlin leader Krause's Sports Palace speech in November 1933 as the outgrowth of a "Jewish" spirit, typical of a "materialist" position.[43] The machinations of Jews, another German Christian claimed, had rent asunder church and state in 1919.[44]

German Christians called on the language of anti-Jewishness to imply sexual licentiousness. In 1935, a German Christian in Hanover described how "the Jews attack the soul of the German *Volk*." In 1927, he recalled, a Jewish director had opened a revue in Bremen "in which lechery and nakedness celebrated a triumph." The affair, he intoned, "ended with the Jew killing a woman."[45] A former Catholic priest turned German Christian closed a 1943 circular by equating Judaism with "irreverence, godlessness, and immorality."[46]

But if "Jewish" connoted secular or immoral to German Christians, it could equally refer to legalistic or dogmatic tendencies. A German Christian pastor from Krauß/Ebingen (Württemberg) in 1935 described the "worst enemy of the church" as the "Jewish nature that has infiltrated us," bringing "intolerance" and building a "fence of orthodoxy as the pharisees once did."[47] German Christians derided their opponents in the Confessing Church by labeling them Jewish. In that way, they further transformed and reshaped the negative associations they fed into the concept of Jewishness. For example, one German Christian pastor denounced the "Jewish" ecclesiology of the Confessing Church.[48] German Christian parents in another town complained that the Confessing Church preached "salvation through Christ as the Jewish sacrificial lamb."[49]

Some German Christians denounced the Confessing Church as Jewish by associating it with individual Jews. In a 1935 meeting in Augsburg, a German Christian vicar lambasted a pastor who, presiding at the burial of a Jewish man, had said, "He died a genuine, pious Israelite." The audience replied with cries of "Behold the slaves to the Jews" ("*Schaut die Juden-knechte*").[50] Another speaker in Bavaria in 1935 ended his denunciation of the Confessing Church with a call for a "Jew-free German Protestant Reich church."[51] By labeling the Confessing Church Jewish or "on the same wavelength" with Judaism, German Christians hoped to anathematize and immobilize that group.

German Christians used the term *Jew* to suggest an international conspiracy against National Socialism and against their own movement. In 1934, a pastor traveling in America reported considerable opposition among American Lutherans to the German Christians. In America, he wrote, "everything pro-Hitler has the enmity of the Jews, and that applies to German Christians as well." He said he had heard horror stories about Jews in Germany whose hands had been cut off, Jewish girls who had been molested, Jews whose windows had been smashed. Because such propaganda seemed to have lost its effect, he claimed, a "new buzzword has been found: persecution of Christians." German pastors disciplined by the National Socialist authorities, he predicted, would "likely be presented by the Jewish press as martyrs for their faith."[52]

For German Christians, Jewish often joined a list of "foreign" elements to be resisted in the church. According to a Stuttgart pastor in 1936: "We are, namely, German Christians, not Jewish, not Roman, not Calvinist, etc., who are striving for a Christianity free of Jews and free from Rome."[53] A Bavarian German Christian pastor was less subtle. "In the Confessing Front," he remarked in 1935, "it stinks like garlic and that is serious." Even more serious, he contended, was the "smell of incense." "When it smells that way," he continued, "like garlic and incense, there is only one solution: a hefty storm must sweep in. Those storm troops are the German Christians."[54]

Often German Christians blurred distinctions between their foes, naming Confessing Church, Catholics, foreign nations, and Jews in one acrimonious breath. That practice became especially pronounced during the war. In September 1939, a German Christian superintendent reported that the bishop of Chichester had held a prayer service for the imprisoned Confessing Church leader Martin Niemöller. At the service, the German Christian scoffed, "prayers were offered for Niemöller and for all the inmates of the concentration camps (!that is, common criminals, antisocial elements, Jews, and the like)." He went on to accuse the Confessing Church of serving "Yahweh, the God of the Jews" and cooperating with the "international, Jewish, and Jewish-related participants in the encirclement of Germany."[55] By using the term *Jewish* as a means of attack in such different ways, German Christians consolidated their definitions of Jewishness and its opposite, Germanness, and brought new associations into the racial glossary.

German Christian statements about race also illuminate the movement's relationships with coreligionists and neopagans outside the church. Within German Protestantism, racial thought separated the German Christian movement from some other *völkisch* Christian groups. In the German Christian camp stood those who endorsed the National Socialist view of race as the fundamental reality of human existence. Outside were people who, despite their own *völkisch* enthusiasms, remained reluctant to replace the idea of God's will as the basic value and standard with a theory of race. In 1932, one group, the League for the Free People's Church (Bund Freie Volkskirche) in the province of Saxony wrestled with the proper relationship of the Protestant church to National Socialism. Spokesmen of the group agreed with Hitler's nationalist goals but stumbled over the Nazi teaching of race. Their deliberations appear tormented. On the one hand, they heralded racial thought as "a protest against a certain deformed, passive . . . kind of Christianity" and a "belief in material forces, bestowed and determined by race and blood." On the other hand, they recognized the uncompromising nature of Nazi racial demands. In the end, they rejected the teaching of blood and race, declaring it contrary to Christianity and the spirit of the Sermon on the Mount. They broke with the German Christians.[56]

Another group, the Christian-German movement (Christlich-deutsche Bewegung) shared more of the German Christian ideas about race. Until 1933, Reich Bishop Müller himself had been a member.[57] But according to the German Christian chronicler Wieneke, the issue of race marked the boundary between the Christian-German movement and the German Christians too. Those like Ludwig Müller who accepted race as at the heart of creation joined the German Christians. Others who rejected that attitude remained Christian-Germans.[58]

Ideas about race also delineated the German Christians from their main rival, the Confessing Church, although the difference was not as great as one might expect. The Confessing Church grew out of the Pastors' Emergency League (Pfarrernotbund), established in 1933 by the Berlin-Dahlem pastor Martin Niemöller. In April of that year, the National Socialist regime introduced legislation to remove Jewish civil servants from office. German Christians hoped to enforce a similar clause in the church that would expel converts from Judaism and their children and grandchildren from the Protestant clergy. Niemöller mobilized pastors in the Emergency League to protest those designs.[59]

Despite its origins, the Confessing Church was not vocal in opposing the German Christian view of race and was by no means a champion of Judaism. Uriel Tal has shown that many Lutherans associated with the Confessing Church compared and equated Judaism with the *völkisch* movement, even with National Socialism itself. Such people, Tal indicated, "resolutely opposed racial antisemitism, and yet drew a common denominator between the Jew and the racist."[60] Both the *völkisch* movements and the Jews, anti-Nazi Lutherans charged, destroyed the traditional authority of family, society, economy, and politics; both, they accused, defined themselves by blood in ways that led to chauvinistic ethnic racism. According to one of their number, "der Rassengedanke ist Judentum [the racial idea is Judaism]."[61] In 1938, Martin Niemöller explained how he, a self-professed antisemite, had come to oppose plans to exclude non-Aryans from the clergy. Even his personal antipathy toward Jews, Niemöller indicated, had not blinded him to the realization that acceptance of an Aryan clause in the church would effectively negate the teaching of baptism.[62]

Dietrich Bonhoeffer, who early on recognized that Nazi antisemitism posed a fundamental challenge to Christianity, expressed frustration with the unwillingness of most people in the Confessing Church to grasp the issues at stake. Still, some others did call into question the German Christian view of race. For the pastor Theodor Haug, the movement's ideas about race made support of German Christianity impossible. "Can one so simply speak of 'German blood and the holy gospels' as the 'roots of German Christianity,'" he asked, quoting from German Christian principles, "as if the two stood as equals next to each other?" No, he answered; the church had only one unconditional "yes": for the gospel.[63] Another Confessing Church pastor realized that the German Christian view of race rendered the Holy Spirit a farce, the story of Pentecost an "offensive tale" of "evil cosmopolitan tendencies."[64] The Bochum Confessing Church pastor, Hans Ehrenberg, himself a "non-Aryan Christian," spoke out courageously against the German Christian view of race. Ehrenberg recognized issues of race as the heart of the church struggle. It was the incorporation of "Jewish Christians," he argued, that affirmed a church as an authentic community of the spirit.[65]

Some of the harshest criticism of the German Christian view of race came from people outside the churches altogether: the neopagans. Because they rejected Christianity in any form as a product of Judaism, neopagans considered German Christian attempts to separate the two misguided and pathetic. Gleefully they lumped Confessing Church and German Christians together as Jewish-infiltrated groups that perpetu-

# Öffentliche Kundgebung
## des Merseburger Kirchenvolkes!

Antwort an die „Deutsche Glaubensbewegung"

## am Mittwoch, den 10. April 1935
### im großen Saal des „Kasino", abends 8¹⁵ Uhr.

## Deutsche Christen und Bekenntnisfront
### in Merseburg einigen sich in der Abwehr des Neuheidentums!

# Keine Kirchenpolitischen- oder Konfessionellen Streitigkeiten!

Es sprechen:

Superintendent **Berckenhagen** (Eröffnung)

Pfarrer **Riem**

Pfarrer **Ziehen** (Antwort auf den Vortrag der „Deutschen Glaubensbewegung" am 27. März 1935 in Merseburg)

00325

**Eintritt frei!**　　　　　　　　　**Erscheint in Massen!**

## Die Evangelischen Kirchengemeinden Merseburgs

Poster announcing a joint rally of German Christians and the Confessing Church to protest the rise of neopaganism—a rare example of cooperation between antagonists. "Public Announcement of the Church People of Merseburg! *A Response to the 'German Faith Movement' on Wednesday, 10 April 1935, in the large room of the 'Casino,' 8:15 P.M. German Christians and the Confessing Front in Merseburg unite in defense*

ated the invasion of "foreign elements" into German spiritual life. "We no longer believe in the Holy Spirit," boasted "The A.B.C.s of the German Pagans"; "we believe in holy blood."[66]

In responding to the neopagans, German Christians confronted the shaky logic of their own position. If they conceded that race was subject to the limits of biblical teachings, they left themselves open to charges of Jewish-Christian complicity. If they posited race as the highest good, they sacrificed any meaningful distinction between themselves and anti-Christian elements. As a result, they followed a mixed strategy, sometimes emphasizing their common ground with the neopagans on the issue of race, at other times protesting their differences. In 1935, the mayor of Stuttgart, a proponent of the "German people's church," wrote to the neopagan leader Hauer stressing mutual opposition to Judaism. "Blood is thicker than water," the German Christian assured his neopagan correspondent.[67] Elsewhere relations were less cordial. In Merseburg in 1935, German Christians even planned a joint rally with the Confessing Church to protest attacks on Christianity by the neopagans.[68]

In the Rhineland, differences between neopagans and German Christians erupted in 1935 in a public dispute over the issue of race. Pastor Otto Brökelschen, a German Christian from Oberhausen, wrote to the editor of a neopagan paper to protest his characterization of Christianity as disguised Judaism. Christianity, the German Christian insisted, was the sworn enemy of Judaism. The neopagan editor ridiculed the German Christian position. "The Jew," he scoffed, "is beginning to grin. He shows a devilishly contemptuous grimace full of inner glee, because once again he sees how well suited the teachings of Sinai are to confuse the senses of the hated Goyim-Gentiles."[69] Brökelschen's letter had boasted that he was a "fanatical antisemite." That, the neopagan guffawed, "is simply beyond comprehension." He quoted theologians and the Bible itself to demonstrate the intimate relationship between Judaism and Christianity. Citing Galatians 3:7: "They which are of faith, the same are the children of Abraham" and Galatians 3:28: "There [before Christ] is neither Jew nor Greek, there is neither bond nor free, there is neither male nor female," he demanded to know why Brökelschen had not mentioned those passages. The

*against neopaganism!* No Church Political or Confessional Fighting! *The speakers: Superintendent Berckenhagen (Introduction), Pastor Riem, Pastor Ziehen (Response to the Presentation by the 'German Faith Movement' on 27 March 1935 in Merseburg).* Free Admission! Come One and All! *The Protestant Congregations of Merseburg." (Bundesarchiv Potsdam)*

entire German Christian position, the neopagan editor expostulated, was both illogical and antibiblical. How could German Christians deny Jews the right to hold office in the church, he queried, "when the God of this church according to his own words, belongs to the Jewish race?"

The German Christian Brökelschen replied in his own parish newspaper. He attempted to take the high ground but was unable to counter the neopagan logic. "You have done us Christians a great service with your answer to my letter," he wrote. "You have further demonstrated that certain groups cry 'Kill the Jews,' and mean Christianity and the church." There, he concluded, the neopagan and German Christian paths diverged. For German Christians like Brökelschen, it was "impossible for the Germans to become a *Volk* without the power of Christianity."[70]

German Christians repeatedly embroiled themselves in disputes with neopagans over issues of race. In 1937, a Westphalian German Christian pastor charged a speaker from the German Faith Movement with public blasphemy. The speech in question had ridiculed attempts to reconcile National Socialist views of race and Christianity, claiming that even if Christ were "the product of a liaison between a Roman man and a Jewish woman, the Nuremberg Laws would still apply to him." National Socialist Christians, that neopagan scoffed, was as ludicrous a concept as "SS-Semites."[71] Another neopagan derided the German Christians for "looking for the Aryan grandmother of Jesus." It was futile, that speaker sneered; "the Nazarene falls under the Aryan Paragraph."[72]

Throughout the war, German Christians complained that neopagans and anti-Christian elements in the Nazi party attacked the church and derided it as Jewish. In 1941, Walther Schultz, the German Christian bishop of Mecklenburg, complained to Hitler about attacks on Christianity. The bishop was outraged by charges that Christianity opened the floodgate to "judaization." He protested a storm trooper song that derided pastors as teachers of Judaism and pointed irately to an army "grace" that announced, "There will be peace only when the last Jew is hanged by the intestines of the last clergyman."[73] Their theory of race differentiated them from other religious groups and contributed to a distinct identity, yet German Christians also experienced their most intense challenges from outside the church on precisely this point.

## Opportunism, Eugenics, Euthanasia

It is tempting to dismiss German Christians' ideas about race as nothing more than efforts to ingratiate themselves with Nazi authorities. The illogic and offensiveness of German Christian anti-Jewishness make opportunism seem all the more convincing as an explanation. And indeed, although German Christians linked their views of race to God's will, they did consider practical benefits on earth, often presenting proof of racist antisemitism as their entrance ticket into the favor of National Socialist authorities. Yet if we compare the movement's attitudes toward race with its stance regarding eugenics and measures against the handicapped, we find that the explanatory power of opportunism is limited.

Some German Christians emphasized race in an opportunistic way to enlist National Socialist help in their struggle with the Confessing Church. This tendency became especially pronounced at times when the Nazi state had just made a new thrust in its institutionalized attacks on Jews. In 1935, after proclamation of the Nuremberg Laws, a German Christian pastor from the Ruhr wrote to *Der Stürmer*, Julius Streicher's rabidly antisemitic newspaper in Nuremberg. It was a special joy, the clergyman effused, that the *Stürmer* denounced the "so-called 'Confession Church' or 'Confession Front.'" He voiced his bid for Nazi action against the Confessing Church in racist language. "Men who babble about God's 'sparing of the Jews for one last great world-historical deed,'" he wrote, and pastors who "scorn the racial sensibilities of the German *Volk*" should not be allowed to continue preaching.[74] The implication was clear. That German Christian hoped Nazi measures against Jews would affect enemies of the German Christian movement as well.

In other cases, German Christians highlighted anti-Jewish thought so as to attempt to make Christianity palatable to National Socialism. A German Christian publication of 1938 urged women to espouse German Christianity to avoid "conflict with the National Socialist worldview." If German Christian women brought the movement's ideas about race into all circles of the population, the author suggested, "then the basic demand of the Führer, to purify the German race and to maintain its purity," would not be perceived as "un-Christian," but rather as a central task for all Christians in Germany.[75]

Although German Christians undeniably used race as a password to effect entree into the good graces of National Socialist powers, it would be a mistake to assume that such opportunism alone explains the movement's anti-Jewishness. Nazi party and state organs did not reward German Christians in any consistent way for their enthusiastic antisemitism; if anything, individual German Christians risked reprimands for dragging National Socialism into church affairs. The limits of opportunism as an explanation for the German Christian theory of race are illustrated in the movement's response to Nazi eugenics policies. In Nazi theory and practice, racial and eugenic doctrines formed related parts of an ideology of the master Aryan race.[76] If opportunism motivated German Christian engagement in Nazi racial policy, we would expect to find members of the movement among the vocal supporters of the eugenics and so-called euthanasia programs as well. Instead, German Christians generally showed reticence on those subjects.

The Sterilization Law of 14 July 1933, officially titled the "law for the prevention of hereditarily diseased offspring," provided for the compulsory sterilization of all people afflicted with a wide range of diseases or disabilities, such as deafness, feeble-mindedness, alcoholism, and schizophrenia.[77] It sparked considerable discussion in Christian—particularly Catholic—circles, but German Christians remained silent. Nor did they respond with any volume to the euphemistically named Euthanasia Program of 1939 and the years to follow, when Hitler, top aides, scores of doctors, other medical personnel, institutional administrators, and social workers cooperated to murder some seventy thousand Germans deemed "lives unworthy of living."[78] As Henry Friedlander has pointed out, the Nazis began their program of mass murder with people they deemed handicapped.[79]

In general, German Christians who publicly addressed issues related to eugenics were the exception rather than the rule. Some spokespeople for the group paid lip service to Nazi attacks on the handicapped or alleged carriers of genetic defects, but they lacked the engagement and enthusiasm that members of the movement showed on the "Jewish question." One prominent German Christian told a meeting in Münster that "God created humans in his own image! All the miserable ones and cripples in the institutions do not fit. That is not order, but disorder."[80] In 1935, a German Christian schoolteacher from Silesia urged the Reich bishop to institute seminars for pastors on the new racial thinking, with instruction in genetics, racial biology, and race studies.[81] An article in the German Christian Reich calendar of the same year reminded readers that the "race question" made difficult demands. Of course, it conceded, "no reasonable representative of the racial idea would dispute the human obligation and the Christian duty toward the sick, the old, and the weak." But those obligations, it suggested, were only one side of the command to love one's neighbor. After all, the author asked, "Is it not a healthy thought that there, where in accordance with God's will a beautiful flower can bloom, no thistle or nettle is standing?"[82]

In contrast to the torrent of literature on the Jews, German Christians produced few publications on eugenics. A 1936 booklet titled *Blut und Rasse im Licht der Bibel* (Blood and race in view of the Bible) devoted twenty pages to the subject. With unusual candor, the author affirmed the Sterilization Law, "under the terms of which a minor surgical intervention prevents criminals from producing a harmful line of descendants." But within a few pages, that writer abandoned the discussion of eugenics per se and returned to the more familiar—perhaps safer—ground of anti-Jewish racial policy.[83] A religion textbook from 1936 titled *Licht und Leben* (Light and life) was equally parsimonious in allotting space to eugenic concerns. It did, however, remind readers that there need be no conflict between Christianity and eugenic "imperatives." The "law for the prevention of genetically ill progeny," it pointed out, aimed to "protect our people from the curse of ongoing evil and from the harmful consequences and dangers of inferior and criminal humanity." Therefore, it concluded, that law reflected true Christian love.[84]

Only one full-length book sought to justify Nazi eugenics in German Christian terms. *Erbpflege und Christentum* (Genetic cultivation and Christianity) by a Protestant theologian appeared in 1940. The author posited race consciousness as the core of "positive Christianity," which he defined as "bound to the *Volk*" and committed to "racial purity."[85] Yet even he acknowledged the complexity of eugenics issues and rejected coercive measures. The book was placed on the index in Rome but received high praise from Protestant circles in Germany.[86]

Instead of embracing Nazi policy about eugenics and euthanasia, German Christians seem to have ignored it as much as possible. In December 1941, a German Christian pastor in Westphalia addressed a regional conference on "Principles on the Question of Euthanasia." Given the timing of that talk, one might expect its theme to have attracted considerable attention. Just months earlier, in August 1941, the Catholic bishop of Münster, Cardinal August Count von Galen, had denounced murder of the handicapped in a sensational sermon that was duplicated and circulated all over Germany.[87] But the German Christian speaker does not appear to have taken a stand against Galen; reports of the event suggest that he touched on the topic of euthanasia only briefly.[88] Perhaps their view of the *Volk* as a gift of God made German Christians reluctant to endorse tampering with it in the way that eugenics as social engineering or "euthanasia" as purification implied. In any case, members of the movement saw no contradiction in coupling active promotion of the anti-Jewish side of the racial coin with indifference and even suspicion toward measures against those deemed handicapped.

Germans outside the German Christian movement also seemed able to separate attacks on the disabled from anti-Jewish policies. A 1941 letter to military authorities in Germany provides a telling illustration. The author indicated the subject of the correspondence clearly: "Re: Elimination of the Mentally Ill." He was equally frank regarding his standpoint: "Whatever possessed our government to adopt this course—no one knows. Some say the institutions had to be cleared because of the *many air force officers with nervous illnesses*, others talk about *economic measures with a view to feeding our population*. But that misses the point. One counters these arguments simply by pointing to *the many millions of Jews* who are still in the country. Why do these dregs of society still live while our sick are simply being murdered?"[89]

Army officials in Münster forwarded the letter to Berlin, with the remark that from it one could reach certain conclusions about the "mood of the population."[90] Judging from that letter and the German Christian position, the population—at least elements of it—was eager to assert an anti-Jewish stance but less enthusiastic about measures against the handicapped. German Christians and like-minded Germans accepted and endorsed Nazi policies against Jews but were reluctant to implement racial purity at the expense of members of the German *Volk*, even the handicapped. The German Christians may have been willing to use their anti-semitism in opportunistic ways, but that opportunism rested on a firm commitment to their project of an anti-Jewish church.

German Christian efforts to create an anti-Jewish church reflected the fundamental illogic of the Nazi definition of Jewishness. The Nazi worldview posited Jewishness as an immutable, biological fact; German Christians showed they shared that conviction by rejecting baptism as changing the status of a former Jew. But the Nazi definition of Jewishness implied religious dimensions as well; under Nazi law, the religion of one's grandparents determined one's race.[91] That religious component constituted both a threat and an opportunity for German Christians.

If Jewishness was a religious force, then Christianity, an outgrowth of Judaism, was implicated through that relationship to the enemy. The connection between Christianity and Judaism provided an inexhaustible store of ammunition for attacks on the churches by Nazi theorists and neo-pagans. They sneered publicly at Christianity as nothing but diluted Judaism. Their derision egged on the German Christians' offensive against Jewish elements in their religious tradition while putting them on the defensive against the very Nazi worldview they embraced.

But the notion of Jewishness as an intangible spiritual force that had infiltrated Christianity presented opportunities to the German Christians as well. It gave them an unlimited sphere of activity in which to prove allegiance to Nazi goals while demonstrating the ability of their people's church to adapt to its clientele. As antisemitic measures escalated in Nazi Germany, the attack on Jewish influence in Christianity became for German Christians an area of endeavor guaranteed to be immune to open opposition. They could point to their anti-Jewish activities as evidence of their loyalty to the Nazi regime; they could silence critics with accusations of treason. Finally, the notion of Jewishness as racial and religious lent credence to German Christians' own conviction that Germanness contained both categories of identity; only Christianity, they maintained, could provide the spiritual content of true Germanness.

CHAPTER 3

The Antidoctrinal Church

*National Socialism is positive Christianity.*
*—Hanns Kerrl, Minister of Church Affairs, 1935*

*Caution—Heresy!*
*—sign on a German Christian bus, 1936*

*For us, what Jesus said is not decisive. And church*
*councils too err and have erred. We gladly let ourselves*
*be labeled heretics for this knowledge, for it has always*
*been heretics who have saved the church's life.*
*—German Christian Pastor Georgi, 1937*

The German Christians marched under the banner of the people's church. They desired an exclusive church, its doors shut to all who did not count in the Third Reich as true Germans. At the same time, their church was to be inclusive, drawing all designated Germans into its spiritual embrace. In keeping with that dream, the German Christians declared war on potential barriers to spiritual unity and proclaimed themselves the champions of antidoctrinal Christianity. At the heart of their vision of the church lay not affirmation of certain tenets of faith but the insistence that adherence to particular religious beliefs played no role in determining membership in the spiritual community.

German Christians spread their ideas in gatherings that ranged from monster rallies with thousands of the faithful to skat games around the

*Stammtisch.* A meeting in Herford (Westphalia) in November 1934 followed a common pattern. A medium-sized group of German Christians and friends—probably around eighty people, women and men—met at the local rifle club. At about 4:00 P.M. the speakers, two men, arrived. The audience applauded as they made their way to their seats on the stage. German Christian flags flanked the podium; above it hung a banner that read, "*Volk, Volk,* hear the word of the Lord." Across the hall another banner urged those present to "fear God, honor the Führer, love your brothers."

The program boasted a brass ensemble, but its members failed to show. Instead, a lone bugle provided accompaniment for the audience and choir. The speakers, one a nationally prominent German Christian, the other a regional figure, preached the familiar message of the people's church. The German Christians wanted no confessing congregations, the Westphalian insisted, no isolated communion of the saints. Instead they fought to win every last true German back to the church. As if to remind themselves that their gathering had religious significance, the assembled closed by singing the fourth stanza of Luther's "A Mighty Fortress": "That word above all earthly powers, no thanks to them abideth."[1]

The German Christians' relationship to church doctrine was essentially paradoxical. Their aim to build a people's church reflected a commitment to religious tradition and a conviction that the church constituted a profound expression of human community. Almost all German Christians remained within the official German Protestant church. They continued to organize as congregations led by clergy, to hold services in church buildings, and to use the vocabulary and symbols of Christianity. Yet while they retained elements of Christian tradition, the German Christians' project was fundamentally destructive. They dissociated those cultural trappings from the tenets of Christian faith. They denied the universal claims of Christianity and attacked the notion of the church itself as independent from the nation. Their antagonism to doctrine ensured that the church they promoted would be a hollow affair, prone to collapse.

German Christians took the assault on doctrine seriously. One searches their utterances in vain for any attempt to grapple with theological concerns that have shaped Christian discourse since the time of Paul. They did not address in any systematic way questions about the relationship among the persons of the trinity, the significance of the sacraments, free will, the role of the priesthood, or the resurrection of the body. Even the issue that had divided German Protestantism since the sixteenth century—the nature of Christ's presence in the Eucharist—elicited no explication from representatives of the movement. Reich Bishop Müller summed up

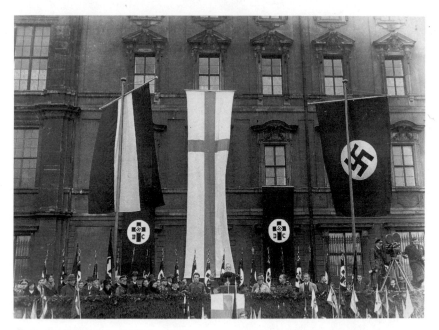

*German Christian flags featuring cross, swastika, and the initials*
*"D.C." for "Deutsche Christen." Here in Berlin on German Luther Day, 19*
*November 1933, celebrating the 450th anniversary of Martin Luther's birth.*
*The speaker appears to be Wilhelm Fahrenhorst, president of the Protestant*
*League. Nazi authorities later forbade the German Christians to use the*
*swastika in conjunction with the cross. (Bundesarchiv Koblenz)*

the German Christian view of the difference between Calvinists and Lutherans with the glib formulation: "One group prays: 'Our Father!,' the other 'Father of Ours!' "[2]

Doctrine, German Christians contended, had no place in the people's church because it led to dissension. According to one German Christian hymn, the people's church was called to transcend the limits of orthodoxy in the interest of unity: "Not courts of inquisition, not squabbling among pastors; No! Consecrate the community of the people through Christ's gift of salvation."[3] German Christians stressed that, like National Socialists, they were not a faction bound to specific beliefs but a movement that signified the end of petty bickering. In April 1933, two Lübeck pastors, fresh from meeting with German Christian leaders in Berlin, announced that the movement wanted "no new dogmatism and theology."[4] In February 1934, Christian Kinder, at the time German Christian Reich leader, explained at a rally in Berlin that "quarrels about dogmas and forms of the confessions of faith" only frightened people away from the church.[5] The following year, Minister of Church Affairs Kerrl tried to legislate anti-doctrinal Christianity: in an attempt to impose peace in the church struggle, he banned use of the word *heresy* (*Irrlehre*) for two years.[6]

Opposition to church doctrine facilitated German Christian efforts to synthesize Nazi ideology and Christianity because it implied denial of the sanctity of biblical texts. In 1937, a meeting of German Christians in the Rhineland endorsed a resolution that blended rejection of doctrine with destruction of Scripture itself. "A demon always resides in the written word," the Rhenish German Christians announced. "The devil values the printed page and stretches it out to demand signatures, while God reaches out his hand. Whereas the Jews were the first to write out their faith, Jesus never did so."[7] Unbound by loyalty to tenets of faith or scriptural authority, German Christians looked elsewhere for forces to unite their people's church. They identified alternative sources of unity in ritual, ethnicity, the state, and war. In each case, the German Christians met with disappointment; their movement proved more effective at destroying unity than promoting it.

## Ritual and Unity

For the German Christians, church ritual, emptied of its doctrinal associations, provided an opportunity for emotional displays of a fellowship that claimed divine blessing. Instead of expressing sacred truths, worship services, baptisms, confirmations, and congregational singing were to function solely as affirmations of the community. According to an essay on liturgical reform by the German Christian Wilhelm Bauer, creation of a genuine spiritual community depended on access to the irrational. Bauer served as the main source of theoretical writing about German Christian liturgy and practical models of new services in the spirit of the movement. If preachers wanted to reach their audiences, he maintained, they needed to "tap into the layer of awareness and experience" that stored both "the language of the Bible" and the "fairy tales and myths of earlier times."[8]

German Christians tried to implement such insights by developing rituals appropriate for the people's church. They preserved elements of Christian tradition as it had evolved in Protestant Germany yet added their own innovations. To involve the congregation, they relied especially on responsive readings and choral speaking, mixing biblical texts with hymns and passages from German heroes.[9] The goal was to create a sense of community by appealing to the emotional ties many Germans felt to the familiar words, actions, and melodies of church ritual. At the same time, the formalized structure of the worship helped conceal the movement's doctrinal nihilism.

Events such as Advent gave German Christians opportunities to hone their unifying ritual while claiming to be bearers of true Christianity. The mid-1930s, when the movement struggled to rebuild a central core from its fragmented parts, turned out to be particularly productive in generating new forms of worship. A 1935 Advent service of German Christians in Berlin-Tegel is illustrative. The pastor called on believers to light Advent candles that, displayed in their windows, would announce: "A Christian lives here. In this home, we pray for Führer and *Volk*!" The services blended traditional Advent symbols like the wreath, ritual acts such as lighting candles, familiar hymns of the season, choral speaking, and songs about German blood, soil, and the flag. That combination reflected the way German Christians transformed the meaning of Christianity from a religion built around an act of atonement to a ritual empowerment of Nazi ideology.[10]

In 1936, Berlin German Christians celebrated the third anniversary of the "national revolution" with a special service. The opening hymn proclaimed that the enmity of the world meant nothing if God were on one's side. In the context of a ceremony honoring the Nazi revolution, those sentiments could only be taken to apply to the Third Reich. In the liturgy that followed, the opening lines of the familiar Psalm, "Lord our Lord, how glorious is thy name in all the earth," prefaced a reading in the same style, praising God for National Socialism. "You have practiced your work on our people," went the pseudo-psalm, "although we neither earned nor deserved it. You have led us throughout our history according to your counsel and your will, although we may not always have understood your guidance." The text extolled Hitler as God's emissary, pledged God's constancy to his people, and elevated the Nazi revolution to a divine revelation. Echoing the history of the Children of Israel, the liturgy enumerated Germany's trials in the past, from the "enslaving chains" of the Treaty of Versailles, to unemployment, party infighting, and the temptations of "people of alien blood and an alien race." The service closed with congregational recitation of a piece by a German Christian poet that called on God to "send us the Führer" to "lead his Germany in faith into the young dawn."[11]

In German Christian hands, every Christian holiday and symbol became a celebration and sanctification of the *Volk*, an opportunity to display and promote the spiritual unity of the nation. One German Christian described Easter as both a "symbol and a reality," representing "the divine miracle of resurrection within our own *Volk*," yet calling Germans to "accept with faithful hearts the message of the crucified and resurrected Lord."[12] German Christians called their religious events "divine celebrations" (*Gottesfeiern*) rather than "worship services" (*Gottesdienste*). The new label was indeed more appropriate to rituals that, as a Confessing Church circular pointed out in 1937, retained nothing but the "old expressions" from the Bible and turned those to new purposes.[13]

German Christians reinterpreted the sacraments, too, transforming baptism into a celebration of the unity of blood. One pastor spoke of being baptized "into the community of the *Volk*—baptized into the worldview of the Führer." Baptism did not bring the infant into a church defined by a confession of faith, he explained, but expressed the community's "belief in the law of blood and in the race" and the parents' pledge to "raise this child in German discipline and customs and in positive Christianity."[14] In that analysis, Christian baptism served to remind parents that their children did not belong to them but to the German *Volk*.[15]

For German Christians, the Communion service too represented a mystical moment of unity. Generally German Christian celebrations retained the traditional bread and wine but attached a new world of meaning to them. One pastor suggested to his congregation that the bread symbolized "the body of the earth that, firm and strong, remains true to the German soil." The wine he called "the blood of the earth," representing "loyalty unto blood" and total dedication to the *Volk*.[16] A colleague in Stuttgart proposed replacing the bread and wine with a communal meal of stew on certain Sundays.[17] After all, he explained, the original Lord's Supper had involved a formative moment in the creation of a community of believers.[18]

German Christians proved to be energetic reformers of church ritual. Members of the movement produced reams of proposals for new ceremonies such as the plan for a celebration of the solstice that combined songs about comrades, torches, and Germany's future with readings from Goethe, 1 Corinthians, and German Christian poets.[19] In early 1943, when the prominent Thuringian German Christian Julius Leutheuser died at the front, German Christians devised a ceremony in his honor. They decorated the sanctuary with pine branches; flames burned in pylons; the pastors present wore either military garb or what by then had come to be known as the German Christian uniform—boots, black jacket, riding trousers. The service included no words from the Bible and no prayers. According to an eyewitness, the one exception, the Lord's Prayer, appeared at the end of the ceremony, "like a museum piece."[20] Only those elements of Christian tradition that created a spirit of Germanic unity found a place in German Christian ritual.

Music served the German Christians in special ways, as a metaphor and a medium for antidoctrinal Christianity. The act of singing together implies both emotional involvement and intellectual detachment. But through congregational singing, German Christians gave voice to their own teachings of *Volk* and race. For example, one German Christian hymnwriter produced a Christmas song to express the movement's interpretation of that holiday as a celebration of German chauvinism: "Christmas! Christmas! Blood and soil awake! Above you God's stars shine; Below you sing the seeds in the fields: *Volk*, from God's light and power, Your honor and heroism come."[21] In that song, references to Christmas served merely to introduce and legitimize the blessing of the *Volk*. Before his death, in a letter from the eastern front in May 1942, the Thuringian German Christian Leutheuser offered a key for decoding the language of German Christian song. "The most beautiful thing," he effused, "is when German people sing new songs about God, the *Volk*, and the Führer." He explained the association of each term: "God, that means goodness and power of life; the *Volk*, that means God's commandment and loyalty, and the Führer means he who has led us to God and *Volk*."[22]

Treatment of the Holy Spirit provides an example of how German Christian innovations in ritual revolutionized church doctrine even as they denied its relevance. The Holy Spirit might seem to have little potential for incorporation into the German people's church. After all, the message of Pentecost was universal: speaking in tongues allowed everyone to understand; the Holy Spirit created fellowship among believers of all nations. But instead of a stumbling block to creation of an exclusive church, the Holy Spirit proved a useful ally for German Christian rituals of unity.

German Christians found the Holy Spirit to be a concept vague enough to fit the loosely defined contours of their own faith. Their hymnbooks included new songs for Pentecost that celebrated the coming of spring, the "flaming steps" of the spirit, the "tumultuous music of the heavens." "O *Volk* of Germany's soil," a stanza of one such hymn concluded, "may God's power move you, so that there will be a springtime for you that brings peace and joy."[23] In 1942, Westphalian German Christians circulated meditations for the Pentecost sermon. "Pentecost," the text explained, was "the day on which God testified to His people in fire and wind, and sent them His spirit. That spirit bound them together in a congregation and a community."[24] Two years later, the meditation in the same publication linked Pentecost to the trials of war. "The church of Luther today must pass with our people through fire and wind," that devotional claimed. "If it struggles in the stormwinds and fire of God through our days, then it stands in the power of the spirit that Jesus Christ promised to his congregation."[25]

Few of the movement's innovations in church ritual and music caught on, and congregations tended to revert to more familiar practices. Still, German Christian publicists, clergy, musicians, and lay people continued to come up with new forms of worshiping God while praising the state. In German Christian hands, church ritual became a vehicle to express the spiritual unity of the nation.

## The Myth of the *Volksdeutschen*

German Christians found another model of antidoctrinal unity in the myth of religious harmony among ethnic Germans outside the Reich. The ethnic Germans or *Volksdeutschen* were self-identified members of the German cultural "nation" living outside Germany and Austria, in places from Romania and Poland to Turkey and South America. Many ethnic Germans considered piety intrinsic to their German identity, whether they were Baptists or Mennonites in Ukraine, Lutherans living among Polish Catholics and Jews, or Roman Catholics surrounded by Orthodox Romanians. The German Christians, like many other Germans, looked to these communities as examples of the perfect fusion of faith and ethnicity. Just as ethnic Germans outside Germany were of one heart and soul, devoted to preservation of Germanness without regard to sectarian considerations, German Christians maintained, so too could the people's church at home eschew divisive doctrine.

According to a German Christian from Merseburg in October 1933, the "firm bond between faith and homeland, between church and *Volk*" that German Christians sought was a "reality on the other side of the borders of the Reich!" For centuries, he concluded, the Protestant church abroad had "proven itself to be the most loyal and best guardian and nurturer of German ethnicity."[26] The 1935 German Christian Reich calendar further explained the link between German Christian goals and the situation of ethnic Germans outside the Reich. Particularly in South America, the author claimed, the experience of ethnic German pastors in the 1920s anticipated what came to be called German Christianity. Abroad, he contended, "Germanness and Christianity find each other in the best, most harmonious bond." The German Christians, he declared, were true heirs of the German pastors overseas. Indeed, in some cases, the calendar author pointed out, overseas pastors became German Christians. The most prominent example, Friedrich Kessel, the German Christian bishop in Königsberg, had been active as pastor to ethnic Germans in South America in the 1920s.[27]

In comparing their own efforts as unifiers of *Volk* and church to the ethnic Germans, German Christians hoped to capitalize on the positive image that ethnic Germans enjoyed in Nazi Germany. In June 1938, a Sudeten German pastor called the Protestant church "the last bulwark of the *völkisch* idea in Sudeten Germany" and reminded his audience that the Sudeten Nazi leader Konrad Henlein had converted to Protestantism out of "conviction and love for his *Volk*." The Sudeten church, he concluded, was a people's church "in the best sense."[28]

According to Wilhelm Staedel, an ethnic German pastor in Romania, until World War II the Lutheran churches from the Baltic to the Black and Caspian seas were "people's churches" to such an extent that, in some cases, Germanness and Protestant faith appeared to be two sides of the same coin.[29] Staedel, born in 1890 in Romania, was educated in Jena, Budapest, and Berlin. Devoted to the Nazi cause, he joined the German Christian movement as well and promoted it among the German-speaking community of Transylvania. In 1941, he replaced a more traditionally nationalist clergyman as bishop of the German church in Romania, a position he held until 1944. During his tenure, Staedel promoted a fusion of German identity, anti-Jewishness, and Protestant Christianity, even establishing a branch of the German Christian Institute for Research into and Elimination of Jewish Influence in German Church Life in Romania in 1942. After 1945, Staedel, active in the circle of former German Christians in Minden, retained his conviction of German ethnic superiority and his suspicion of Jewish elements within Christianity.[30]

German Christians got considerable mileage from the image of perfect spiritual solidarity among ethnic Germans outside the Reich. That vision of the people's church triumphant, however, was a myth. The same complaints of indifference toward church life that typified church publications in the Reich also appeared in ethnic German communities elsewhere. For example, in 1941, an ethnic German in Romania reported on the situation of the church in his district. Church attendance was high on important church holidays, he conceded, but abysmal at all other times. A typical Bible study group, he lamented, consisted of six women, an "invalid boy," and a "crippled man."[31]

Confessional and even ethnic differences impinged on and divided Germans outside the Reich too. After 1918, for example, changes in borders suddenly made the so-called Siebenbürger Saxons in Transylvania, a Protestant group whose presence in the area dated back hundreds of years, part of a predominantly Catholic, ethnic German minority in Romania. In the words of the German Christian bishop Staedel, "Faith and ethnicity no longer overlapped, as we Siebenbürger Saxons had considered natural for many centuries."[32] And finally, those ethnic Germans outside the Reich who interested themselves in the fate of the "mother church" were as divided as their counterparts inside German borders over how close a relationship between Christianity and National Socialism was possible or desirable.

German Christians in the Reich expected ethnic German Protestants elsewhere to sympathize with their cause, but they were often disappointed. Some ethnic Germans were interested. By late 1933, sixty-six German Protestant pastors active in South America had endorsed the German Christian movement. Copenhagen boasted more than fifty German Christians; a group formed in Paris as well. According to German Christian sources, "requests for membership were coming in from all over the world."[33] In other cases, despite German Christian overtures, ethnic Germans rejected the movement. In late 1936, the German Christian Erwin Balzer, bishop of Lübeck, was outraged by news that one of the pastors in his jurisdiction had joined the Confessing Church. The leader of the Lübeck German Christians had recruited that pastor in Czechoslovakia, where his engagement in *"völkisch* life" among ethnic Germans had created the impression that he was sympathetic to the German Christian cause. Bishop Balzer considered the pastor's decision to join the Confessing Church a betrayal of his earlier commitment to the *Volk*.[34]

German Christians failed to find either perfect unity or unmitigated support among ethnic Germans. At the same time, Nazi authorities further obstructed outreach in that direction. Some state offices were more sympathetic than others. The German Foreign Office recognized the role that Protestant pastors played among ethnic Germans abroad, and funds moved frequently from Foreign Office treasuries to the Protestant church's own foreign office under the leadership of Bishop Theodor Heckel, a German Christian sympathizer.[35] But in other cases the German Christians encountered resistance. In September 1941, the Reich Chancellery informed governors of territories annexed or occupied from Poland, Austria, and Czechoslovakia that, in accordance with Hitler's wishes, the Reich minister for church affairs would restrict his activities to the territory of the Greater German Reich.[36] With that pronouncement, Hitler made it clear that existing church policies, authorities, and struggles were to be contained within Germany's borders. In April 1942, Reinhard Heydrich, chief of the Security Police, head of the SS Intelligence Division, and acting Reich protector of

Bohemia-Moravia, complained that Heckel and the Protestant foreign office had built up too much power. Heckel and his accomplices, Heydrich maintained, could not be trusted to represent the Reich's interests abroad, "not even in the ecclesiastical sphere."[37] Coming from the man who served as de facto administrator of the so-called final solution, this condemnation dealt a heavy blow to German Christian ambitions. Nazi authorities made sure that the movement would not witness a rejuvenation of Christianity through union with ethnic Germans. Nor would it be permitted to play any significant role in the expanded Nazi empire that Hitler, Heydrich, and their henchmen were constructing in the east.

## Cultivating the State Church

The German Christians agreed that the antidoctrinal church would be at all costs a state church. Most Germans were so committed to the notion of a state-sponsored church that they articulated it only rarely. Like most Confessing Church people, German Christians assumed that any legitimate church had close ties to the state. Adherents of both groups demonstrated their endorsement of state-church relations by remaining in the established Protestant church and continuing to contest ownership of its resources and its authority. Only a very few daring thinkers in Confessing Church circles argued that the church needed to sever all ties with the National Socialist state if it were to remain a genuine community of the Holy Spirit.[38]

Much more common was the approach of a German pastor in the Netherlands. In 1934, as the Confessing Church gained ground in Germany, he worried that the state would withdraw completely from church affairs, ending the church struggle in a "decline into American-style free churches." The only way to prevent that catastrophe, he argued, was to oppose the Confessing Church and support Reich Bishop Müller's church government.[39] Dietrich Bonhoeffer replied to the man's concerns. "American-style free churches," he retorted, were eminently preferable to the German Christian church of Müller, the " 'people's church.' "[40] But few German Protestants were willing to follow Bonhoeffer in sundering the bond that had existed since Luther between the Protestant church and secular government. The German Christians especially clung fiercely to the notion of state sponsorship and sanction of the church. The concept of a state church reflected the identity they claimed between the people's church and the nation.

German Christians tried to use assumptions about the necessity of a state church to convince the Nazi regime to fight their battles for them. In 1934, a German Christian curate in the Rhineland wrote to Hitler protesting that the Confessing Church sought to dissolve ties between state and church. The very concept of free churches, the German Christian huffed, was "un-Lutheran, un-Christian, and unbiblical." It was no coincidence, he contended, that free churches existed in the Netherlands, France, and the United States, all "liberal, private" societies. If introduced in Germany, he warned, free churches would herald the end of National Socialism and its emphasis on the "organic" unity of communal life. To prevent either the triumph of liberalism or the victory of neopaganism, the curate concluded, National Socialists had only one option: retention of a Christian church bound to the state.[41]

In the mid-1930s, German Christians did have some reason to assume that the National Socialist regime shared their commitment to a state church. Confessing Church critics pointed to incidents in which the Nazi party supported German Christians in their pastoral offices despite opposition from congregations, or to Church Minister Kerrl's appointment of a radical German Christian as his sole theological adviser. "The state church as we now have it," the Confessing Church authors of one pamphlet announced, "is externally and internally the realization of the German Christian agenda."[42]

But German Christians discovered that they could not rely on Nazi loyalties to the state church for support in their struggle to control German Protestantism. In late 1936, lay German Christians in Westphalia, outraged by Confessing Church refusals to open church buildings for their use, decided to take action. In a public statement, they announced that members of the German Christian movement were prepared to cease payment of church taxes.[43] Two German Christians visited the president of the district government in Minden to present their concerns. German Christian lay people, they warned, sought decisive action against Confessing Church usurpers of the state church. Given the "disappointed and excited mood in their congregations," the spokesmen threatened, even "violent outbreaks" were to be feared. The results would be serious, they implied, claiming that their two congregations alone held 2,500 German Christians and membership in Westphalia as a whole reached 250,000.[44] Those German Christians' protests fell on deaf ears. Like their counterparts elsewhere, they discovered that Nazi authorities were all too willing to allow them and the Confessing Church to fight it out on their own in the hope that both camps would lose.

In 1940, General Superintendent Otto Dibelius, an adherent of the Con-

*Reich Minister of Church Affairs Hanns Kerrl and his wife. Kerrl held that position from the establishment of the ministry in 1935 until his death in 1941. He promoted "positive Christianity," which in his assessment was identical with National Socialism. Many of Kerrl's policies benefited the German Christians or at least acknowledged them as a significant interest group within German Protestantism. (Bundesarchiv Koblenz)*

fessing Church, proposed a compromise to restore peace in the Protestant church. Dibelius's scheme involved legal and organizational separation of the Confessing Church from the German Christians. Under his plan, each congregation would choose its allegiance, and both umbrella church organizations would enjoy the benefits of state affiliation.[45] The Westphalian German Christian Karl Wentz denounced the proposal out of hand; Dibelius, he snorted, was "out of touch with the mental world of National Socialist Germany.... He has not yet observed that in a total state, there can be only one church *in* the state, not against the state."[46] Wentz, a teacher and German Christian theorist of sorts, devoted considerable energy to maintaining ties among members of the movement, both during and after the Nazi period. From his vantage point in 1940, he advocated holding out for a unified state church that would be the bearer of German Christian ideas.

Wentz's optimism may seem farfetched, and arguably, he consistently overestimated the movement's strength. Even so, however, evidence suggests that at least some elements in the Confessing Church were moving in the direction Wentz foresaw. Most significant was that Dibelius, as Wentz did not fail to note, included implicit recognition of the Aryan clause in the church. "Only citizens of Germany," Dibelius's proposal stipulated, could be ordained.[47] That rather banal statement brought the Nuremberg Laws directly into the church. Seven years earlier, the Confessing Church had originated in protest to the removal of non-Aryans from pastoral office. By 1940, such exclusion was taken for granted. And even an outspoken individual like Dibelius considered it an acceptable price to pay for affiliation with the state. The decisive unity that German Christians hoped state sponsorship would provide to the people's church failed to materialize. Instead, the Nazi state had determined the limits within which any officially sanctioned church could function.

## War as the German Christian Pentecost

For the German Christians, war represented the ultimate moment of antidoctrinal, spiritual unity. In the heat of battle, they proclaimed, all Germans—pious or atheist, Catholic or Protestant—were as one. That same spirit of unity, German Christians insisted, must permeate the people's church. War was a sacrament and a celebration of the German Christian people's church, the formative moment that replaced Pentecost. According to the Pentecost sermon of a German Christian pastor in 1933, the Holy Spirit had revealed itself "in the trenches of the World War." Just as the "pure flame" at Pentecost had forged the disciples into "one heart and one soul," he announced, the Holy Spirit, in the fire of war, had completed the work of unifying the German *Volk*. The challenge now, he exhorted his audience, was to recapture that unity in the people's church.[48]

Another German Christian publication presented the "grand old man," Paul von Hindenburg, as antidoctrinal Christianity personified. The warrior Hindenburg, the author insisted, captured the imperative of spiritual unity between fighting front and home front in his words: "We feel here at the front that those at home are not praying enough."[49] That community of spiritual devotion to the embattled fatherland, German Christians asserted, was the most profound expression of the people's church.

Convinced that the people's church found realization in the solidarity of a *Volk* under arms, German Christians showed a good deal of interest in the military chaplaincy. Clergymen in the movement believed their intense loyalty to National Socialism made them natural candidates for jobs as chaplains. Ludwig Müller, the movement's most prominent public figure in the early years, experienced World War I as a naval chaplain and served as military district chaplain in Königsberg until he became Reich bishop in mid-1933. Throughout the 1930s, pro-Nazi pastors from as far away as Luseland, Saskatchewan, begged German church authorities for a chance to serve the new regime as military chaplains.[50] At least one request reached Reich Bishop Müller from a Baptist preacher, Otto Jäger in Pillkallen. Local Nazis assumed Jäger was a German Christian because, in the words of a party report from Pillkallen, "the Baptists are German Christians."[51]

Some German Christians managed to enter the chaplaincy. Their most influential representative, Heinrich Lonicer, rose from a military base chaplain in 1935 to a superintendent of chaplains during the war.[52] Lonicer's bid to become Protestant military bishop in 1939 failed,[53] but he still found ample opportunity to propagate antidoctrinal Christianity. For example, during the war, he criticized a subordinate for reciting the confession of faith in his services because "no one understood it any more." That same chaplain's sermon, Lonicer carped, had been "much too Christian"; one could still preach about God, he said, but not about Christ.[54] In 1942, Lonicer boasted that he violated military prohibitions against compulsory attendance at religious services by effecting enforced participation in three camp services he held in honor of Hitler's birthday.[55] Such an event provided the ultimate expression of antidoctrinal Christianity: it was not religious beliefs but ritual, a shared German identity, official coercion, and wartime spirit that unified Lonicer's audiences.

After 1939, German Christians had a chance to put into practice their notions about war as the great unifier of the people's church. While some German Christian clergy obtained positions in the chaplaincy, others seized informal opportunities to preach to the armed forces. One theologian reported in October 1939 that he had accepted an invitation from his commander to hold devotions for the troops.[56] Another pastor offered a lecture series in the military hospital at Lake Constance in 1944; he used that forum to agitate for the German Christian cause and stirred up considerable controversy.[57]

The amount of German Christian literature cleared for distribution to soldiers was far out of proportion to the movement's size. The press office of the Protestant church, military authorities, and the Protestant military bishop prepared a list of religious publications Protestant chaplains could hand out to the troops. The 1940 list included approximately one hundred titles. Twenty-four of them are immediately recognizable as German Christian items—works by well-known German Christians or products of German Christian presses. No publications from the Confessing Church were listed.[58]

German Christians found ways to send unapproved religious propaganda to members of the armed forces as well. At least two regional groups, in Westphalia and in Thuringia, mailed newsletters to soldiers at the front throughout the war. Pastor Walter Fiebig in Westphalia put out a monthly newsletter called the *Theologische Arbeitsbrief* (Theological working letter) that he also sent to members of the armed forces.[59] Fiebig, the self-styled spiritual leader of Westphalia's German Christians, maintained close contacts with a widespread network of pastors and German Christian luminaries, including his ally Karl Wentz in Minden. In Thuringia, the *Deutsche Christen Nationalkirchliche Einung Informationsdienst* (Information service of the German Christian National Church Union), under the direction of Pastor Heinz Dungs, Weimar, was a monthly bulletin that included news of soldiers in the German Christian movement—promotions, engagements, births—as well as religious propaganda in the form of meditations, sermons, and book reviews.[60]

German Christian literature emphasized war as the supreme test and the ultimate opportunity for the national, spiritual community. The people's church, German Christians insisted, was not a community of belief but a unity in battle. Typical is the following excerpt from a sermon of 1942: "Judaism has been dashed to pieces on the person of Christ. And the Soviet state too will shatter on Christ: this state that crucified Christ for a second time, that erected a monument to Judas Iscariot—and has demanded the blood of thousands upon thousands of martyrs. . . . But the life of our *Volk* too will be decided on the basis of Christ. . . . So we stand in the midst of the fires of the world . . . as protectors and defenders of the German Christian legacy. We stand before God as Germans and as Christians."[61]

On the home front, too, German Christians presented war as an expression of spiritual unity. The basis of a German people's church, Ludwig Müller argued, could not be "speeches about dogma" but a "positive Christianity" built on the "spiritual, godly values" represented by the "graves of soldiers and of victims of air attack on the home front."[62] "But only graves create a homeland," began one German Christian hymn: "Only our dead give us light. Only on mounds where mourners kneel, Only over coffins do you become a *Volk*."[63]

German Christians preached that war would forge an unbreakable unity of *Volk* and church, faith and nation. That solidarity proved elusive as conflict within the church continued. Under pressure of war, Westphalian German Christians lamented in 1943, opposition between their movement and the Confessing Church had if anything intensified.[64] And during the war, the Nazi regime increasingly revealed its antagonism to Christianity, even attacking the military chaplaincy. The offices of Martin Bormann, Heinrich Himmler, and Joseph Goebbels issued numerous orders prohibiting chaplains' activities, reducing their numbers, ordering them to locate themselves in areas of heaviest fighting—the so-called Uriah law—and refusing to award them the Iron Cross.[65]

Even among the fighting men, German Christian hopes for a spiritual breakthrough proved unfounded. One German Christian theologian at the front pointed to "vast, even grotesque" ignorance of the Bible and told of an individual who, seeing a picture of Jesus' mother, explained that was Mary, Jesus' wife. Both Old and New Testaments, he remarked, had lost all authority, and a similar "demystification" applied to the church and Jesus and even to death itself. The people's church, he argued, could rise above this disinterest only by adjusting its message to resonate with the remaining traces of religiosity in the *Volk*. That adaptation meant presenting God as "the father in whose hands we are safe" and the source of the "vital desire to be good"; the cross as a "witness of God's love for all brothers."[66] The triviality of that summary of the message of the church indicates that, when it came to antidoctrinal faith, German Christians were reaping what they had sown. They had replaced belief with ritual, ethnicity, state sponsorship, and war as the core of their spiritual community. In the process, they perpetuated a church with neither authority nor integrity.

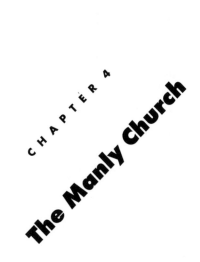

CHAPTER 4

The Manly Church

*We want a kind of Christianity*—with which one can do something in life, *a Christianity of which our youth will say: that is alive, there is heroism there. That is not "only" for old women, but for the life-affirming men of the Third Reich.*
—*German Christian flyer*

The German Christians aimed to include all Aryan Germans in the people's church. Within that institution, however, they foresaw a hierarchy based on gender. The people's church, German Christians insisted, would be a "manly" church that enshrined and promoted masculine qualities. With that stance, German Christians both expressed their view of proper gender relations and responded to attacks from denigrators. Nazi and neopagan critics accused Christianity of preaching weakness, humility, and defeatism, feminine traits antithetical to National Socialist values. In their efforts to defend against those charges, German Christians showed how they shared the principles of their attackers. True Christianity, they argued, was not feminine and weak but manly and hard.

Accounts of German Christian events provide some glimpses into the movement's version of manly Christianity. In January 1935, German Christians met in the pub of the Pschorr brewery in Munich to found a new local group. A young vicar from the Confessing Church and twelve of his friends attended as well; the vicar prepared a report. Between fifty-five and sixty people were present, he noted, most of them elderly. An engineer opened the meeting; two pastors were also on hand. The German Christians tried to get the Confessing Church interlopers to leave. When they refused, some of their hosts attacked them so viciously that, according to the reporter, "even two German Christian women" fled in shock. The account mentions no other female participants. The vicar was shoved to the door; a deacon received a punch in the face. Among the most forceful of the aggressors were a German Christian organist and the son of one of the pastors.[1]

German Christians tried to promote a manly image through their deeds and words. Statements from the movement, in particular those made by leading men, often used the adjectives *männlich* and *mannhaft* to modify the nouns *church, Christianity,* and *faith. Männlich* and *mannhaft* also appear as adverbs describing desirable behavior or praising actions of admired leaders. Both words can be translated as *manly* or *masculine*; they connote virility, bravery, and resoluteness.

The German Christian vocabulary of manliness also included words denoting the opposite condition. German Christian remarks often contrasted *Männlichkeit*—manliness—with qualities described as *schwach*—weak—or *weichlich*—effeminate, soft, or weak. The word *weichlich* is an especially telling foil to *männlich* because it sounds so much like the German word for female: *weiblich.* Although *weiblich* and *weichlich* stem from different roots—the former from *Weib* (woman), the latter from *weich* (soft)—their relationship is roughly equivalent to that between the English words *female* and *effeminate*, the first linked to biological femaleness, the second implying inappropriate or improper presence of traits associated with femininity, such as weakness and softness. In any statement in which *weichlich* and *männlich* appear as contrasts, *weiblich* is present too, first through its phonetic proximity to *weichlich*—we can almost hear it—and second by dint of the cultural link between the traits of femaleness—*Weiblichkeit*—and softness—*Weichlichkeit*.

Attention to notions of manliness illuminates ways that the German Christian movement situated itself with respect to the German past and political present. The concept of a *manly church* can help us to understand the significance of militarism in the German Christian self-image and to explore how members regarded the church's role in Germany's defeat in 1918. Sensitivity to issues of gender can shed light on the spread of racial thought in the church as well and make some sense of German Christian plans for ecclesiastical and liturgical reform.

## Code Word: The Soldier's Church

Images and associations that appear around the term *manly* in German Christian pronouncements are strikingly consistent. For proponents of the manly church, masculinity connoted a well-defined canon of soldierly qualities: it was manly to fight ruthlessly, to exhibit hardness and heroism, to follow orders with discipline and enthusiasm. Men too old or too young to be soldiers, homosexuals, and men unwilling or unable to fight did not fit the bill. German Christian spokespeople made it clear that the manly church would not simply be dominated by males but would house "real men." In 1935, a German Christian pastor from Oberbreidenbach (Hesse) made that distinction explicit in his call for "a church of men, not a church of women of both sexes."[2]

Images of combat and the collective memory of the Great War furnished the language and the metaphors for the manly church. German Christians compared the church struggle to the glorified experience of 1914 to 1918, identifying their cause with the front. In December 1933, the German Christian–dominated presbytery of the Reformed congregation in Dinslaken-Hiesfeld (Rhineland) used such an analogy to defend aggressive German Christian tactics. The German Christians, the presbyters maintained, stood at the "forefront" of the "struggle against atheists and against Rome." In wartime, the declaration pointed out, wartime rules applied. Deserters, saboteurs, and traitors were "stood up against the wall!" According to the presbyters, stricter enforcement of that rule after 1918 would have prevented "years of shame and misery." They closed with a call to the Protestant church to "learn from Germany's past!"[3]

A 1934 article in the German Christian bulletin of Saxony and Anhalt exemplifies the movement's use of military imagery. Titled "With God's Help, Advance and Break Through!" it phrased its challenge to German Christians in "the language of the front." Urging German Christians to "break through" to the unified Protestant church and to the *Volk*, the author closed with an exhortation: "The heroic attitude toward life is not an empty delusion, at least not for us people of the war generation."[4]

For German Christians, the manly church would not simply be like the war experience; it would recreate that experience, it would inspire true manliness in the form of courage and single-mindedness, and it would offer to the faithful the all-absorbing community of comrades. Remembering is an act of will. It was not without effort that, for so many Germans in the early 1930s, including those too young to have personal recollections, the memory of the world war remained an open wound. With their call for a manly church, German Christians tried to capitalize on the emotions and

*Procession of clergy with flags of the "Deutsche Christen"—German Christians—in Berlin for the official induction of Ludwig Müller into the office of Reich bishop. The German Christian movement used flags, uniforms, and other military trappings to promote a masculine image. (Evangelisches Zentralarchiv in Berlin)*

energy bound up with the wartime experience while expressing their own conviction that war represented the ultimate moment of German unity. At the same time, by praising soldierly values and enshrining them in the cry for a manly church, German Christians did their part to stoke the fires of resentment toward the Versailles settlement.

In the German Christian code, to be manly meant to be a National Socialist. Nazism itself was linked to soldierliness, and Nazi identity drew heavily on military trappings and symbols: flags, boots, marching formations, physical violence, songs and slogans that used wartime rhythms, language, and images. With the code word *manly*, German Christians sought to enhance their own profile through association with the masculine image of National Socialism. In 1933, German Christian leader Joachim Hossenfelder fondly proclaimed the German Christian Faith Movement the "storm troopers of the church," explaining that "both groups fight in the spirit of National Socialism for the manly external and internal realization of the Third Reich."[5]

German Christians perceived the stepped-up manliness they urged on the church as a temporary expedient, directly tied to the needs of the moment. This sense of urgency came across in a series of essays titled *Gnade und Männlichkeit* (Grace and manliness), published by the German Christian–dominated Office of Home Missions in Silesia. One author derived the pressing need for German manliness from the destitution of the German *Volk* after defeat in the world war.[6] Another item in the book associated manliness with both the Great War and the National Socialist struggle. To that author, war was the force that created German manliness. "Twenty years ago," he wrote, "the thunder of history roused our people. . . . We became a people of fighting men. In everyone a new image appeared: the image of German manliness. . . . The image of the hero storming forward grew into that of the man who endures to the end." National Socialism perfected German manliness, that writer continued. "The image of this manliness has engraved itself deeply on the hearts of men and youths. It nurtures the burning desire of our *Volk* to renew itself. . . . The unknown soldier of the world war and the unknown fighter for unity and purity of the *Volk*, those are the images of manliness that move our hearts."[7] As a code word, the manly church represented German Christian efforts to link their movement to the world war veteran who had not given up the torch and to the National Socialist fighter whose struggle formed part of Nazi mythology.

The association of the church struggle with the war experience of 1914 to 1918 highlights a crucial aspect of the manly church slogan. The German

Christian notion of a manly church seemed to offer defeated soldiers and those who identified with their failure a chance to redeem themselves on the home front by reasserting manly qualities. This act of redemption had special significance for the church and the men associated with it. If one believed, as many Germans did, that the fighting front had been stabbed in the back by the weak-willed at home, then the church was implicated on the side of the home front. Moreover, the stab-in-the-back-myth had its own gender dimension: those doing the stabbing were, by definition, women and unmanly men because, according to the terms of the myth, real men, that is, soldiers, had been at the front.

Reich Bishop Müller shared the view that the church had been allied with the feminine home front during the world war. In a 1936 speech in Oberbarmen (Rhineland) he made these remarks about 1914: "Then came the war. Everyone returned to church. And the good, dumb pastors thought the people were becoming pious again. (laughter, applause!) But I have another opinion and am not afraid to tell it to you. The people had no ecclesiastical or religious interests. They came for a very selfish reason: their husbands, their sons, their fiancés were out there at the front. And they didn't want them to die. So they prayed—in the church and at home, too."[8]

By labeling the church manly, German Christians hoped to wrench it out of the feminized home-front category—the side of the weaklings who had allegedly betrayed Germany—and ally it with the soldiers, the thwarted heroes. For the German Christians, the ideal of a manly church offered both compensation for the emasculating experience of the lost war and a chance for the church to absolve itself of complicity in the stab in the back. It was almost always men, and most often clergymen from the cohort of participants in the world war, who extolled the manly church as a soldierly church. That is not surprising given the vulnerability of their own masculine identity to attacks on the church for its supposed contribution to defeat.

German Christians offered the manly church as a corrective to the feminine church they believed had failed in the war. In his speeches on behalf of the German Christian cause, Hossenfelder stressed the compatibility of masculinity and faith by urging "aggressive Christianity." This new manliness, Hossenfelder explained, contrasted sharply with older presentations of Christianity as "something for the weak," "inappropriate" for men. Those associations, he claimed, were fundamentally wrong. "The origin of Christianity is anything but effeminate and weak," Hossenfelder argued. "Jesus Christ stood alone without any external

*Flanked by storm troopers, Friedrich Wieneke, German Christian
cathedral pastor in Soldin, addresses the Student Fighting League of German
Christians in the summer of July 1933. Wieneke later became the movement's
chronicler. (Evangelisches Zentralarchiv in Berlin)*

means of support in the tumult of his time. . . . He is a shining example of heroic courage. . . . Christian faith is a manly, heroic matter."[9]

According to German Christians, the church had failed to rally the people during the war and in the years to follow because it had fallen victim to emasculating forces. Speaking in Breslau in 1934, one German Christian bishop blamed "the liberalism of the nineteenth century" for producing a style of worship that was "un-German," "feminine," "decadent," and "in keeping with the general alienation from the Word of God."[10] A year later, a German Christian women's leader contended that feminization of the church had even alienated women. In her view, "a strong, vital Christianity" would attract people of both sexes, whereas "a soft Christianity of feelings . . . did not interest the *Volk* as a whole at all!"[11]

## Gender and Race

In important ways, the manly church slogan bound German Christians to the racialist worldview of National Socialism. Sexism and a sharp division of gender roles helped pave the way for racist antisemitism in the church. According to the German Christians, only a church devoid of such feminine qualities as compassion and capable of hard, manly resolve could become a front-line fighter against racial impurity. Ludwig Müller voiced the connection between manliness, race, the *Volk*, and the church in a 1939 publication. By keeping their "German blood pure from the blood of alien races," he argued, and especially by banning "the Jewish influence that is foreign to our nature from all areas of German life," Germans were demonstrating their "love for the German homeland and the German people." Such love, Müller contended, had a "hard, warrior-like face. It hates everything soft and weak because it knows that all life can only then remain healthy and fit for life when everything antagonistic to life, the rotten and the indecent, is cleared out of the way and destroyed."[12]

German Christians used divisions between the sexes to justify the introduction of racial distinctions into the church. Just as Christian faith did not eradicate physical differences between male and female, they argued, it did not negate the "biological fact" of race. Wilhelm Stapel, a prolific German Christian theologian, spelled out this line of thinking in 1934. "In the earthly congregation," he wrote, "one cannot revoke the difference between the sexes, even though, 'in the resurrection they neither marry nor are given in marriage' (Matthew 22:30)." It was just as impossible, Stapel contended, "to declare invalid physical, mental and spiritual differences among peoples, simply because, 'by one Spirit are we all baptized into one body, whether we be Jews or Gentiles' (1 Corinthians 12:13)." For Stapel, the analogy from gender to race justified exclusion of non-Aryans from the pastoral office. Just as Paul, "for very earthly reasons," forbade women to speak in the church,[13] he argued, German Protestants could "forbid the Jews to speak in our German congregations." Paradoxically, as final proof of the "rectitude of this analogical conclusion from sex to race [*Volk*]," Stapel quoted Galatians 3:28: "[In Christ] there is neither Jew nor Greek . . . there is neither male nor female."[14]

A German Christian circular from 1935 again referred to Galatians 3:28 and its claim that salvation through Christ transcended differences among people. The publication conceded that some people tried to use that verse to "deny the validity of the racial idea in the church" and to resist introduction of the Aryan clause. "Any child," the circular's author scoffed, could see the foolishness of such a claim: "When there is no longer 'man and woman' in the earthly church, then we will also believe that there is no longer any difference between German and Jewish." It was a mistake, the writer insisted, to "confuse the spiritual unity of the church, which we German Christians have always represented, with denial of racial differences." He saw "no contradiction" in accepting other races in "the spiritual community of word and sacrament" while rejecting them as "members of the *Volk* in the people's church."[15] By stressing the gap between the invisible, universal church and the visible church, where race and gender reigned, German Christians attempted to legitimize the exclusion of non-Aryans from the people's church.

Instead of repudiating this line of argument outright, many neutrals and Confessing Church people tacitly accepted the German Christian assumptions about gender and race. They concentrated on trying to show that the church had in fact been a bulwark against the encroachment of Jewish influence. Only a few individuals cut through to the heart of the issue. Dietrich Bonhoeffer, for example, attacked the German Christians' gender-to-race analogy in a 1933 essay opposing the Aryan Paragraph. There was no getting around it, he argued, excluding the "Jewish Christian" from the pastoral office relegated him to an inferior position in the church. It proved nothing, he continued, to point to the biblical instruction, "Let your women keep silence in the churches" (1 Corinthians 14:34). Either one read that verse as a law, in which case it said nothing about "Jewish Christians," or one did not read it as a law, which would mean that women too could speak in the congregation. Bonhoeffer considered any subjection of the pastoral office to "the arbitrariness of the congregation" unacceptable.[16] For the German Christians, in contrast, nothing but the congregations' preferences mattered.

## The Brown Man in the Church

German Christians hoped to promote religious revival by latching onto the manly spirit of National Socialism. The church's task, Hossenfelder stressed in November 1933, was to preach the gospel "to those who are alive today, to the brown man, who personifies the age in which we live."[17] Only within the manly church, Hossenfelder and other German Christians contended, would National Socialism find its synthesis with Christianity. To many members of the movement, that synthesis offered the church's sole chance for survival. According to Magdeburg's German Christian bishop Friedrich Peter, only one thing mattered: *that the brown army of Adolf Hitler not be lost to the church.*"[18]

To Friedrich Coch, the German Christian bishop of Saxony, National Socialism, Christianity, and manliness were inextricable. In a 1936 speech in Dresden, he said a woman had asked him, "What is one first—a Christian or a National Socialist?" When he responded, "a National Socialist," she was "shocked," but he explained: "In order to be a Christian, I first have to have been born and if I've been born in this country, I'm a German and every German today, if he is a decent guy [*ein anständiger Kerl*] is a National Socialist (applause)."[19]

As Coch's response indicated, German Christians' manly faith easily deteriorated into nothing more than a restatement of National Socialist ideology. A fictional piece in the German Christian organ "The Gospel in the Third Reich" from November 1933 illustrates this tendency. The wife of a storm trooper, in obedience to her husband, Fritz's, last request that she "save" the communist who killed him, convinces the communist to join the SA. He in turn is killed by former comrades, but, she recounts, "he died a hero"; over his grave hung a swastika, the "sign that God forgave him, just as Fritz forgave him."[20] In this story the National Socialist epitomizes manly Christianity; his forgiveness toward his enemy provides the model for God's forgiveness of sin.

The call for a manly church expressed German Christian efforts to bring men into more active involvement in church life. Organizers worried about the absence of men at their events. In 1936, the German Christian parish paper in Wetten-Ruhr addressed a question directly to men: "Where are you? Where were you during our last German Christian evening? We know there are many demands on you, but we cannot and must not discuss and take action without sufficient participation from you and without your cooperation. It's your own fault when afterward you are 'not in the know.' "[21]

Neutrals and Confessing Church people joined the German Christians to decry the physical absence of men from church services. In a report from 1937, a non–German Christian pastor from Duisburg attributed male alienation from Christianity to man's superior rationality, active sex drive, and independent will. Men, the author claimed, as the "bearers of public life," were more susceptible to anti-Christian trends; moreover, they lacked "civil courage."[22] Among the neopagan groups, too, it seems women were more active than men. A male medical doctor in Hauer's German Faith Movement grumbled about this phenomenon in 1932. "Something else has struck me," he wrote Hauer, "the overrepresentation of the female element at our meetings . . . I'm not 100% in agreement with . . . [the] view of the 'physiological feeblemindedness of the female' (!) but without a doubt among women feeling is dominant . . . and it would seem to me rather risky, given the serious problems and questions that have brought us together, to take a position that emphasized feeling unduly."[23] Hauer's response conceded the numerical preponderance of women, but unlike his Christian contemporaries, he did not consider that situation a problem. In his view, women's "superior religious intuition" was to be respected.[24]

The most obvious way to institutionalize manliness in the church was to bring more males into the services. German Christians found that the easiest method involved exploiting contacts with local storm trooper or Nazi party units and ordering the ranks to appear. Such shows of strength, or what a neopagan derided as "commandeered Christianity,"[25] occurred often in early 1933. German Christians tended to interpret those events as signs of religious revival.[26] Over time, however, that method ceased to be an option as Nazi authorities sought to avoid anything that might strengthen the churches.

Beginning in late 1933, a series of directives from party and state offices tried to ensure the independence of Nazi organizations from church matters. On 13 October 1933, Hitler's deputy Rudolf Hess issued a decree stating that no National Socialist was to suffer disadvantage for not belonging to a particular denomination or church party.[27] In November 1935, party headquarters in Munich ordered strict reserve toward church affairs and dissociation of party members from church activities; in 1936, it prohibited party uniforms at church services or events.[28] Himmler removed the SS from church concerns as well. In 1934, he ordered the "honorable discharge of clergymen of any confession" from the SS. A year later, he forbade members of the SS to play a leadership role in religious or faith organizations.[29] As of August 1936, SS musicians could not participate in any religious services, even out of uniform.[30]

German Christians floated various schemes to attract men into the church. In December 1933, Hossenfelder introduced the "Sunday of the Fathers," whereby the service on the first Sunday of each month would be geared especially toward men.[31] A German Christian pastor in Upper Silesia proposed obligating all men in the movement to hold daily devotions with their families, attend church services and Bible studies, and witness for Christ at their jobs and among their comrades.[32] Some German Christians tried to organize special men's groups, similar to women's aid circles, in support of the cause. In 1935, for example, a German Christian congregational representative and postal inspector in a Ruhr community set up an anti–Confessing Church men's group. The only record of its activity involves disputes over church property: evidently the postal inspector moved thirty-seven chairs and seven tables from the church meeting room to the local Hitler Youth house and, together with an accomplice in party uniform, walked off with some of the instruments from the brass ensemble.[33] In general, it seems it was considerably easier to get women's groups going than men's. Of the churches covered in the news column of one Westphalian German Christian paper, only St. Paul's in Dortmund had a men's group, while some churches had a German Christian Women's Service, a mothers' circle, and a young girls' group, in addition to boys' and girls' clubs.[34]

If German Christians found it difficult to attract large numbers of men to their events or to institutionalize their male involvement, they could at least seek to create the impression of manliness. Physical arrangement of meetings could serve to produce a masculine effect: German Christians often gathered in veterans' halls and pubs and decorated their space with national flags. Frequently participants smoked and drank beer during the proceedings.[35] Organizers paid close attention to the numbers of males and females present, measuring the success of a gathering by the percentage of men in the audience. The more men the better, and the more manly the men present, the better still, so that young men counted for more than old men, and men in uniform topped the list.

Concern with attendance rates by gender was both an attempt to quantify manliness and an effort to convey a manly image, even if it meant distorting the facts for public consumption. German Christian publications pay so little attention to women that one tends to imagine the gatherings as exclusively male.[36] Reports of the movement's Reich Conference in Berlin in April 1933, for example, mention very few women, yet a photo of part of the assembly hall shows 47 of the 112 people captured by the lens to be women.[37] In the years before the war began in 1939, women only rarely

*First Reich Conference of German Christians, Berlin, 3–5 April 1933.*
*On the banner behind the podium: "Read the 'Gospel in the Third Reich'!"*
*(*Evangelium im Dritten Reich, *the German Christian newspaper). The*
*photograph reveals the participation of significant numbers of women.*
*(Kommunalarchiv Minden)*

assumed any public role at German Christian events. At most, they graced the audience with a poem or a solo, like the woman who sang "Heil'ger Gott wir treten an, deines Geistes Sturmgeschlecht" ("Holy God we come before you, storm troops of your spirit") at the induction of a German Christian pastor in Fürth (Bavaria) in April 1939.[38]

Accounts from the Confessing Church and from state and party offices consistently show that, contrary to German Christian claims, women outnumbered men at the movement's events, often by a wide margin. A 1934 police report on a German Christian meeting in Berlin described the ratio of women to men as more than three to one (one hundred to thirty).[39] In March 1937, a German Christian meeting in Hanover drew twelve hundred people, almost two-thirds of them women.[40] These observers often intended the attendance figures they provided to embarrass the German Christians, but even so, it seems that at best the audiences consisted of women and men in equal numbers. There are few more telling admissions of this than the 1937 account of a church service in Dortmund in the Westphalian German Christians' publication. It was "a joy," the author noted, "to see that about half of those attending the church service were men!"[41]

## Plans for Manly Reform

The quest for manliness demanded alterations to Christian teaching. In the interests of manliness, German Christians searched for masculine role models. Some found the ideal of "a hard, manly piety" in the Old Testament. According to a Marburg professor of theology, a proper reading of the Old Testament could "sweep sweetness and sentimentality out of the parish and out of the church service."[42] For the movement as a whole, however, even the most manly figures of the Old Testament were too Jewish to fit the bill.

One advocate of manly Christianity, a retired major, argued that the Bible was the ideal handbook of a soldierly faith. In his view, "Those who pronounce as repulsive everything unnatural, effeminate, overly sweet or affected, who condemn the bloodless impotence of some pictures of Christ or the 'unctuous' tone of some sermons, can only have the heartfelt concurrence of those who truly have their roots in the Bible." He praised the manly piety of Friedrich the Great and his army, attributing "Old Fritz's" triumph against all of Europe to his "Christian spirit." Lack of that spirit, he continued, had brought ruin and betrayal in 1918.[43] Other German Christians pointed to certain Bible verses for a link between manliness, strength, and Christianity. A particular favorite was 1 Corinthians 16:13: "Watch ye, stand fast in the faith, quit you like men, be strong."[44]

The New Testament posed serious challenges as a manual of masculinity for the German Christians. Soldiers and warriors are scarce on its pages; Paul was a problem for proponents of manly religiosity, and Jesus too presented difficulties. German Christians devoted considerable attention to revising the image of Jesus to fit the demands of a manly religion. They stressed his heroism and viewed as anathema the aspects of his nature captured in the phrase "Lamb of God." In 1933, an engineer from Lüdinghausen (Westphalia) sent his comments on German Christianity to Hitler. He argued that German nature demanded a "fighting Christ," not "a cowardly sufferer" who assumed the guilt of others and turned the other cheek to his enemies.[45] A leading Thuringian German Christian was even more explicit in a 1936 statement. "We can naturally have nothing to do with a little lamb kind of Christianity or with any pietistic or petty-bourgeois view of Jesus," he maintained. "That view was in any case never anything but a nasty degradation of Jesus's greatness into the realm of sentimentality. The man from Nazareth, who represented pure love to those suffering inwardly and outwardly, was at the same time, an unprecedented warrior."[46]

Heroes of German history proved more amenable to manly revision than biblical figures. For many German Christians Martin Luther exemplified the fusion of manliness, Christianity, and Germanness. Although he was not a soldier, Luther's rejection of monasticism and celibacy gave him solid potential as a paragon of manliness. In a publication of the German Christian Women's Service in 1937, a leading German Christian described Luther's marriage as a "defiant declaration of war on a totally mistaken kind of piety." Luther, that author maintained, demonstrated no "sultry sensuality," only "healthy, straightforward, strong masculinity."[47] Another German Christian blamed the emasculation of the church in Germany on neglect of Luther. He decried the "effeminacy" that had invaded the church through "sentimental" sermons, "religious kitsch," the "overly sweet picture of Jesus that the Nazarenes and others have produced," and a "pious English singsong" form of church music. Since the German Enlightenment, he argued, appreciation of Luther had declined and, in his view, that was why the church had "lost so many men."[48]

The German Christian list of manly heroes was long and varied. From the artist Albrecht Dürer to the nationalist poet Ernst Moritz Arndt, such figures provided material for innumerable sermons, lectures, and devotional books.[49] The more recent past also offered models of manly piety and pious masculinity. In 1934, *Evangelium im Dritten Reich* printed an article by Horst Wessel's sister titled "On the Faith of My Brother Horst." Here the dead Nazi hero became manly Christianity personified. Horst, his sister wrote, "never considered Christianity to be something reactionary or alien to German nature." According to Ingeborg Wessel, their father, "the war veteran and Pastor Dr. Ludwig Wessel," refused to accept the Weimar Republic and "continued to fight for Germany against the new system." As a result, she asserted, "my brother Horst certainly never experienced the church as some relic of the distant past. Our father was far too much a willing warrior of God for that."[50] As the quasi-canonization of Wessel suggests, in their quest for the manly church, German Christians added new "patriarchs" to the Christian tradition. With manliness as the criterion, Wessel surpassed Abraham or the apostles as a figure of religious significance.

German Christians portrayed their own leaders as manly heroes. This proclivity is most obvious in the case of Reich Bishop Müller. In German Christian propaganda, Müller embodied manly Christianity. He made public appearances in military uniform, spoke in a coarse manner, and referred often to his wartime experiences. In all of the telegrams from various camps in the church thanking the Reich bishop for his response to the Sports Palace affair in November 1933, the adjective used most commonly

*Ludwig Müller became Germany's first and last Protestant Reich bishop in 1933. A staunch German Christian and former naval chaplain, he cultivated a manly image. Shown here with Prussian commissioner of churches August Jäger. (Evangelisches Zentralarchiv in Berlin)*

to praise his reaction was *manly (mannhaft)*.[51] A German Christian circular of 1935 continued the earlier trend of identifying the Reich bishop as the incorporation of Christianity and masculinity. Ludwig Müller, it was reported, closed the church leaders' conference in November 1934 with a "word on the current situation that was both deeply Christian and manly."[52]

Müller presented himself as something of a "ladies' man." Rumors about his marital infidelity and questionable sexual morals may have added to his aura of virility. According to a Confessing Church report on his visit to Bad Oeynhausen in 1935, Müller enjoyed some success with the "weaker sex": "The Reich bishop appears! He is greeted with extraordinary enthusiasm. He seems especially to have captured the fancy of the female participants of the event. . . . He receives enthusiastic ovations, namely from the female guests."[53] Such remarks are admittedly ambiguous, and the writer's disdain could well be interpreted as an attempt to explain the inexplicable, that is, that only dupes like women could possibly support Reibi Müller. German Christian sources, however, echoed the claims that Müller had a special appeal to women. In 1936, one young woman from Baden even wrote a poetic tribute for him in a Black Forest dialect and sent it to his office.[54]

Language was Müller's main tool in the construction of a manly image. In August 1933, while still Reich bishop–designate, he received accolades from the German Christian press for "speaking the language of these men to an emerging *Volk* in an age of manly uprising."[55] According to the Reich bishop, a true pastor "spoke from the pulpit in the language of the people, above all, the language of the brown man."[56] One gets a sense of Müller's use of language from his versions of Bible stories. In retelling the story of the Samaritan woman at the well (John 4:5–30), he presented the woman as a fool, Jesus as crude. "God is good," Müller began. "Once a woman from Canaan came to Christ to ask where she should worship God. Christ told her what God is. The Savior said to her: Oh woman, are you stupid! [*Ach Weib, bist du dumm!*] God is spirit, and those who worship him must worship him in spirit and in truth."[57] Müller further illustrated the use of manly themes in a parable he told at a 1934 appearance in Dortmund: "When the young soldier comes into the city, they say to him—let's have one on you—and then they drink more than they can handle—and they go to still other bars, and the next day, they have a bad conscience. Many a man wants to get away from it all when he thinks of the things he's done; he's ashamed before his mother and before his girl in his hometown. Then he goes the next morning to church. If a pastor is there who talks about

*Reich Bishop Müller on tour in Westphalia in 1935. Behind him to the right is Friedrich Tausch, Reinhold Krause's successor as leader of Berlin German Christians. In his public appearances, speeches, and writings, Müller promoted a folksy view of Christianity intended to appeal to ordinary people. (Kommunalarchiv Minden)*

some religious theme and finds no words to comfort him, he says to himself, I'll never go back there again."[58]

German Christians undertook liturgical renovations intended to reflect and promote manliness. In June 1934, the *Evangelische Beobachter* (Protestant observer) raved about an outdoor church service for farmers that featured a male choir, a brass ensemble, and proclamation of a blessing on the fields.[59] Events such as the Day of Mourning for the World War dead (*Volkstrauertag*) provided a perfect opportunity for proclaiming the compatibility of Christianity and manliness. These commemorative spectacles inspired a corpus of German Christian liturgical guides and pseudo-military hymns, like the chorale "Death, You Are the Pale Comrade" (*Tod du bist der bleiche Kamerad*):

> Death, you are the pale comrade,
> whom the drum calls to the final fray;
> With the dead on the path to the stars

boldly advancing on the gates of eternity.
Hush! The flags are being lowered
as the silent brothers pass.
He who calls the brave to the stars
insists they reawaken in honor.
And he draws the flags up to the light,
so that they blaze in glory, holy, grand!
And the face of death is shining
and the womb of mother earth is blooming.[60]

For German Christians, church music was a particularly fertile area for the transformation from an effeminate to a manly style. *Evangelium im Dritten Reich* devoted special attention to the new German Christian emphasis on manly singing. "We sing our songs," the paper announced, "the rediscovered masculine notes of faith from ages past, and the new songs too, that grew out of the experiences of the people in the days of the National Socialist revolution."[61] A 1934 German Christian program for an Advent church service described the music as "manly and powerful. The rhythm of marching columns conjures up the image that an awakened *Volk* is marching toward the light."[62] By 1937, a prominent German Christian publicist stressed the new liturgical forms, especially the hymns, as the crowning achievement of German Christianity. In these "*new forms of celebration*," he exulted, "we hear the free, joyous, invigorating message of the fatherly love of God, as witnessed in Christ, from men who are truly alive and who therefore *serve life*."[63]

A handful of German Christian lyricists and musicians produced numerous manly hymns. The melodies were sharply rhythmic, the lyrics heavy on words and phrases like *comrade*, *the battle*, and the *Führer*. German Christians sang of "calling to combat" and announced the "storm troops of God's Spirit."[64] An example from the German Christian National Church Union song sheets typifies these traits:

We need men, with tumult in their blood,
and heaven in their hearts;
who rise like shining arrows
from the rushing floods of the day. . . .
Men who look out at life
from their armor reverberating with masculinity;
who bow their knee before God,
but never their heart or their head before anyone.[65]

*Ludwig Müller addressing a rally of twenty thousand German Christians and supporters in Berlin's Sports Palace, February 1934. The large banner in the back reads: "For the German People's Church." (Landeskirchenarchiv, Bielefeld)*

All such hymns shared a military preoccupation and a concomitant deemphasis of usual Christian themes: Jesus, salvation, sin, heaven, forgiveness, grace, mercy, the church.

Lay people also participated in liturgical innovations that celebrated manliness. For example, a German Christian teacher, choirmaster, and local group leader in Schönau, Lower Silesia, composed a hymn titled "Life Is an Eternal Struggle." "Life is an eternal struggle," he wrote, "with people, cares, sickness, sin. A German Christian must be able to find his way in every situation. With manly decisiveness, never wavering, he will bear his burden. Fate can never overcome him; With faith in God, all will go well!"[66]

But whether clergy or lay, it was men who produced the new manly hymns. Some German Christian women wrote poems and songs as well, but they tended to focus on nature, the family, and motherhood. Few of their works made it into the new German Christian songbooks. The main German Christian hymnbook, *Großer Gott, wir loben Dich!* (Holy God, we praise Thy name!), included more than three hundred hymns, but women wrote the lyrics to only seven of them. Of those seven, only one appeared in the section of songs for the fatherland. The other six appeared under headings such as thanksgiving, bereavement, and repentance.[67]

German Christians did not invent the ideal of the manly church, and concern that Christian virtues were somehow antithetical to soldierly qualities predated establishment of their movement. After 1918, pastors and theologians of all political persuasions had rushed to prove the church's loyalty to the fighting front by stressing how many Protestant clergy had died in uniform.[68] During the 1930s, the Confessing Church too demonstrated concern with its manly image. For example, in 1937, a Confessing Church flyer from the Rhineland closed with 1 Corinthians 16:13, a favorite Bible verse of German Christian publicists: "Watch ye, stand fast in the faith, quit you like men, be strong."[69] Not surprisingly, the manly component of the German Christian program attracted little attention and elicited almost no criticism. With their yearning for a manly church, the German Christians could claim to be the heirs of Ernst Moritz Arndt, the nationalist poet of the Napoleonic era, whose poem they often sang at their gatherings:

> Who is a man?
> He who can pray and trusts the Lord his God;
> Though all should fail, he'll never quail,
> The brave man knows no dread.
> Who is a man?
> He who believes, with passion, true and free;
> For this his shield shall never yield
> to earthly enemy.
> Who is a man?
> He who can love, heartfelt, pious, warm;
> The holy fire grants courage divine
> and steels his mighty arm.
> This is the man,
> He who can die for God and fatherland;
> He'll fight on, brave until the grave
> with heart and voice and hand.
> So German man,
> Oh man so free, To arms! With God the Lord!
> For only He gives victory
> and aid, and fortune good.[70]

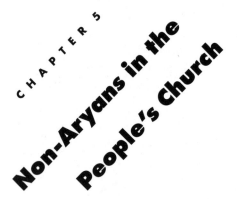

CHAPTER 5

Non-Aryans in the People's Church

*A godless fellow member of the* Volk *is closer to us than an alien, even if that alien sings the same song or prays the same prayer.*
*—German Christian leader Joachim Hossenfelder, 1933*

In October 1933, an Erfurt man wrote to Reich Bishop Müller. His son, he explained, had been a student of Protestant theology in Halle until regulations against non-Aryans forced him to leave the program. The young man had assumed he was fully Aryan, but events required his father to tell him the truth: his grandparents had converted from Judaism as youths. Could the Reich bishop make an exception, the father now asked, so that his son could complete his studies and become a pastor?[1]

A German Christian theologian in Jena answered the letter on Müller's behalf. His response upheld the prohibition against theological studies for non-Aryans. The church had "pledged itself" to uphold the "*völkisch* state," the professor explained; it was not possible "to deviate from the rule."[2] Denial of his petition aroused the father to the issues at stake. For him, he wrote back, the church had ceased to exist. Restrictions against non-Aryans had erased the welcoming "Come unto me" from above the door and replaced it with the flaming letters: "lasciate ogni speranza voi ch'entrate!" Abandon all hope you who enter here![3]

The experiences of the Erfurt man and his son reveal some of the ways that the German Christians implemented their vision of a racially exclusive church. They targeted people defined as non-Aryan Christians and attempted to hunt them out of the clergy and eventually out of the congregations. At the level of principle, German Christians applied their racial notions energetically and consistently. The movement demonstrated remarkable unity, for example, in rejecting the idea that baptism could change the status of a former Jew. In contacts with individual non-Aryans, however, the German Christians sometimes showed uncertainty and even flexibility in applying their racial ideology. Such incidents do not suggest that German Christians took their racist ecclesiology lightly. Instead, they reflect how rarely German Christians faced challenges to the practical implications of their racial doctrine and how fully they could count on support from other elements of their society.

The National Socialist state, pursuing its own anti-Jewish program, implemented measures that executed many of the German Christians' exclusionary plans for them. Even opponents in the Confessing Church presented no organized front against the German Christians' racial assumptions and offered little opposition to their treatment of non-Aryans. Like the German Christians, almost all other Protestants referred to converts from Judaism and their descendants as "Jewish Christians" or "baptized Jews." By using those labels, representatives of all camps in the church struggle indicated that they too regarded "Jewishness" as an immutable biological fact that was perhaps modified but not transformed by conversion to Christianity. This rather broad consensus meant that German Christians, having designed a wall of racial exclusion around their ideal spiritual community, could leave much of the construction and maintenance work to other elements within German society and inside the Protestant church.

German Christians had few contacts with Jewish people and almost never mentioned actual, individual Jews in their speeches and writings. Germany's Jewish population was small: 582,000 in 1934, by widely accepted figures.[4] The German Christian movement opposed missions to the Jews so its members had no reason to seek interaction with them. Non-Aryan Christians were another matter. Those people, converts from Judaism to Christianity, or children and in some cases grandchildren of such converts, drew intense scrutiny from German Christians. The number of non-Aryan Christians in Germany was small, too, despite the impression created by German Christians' urgent calls for racial exclusion. Interior Ministry statistics from April 1935 showed non-Aryans to be 2.3 percent of the German population. "Religious Jews," the report specified, numbered 475,000; the category "Jews not of the Jewish faith" included 300,000 peo-

*Joachim Hossenfelder, German Christian Reich leader, vice-president of the Prussian Upper Consistory, and bishop of Berlin-Brandenburg. Hossenfelder, who liked to refer to the German Christians as "storm troopers of Christ," led the movement at its peak in 1933. After he was ousted as Reich leader, he remained active in various splinter German Christian groups. (Kommunalarchiv Minden)*

ple; and an estimated 750,000 "Jewish-German halfbreeds (first and second degrees)" made up the balance.[5]

German Christians pointed hysterically to marriages between Christians and Jews, warning that the time had come to dam the flood of racial defilement. Here too the numbers told a different story. In 1937, only about forty thousand such unions existed in all of Germany. Before 1933, Germans had tended to use the term *mixed marriage* to describe Protestant-Catholic couples. After the National Socialist revolution, the Protestant church, its "responsibility for *Volk* and race aroused," began to devote more attention to marriages between Christians and Jews. At the same time, the Nazi state appropriated the term *mixed marriage* (*Mischehe*), restricting its application to Christian-Jewish unions.[6]

Statistics on numbers of Jews converting to Christianity also fail to substantiate German Christian fears of the de-Aryanization of Protestantism. In the 1940s, a German Christian report indicated that between 1934 and 1939, only 852 converts from Judaism joined the Protestant church in Brandenburg. Pomerania had seen 6 such converts in that period, the Rhine Province 49, Westphalia 8. Of the regional churches outside the Old Prussian Union, Nassau-Hesse, with 65, had the most converts from Judaism during those years; Mecklenburg, Oldenburg, and Braunschweig had none. In Austria, the report mentioned, 594 Jews converted to Protestantism over the same time period, although the annual number dropped from 126 in 1937, to 85 in 1938, down to 2 in 1939.[7] Altogether since 1900, only 14,461 German Jews had converted to Protestant Christianity.[8] Small wonder that though German Christians had a great deal to say about Judaism in general, they rarely discussed individual Jews, and even the subject of non-Aryan Christians came up most frequently in an abstract rather than specific context.

The rest of this chapter looks at German Christian encounters with people defined as non-Aryans, focusing on five points of contact: baptism, the Aryan Paragraph, non-Aryan clergy or clergy with non-Aryan wives, non-Aryan lay members of the Protestant church, and church musicians. The first two issues reflect efforts to establish principles of exclusion from the Christian community. The other three topics illustrate how, on the basis of racial criteria, German Christians tried to expel or restrict certain individuals in the Protestant church.

## Baptism

German Christians recognized baptism, the symbol and proclamation of church membership, as a pivotal point for imposing their racial policy on the Christian community. Baptism was crucial to the Nazi system, too, because the definitions of Aryan and non-Aryan depended on it, or at least on whether one's grandparents had been baptized. By echoing the state's interest in baptism, German Christians not only voiced support for the system; they helped ensure that it could function at all. Without the cooperation of the Christian churches, whose officials recorded baptisms, issued baptismal certificates, and provided proof that relatives and ancestors had been baptized, it would have been impossible to enforce any distinction between Aryan and non-Aryan Germans.

Members of the German Christian movement denied that baptism changed the status of a former Jew. Because the German Christians sought to fuse church and nation, they tended to blur the two contentions inherent in their stance on baptism: baptism could not make a Jew a German, they argued, and baptism could not make a Jew a Christian. Just as Jewishness for German Christians was both a religious and a racial category, so German Christianity, its polar opposite, encompassed both a religious and a racial identity.

German Christians warned that baptism could become a portal through which alien elements entered the Aryan bloodstream. In January 1933, *Deutsches Volkstum* (German ethnicity), a periodical coedited by a German Christian, addressed what it called the "problem of Jewish converts." In a system based on distinctions of blood, the author intoned, baptism must be denied any efficacy. In his view, baptism provided a "wedge" for Jews who sought to improve their standing by assimilation and deception. Converts from Judaism to Christianity, he emphasized, belonged in the official category of Jews.[9]

Public statements by German Christians stressed that baptism could not bring a non-Aryan into the people's church. When the German Christian chronicler Friedrich Wieneke called for a "truly German Church" in 1933, he specified that it was to be based on blood not baptism. "The baptized Jew does not belong," he pointed out, "nor for that matter do the baptized Chinese and Negro." They could be "Jewish Christians or Christians of another race," he conceded, but they could never be "German Christians or members of the German church community."[10] A signboard hung in Lippe (Westphalia) crudely and accurately summed up the German Christian view of baptism: "Baptism may be quite useful, but it cannot straighten a nose [Die Taufe mag ganz nützlich sein, Doch glattet sie kein Nasenbein]."[11]

Some German Christians took the initiative to prevent baptism of non-Aryans even though neither Protestant church law nor the National Socialist state forbade it. In late 1935, a German Christian church council member in Breslau boasted that he and colleagues had blocked baptisms of non-Aryans in Silesia. According to his account, pastors gave church councils names of Jews who requested conversion to Christianity to decide whether they should be baptized. German Christian church representatives found ways to complicate and obstruct the process so that "the baptisms practically never occurred."[12] In October 1935, a German Christian–dominated parish council in Berlin forbade baptism of non-Aryans in its church facilities. The council further ordered that any such baptisms performed privately or secretly not be entered in the baptismal registry.[13] Because church offices controlled the evidence needed to establish Aryanism, refusal to register a baptism could have significant implications, particularly in the long term.

It was not impossible for Christian clergy to carry out baptisms of non-Aryans. In his memoirs, a pastor from Danzig, who was neither a German Christian nor a Confessing Church adherent, mentioned that he baptized several former Jews, "despite the prohibition." It is not clear which prohibition he meant. That pastor reported no negative consequences of his actions, which he attributed to the loyalty and discretion of his co-workers in the church, especially the man who maintained the baptismal and marriage records.[14]

For German Christians, moves to obstruct baptism of non-Aryans formed part of a broader agenda of excluding them from German society. That project picked up steam after promulgation of the Nuremberg Laws in 1935. In 1937, the German Christian group in the Reformed congregation of Siegen (Westphalia) called for establishment of a "German Protestant people's church" that would be "free of Jews." If the church wanted to retain the trust of the National Socialist state, the statement warned, then it was untenable that "Jewish Christians, whom the state for the sake of the principle of race has had to exclude from our community of the *Volk* as a disruptive element," be recognized as church members with equal rights. For a model of successful incorporation of racial distinctions into Christian life, those German Christians looked to America. "The Jewish Christian himself should muster as much character and Christian love as the Negro Christian in America," the Siegen statement suggested. Borrowing racial ideas from the missionary experience, they pointed to what they called the "African church" where "Protestant Negroes" in America "preached the gospel in their blood-bound, racially special manner, a manner that is just as alien to an Aryan as is that of the Jews."[15]

In the 1940s, as the Nazi state implemented its policies of isolation, deportation, and annihilation, it effectively institutionalized German Christian racial preoccupations. The Nazi definition of Jewishness denied the efficacy of baptism, at least in the present generation. When police regulations in September 1941 forced Jews in Germany to wear the identifying Star of David or when general deportations of Jews to the territory of Poland began in October 1941, the people targeted by those measures included converts to Christianity and their children as well as observant and nonobservant Jews. With or without German Christian efforts, the racial exclusivity of the people's church was practically assured. Yet their endeavors helped legitimize Nazi measures, and they even urged more stringent restrictions on non-Aryans. In late 1941, the central office of the German Protestant church, dominated by German Christians, sympathizers, and neutrals, acknowledged that the exclusion of Jews from German society had been achieved. Now, the declaration urged, the church needed to follow suit to ensure that "baptized non-Aryans will remain out of the ecclesiastical life of the German congregations."[16]

The German Christians insisted on the primacy of race over grace. They rejected baptism as capable of changing the status of those defined as racial outsiders for either political or religious purposes. To a significant extent, their self-assigned task of denying the efficacy of baptism was accomplished by state policies that premised genocide on racial categories.

## The Aryan Paragraph

Non-Aryans, German Christians agreed, would be at best inferior members of the people's church. Defining that position precisely, however, proved contentious. For the most part, the movement focused on restricting non-Aryans from pastoral office. In 1933, German Christians proposed imposing an Aryan Paragraph in the Protestant church. Such a regulation would have meant dismissal of all clergy and church officials deemed non-Aryan. Its backers intended it to echo the state's exclusion of non-Aryans from civil service positions in April 1933.[17] No exact definition of non-Aryan accompanied discussions of the clause.

On the issue of the Aryan Paragraph, the first public test of German Christian ideas about race and Christianity, members of the movement showed less unity than on the principle of baptism. Particularly in the early stages of the church struggle, German Christians failed to agree about the proposed clause. In July 1933, a German Christian pastor speaking in Dortmund publicly "welcomed" the fact the new Protestant church constitution had not included an Aryan Paragraph. Although he believed that "international Judaism" had been the "misfortune of the German people," he still considered the decision not to legislate dismissal of non-Aryan clergy to be a triumph of "true Christian teaching."[18] In October 1933, a Berlin woman whose brother was a German Christian pastor wrote to the Reich bishop expressing her support for the German Christian cause. "Only the application of the Aryan Paragraph," she admitted, "gives me great difficulty."[19]

The German Christian movement could tolerate some hesitation about the Aryan Paragraph in its ranks because its opponents were disunified on that score as well. In October 1933, representatives of the Gospel and Church party (Evangelium und Kirche), many of whom ended up in the Confessing Church, met with German Christian leaders in Westphalia to discuss church affairs. When the subject of the Aryan Paragraph came up, conversation disintegrated into debate about one particular non-Aryan pastor. Instead of rallying around their colleague, some of the Gospel and Church representatives made excuses for his Jewish background or tried to wrangle an exception. One of them argued that the pastor's involvement in the revolution of 1918–19 was not "necessarily attributable to his Jewish blood." Martin Niemöller's brother Wilhelm, also with the Gospel and Church group, proposed adopting the Aryan Paragraph in the church but exempting veterans of war. Only one representative attempted to steer the conversation back to issues of principle, pointing out that German Christian anti-Jewishness amounted to rejection of the New Testament because Paul, the apostles, and Jesus were Jews.[20]

German Christian leaders failed to get the Aryan Paragraph enshrined in the new church constitution of July 1933. Nor could they ram it through at the national synod held that September.[21] Many of the movement's rank and file expressed disappointment, and the Reich bishop's secretariat warned of rumblings owing to rumors that "the new church was not thinking seriously about imposing the Aryan Paragraph."[22] Two months later, at the Sports Palace rally in November 1933, Berlin German Christian leader Reinhold Krause gave loud and belligerent voice to that discontent. Krause's call for "rapid, unqualified implementation" of the Aryan Paragraph drew thunderous applause from the crowd of twenty thousand.[23]

But Krause's speech backfired. In the wake of the Sports Palace uproar, German Christian leaders, nervous about the movement's radical image, withdrew demands for immediate implementation of the Aryan Paragraph. That retreat in turn elicited bitter criticism from some members.[24] A genuine people's church, German Christian statements argued, had to keep step with the racial consciousness of the *Volk*. "The comradeship of blood and faith," one press release insisted, "demands a clear stance on the Aryan principle on the part of the church." The church, it continued, must preach God's word in a manner pitched to an audience that included "all members of the *Volk*: the worker, the farmer, the craftsman, and also the lowliest comrade of the brown battalions."[25]

Voices outside the movement echoed those concerns. Quite apart from the question of equal rights, one man argued in the *Deutsches Pfarrerblatt* (German pastoral paper), "aversion for the Jews as an alien element in the body of our *Volk*" made non-Aryan clergy unacceptable to German congregations.[26] In early 1934, another article in the same paper called it the "right of Christians who are German to demand that pastoral care be provided to them by pastors of German ancestry," just as people in the mission fields had the "right to pastors of their tribe: Chinese for Chinese, Japanese for Japanese, Negroes for Negroes."[27]

Even the Confessing Church leader Martin Niemöller, who had organized opposition to the Aryan Paragraph, believed there was some validity to arguments that the clause was a necessary response to congregations' prejudices. For Niemöller, Jewishness was a disagreeable racial fact that the church had to endure to "demonstrate whether it is serious about being a community that transcends national groups." Niemöller proposed his own solution to the non-Aryan "problem." In his view, "officeholders of Jewish ancestry" should spare their fellow Christians difficult decisions by not accepting prominent positions in the church.[28] Dietrich Bonhoeffer, however, rejected outright the racial thought that underlay the Aryan Paragraph. To him, German Christian demands for Aryan church leaders, "for the sake of *völkisch* sensibilities," typified "the weak in faith."[29]

After early 1934, national debate on the Aryan Paragraph waned, although German Christian agitation continued at the regional level. The church of Nassau-Hesse imposed its own Aryan clause in 1934, a measure Berlin church authorities suggested was "probably not legally valid."[30] The following year, the German Christian–dominated church government in Schleswig Holstein required candidates for theological examinations to furnish proof of Aryan ancestry.[31] In 1937, Eleanor Liebe-Harkort, the German Christian women's leader in Westphalia, announced her support of the Aryan Paragraph.[32] Her declaration carried considerable weight. Liebe-Harkort, born in 1884, had been involved in church work since 1917. Although she chafed at the restrictions some German Christian men placed on her work, she was an enthusiastic proponent of the cause from 1933 down to the end of the war and even beyond. She served as a go-between linking various factions within the German Christian movement and, at the peak of her power in 1935, led twenty-five thousand women in the Protestant Women's Service of Westphalia.[33] In Braunschweig, German Christian bishop Helmut Johnsen used the Kristallnacht pogrom in 1938 to effect exclusion of non-Aryan clergy in his jurisdiction: he suspended two pastors whose mothers were described as "purely Jewish."[34] By the immediate prewar years, German Christians in many parts of the country had achieved de facto implementation of the Aryan Paragraph, often less by their own efforts than as a product of institutionalized anti-semitism in Nazi Germany.

De facto racial exclusion was not enough for some German Christians. By the end of the 1930s, however, their tactics for formalizing the Aryan Paragraph had evolved from direct assault to reliance on unobtrusive administrative measures. The success of those new methods reflects the degree to which German Christians and their ideas had infiltrated the offices of the established Protestant church. In March 1939, Protestant church authorities in Posen–West Prussia urged the Upper Consistory in Berlin to require every candidate for ordination to furnish proof of Aryan ancestry for himself and his wife.[35] Two months later, the Berlin Consistory, under its German Christian president Friedrich Werner, produced a questionnaire on ancestry, to be filled out by every theologian before ordination or admission to the examinations. Prospective wives were required to complete the form as well.[36]

The Upper Consistory of the Protestant church in Prussia initiated its questionnaire on race independent of pressure from the state. In fact, a memo of July 1939 from the Reich Office for Genealogical Research (Reichsstelle für Sippenforschung) indicates that office only learned of the measure from a press release.[37] Church authorities in Berlin soon upgraded their request for information to an order and expanded it to include already practicing as well as prospective clergy. They gave regional churches two months to collect proof of "ancestry from German blood" for all pastors and their wives.[38]

Responses from regional churches suggest there was some flexibility in implementing the order, if only because of inefficiency on the part of church officials. For example, the questionnaire of a candidate in Silesia revealed a Jewish grandparent, but because the order had not said what would happen to individuals without purely "German" ancestry, Silesian church officials now wanted to know if they could admit the man to the theological examinations.[39] Ecclesiastical authorities in Berlin finally responded a year later, after the man in question had already been accepted to the first examination in the church in the Rhineland. If the state deemed the candidate worthy to bear arms, the answer went, nothing prevented his acceptance into the service of the church. At least two of the church officials in Berlin who initialed that decision were German Christians.[40]

Most pastors complied with the order to provide proof of ancestry. Even those who refused often declared themselves prepared to produce such documentation at the request of the state but not the church. In Bremen all but eight pastors submitted the required papers;[41] in Grenzmark Posen–West Prussia only a few clergy declined "for reasons of principle."[42] All but ten pastors in Saxony produced proof of their Aryan ancestry.[43]

In December 1939, the Upper Consistory sent a circular to regional church offices, trying to justify its demand that pastors prove Aryan ancestry. Under current circumstances, the circular claimed, "non-Aryans have no prospect of being able to develop fruitful activity" in "the almost completely pure, Aryan church congregations of Germany." They would face "rejection and mistrust," obstructions to effective preaching. In that sense, the circular assured its readers, the "Aryan certificate" was simply another credential, "equivalent to proof of citizenship in the Reich and the diploma for theological studies."[44] That line of argument was vintage German Christian: rooted in the ideal of a people's church, it eschewed everything that might offend the "people," even if it meant elevating their "weakness" to a law in the church.

Enforcement of the Aryan Paragraph was never total. For one thing, the magnitude of paperwork involved was staggering. Forms from a pastor in the province of Saxony who listed a Jewish grandfather included forty-two attachments verifying births, deaths, baptisms, and marriages of his ancestors and his wife's.[45] In rare cases other factors outweighed considerations of race. The Consistory in the Mark Brandenburg, for example, petitioned for an exception in the case of a pastor with one Jewish grandparent. That man's father, grandfather, and great-grandfather had been Protestant theologians, although the grandfather now counted racially as a Jew. The man himself, Brandenburg church authorities effused, had fought in the Polish and French campaigns, "looked completely German," and was engaged to be married to a "pure German-blooded" woman. Now he sought ordination. As the petition pointed out, no church law prohibited one-quarter non-Aryans from holding church offices, nor were they banned from the study of theology at the universities.[46] The Upper Consistory agreed to the proposed ordination.[47]

In August 1944, the Upper Consistory relaxed its requirements for proof of Aryan ancestry. The reasons involved practical considerations, not principles. Given difficulties with assembling documents in wartime, central church authorities decided that, for the time being, clergy and church officeholders need only sign a pledge that they and their spouses did not have Jewish parents or grandparents. Presentation of documentary proof could wait until the war was over.[48] The Upper Consistory explicitly patterned its relaxation of proof of Aryanism requirements on measures adopted by the Ministry of the Interior in September 1943.[49]

Thus the struggle over the Aryan Paragraph in the Protestant church ended not with a bang but a whimper. The result was what German Christians had sought since 1933: effective exclusion of anyone defined as non-

Aryan from pastoral office in the Protestant churches of Germany. Yet German Christians could hardly take credit for that outcome. There had never been more than a few non-Aryan pastors in any case, and many of those had left on their own. For example, Hans Ehrenberg, the outspoken and energetic non-Aryan pastor from Bochum, was incarcerated in Sachsenhausen in 1938. His wife managed to secure his release, and the family moved to England. Ehrenberg had been active in the Confessing Church but found that elements in the organization repeatedly pushed him to the background and urged him to restrain himself. For them, his non-Aryan status was something of an embarrassment.[50]

Nazi policies ensured that people defined as Jews were shut out of German society, while church organs, and not only those controlled by German Christians, added their own administrative measures to restrict non-Aryan clergy. By the onset of World War II, even Germany's military chaplains, often mistakenly believed to have been isolated from German Christian influence, were required to prove that they and their wives were of "German or kindred blood."[51]

## Non-Aryan Clergy and Clergy with Non-Aryan Wives

While German Christians debated the Aryan Paragraph, they also interacted with individual non-Aryan pastors and pastors with non-Aryan wives. Both categories were small. Alarmist reports in 1933 claimed that "500 to 600 pastors of Jewish ancestry" served the Protestant church, but the *Evangelisch-kirchliche Anzeiger* (Protestant church bulletin) debunked such rumors. In fact, it informed its readers, only twenty-nine of Germany's eighteen thousand Protestant pastors had "Jewish ancestry." Seventeen of those belonged to the Prussian Protestant church, which had introduced its own Aryan clause in September 1933. Eleven of them were exempted because they had held office since before 1 August 1914 or were veterans of the front. The Prussian law, subsequently revoked in any case, thus applied to all of six people.[52]

No non-Aryan clergy held membership in the German Christian movement. Evidence of German Christian pastors with non-Aryan wives suggests few people fell into that category as well. Two cases that do appear in the archival record demonstrate an uncompromising attitude on the part of German Christian church authorities. Both marriages had already ended in divorce by the time the clergymen involved came to the attention of their ecclesiastical superiors. Still, both lost their positions. One of those men was a National Socialist and German Christian pastor from Baden.

His involvement with the Nazi party, he wrote, had estranged him from his wife; the two divorced because of the "racial contrast." The church government in Baden, controlled by a group of German Christians with particularly close ties to the Nazi party, suspended him effective 1 November 1933. The pastor, whose German Christian membership card bore the number 754, begged the Reich bishop for help, pleading with him "not to leave an old fighter in the lurch."[53] The Reich bishop's office offered no sympathy and suggested that he seek a new position.[54] Another pastor, a party member in Stuttgart married to a "half-Jew," lost his church job as well.[55]

For the most part, German Christian encounters with non-Aryan clergy or clergy with non-Aryan wives involved individuals outside the movement. German Christians never relinquished their conviction that race was central to the people's church, but they showed some flexibility in manipulating specific situations to their own ends. In 1935, a small group of German Christians in Soest (Westphalia) charged that the wife of Pastor Seidenstücker there was not an Aryan.[56] Minutes of a meeting of the presbytery reveal that those German Christians were less interested in racial purity than in replacing an unsympathetic clergyman with a member of their own movement.[57] Attacks on Seidenstücker seem to have formed part of a plan to get a post in the St. Peter's Church for the German Christian director of the seminary in Soest.[58] Evidence of the Jewish ancestry of the pastor's wife was clearly fabricated.[59] When Seidenstücker disproved the allegations, his opponents simply added a new charge: that he had not denied his wife's non-Aryanism immediately.[60] And when that tactic failed, the German Christians drummed up other accusations. They used their dominance of the parish council to fire Seidenstücker's sister as church bookkeeper (*Rendantin*), claiming that she was too closely related to the pastor, lived outside the parish, and failed to return the "German greeting."[61]

Sometimes German Christians used issues of race to get party and state organs to help them achieve their own ends. The case of the non-Aryan Pastor M. Goosmann in Berlin-Adlershof illustrates such collusion. In February 1936, Goosmann complained that a schoolteacher had encouraged her students to boycott his confirmation classes. Leaders of the local party organization, the League of German Girls, and the Hitler Youth all cooperated to sabotage Goosmann's confirmation ceremony, threatening to report the children involved and their families to Gau party leadership.[62] Meanwhile, a German Christian student pastor offered alternative confirmation instruction.[63] In that situation, German Christians exploited Goosmann's non-Aryan ancestry to drum up candidates for their own group.[64] They then pointed to the lack of support for Goosmann in the congregation as evidence that the non-Aryan pastor was "unsuitable." Unless Goosmann's activities were curbed, a German Christian lawyer threatened in 1936, the "racially sensitive part of the congregation" would leave the church.[65]

As a veteran, Goosmann had special status under the Nuremberg Laws. He fell into a category of non-Aryans initially allowed to retain their citizenship, including the right to vote. But his German Christian opponents showed no interest in the fine points of his racial classification. As with Seidenstücker in Soest, attacks on Goosmann were motivated less by considerations of racial purity than by schemes to get a German Christian pastor into the congregation.[66] Goosmann's Jewish grandparent made him an easy target. Not mere tools of National Socialism, German Christians used the antisemitism of those around them to implement their own agenda and bolster their local positions.

In their dealings with non-Aryan clergy, German Christians reflected common attitudes in the surrounding society. In 1935, Minister of Church Affairs Kerrl established the Reich Church Committee (Reichskirchenausschuß) and charged it with restoring peace in the Protestant church.[67] The neutrals who dominated the committee and its regional offshoots sought to minimize conflict both within the church and between church and state. Pursuance of that goal often furthered the German Christian cause. For example, in July 1936, a student in Rostock demanded admission to the theological examination of the Protestant church in Hamburg. He was a "full Jew" under the race laws, but his father had fought in the world war. The Reich Church Committee allowed the man to sit the test, as long as he declared in writing that he did not expect employment as a pastor.[68] Heinz Brunotte, the senior consistory councillor who prepared the decision, belonged to the Confessing Church. Nevertheless, though not siding with the German Christian view of race in principle, decisions such as this one helped enforce racial exclusion in the church.

## Non-Aryan Church Members

Because only Aryans could join the German Christian movement, its members had no interaction with non-Aryans within their ranks.[69] One known case of a German Christian lay person with a non-Aryan spouse ended in divorce. Klara Schlossmann-Lönnies, a German Christian women's leader, had been married to a non-Aryan,[70] but that did not seem to affect her participation in the movement. To the contrary, in the summer of 1933, she held the position of director of the Mothers' Service Enterprise of the Protestant Reich Women's Aid (Leiterin des Mütterdienstwerkes der Evangelischen Reichsfrauenhilfe). In that capacity, she was charged with alerting the population to the dangers facing girls and mothers unless immediate steps were taken to promote "national rebirth, eugenic improvement, and spiritual renewal."[71] It is difficult to assess whether the difference in her experience from that of the two clergymen with non-Aryan wives reflected a double standard for women and men, for clergy and lay people, or some other considerations.

Some German Christians did encounter non-Aryans within their congregations. Often they acted toward them in precisely the exclusionary way their doctrine of race would suggest. For example, a Protestant woman from Neuss, daughter of a Jew who had converted to Christianity, described how two "enthusiastic National Socialist women" forced her out of the Protestant Women's Aid, during the time when, as she put it, the German Christians "had the say."[72] The German Girls' Bible Circle in Danzig expelled an Afro-German member.[73] German Christians showed less decisiveness in other cases. In October 1933, Reich Bishop Müller and the German Christian leader Hossenfelder intervened with the disciplinary wing of the Nazi party on behalf of a Protestant woman who had adopted the "half Jewish son" of a friend. When the party responded with a reprimand, reminding the German Christian leaders that National Socialism could not "tolerate interaction with those of Jewish blood,"[74] the Reich bishop's office apparently dropped the matter.

Issues involving non-Aryan lay people served as a way to induce state or party officials to take action in the German Christian interest. In early 1936, the mayor of Berlin-Schöneberg complained that a "racial Jew" belonged to the Protestant congregation in Friedenau and sat on the parish council. The mayor ordered "the Jew" removed from the council. German Christians had inspired that attack. The mayor drew his information from the German Christian paper *Positives Christentum* (Positive Christianity), and he sent copies of his letter of complaint to German Christian members of the parish council in Friedenau.[75]

German Christians may also have influenced other church-related organizations to set up barriers against non-Aryans. The Protestant League, an organization devoted to "protecting" German Protestantism from Catholicism, remained formally independent of the German Christian movement. But in 1937, when the Protestant League in Thuringia issued a new constitution, it limited membership to "all Protestant Christians of Aryan ancestry who accept the goals of the Protestant League and want to further them."[76] It is no coincidence that in Thuringia, where German Christians retained their firmest hold throughout the National Socialist period, the Protestant League saw fit to proclaim its own commitment to a pure Aryan church.

German Christian dealings with non-Aryan lay people demonstrated inconsistency as well as adherence to exclusionary principles. In February 1939, the parish council of St. Gertrud in Lübeck, under German Christian leadership, wrote to the consistory in the same city regarding an old couple in the congregation. The husband had converted from Judaism to Christianity when he married his Lutheran, Aryan wife. The two were poor, and the pastor periodically gave them small sums from parish funds. By early 1939, the pastor had become nervous about supporting a non-Aryan. He wanted to know what to do. The council decided the question involved significant principles. Could a non-Aryan parishioner receive support from parish funds, raised from "Aryan parish members"? Could non-Aryan church members be involved in church life? Could they receive communion? Could they be buried by a clergyman? It requested a prompt reply from the Lübeck Consistory,[77] but there is no evidence that those authorities, many of them German Christians, responded. That German Christians raised such questions as late as 1939 illustrates how the movement's decisiveness on matters of race at the level of principle could turn into uncertainty when it came to dealing with individuals.

With their vacillation on individual cases, German Christians fit Himmler's 1943 description of the "worthy eighty million Germans," each of whom talked about the need to exterminate the Jewish people but then produced "his decent Jew."[78] Himmler used that point to motivate SS leaders to put aside compassion or personal attachments in the assault on Jews. But the history of the German Christian movement shows that such sentiments about individuals, when coupled with general acceptance of Nazi racial policy, did little or nothing to stem the tide of isolation and annihilation.

Shortly after the Kristallnacht pogrom, in the early months of 1939, German Christian–dominated regional churches began passing regulations excluding non-Aryans from the religious community. In February 1939, the Thuringian Protestant church ruled that people defined as Jews could not become members. The decree freed pastors from any obligation to perform services for "Jews" already in the church. It prohibited use of church rooms and equipment for services or sacraments for non-Aryans, and it released non-Aryan Christians from payment of church taxes.[79]

Within months, the churches in Mecklenburg, Anhalt, Lübeck, and Saxony produced similar legislation.[80] All of these regional churches had extremely small numbers of non-Aryan members. But that symbolic action sent an incontrovertible message to German church people: German Christians supported forcible and complete exclusion of Jews and non-Aryans from every sphere of German life, by whatever means possible.

## Church Musicians

More than ordinary lay people, non-Aryan church musicians attracted German Christian attention. In this regard too, we see the combination of dogmatic adherence to their racial doctrine and inconsistency that characterized German Christian dealings with individual non-Aryans. In 1934, German Christian church authorities in Zittau (Saxony) denied use of the church building to a choir whose director had converted from Judaism to Protestant Christianity. Instead of siding with the Zittau German Christians, the German Christian Walter Birnbaum in the Reich bishop's office intervened on behalf of the choir director, asking the Reich Chamber of Music whether he might not be permitted to perform. Birnbaum's reasons are unclear, but it appears that he considered the director a fine musician whose services warranted retention. The Reich Chamber of Music overturned Birnbaum's decision and upheld the Zittau church's view.[81]

In September 1935, the Reich Chamber of Music produced a list of non-Aryan organists in the service of the Protestant churches of Germany: a grand total of fourteen people.[82] That small number notwithstanding, some Germans leveled hysterical attacks against what Hans Hinkel, a prominent figure in the Reich Ministry of Propaganda and Public Enlightenment, called "conditions that are really too grotesque and outrageous in the nurturing of music in the church." There were Christian churches in Germany, Hinkel claimed, where "for years full-blooded Jews have been playing the organ for German people of the Christian confessions."[83]

German Christians rushed to defend their movement. When it came to church musicians, however, they sometimes subordinated considerations of race to practical matters or concerns with ecclesiastical autonomy. In 1935, the Bremen Protestant church, dominated by one of the most outspoken advocates of radical German Christianity, Heinz Weidemann, defied the Reich Chamber of Music in an attempt to retain the services of a church organist who was "one-quarter" Jewish. The musician in question had the firm backing of his congregation.[84] The Reich Church Committee in Berlin backed the Bremen church's position. Neither the Bremen German Christians nor the neutrals in the Berlin church office addressed the basic rights of non-Aryans in the church. Local considerations governed the Bremen case: the congregation needed an organist and the man in question had served well. As for the central church authorities, they wanted to protect their jurisdiction over church music. The Reich Church Committee recommended the organist's continued employment, with the caveat that he be warned "to confine his church musical activities to the worship service."[85]

In July 1936, the Upper Consistory of the Prussian church, under the presidency of the German Christian Werner, articulated its position on non-Aryan church musicians in a memo to the Reich Chamber of Music. The memo expressed a clear bid for ecclesiastical autonomy in the area of church music. Of the ten thousand musicians employed by the Protestant church in Prussia, it reported, only seven were non-Aryans. The Prussian Consistory expressed pride that "musical life within the church had kept itself almost completely pure of Jews." Of course, it continued, despite the numbers, the question was important in principle. But that did not change the fact that church musicians were employees of the church: exclusion from the Reich Chamber of Music need not mean automatic dismissal from church posts. Any difficulties that might arise, the memo assured its readers, could be overcome by differentiating between church work and other public activities of the non-Aryan church musicians. And in any case, the consistory pointed out, the Reich Chamber of Music imposed Aryan requirements that went beyond the Nuremberg Laws, something the "church could not do."[86] German Christians and even neutral church offices had been quite willing to go beyond the Nuremberg Laws in defining non-Aryan for other purposes. But they became proponents of a more modest definition when it came to protecting the jurisdictional territory of the church.

The issue of non-Aryan church musicians came up again in 1941. This time it was owing to the publication of the *Lexikon der Juden in der Musik* (Encyclopedia of Jews in music), sponsored by the Nazi party's Institute for Research on the Jewish Question. The Protestant Church Chancellery proudly noted in its files that the book listed only nineteen Jews and "half Jews" who were active in church music or as church organists in Germany. Oskar Söhngen, the well-known church musician who wrote the file notation, was not linked to the German Christian movement. Yet he closed his remarks with an endorsement of efforts to "purify" church music from all non-Aryan elements. "On the whole the result is most gratifying," he wrote of the study, "because it shows clearly how pure of Jews church music has been. If only other areas of musical nurturance had even come close to keeping themselves so free of Jewish influence, it would never have come to such a decline in our public musical life!"[87]

Discussion of non-Aryan organists in 1941 illustrates again how non–German Christians helped construct racial barriers around the church. Church authorities busied themselves checking up on each of the nineteen persons listed in the lexicon, writing to regional churches to request information.[88] Once compiled, results were sent to the Reich Ministry for Church Affairs. Of the nineteen names, the Church Chancellery reported, twelve were "full Jews," one "three-quarters," and six "half." Of the twelve "full Jews," nine did not work for Protestant congregations. Some had been musicians in synagogues. One of the remaining three lived in Switzerland, leaving only two in office, one in Cologne, the other in Königsberg. Both had been dismissed "years ago"—the Königsberg man in 1936. Of the six half-Jews, by 1933, only four had worked for the Protestant church, and two of those had since resigned.[89] So the entire tempest over non-Aryan church musicians in 1941 was about two individuals, each of whom had one parent deemed Jewish. More significant, however, was that a range of participants in church life and decision making accepted as legitimate the social, political construct of race and tolerated or even actively aided German Christian construction of racial barriers around the people's church.

The archival record is sketchy on German Christian interaction with non-Aryan church members. Still, a general pattern emerges. German Christians sought to impose their doctrine of race by excluding non-Aryan Christians from religious fellowship. At the level of principle, they were decisive and consistent. Regarding individual cases, they showed less certainty, even going out of their way at times to make exceptions. Yet such flexibility in no way suggests that German Christians violated their own racial doctrines. Rather, because they faced so few challenges to their position on race, they never needed to develop a coherent set of regulations. Moreover, they could afford to compromise when it suited particular needs. Most significantly, they could count on the support not only of state and party offices but of many other members of the Protestant community. The Christian churches made a major contribution to the exclusion of non-Aryans from German society by providing the information needed for certificates of Aryan purity. Almost no one, German Christian or otherwise, questioned the rectitude of that activity or the duty of the church to perform it. They did not see its danger because they shared its underlying assumptions.

**CHAPTER 6**

**Catholics, Protestants, and Dreams of Confessional Union**

*German Volk are building*
*a new German dome,*
*the new church of Christ,*
*in battle against Rome.*
*Faith is the power,*
*Faith provides the skill.*
*From us the Lord demands it;*
*Through us He works His will.*
*—German Christian hymn*

In 1958, a former German Christian church superintendent contacted an old colleague from the movement. Was it true, he wanted to know, that "at first there were very many Catholics in our ranks, or that many, after they converted from Catholicism to Protestantism, came to us?"[1] No reply is recorded. This brief monologue captures some important dimensions of the German Christian movement's relationship to Catholics and Catholicism. In keeping with their vision of an inclusive people's church, German Christians attempted outreach to the Roman Catholic community. Yet their efforts remained ill-defined, replete with misunderstandings, and ultimately unsuccessful.

The reality of confessional division challenged the ideal of a people's church that would encompass all Aryan Germans. More than twenty million Catholics constituted about one-third of Germany's population in the

1930s.[2] The German Christians could hardly claim to embrace all Germans in their spiritual community yet disregard Catholics. Nor could they exclude Catholics with the argument that only Protestants were true Germans. That contention would have shut out Hitler himself, a possibility no German Christian would have entertained.

The logic of the people's church forced German Christians to look beyond Protestant circles. Increasingly throughout the 1930s, members of the movement described their goal as creation of a national church, a supraconfessional church that would transcend the boundary between Catholics and Protestants as well as the divisions within Protestantism. German Christians never achieved consensus as to the nature of that national church or the timetable for its realization. They did agree, however, that in the long term, ecclesiastical unity was not only desirable but essential for the strength and survival of the German nation. At the same time, they encountered intense opposition to their supraconfessional schemes from Catholics and Protestants alike.

This chapter examines what happened when the German Christian movement confronted Catholicism and Catholics. Attempts to create a supraconfessional church failed, but that failure itself is instructive. German Christians built their vision of the church on illusions, prejudices, and confidence in the unifying potential of their rejection of doctrine. They made little attempt to engage the Catholic community, and plans to include Catholics in the people's church alienated rather than attracted many Protestants. Much of that resistance reflected not doctrinal considerations but pervasive anti-Catholicism that many German Christians shared, too. Finally, the failure of the supraconfessional church reveals the bankruptcy of the German Christians' antidoctrinal stance. Self-proclaimed enemies of religious doctrine, German Christians could not grasp Catholics' commitment to their own beliefs or even recognize the extent of Protestant hostility to Catholicism.

## The National Church and Its Sources of Unity

If the church were to be a church of the *Volk*, German Christians reasoned, it could recognize no boundaries but those of blood. If belief played no role in determining membership in the spiritual community, then confessional divisions were inauthentic and obstructed genuine fellowship. Contemporary observers and subsequent commentators on German Christianity often assume that only the Thuringian wing of the movement, sometimes called the National Church Union,[3] advocated the fusion of

Protestants and Catholics into one church. Certainly that group around the Thuringian pastors Siegfried Leffler and Julius Leutheuser consistently and stridently preached that message. As a district leader from Gera explained in late 1933, the Thuringians sought "not the German Protestant Church, but the German National Church."[4]

But other German Christians also advocated abolition of confessional boundaries. From the movement's beginnings, adherents called for an end to the Catholic-Protestant division within Germany. The goal of a national church came through loud and clear in Reinhold Krause's controversial speech at the Sports Palace rally in November 1933. Luther, Krause announced, had left Germans with a "priceless legacy: the completion of the German Reformation in the Third Reich!" To enthusiastic applause, the Berlin German Christian leader called for "a dramatically new, all-encompassing German people's church."[5] The deacon and organist who addressed another German Christian service in Berlin a week after Krause's speech concurred. "Political and military upheavals" had prevented fulfillment of Luther's work, he contended, but through the German Christian movement and under Hitler's leadership, that task would be brought to fruition.[6]

The dream of a supraconfessional church found resonance even in more respectable theological circles. In late 1934, a German pastor serving in the Netherlands shared his thoughts on the issue with his colleague Dietrich Bonhoeffer in London. Although he claimed not to be a German Christian, that pastor considered the "validity of the confessions of the Reformation" to be "limited, indeed expired." Thuringian German Christians might be "fanatical," he conceded, but in his view, they demonstrated more potential for religious renewal than did a church that "no longer represents the will of the people as a whole."[7]

True to that potential, the Thuringian wing, from its isolated position in 1933, expanded to attract regional German Christian organizations from all over the country to its goal of a national church. In July 1936, German Christians from the Rhineland announced their commitment to "defeat of the confessional division in the church."[8] Groups from Bavaria to Mecklenburg and Westphalia issued similar declarations. Such statements reflected no grueling theological struggle; the movement sidestepped the difficult issues at stake by resorting to denial of doctrine. German Christians, explained the Thuringian leader Leutheuser, would not "quarrel about Luther or the pope," dispute the "right or wrong teachings of sin and grace," or bicker about "the numbers of sacraments." Instead, he asserted, they would "learn how to believe as Germans in one Savior."[9]

Christ himself, Leutheuser assured his followers in 1937, was the "mightiest foe of the sterile religiosity of the Christian confessions."[10]

By the war years, even self-proclaimed moderates within German Christian ranks endorsed the supraconfessional church. In 1941, a group of German Christians formed the Schlachtensee Circle. That organization, named for the Berlin suburb where it first met, claimed to occupy the middle ground between Thuringian German Christians and the Confessing Church. As its first principle, the Schlachtensee Circle professed allegiance to the "unified German people's church through the defeat of confessionalism," a church "publicly and legally acknowledged and recognized in the National Socialist, Greater German Reich, unified in its constitution, leadership, and administration."[11] Whether they labeled themselves National Church Union or not, German Christians dreamed of adding to the Nazi demand for "One *Volk*, One Reich, One Führer" the words "One Faith!"[12] In keeping with their repudiation of doctrine, German Christians did not seek a basis for their supraconfessional church in theology or Scripture. Instead, they relied on four familiar sources of unity: ritual, ethnicity, the state, and war.

Enthusiasts for confessional union found little common ground in the sphere of ritual. Protestants and Catholics worshiped differently; they understood and performed the sacraments in diverse ways. In September 1936, a German Christian paper announced the emergence of new ritual forms to unite the confessions. It offered only one concrete example: the Lord's Prayer. A testimony from a German Christian pastor described the supposed magical unifying quality of that prayer: "'After this manner therefore pray ye: Our Father who art in heaven.' . . . Suddenly it all appeared in a new light, in the joyful recognition that on this point, someday the entire German *Volk* would stand together, in the most profound depths of its German nature, of one mind and one spirit, free of the divisive trenches and confessional fences of its past."[13] Reich Bishop Ludwig Müller tried to produce that mystical fellowship in a sermon in 1942. The German *Volk*, he proclaimed, "cannot remain torn into confessions, sects, and associations. There is only one God and there is only one Germany." He too closed with the words of the Lord's Prayer.[14]

Powerful as it might be, one prayer alone failed to provide the ritual underpinnings for a national church. The German Christians presented sacred music as an additional ritual to join Catholics and Protestants. In this regard too, however, the unifying potential was limited. Many of the familiar hymns of German Protestantism originated with Luther or the Thirty Years' War, hardly a tradition that Catholics regarded fondly. In addition to Protestant classics, German Christians offered new hymns composed by their members. According to a 1936 publication, the "fiery rhythms and themes" of such songs drew singers into the "final struggle against the last enemy of the *Volk*: confessional strife."[15] Sacred music, an article in the German Christian press claimed in 1937, constituted a sphere "untouched" by confessional struggles." As an example of music that transcended confessional boundaries, the author referred to Johann Sebastian Bach. German Christians used Bach to promote the supraconfessional church, sponsoring a tour of "first-class artists" playing Bach fugues throughout Thuringia and providing a space where "all can meet," regardless of belief.[16]

If German Christians had little to offer by way of unifying ritual, ethnicity too proved unsatisfactory as a source of models for Catholic-Protestant solidarity. In their quest for symbols of ethnic unity between Protestant and Catholic Germans, German Christians focused on Martin Luther, a preoccupation indicative of their disregard for even the most basic issues of church history. German Christians elevated Luther's image as the paragon of Germanness above his significance as the founder of Protestantism. They therefore saw no contradiction in presenting him as the champion of the supraconfessional church. At a 1934 rally in Herford (Westphalia), German Christians called for a church that would overcome confessionalism and win over "every last German member of the *Volk*" and then closed by singing Luther's battle hymn, "A Mighty Fortress Is Our God,"[17] a declaration of war against Roman Catholicism.

According to a German Christian lecture in 1933, the "language of the German Bible" in Luther's translation had united the Germanic tribes and led Germans to "common ways of feeling and thinking." Catholic members of the *Volk*, too, that professor pointed out, "feel and think in that language."[18] Thuringian German Christians claimed that "Luther himself laid the foundations for the national church, in his German Bible, in the German language of the worship service, and in the German songs."[19] Such references to Luther reveal the German Christian propensity to appropriate and transform elements of religious tradition to their own ends. As one critic of the movement observed, such manipulation created a "new Luther," a "mirror image of their own fantasies and vanities."[20]

Some German Christians sought models of unity for the supraconfessional church in ancient German history. In 1936, a pastor and a schoolteacher solicited support for their research into the "anti-Roman" or pre-Roman roots of Christianity in German lands. Boniface, the men contended, had brought to German lands the "alien," "Roman," and "Jewish" influences in Christianity. But the period before his activities, they maintained, had witnessed the "founding of the first, Rome-free national church in what is today Germany."[21] During the war, a German Christian poet devised a scheme to draw Catholics in Alsace into the national, spiritual community. He urged construction of a Germanic shrine on the Odilienberg in the Rhineland[22] and hoped to infuse Alsatians with "German feeling and thought" by appealing to a "unique past" that predated Roman Catholicism.[23] Such fanciful plans did little to win support for the supraconfessional church.

German Christians identified loyalty to the fatherland as more promising common ground between Catholics and Protestants. In 1935, at a service in Frankfurt/Main, a speaker insisted that German Christians did not ask whether someone was Catholic or Protestant; rather, "Do you believe in eternal Germany, and do you believe in the power that works through our Lord and Savior?"[24] According to the Thuringian leader Leffler, German Christians could transcend confessional division in an undogmatic way, "based only on Germany and Christ."[25]

Above all, German Christians relied on war as a potential source of unity for the national church. According to a speech in 1936, during the world war, "the Protestant stood next to the Catholic, next to the member of a sect; they were all one in combat and one in their will to protect the German homeland."[26] That German Christian orator seemed to forget that from 1914 to 1918 Jewish Germans had fought alongside Catholics and Protestants as well. Dreams of a supraconfessional church reflected the myth of perfect unity in battle. According to Reich Bishop Ludwig Müller, the Wehrmacht exemplified the "unity of the entire *Volk*."[27]

To German Christians, the military chaplaincy in particular constituted a paragon of confessional unity and a microcosm of the supraconfessional church. Army orders to German chaplains during World War II stressed the need to overcome confessional divisions; the 1941 and 1942 guidelines for chaplains mandated interconfessional services that sought to reproduce at the altar the unity of the battlefield.[28] A 1940 memoir by a German chaplain in Poland described the "genuine, beautiful, complete cooperation and mutual support of the Protestant and Catholic military pastors." The two chaplains, he explained, wore identical uniforms and were "of one heart and one soul."[29] The interconfessional schemes of military authorities responsible for the chaplaincy reflected practical considerations. But such attempts to meld Protestant and Catholic Christians also showed the influence of the supraconfessional ideal, both in the military office for the chaplaincy and in the Ministry of Church Affairs.

War, German Christians discovered after 1939, did not automatically produce confessional fusion. Nevertheless, related developments fueled their vision of a supraconfessional church. On 5 September 1939, the deputy leader of the National Church Union of German Christians, Mecklenburg bishop Walther Schultz, announced his appointment to the new, three-man "spiritual council." The Ministry of Church Affairs and Protestant church offices had established that council to govern the Protestant church for the duration of the war. Members of the council represented the three main camps in the church struggle: Confessing Church, neutrals, and Thuringian German Christians. Schultz made it clear that he intended to use his new post to promote the national church, or in his words, to "lay new foundations for the one Christian church of all Germans."[30] With a representative of their movement occupying one of the highest church posts in the country, German Christians and their notion of the supraconfessional church gained authority and legitimacy. But even the promise of spiritual unity through war proved illusory. At most, German Christians managed to exploit the situation to improve their own position in Protestant church politics.

## German Christian Outreach and the Catholic Response

German Christians proclaimed the supraconfessional church, but they developed no concerted program to win Catholics to that cause. Members of the movement seemed unclear as to how Catholics fit into their plans. And telling silences suggest a low level of Catholic involvement in the German Christian movement. After 1933, the annual number of converts from Catholicism to Protestantism in Austria increased dramatically. In the first half of 1934 alone, twenty thousand Catholic Austrians switched to Protestantism. Since 1898, the highest annual number of such transfers in a year had been six thousand.[31] German Christians involved themselves in that development and took as much credit for it as they could.[32] Certainly they would also have reported any detectable influx of German Catholics into their own ranks. No such reports ensued.

The German Christian movement even failed to capitalize on the existence of potential sympathizers within the Catholic community. German Catholics had their own small, national Catholic movement, under the clergyman Heinrich Hütwohl in Essen.[33] That group, part of the Old Catholic church (Altkatholiken), originated in 1870 in protest against the declaration of papal infallibility. At least some Old Catholics shared the German Christians' intense devotion to National Socialism. During the Third

Reich, they began calling their group the Catholic German National Church (Die katholisch-deutschnationale Kirche). In 1937, the Old Catholics numbered between twenty and twenty-five thousand; the group's publication, *Der romfreie Katholik* (The Catholic free of Rome), circulated to about thirteen thousand readers.[34] While other Catholic papers endured seizure and prohibition, *Der romfreie Katholik* continued to appear until 1941.[35]

German Christians were aware of those "national church Catholics," but nothing suggests that they initiated contact. At most some German Christians tried to monitor the activities of their Catholic counterparts. For example, German Christians in Mecklenburg circulated material on the Catholic National Church Movement, also known as the Away from Rome Movement in Germany. In May 1937, German Christians reported, the Catholic movement held its first Reich conference in Mannheim. An Old Catholic bishop presided over the worship service.[36] In any case, the Old Catholics were not promising as allies. Although they desired a German Catholic church independent of Rome, they did not renounce Catholicism or express supraconfessional goals.

An English Catholic observer identified an Austrian group, the Fellowship of Work for Religious Peace (Arbeitsgemeinschaft für den religiösen Frieden) as the "Catholic counterpart of Evangelical 'German Christians.'" That somewhat mysterious group apparently based itself on the conviction that Catholic faith and National Socialist belief were not contradictory. Its membership included priests and lay people.[37] It is unclear whether German Christians made any effort to establish contact with that group in Austria.

For the most part, German Christians tried to create a supraconfessional church not by seeking out Catholics but simply by trumpeting the ideal of unity. They did not hold meetings in Catholic church buildings, nor is there evidence that they attempted to do so. Rather than develop a plan to realize the national church, they preferred to operate as if it were already a reality. Typical of that approach was a 1938 decision of German Christian leaders in Saxony. Delineation and naming of church congregations along established lines, they announced, was to cease; new boundaries and new names would express the "supraconfessional nature" of the National Church movement. Renaming began in Dresden.[38] Although they had done nothing to win Catholic members for the projected supraconfessional church, German Christians maintained the fiction of its impending realization.

Catholics could hardly fail to recognize the supraconfessional schemes of the German Christian movement as fundamentally hostile to their own religious traditions. In September 1934, when Protestant Reich bishop Müller called for "one state, one people, one church," he aroused considerable uproar among the Catholic population.[39] Episcopal authorities in Speyer announced that any Catholics who joined the German Christian movement shut themselves out of the Catholic church.[40]

Beginning in the mid-1930s, prominent Catholics spoke out against the idea of a national church. In his end of the year sermon for 1934, Archbishop Jacobus von Hauck of Bamberg denounced supraconfessional schemes in terms that made it clear he had the German Christian movement in mind. "People are trying to create a counterfeit Christ," Archbishop Hauck told his audience, "to make him into an Aryan hero whose teachings were falsified and perverted by the Jewish Rabbi Paul." He denounced such "fake Christianity" and linked it with "the idea of a national church" that had "appeared here and there" across Germany. "People say it expresses a profound unification of the German people," Hauck continued. But he left no doubt as to his stance: "That idea of a national church stands in absolutely glaring contradiction to the nature of the Catholic church."[41] A schoolteacher from Speyer made similar comments in October 1934 in a speech before an audience of ten thousand in Maria Rosenberg.[42]

In their pastoral letter of 20 August 1935, German Catholic bishops protested Nazi attempts to encourage a "national church free from Rome." The bishops interpreted strivings for a national church as a direct attack on Roman Catholicism.[43] Two years later, the office of the bishop in Speyer published and distributed a pamphlet titled "A German National Church? A Word of Enlightenment to German Catholics." It condemned the supraconfessional church as an "inauthentic invention," a "betrayal of Christ," and a "misfortune for the German people."[44] In 1938, Catholic bishops described the call to a supraconfessional church as part of the Nazi propaganda campaign to convince people to give up church membership altogether.[45]

German Christian inroads into the Catholic community stand out as exceptions rather than the rule. In 1937, a Westphalian Catholic who wished to convert to Protestantism asked that a German Christian vicar, not the local pastor, provide the necessary instruction and counseling.[46] That same year, several German Christian groups reunited under the leadership of the National Church wing. The following year witnessed numerous rallies under the slogan "*Volk*, break through to unity in the faith!" along with increased efforts to attract Catholics.[47] German Christian propaganda reported that in the south and west, the movement had won "numerous Catholic members of the *Volk* for the National Church Union."[48] No statistics substantiated that claim.

In 1938, German Christians established an office called Roman Catholic Church to coordinate outreach efforts. Its director had been a Catholic priest in Freiburg for twenty-one years before he enlisted in the German Christian cause. In his view, of all the movements in Germany, only the National Church Union of German Christians "clearly and unambiguously" represented the "dual ideal of religious renewal and national unification."[49] Early in 1944, that former Catholic priest became interim leader of the National Church German Christians in Franconia.[50]

Despite a flurry of activity in the late 1930s, German Christian agitation resulted less in Catholics joining the movement than in Protestants leaving the church altogether. During the war, some groups of German Christians, notably in Bavaria, announced their departure from the "splinter church of the confession." God, they proclaimed, called Germans to be "one community, also in the faith!" Attached to their declaration was a questionnaire regarding church taxes. Would the undersigned pay church taxes to the National Church Union of German Christians, it asked, and if so, was monthly collection or bank debit preferred?[51] Instead of uniting Catholics and Protestants in a revolt against church taxes, the Bavarian German Christians' "away from the church!" campaign fizzled. According to church superintendents' reports in 1941, only a few German Christians left the church: Bayreuth, for example, reported fifty-nine such withdrawals, Hof only seven. In rural parishes, the campaign appeared to have no impact at all.[52] The supraconfessional church could not be bought at that low a price.

In general, the figures available point to very small numbers of Catholics in the German Christian ranks. In 1936, the National Church group of German Christians in the Palatinate claimed only two hundred members who still belonged to the Catholic church. A government report from Speyer in 1937 noted that although the struggle over a unified Christian national church occasioned heated debate among Protestants, the Catholic church was "practically not worth naming in this regard." Few of its people had joined the German Christian movement, the report added.[53] Five years later, after an aggressive program of outreach in Bavaria, German Christians had made few gains in Catholic circles. In July 1942, a group of Franconian German Christians in the Nuremberg region provided membership figures for seventeen localities. The region boasted a total membership of 6,409 German Christians. Of those, 5,758 were Protestant-

Lutheran; 499 outside a church (*gottgläubig*); and only 152 Catholic. Eight of the seventeen local groups described included no Catholics at all; members outside the churches outnumbered Catholics in all seventeen of the groups.[54]

At best, the German Christians picked up some Catholic stragglers whose attachment to their faith was particularly weak. Those Catholics who did join found their common ground with Protestants in the movement was less allegiance to a supraconfessional church than rejection of any recognizable form of Christianity. In late 1943, a former Catholic priest served as German Christian pastor in Kulmbach (Bavaria). He preached his Advent sermon that year in the black uniform of the German Christian clergy: high boots, black military-style jacket, riding breeches. He did not use the Bible, say Amen, or pray. Christ, he announced, "did not have a home in the Catholic Church, because it has a pope." Nor did Christ find lodgings in the Protestant church, he contended, "because it has a paper pope, the Bible."[55] Only in the antidoctrinal sanctuary of the German Christian people's church, he implied, did true Christianity reside.

## The Failure of Supraconfessionalism

For the German Christian movement, supraconfessionalism proved ineffective as a plan of action and counterproductive even as a slogan. The idea of a people's church that would transcend confessional boundaries not only failed to attract Catholics; it contributed to dissension within German Christian ranks, alienated fellow Protestants from the cause, and earned suspicion and hostility from Nazi authorities.

The blatant anti-Catholicism of many German Christians precluded confessional reconciliation. Although they claimed to be the voice of unity, German Christians presented Catholicism as the enemy of their projected people's church. In 1933, the national conference of the movement's student organization included a session on the Catholic church. By scheduling that topic in a series with discussions of Jews, Socialists, Freemasons, and Bolsheviks, organizers made it clear that they considered Catholicism just as antithetical to their cause as those familiar foes.[56] In June 1935, the German Christian leader of Mecklenburg identified "eternal Rome and the Confessing Front" as chief enemies of the movement, pointing to the "religious confusion and hatred" they sowed.[57] Elsewhere, German Christians contrasted the "Catholic 'Power-Church'" with the German Christian "People's Church."[58] A German Christian publication in 1938 warned that "the Catholic church is and will remain the archenemy and the ancient foe of the Church of the Reformation."[59]

The German Christians' vocabulary relied on anti-Catholic slurs. They denounced opponents as "Jesuits" or "papists"[60] and used allusions to Catholicism to discredit competitors. In December 1934, when German Christians complained that Confessing Church "hordes" disrupted their worship service in a Berlin-Schöneberg church, they noted especially the presence of "a Catholic director" and a "non-Aryan, baptized lawyer."[61] In 1935, Leffler, champion of the supraconfessional church, lambasted a Confessing Church pastor who, planning a trip with his youth group, arranged lodgings through a Catholic priest. It was "unbelievable," Leffler insisted, "that these pharisees accuse us of betraying Luther, of harboring in our German Christianity the insidious tendency to make our *Volk* Catholic, while they themselves in word and deed are a limb of eternal Rome."[62] When German Christians reached for a slur or an insult, they often resorted to the language of hostility toward Catholicism. Small wonder that Catholics did not flock to their cause.

The supraconfessional church divided the German Christian movement itself. Some German Christian clergy hesitated to embrace unequivocally the supraconfessional ideal. A pastor in Dresden lamented that as a German Christian, he was "defenseless" when people discredited the movement by pointing to schemes for a national church. He pleaded with German Christian leaders to distance themselves from supraconfessionalism.[63] The promise of a national church both attracted and disillusioned rank-and-file German Christians. In February 1942, a Bavarian pastor reported that German Christians in his community had misunderstood the implications of supraconfessionalism. They had believed "nothing about the faith would be altered," he reported, and had only wanted a "unified organization of the German churches with a common hymnbook." They favored Protestant-Catholic reconciliation for practical reasons to "overcome difficulties with regard to confessionally mixed marriages." German Christian lay people, the pastor concluded, had simply not thought through the implications of their movement's agenda. For example, they "more or less left open" the question as to whether the projected "German Church" would be Protestant in nature or the product of genuine confessional union.[64]

If the idea of a supraconfessional church proved divisive and confusing in German Christian ranks, it was explosive within German Protestantism as a whole. Many Protestants, anxious about Catholic encroachment, feared that the German Christians played into Catholic hands. After the Sports Palace affair in 1933, some people worried that "confusion and uncertainty" in Protestant circles would induce migration to the "Roman Church."[65] Two Lippstadt pastors, for example, complained that German

Christians bred strife in the community, and the *"tertius gaudens"* (rejoicing third party) was "Rome." Rumors already circulated, they fretted, that the "Roman Church" planned to take over a Protestant church building within two or three years.[66]

For Confessing Church circles, the supraconfessional church provided a convenient stick with which to beat German Christians. Those critics often expressed a horror at German Christian plans to incorporate Catholics into the spiritual community that far exceeded their shock at intentions to exclude converts from Judaism. According to one Confessing Church account, the supraconfessional church constituted the surest proof of German Christian heresy. Moreover, the author accused, that notion was "an obvious product of nineteenth-century liberalism." It was "undeniable" he asserted, "that the idea of the national church bears characteristic Jewish tendencies." Supraconfessional schemes were neither "German nor Aryan, and certainly not Christian," he concluded; "they represent a return to Jewish speculation and hopes for the future."[67]

To win support for their own cause, Confessing Church circles encouraged rumors that German Christians wanted to "turn everyone into Catholics."[68] In Hanover, for example, German Christians complained in 1935 that a senior churchman had gone door to door, "to hoodwink the innocent population into believing that their German Christian pastor had been sent to make them all into Catholics."[69] "Are German Christians true to the confession?," asked a flyer from the Confessing Church; "No!," came the emphatic response. The proof: "in many local groups Catholics are members."[70]

In 1935, when German Christians founded a series of local groups in Bavaria, Confessing Church observers emphasized that those groups, though small, contained "many Catholics."[71] Protestant Bishop Theophil Wurm of Württemberg remarked critically that "many non-Protestant people" numbered among the members and officers of the German Christian movement.[72] In 1940, his counterpart in Bavaria, Bishop Hans Meiser, described the German Christian movement as "heavily infiltrated by Catholics."[73] All of those commentators had access to more precise information that would have revealed the paucity of Catholics in German Christian ranks. But the specter of a Protestant movement dominated by Catholics worked well as a propaganda tool for opponents of German Christianity. Mere mention of Catholicism inspired fear among Protestants, revealing both pervasive anti-Catholicism and profound insecurity within the German Protestant community.

## The Protestant League and Opposition to Confessional Unity

In addition to providing ammunition for Confessing Church attacks on German Christianity, the supraconfessional church alienated from the movement some Protestants otherwise sympathetic to its cause. A look at the Protestant League illustrates this point. Formed in 1887 as an offensive against Catholicism, the Protestant League for the Protection of German Protestant Interests (Evangelischer Bund zur Wahrung der deutsch-protestantischen Interessen) had 260,000 members in 1934 with local groups across the country.[74] The language and rhetorical style of the league's spokesmen bear an uncanny resemblance to those of German Christians, in the sense of urgency and impending doom, intense hostility to democracy, celebration of a cult of Luther, and chauvinistic enthusiasm for Germanness. The Protestant League had developed its aggressive style early. The declaration of the league's foundation in 1887 warned of the "most severe dangers" threatening the German Protestant church, "and with it our German fatherland." On one side, it intoned, "stands the mighty unity of Rome, on the other, woefully divided German Protestant Christianity." It decried the factionalism within Protestantism that caused splintering over "internal church questions," while "the enemy advances, in its inexorable attempt to destroy us."[75]

The Protestant League did not create the German Christian movement, but it fostered a climate of hatred within German Protestant circles that both encouraged and legitimized collective resentments. At the 1924 annual meeting, for example, the league's president, Court and Cathedral Pastor Bruno Doehring of Berlin, declared war against Rome, calling members to join the "storm troop" of Martin Luther.[76] German Christians appropriated the Protestant League's vitriolic vocabulary and strident style, substituting Jews for Catholics as the mortal foe of Protestant Christianity in Germany.[77] The league also contributed to the German Christian movement through links of personnel. In some cases, it literally fathered German Christians: for example, a pastor from Herford (Westphalia) who was active in the league after World War I[78] had a son who became a German Christian pastor.[79] Some members of the Protestant League themselves joined German Christian ranks. Wilhelm Fahrenhorst, prominent in the league from the 1920s, later attracted attention because of the German Christian tone he lent to league publications.[80] A pastor from Berlin-Charlottenburg who addressed the league's annual meeting in 1930 on the subject of "German piety" also ended up among the German Christians.[81]

In its early stages, the German Christian movement enjoyed congenial relations with the Protestant League. Representatives of the two organizations met in January 1933. According to a league report of the encounter, the German Christians showed "great understanding" for the Protestant League's stance against Rome. At the 1933 and 1934 meetings of the league's executive, President Friedrich Conze and head of publications Wilhelm Fahrenhorst, both sympathetic to the German Christian cause and active in its interests, emphasized that German Christians had given considerable impetus to the conversion of Austrian Catholics to Protestantism.[82] A pastor in Berlin-Wilmersdorf invited German Christians there to join the league, apparently with considerable success.[83]

Despite that initial cooperation, the Protestant League eventually broke with the German Christians over the issue of the supraconfessional church. Leading figures in the league interpreted schemes to abolish confessional division as a call to increase their vigilance toward Catholicism and to extend that suspicion to those German Christians who flirted with supraconfessionalism. The league's criticism of German Christianity came to a head in 1936 and 1937. A 1936 booklet titled "The National Church: Different Ways to a Goal" urged Protestants to eschew supraconfessional dreams and instead await the withering of Catholicism in Germany. Numbers, the author argued, spoke for the Protestant side. Two-thirds of Germans were already Protestant and all "true Germans" belonged, he reasoned, because the Protestant faith "sees in that which is holy to the German as a German—in race, ethnicity, nation and state—the laws of God's creation." One day, that league representative exulted, the longing of German Protestants would be fulfilled, not in supraconfessionalism but in a "German Protestant National Church."[84]

In mid-1937, the Protestant League issued 130,000 copies of a four-page flyer titled "National Church?" Up until that time, the Confessing Church had criticized the league for its pusillanimous neutrality in the church struggle. But release of that flyer with its unequivocal denunciation of the supraconfessional church brought the league into head-on confrontation with the German Christians. The league's statement began by conceding the desirability of confessional unity. But it then honed in on those German Christians "who want to construct a 'Cathedral of the Germans,' a 'German Christian National Church.'" For the league, such dreams were delusions, the chasm between Protestant and Catholic unbridgeable. "Every Protestant Christian," the pamphlet explained, "knows that the Roman Church has a doctrine of the Lord's Supper that appears to be magical, that Catholics interpose the priests between God and humanity, that they have a different attitude toward *Volk*, work, and earthly realities—Protestant monks are an abomination!—and above all, that they honor the Pope as the highest authority, as the supposed deputy of Christ on earth, who in an infallible way can decide on matters of faith."[85]

To illustrate irreconcilable differences, the flyer pointed not to the explicitly doctrinal concerns it had mentioned earlier but to a "burning issue so important for our *Volk*": the Sterilization Law. The reference was to the Law for the Prevention of Hereditarily Diseased Offspring of 14 July 1933, which ordered compulsory sterilization of all people afflicted with certain diseases or disabilities.[86] The Protestant church welcomed that measure, the flyer indicated, and "an entire congress of Catholic scholars" also recognized its "necessity." Yet the pope condemned it.[87] The Protestant League exaggerated with the reference to a "congress of Catholic scholars." In fact, two Catholic theologians from East Prussia, Hans Barion and Carl Eschweiler, both members of the Nazi party, had issued an opinion that the Sterilization Law did not violate Catholic teachings.[88]

On the basis of the sterilization example, the league's flyer maintained it would be "superficial" to spurn as inconsequential the chasm between the confessions. Unless all Germans intended to become Catholic, the flyer scoffed, "talk of a 'national church'" was "utopian" and "fanatical."[89] The league and German Protestants who shared its views were willing and even anxious to embrace a church intimately linked to the National Socialist regime and its ideology, but they drew the line at inclusion of Catholics in their spiritual community.

Conflict with the German Christians was not without effect on the league's membership. According to a report from Nassau-Hesse, a series of local groups disbanded in protest against rejection of the national church. In several cases, the president, in accordance with his own views, simply declared the group dissolved without consulting members. At least seventeen local groups in Nassau-Hesse alone disappeared.[90]

The Protestant League institutionalized anxieties that Protestantism was becoming obsolete. Some German Christians shared those concerns. In April 1934, a German Christian pastor in Halle (Westphalia) labeled the past hundred years of Protestantism a "story of failure"; the Protestant church, he lamented, was truly "the church of missed opportunities."[91] Similar expressions of a looming sense of irrelevance recur in many German Protestant statements throughout the first decades of the twentieth century.[92] Symptomatic of a widespread crisis of confidence within German Protestantism is the fact that, for many in its ranks, hostility to Catholicism was the single most important reason to reject the German Christian movement.

## Nazi Authorities and the National Church

German Christians considered the supraconfessional church the greatest gift they could offer to National Socialist Germany. Nazi authorities, however, thought otherwise. German Christians found little sympathy from the Nazi regime for their plans to create a national church. In December 1937, Reinhard Heydrich, chief of the Security Police and head of the intelligence section (SD) of the SS, dispatched a curt letter to Siegfried Leffler. Heydrich forbade the German Christian organization any display of the swastika in conjunction with the "Christian cross." The National Church movement of German Christians had been warned repeatedly to desist from that practice, Heydrich threatened; should the renewed order be violated, he reserved the right to undertake "further measures."[93] The Reich Chancellery noted that because the party and state had at one time furthered the German Christian cause and the Ministry of Church Affairs still did so, Minister of Church Affairs Kerrl should also respond.[94] Kerrl accordingly prohibited any religious organizations from using National Socialist symbols.[95]

Rather than uniting Germans in a supraconfessional church, the war brought hard times for Christians of all stripes. Anti-Christian elements in the Nazi party and military leadership opposed the chaplaincy's emphasis on interconfessional services because they feared it would compromise the strictly voluntary nature of religious services in the armed forces and sow discord by bringing "certain disputes that exist in the Protestant church into work at the front."[96] German Christians found themselves included in general attacks on Christian practice among the troops. Dean of Naval Chaplains Friedrich Ronneberger, himself sympathetic to the movement, complained bitterly about obstructions to effective pastoral care for the military. As examples, Ronneberger pointed to military orders that Christmas be celebrated as the festival of the German tree of life and the prohibition of chaplains' visits to barracks.[97]

At home, Nazi party and state organs assaulted Christian ritual in ways that offended even the German Christians. In 1942, a German Christian wrote to the Reich Chancellery expressing alarm that anti-Christian measures were sapping the "spiritual power" of the German *Volk* in wartime. That correspondent considered the German Christian hope for "completion of the Reformation" identical to the National Socialist quest for "unity of faith." Spiritual unification of all Germans, he argued, would provide a "unique source of power" for the nation. Instead of recognizing that power, he complained, the Nazi party denounced believing Protestants and Catholics as unreliable; forbade pastors to hold party posts; disadvantaged church people in the distribution of ration coupons; and attacked Christian holidays, customs, baptisms, church weddings, and funerals. The result, he warned, forced churches into opposition.[98]

Late in 1943, another German Christian, a well-known proponent of the national church, voiced his "most grave concern about the unity of faith of all Germans" and protested the oppression of Christianity in the Third Reich. Even in Thuringia, he asserted, an area not known for its piety, the churches had been full to overflowing on Christmas 1943. That phenomenon, he insisted, revealed how profoundly the *Volk* still needed spiritual power. He quoted a fellow German Christian leader: "If Christianity were taken away from me and my children, at least each Christmas Eve I would be an unhappy person!" The Third Reich jeopardized even that minimalist definition of Christianity. The German Christian's plea to the regime indicates how far members of the movement had lowered their expectations of state involvement in the national church. He no longer anticipated support; he begged only for tolerance. "The path to defeat of the confessions . . . in Germany," he concluded, "will only be secured through the unconditional freedom of conscience guaranteed by the total state."[99]

For German Christians, the supraconfessional church constituted an attempt to construct a spiritual homeland for the German nation. That project failed in every regard. It attracted few Catholics, divided German Christians, alienated other Protestants, and reaped indifference and hostility from Nazi authorities. The fate of the supraconfessional church exposes the essential negativity and the spiritual void at the heart of German Christian ecclesiology. The German Christians could destroy but they could not build. According to the Thuringian pastor Siegfried Leffler, the supraconfessional church would be the willing agent of its own obliteration: "Like a narrow pass that we must go through on the way to that cathedral where Germans, as a nation, pious and free, will look up to God and pray, lies the word and the thing: 'the church.'"[100]

CHAPTER 7

Women in the Manly Movement

*I myself am nothing but a National Socialist of the deepest
conviction. In fact, I want exactly what our Führer wants and what
the best elements of the movement for liberation strive for, only I have
worked it out in a feminine form and in womanly ways, so that my
struggle is directed inward and motivated by inner renewal and
liberation.*
—Guida Diehl, Director of the New Land Movement, 1932

*The soul of the family is . . . and remains the mother. . . . She is the
guardian of the holy fire in the hearth, whose flame shall never be
exhausted. She is the nurturer of the powers of faith, without which
all external success is useless.*
—German Christian Mathilde Wohlert, [1935?]

For about a year, between late 1933 and early 1935, a certain
Miss Wiedemann edited the press organ of the German Christian movement, *Evangelium im Dritten Reich* (The gospel in the Third Reich). But
her name appeared nowhere on the masthead. The publisher, required by
law to identify the individual responsible for the paper's contents, listed a
man in that capacity, even though that person worked with page layouts
and had no editorial functions whatsoever.[1] Christian Kinder, the German
Christian national leader at the time, was candid about the reason for that
deception. "We did not want to appear in the police files as having a woman
editor," he told members of the movement.[2] In the interests of the manly

church, Miss Wiedemann became invisible. Only a conflict between Kinder and Joachim Hossenfelder exposed her position; Kinder revealed her role as a way to discredit his rival German Christian leader.

The German Christians advocated a manly church, not a church of men only. As Miss Wiedemann's case illustrates, women participated in the movement in many significant ways, their low visibility in the sources notwithstanding. In an organization that flaunted a masculine image, however, their involvement was essentially ironic. The survival and success of the movement depended on women and their efforts. But while women strengthened the movement by contributing legitimacy, energy, and numbers to its cause, they undermined its manly mission from within, laying it open to charges of unmanliness and resisting its attempts to transform the practice of Christianity.

Women acted in the German Christian movement from behind a barrier. With the battle cry of manliness German Christian leaders signaled to women and unmanly men that they were to keep a low profile. But just as a barrier implies the presence of a challenge or a threat, the movement's strident and defensive use of the manly slogan suggests that the opposite condition lurked just around the corner. The tension that characterized gender relations within the German Christian movement both reflects conditions in the surrounding society and highlights contradictions inherent in German Christianity itself.

## Mothers and Wives

It was as mothers that women found their most celebrated role in the German Christian movement. German Christians echoed the Nazi adulation of motherhood, adding their own religious dimensions. The image of the mother both opposed and complemented that of the soldier, providing an ideal foil for the manly elements in the German Christian movement. Like the military images associated with the manly church, the German Christian emphasis on motherhood implied liturgical change. The movement's new hymns, poems, and celebrations provided the means to create an appropriate place for mothers.

German Christians stressed sacrifice and selflessness in the image of the ideal mother. A German Christian book on funeral celebrations provided special readings for burial of mothers. One verse depicted the mother as the paragon of ultimate self-sacrifice:

> You carried all our sorrow for us,
> And you gave us all your joys.

You took the sword of our pain without complaint,
and smiling you sank it into your own heart.[3]

Such readings perpetuated and refined the picture of the loving, long-suffering mother, the martyr who sacrifices all for her children. Extending that image, poems, like this one from a German Christian anthology, codified a link between mother, faith, and racial purity:

Hold fast to what your mother taught you
early on, in her lap,
before your little heart had protection against the alien,
the false.
Dead is that which you get from strangers,
To which your blood does not testify.
Flee! It will smother you,
as it has brought many a people to its knees![4]

For the German Christian movement, the mother constituted a link to religious tradition, a legitimizing force for the new manly spirit.

German Christian hymnbooks devoted entire sections to motherhood.[5] Typical of such hymns was a song titled "These Are the Quiet in the Land" (*Das sind die Stillen im Lande*), recommended for German Christian Mother's Day celebrations. The melody, adapted from a spiritual folksong, shows no trace of a marching beat. The lyrics contrast the emphasis on comrades, blood, and flags in the manly hymns. In this song we find mothers "tending the holy fire"; we see their "protective hands" and witness the "pure light" that flows from them.[6] If the manly hymns captured the spirit of struggle that characterized the German Christian movement, the hymns for mothers sought to preserve a sphere of serenity and piety that nurtured those storm troopers of Christ. As Claudia Koonz has shown, mothers and wives "made a vital contribution to Nazi power by preserving the illusion of love in an environment of hatred."[7]

At times the mother cult propagated in German Christian speeches and publications reached dizzying heights of maudlin emotionality. In a world extolling manly virtues, mother represented a site at which men could revert to the helplessness of the child at the bosom. A 1935 article in the German Christian paper *Der Weckruf* (The rousing call) epitomizes such writing. The author described a visit to his ailing mother:

I felt a tear run down my cheek. And I cried out only one word: "Mother!" I held her old, loyal hand, that had worked for me. It seemed to me as though it led me in that quiet hour through all the worlds. And everywhere I felt that I was not forsaken, that the God whom I sought, went with me. . . . I saw only the true, beloved hand of my mother. And yet I was not just in my mother's house, not just in the tiny village. I saw suddenly all of Germany. I knew what it meant to be in Germany. And I said very quietly to myself the word in which I saw all the cities and villages, the mountains and valleys, the rivers and lakes, and I loved them all in that one word: Mother! . . . I was completely happy. But I did not appear happy at all. One teardrop after another fell over my face. I was not ashamed. I cried. And yet I was so happy, for I held quite still the dear, loyal hand of my mother.[8]

For that man, feelings about God, country, and mother were indistinguishable. Mother constituted the link to spirituality and sentimentality, the refuge where tears and dependence need not cause shame but could rejuvenate.

The cult of motherhood provided women with a space and an identity for their work in the German Christian movement. Before the church elections planned for 1937, a Stuttgart German Christian pastor disparaged female candidates with the remark: "It would be more appropriate to let young girls be elected than old maids who have never borne a child."[9] Only mothers or potential mothers, he implied, had a place among German Christian leaders. It is no coincidence that one of the most prominent German Christian woman, the childless and unmarried Guida Diehl, was referred to by her followers, even into the 1960s, as "Mother Guida" or "our beloved mother."[10]

In April 1933, Guida Diehl spoke at the Reich conference of German Christians on the tasks of the woman and mother in the new state. Her talk was a bid to assert women's influence in new areas, particularly in work with youth. Diehl argued that a woman, because of her "motherly soul," was nearer to God and therefore "specially talented and called to the raising of the youth."[11] Her publication, the *Neulandblatt* (New Land paper), printed numerous odes of praise to motherly qualities. A 1934 article, for example, called for the "truly developed female character" to permeate "the soul of the people."[12] Genuine fulfillment of the manly church, such statements implied, depended on the active involvement of women.

In 1934, one German Christian woman, Klara Schlossmann-Lönnies, based an entire scheme for religious revival on the image of motherhood. Lönnies, at one time director of the Mothers' Service Enterprise of the Protestant church (Mütterdienstwerk der Evangelischen Reichsfrauenhilfe), proposed mounting a symbolic action to counter world opinion that National Socialism threatened Christianity. To be effective, she held, the

*From the National Socialist paper, the* Illustrierter Beobachter
*(Illustrated observer), late 1933. On the right, a mass wedding of Nazi women
and men under the heading "For Race and* Volkstum." *The chart shows rising
marriage rates and the text describes the positive effects of new laws
encouraging marriage and procreation. Such mass weddings were common
in the spring and summer of 1933. German Christians often interpreted them
as a sign that the Nazi revolution had effected a revival of interest in the
Protestant church. On the left, the flip side of racial policy: images of the
"hereditarily diseased." (Kommunalarchiv Minden)*

*A church wedding with the groom in SS uniform, January 1934. Himmler later forbade SS uniforms at religious events. (Landesbildstelle, Berlin)*

project needed to appear as unpolitical as possible; hence mothers' work provided the ideal focus. She advocated calling all Protestant women and mothers to help build a church in Bremen. The state would fund construction, she planned, but Protestant women would repay that contribution by collecting a "Mothers' Pence." Even in its architecture the church complex would symbolize "the people's church," she claimed, because it would encompass pastorages, an old people's home, an orphanage, and a school for mothers. The plan, Lönnies rhapsodized, would solve a range of problems: it would secure the authority of the Reich bishop, revise views of National Socialism in the domestic and foreign press, and stimulate job creation. Most important, she exulted, "the German women would come together as mothers of the people in a united deed of faith and thereby give a great example for the fight of a state against heathenism and the dangers of Bolshevist propaganda."[13] By capitalizing on the image of the mother, Lönnies intended to bring women into the center of power in the people's church.

An image of the German Christian wife formed a corollary to the role of motherhood. In this capacity, too, women could enhance the manly spirit of the movement by providing a foil to the combative nature of their spouses. A 1933 German Christian publication alluded to the wife of Fritz Loerzer, a prominent German Christian, as a testimony to his genuine manliness: "This manly, fighting life is penetrated and permeated by the experience of a great, unique love and marriage!"[14] A 1935 circular from German Christian leaders in the Palatinate urged members to bring their wives to a conference to enhance the sense of community.[15] The ideal German Christian wife offered her husband quiet support and respectability. Reich Bishop Müller, for example, never made public appearances with his wife or referred to her in his speeches. Yet it was to Paula Müller that concerned church people wrote in 1934, when rumors of an inordinately large salary assaulted her husband's reputation.[16] Even after his death in 1945, she tried to salvage his reputation by denying that he had committed suicide.[17] Ludwig Müller died of a heart attack, his wife insisted. With that claim she sought to lay to rest charges that he had been a coward, afraid to face the justice of the victorious Allies.

None of the wives of leading German Christian men gained independent prominence in the movement. Still, some of those women took an active interest in church politics. Irma Rehm, wife of Wilhelm Rehm, who led the Reich group of the German Christians in 1935, supported the Reich bishop avidly, if only in private.[18] The wife of another German Christian pastor had herself worked as a vicar in the movement's central office.[19] While the movement venerated the roles of mother and wife, it tended to relegate individual mothers and wives to the margins of its activities.

## The Religious Conscience

As mothers and wives, German Christian women stepped into a familiar feminine role as guardians of virtue, lending respectability to a movement that suffered from a reputation of being riddled with thugs. According to a prevalent stereotype, women were more emotional, less rational, and more spiritual than men. Those traits formed the basis of a view of women as the religious conscience of the *Volk*. German Christian women in turn seized on that empowering vision of feminine nature to expand their involvement in the movement.

Often German Christian women exercised their role as guardians of religious virtue by writing letters, questioning, challenging, and criticizing the men who dominated the movement. As a form of participation, letter writing typifies the place of women in the manly church; sufficiently public to elicit some response, it still allowed women to retain a low profile. After the Sports Palace affair of November 1933, Reich Bishop Müller received a flood of correspondence from German Christians worried about pagan influence in their ranks. Women wrote many of those letters. Three deaconesses from Potsdam were among the early correspondents. They wanted to know if German Christian leaders supported the principles Krause had expressed at the Sports Palace. The response to their query, they warned, would determine whether they would be "willing and able to support the 'German Christian' movement."[20]

A letter from Berlin-Wilmersdorf provides insight into the experience of another woman. Ever since she first heard Ludwig Müller on the radio and in person, that woman explained, she had actively promoted the German Christian cause. But in the wake of the Sports Palace affair, she complained, the responsibility of defending the movement's religious orthodoxy had grown almost unbearable. "Everywhere I run up against the same accusation," she reported. "'You people want to get rid of the Psalms, the hymnbook, even the *entire* Old Testament.' . . . I reply that *you*, Sir, as Reich bishop, do *not* want that. I have felt that in your speeches—only I have no written proof." She closed with a plea to the Reich bishop. "Please allow us to keep the benediction in the church service: 'The Lord make his face shine upon thee, and be gracious unto thee: The Lord lift up his countenance upon thee and give thee peace.' Those of us who were driven out from the country to the big city need to hear these words sometimes."[21] That letter typified responses from many women who sought to protect aspects of the Christian tradition while expressing loyalty to the German Christian cause. A "craftsman's wife" from Prussian Oldendorf (Westphalia) echoed the concern with preserving Christianity. "I might be a simple person," she wrote, "but I hold fast to my Bible, *Old* and New Testaments, come what may."[22]

For some German Christian women, Krause's Sports Palace speech engendered a personal crisis. A party member from Berlin reported that she and her husband had returned home from the event "extremely shattered." She called Krause's ideas antithetical to Christianity, materialistic, and the product of a "Jewish spirit."[23] Another woman wrote that she was especially thankful for the Reich bishop's condemnation of Krause because she had received a "concerned inquiry" from her American relatives, "who fear the destruction of the Protestant church in Germany."[24] By insisting that certain elements of Christian tradition be retained, women enhanced the German Christian movement's credibility. At the same time, women used reference to treasured components of Christian practice as a way to criticize elements within the group, especially among its leadership.

*A group of women from the Spree Forest area in traditional
garb give the Hitler salute to Reich Bishop Müller.
(Evangelisches Zentralarchiv in Berlin)*

In a letter to the Reich bishop in late 1933, a woman from Holtland (Ostfriesland) described the problems she faced as a German Christian. Precisely those people most involved in church work were most skeptical about the movement, she complained. Often, she asserted, local party leaders were to blame for the disastrous politicization of the church. She warned against excesses such as calling Hitler "the good shepherd" and closed with the prayer that "the Lord will grant the right way to the pastors in the movement to preach salvation, so that our people will again become a people after God's own heart."[25]

In 1937, a pastor's wife from Droskau (Niederlausitz) resorted to sending her suggestions on church issues to Minister of the Interior Wilhelm Frick's secretary, in the hope that she would pass them on to her boss. She expressed pathos and not a little frustration in her lines: "Often I've shared my advice and thoughts with the authorities; it is, however, so regrettable, that the men who matter—in our case, the Reich Minister Kerrl—never receive our letters."[26] Ten years earlier, she wrote, she had warned against the woeful inadequacy of church officials, who were promoted solely on their ability to shuffle paper. But she had not been heeded, for as she put it, "what does the voice of a woman count against such important men?"[27]

What kept such women in the German Christian ranks? Critical of the movement's excesses, mistrustful of National Socialist influence, loyal to aspects of the Christian tradition, they nevertheless took a stand for the German Christian cause. Often the reader of their letters would be unable to identify them as adherents of the movement had they not described themselves as such. Perhaps they did not grasp the implications of German Christianity. It is more likely, however, that they agreed with the German Christian goal of religious revival on the basis of a racially defined people's church and sincerely believed in the possibility of a Nazi-Christian synthesis.

A woman who signed herself "a German Christian" wrote to the foreign minister in 1935 with her view of church affairs. Her letter captures both the central themes and the fundamental contradictions of German Christianity:

> Why don't our rulers declare themselves for the *Volkskirche*, which is fighting for a living Christianity? With our great leader Adolf Hitler, our previously dead church also experienced the reawakening of a vital spirit. . . . [Julius] Streicher, the Franconian leader, said in a speech: "The murder of Golgotha is written on the foreheads of the Jews." Yes— and that is why there is a curse on that people. Jesus, however, died for us and so we should believe in him and accept him. He is the way to light, to peace and to love. . . . Only when we stand *united* in genuine faith in Christ will we defeat the priests of this world. . . .
>
> The Kingdom of Heaven is immanent in us—it must be prayed for and fought for. Martin Luther already struggled for this church for us. May we with God's help succeed, to the blessing of humanity. Amen.[28]

For German Christian women like that correspondent, devotion to racial purity and to National Socialist ideology in no way contradicted loyalty to Christian tradition. Their defenses of Christianity generally consisted of attachment to particular practices, not concern about basic Christian teachings.

The role of religious conscience gave women an opportunity to impose their vision on the German Christian movement. In the words of Eleanor Liebe-Harkort, leader of the German Christian Women's Service in Westphalia in 1935: "We women must recognize this great need of the church, the shortage of true spiritual advisers, and we must help our pastors, so that things will be set right again."[29] A year later, Liebe-Harkort expanded that somewhat subversive view of women's role in the German Christian movement. Women, she argued, made the best German Christians. Emphasizing the faithfulness of the Westphalian women despite conflicts within the movement, she praised them as "more courageous than men."[30]

## German Christian Women's Groups

Collectively women entered the German Christian movement through organized women's groups. In that capacity, too, they both bolstered and challenged the manly image of German Christianity. The titles of the German Christian–dominated groups in the Reich Church—the Women's Service (Frauendienst) and Men's Enterprise (Männerwerk)—indicate the respective assignment of roles.[31] Women's groups were responsible to men, indirectly to the Reich bishop, and directly to a member of the clergy. For example, in May 1935, the German Christian bishop of Oldenburg became regional leader of the Protestant Women's Service there; at his side "was the wife of Pastor Börner from Großenmeer."[32] Even women who led the women's service in a certain area often shared their posts with a man.

In 1935, Reich Bishop Müller appointed the German Christian pastor Hans Hermenau from Potsdam to reorganize the women who remained loyal after a number of organizations had broken away to attach themselves to the Confessing Church. Hermenau's credentials included the fact that he had written the lyrics to the "Song of the Women's Aid."[33] In March 1935, Hermenau drew up a set of instructions for Protestant Women's Service groups. The groups, he specified, were to be tied firmly to a man: the pastor or, if the clergy in the area were Confessing Church, the regional pastor.[34] In relying on men to lead women's organizations, German Christians followed Nazi practice. Gertrud Scholtz-Klink's predecessor as Reich leader of the National Socialist Women's Organization (NS Frauenschaft) was a man, although he held the post only briefly in late 1933 and early 1934. That man, a lawyer from the Rhineland named Gottfried A. Krummacher, was also a prominent German Christian, one of the few members of the group to gain a significant post outside the church.[35]

For the German Christian leadership, maintaining control of the organized women's groups was not just a matter of boosting male egos. Given the perception that women dominated religious life, representatives of all camps in the church struggle suspected that whoever had the women ruled the church. As a Confessing Church pastor remarked in August

1933, "Of what use is our fight for the church if our own Women's Aid is ruined?"[36] The male leadership of both camps considered women's groups their chattels, in their possession but liable to be lured away by rivals. A 1934 statement by the German Christian leader Kinder warned Gau leaders that "the effort is being made to hitch the Protestant Women's Aid to the wagon of the Confessing Church synod."[37] Conversely, a Westphalian Confessing Church pastor complained that his German Christian colleague had "tried over and over to lure members of the Linderhausen women's group away," even driving the president of the group to tears.[38]

To boost the credibility of their movement, German Christian leaders encouraged women's groups to operate under a pretext of neutrality in the church struggle. Such neutrality promised to make the groups more useful weapons in church politics, while curbing their ability to initiate action independently. According to a membership letter for German Christians in the Rhineland, Pastor Hermenau, leader of the women's groups, was devoted to creating a "truly neutral" organization. The circular went on to specify that women's groups should send their declarations of loyalty to Hermenau to the German Christian office, Gau Rhineland.[39]

Despite urgings from the German Christian movement that they maintain a show of neutrality, neither women's groups nor individual women remained detached in the church struggle. German Christian women gathered information to use against opponents and helped bring the church struggle into new arenas. In December 1934, a German Christian man from Lübeck reported to his Gau leader that his wife had visited the Women's Aid of the St. Giles Church, which was under the tutelage of a Confessing Church pastor. The pastor announced that an impending Confessing Church rally had been prohibited, but one of the women present urged everyone to go anyway. The German Christian man's wife passed this remark on to him, and he in turn reported the proposed action to his superior.[40] In Bielefeld, a woman wrote to Hitler in late 1934 complaining about the treatment of German Christian women there. "Our opponents are fighting with the dirtiest weapons," she claimed. "They throw our women and mothers out of the Women's Aid even though some of them have been members for thirty years and more, just because they are German Christians and stand behind the Reich bishop."[41] That woman was married to the German Christian district leader.[42]

Through the pretext of neutrality, women's groups helped create a space for the propagation of German Christian ideas. In December 1936, the Women's Association in Lohne (Westphalia) celebrated its twenty-fifth anniversary.[43] The pastor in charge was not formally a German Christian

*The procession leaving the church at a mass wedding ceremony in eastern Berlin, 1933. The accompanying text specifies that all of the fifty couples involved belonged to the Nazi party.*
*(Landeskirchenarchiv, Bielefeld)*

because for some reason he had been denied membership. Nevertheless, he acted like and was treated as a German Christian by colleagues of all persuasions. At the celebration he urged the women of his congregation to cooperate with the "great project of the Women's Organization in the Third Reich." As for the church struggle, he maintained that in Lohne there had been peace so far, and it would stay that way, thanks to women's neutrality. He compared the Women's Association to a tree, "more specifically a 'Lindentree,' under whose shady branches one often drinks a cozy cup of coffee." His remark that "it was after all so nice, peaceful and comfortable to drink coffee under the Lindentree" brought "lively applause in the room." In closing, the pastor noted that "God was not in the Bible, but rather in us. He also revealed himself in history, above all in our people, in blood and race (enthusiastic applause)."[44] Claims of neutrality in no way prevented that pastor from adopting a clear German Christian stance in the women's meetings. He and his wife later withdrew their Women's Association from the Westphalian Women's Aid.[45] By accepting his lead, the women under his tutelage endorsed and advanced German Christianity.

Although the German Christian women's groups marginalized women in a supporting role, they still provided organized and sometimes public ways for women to express loyalty to the movement. Mass weddings provided the most ostentatious of such displays. For example, in October 1933, eleven women were married to storm troopers in a group ceremony at the Protestant church in Schlachtensee, a suburb of Berlin. The event was a triumph for the manly church. A German Christian pastor presided, and members of the SA stood guard. Women were present as brides and as onlookers; their official role as the Women's Group of the German Christians was to provide cake and coffee at the reception.[46]

Like the roles of mother and religious conscience, the women's groups helped create an aura of normalcy and serenity within the German Christian movement. At the festive induction of a German Christian pastor in Lotte (Westphalia) in July 1934, a women's organization decorated the church with flowers and laurel branches, led the procession welcoming the new pastor, and serenaded him with the hymn, "O, That I Had a Thousand Voices."[47] Organized women's activities offered both a means for men to control women's activities in the movement and a space where women could assert their interests in church affairs.

## Women Officeholders

Men had a monopoly on the clergy in Germany in the 1930s and 1940s. By definition, the German Christian movement, a group dominated by pastors, relegated women to the rear. Nevertheless, women did challenge exclusive male dominance by occupying official positions in the German Christian hierarchy. Since the mid-1920s, German faculties of theology had admitted women although their ordination was not permitted. At least two women became German Christian vicars, meaning that they completed degrees in theology and held church positions without being ordained. Little is known about these women. A report from a delegate of the German Christian Women's Service mentions the wife of a German Christian pastor, "known to many of us still from the time she worked in the Reich office under the name of Vicar Ehmann."[48] After the war, when a German Christian man produced a list of twenty-five former German Christians and their fates, he included one woman, a retired vicar named Elfriede Müller. The only information he provided on Elfriede Müller was that she had not been subjected to a hearing before the church denazification boards.[49]

Women could vote in church elections and be elected to church posts. As a result, they exercised some formal power within the German Christian movement. At least at election time, German Christian strategists had to remember the women in their congregations. In July 1933, a German Christian campaign flyer from Aplerbeck near Witten (Westphalia) called on "National Socialists, German Protestant women and men" to register to vote. The attached list of forty-nine German Christian candidates, however, did not include even one woman.[50] That same summer, official election strategy in some regions called for at least some nominations of women. "Women can continue to be elected," read one set of orders for German Christian groups; "we welcome their valuable cooperation. So nomination of women is desirable (approximately 10 percent)."[51]

Women won election under the German Christian lists at every level of church government. In 1933, the General Synod for the whole of Prussia included 229 positions. No woman was the primary holder of any position, but six women were first or second alternates. There is no designation as to which camp these women endorsed with regard to church politics. It seems safe to assume, however, that at least the two alternates for the German Christian Pastor Hermenau were German Christians as well. One of those women was a city councillor from Berlin, the other was managing director of the church-social women's groups.[52]

German Christian women also assumed responsibility as elders and parish representatives. One of four German Christian elders of the Peace and Salvation Parish in Potsdam was a woman.[53] The St. Thomas Church in Berlin had a woman elder who was a German Christian.[54] As of February 1935, one of the four German Christian parish representatives from the St. Peter's church in Bielefeld was a woman.[55] Berlin's Sophia parish had two German Christian women representatives.[56] In 1935, a German Christian woman effectively paralyzed the church council in Münster by declining to take office as a presbyter. She deferred with the request that "it be considered whether it would be better if a man entered the presbytery in my place."[57]

A few women gained positions within the German Christian hierarchy as spokespeople or officials of local groups. As of November 1933, the German Christian parish group in Berlin-Treptow had a spokeswoman (*Vertrauensfrau*) who that month addressed a general membership meeting on "The Woman as a German Christian."[58] The German Christian "officeholder" (*Amtswälterin*) in the Christ congregation in Berlin as of January 1935 was also a woman.[59] It is significant that these women had different titles than did men in comparable posts. "Spokesman" (*Vertrauensmann*) or "Officeholder" (*Amtswalter*) were not labels male local leaders used. It is unclear whether this irregularity is a coincidence, whether it reflected discomfort on the part of the German Christian leadership with women holding posts, or whether the women themselves were reluctant to enter the men's ranks as peers.

Women filled other important offices as well; even the manly church depended on women at the typewriters. Those women left little identifiable trace in the records, but evidence of their presence is everywhere. In 1934, the German Christian Walter Birnbaum, head of the Reich bishop's Secretariat, spent some months without a secretary. His office deteriorated into disarray; the files contain numerous letters hounding him about things he had failed to do, letters he had forgotten or irretrievably misfiled.[60] Birnbaum was reduced to writing apologies like the following to a pastor who had sent in the original of a certificate and now some months later needed a copy of it: "I had at the time no secretary and it is possible that somehow the letter was not properly filed, so that it is now not to be located."[61] His colleagues chided him about his inefficiency. In July 1934, consistory councillor Walter Grundmann in Dresden wrote asking Birnbaum to contribute to a book of devotional meditations. Grundmann minced no words: "I hope that you again have a stenographer at your disposal and therefore the mail will not need to lie around unanswered."[62] Without secretaries the church struggle could not have taken the form it did.

Women served the German Christians unofficially as denouncers and sources of information. When Berlin German Christians demanded removal of a Confessing Church pastor in 1934, they based their case on the testimony of two female witnesses. The women, one an assistant to the pastor, the other a German Christian, reported the pastor for describing the Reich bishop as "Ludwig the Child."[63] Another Confessing Church pastor faced censure in 1934 for claiming that the Reich bishop had bought his clerical robes from a Jew. Again, it was a woman who brought the information forward; she had heard it in Bible study.[64]

Toward the late 1930s and especially during the subsequent war years, women assumed a higher profile in German Christian publications and public events. In February 1939, a German Christian woman proclaimed the importance of female involvement in the movement, pointing out, "Everyone involved in the religious struggle today knows just how much everything depends on women's behavior, too."[65] As the German Christian movement struggled to retain its position vis-à-vis the Confessing Church, neopagans, and Nazi authorities, it could hardly afford to squander the support of half of the population. When regional treasurers of the National Church German Christians met in Eisenach in June 1939, eight of the thirty-three who posed for the camera were women.[66] That same month

*Meeting of regional treasurers of German Christian groups affiliated with the Thuringian National Church leadership, Eisenach, June 1939. Women are well represented. (Evangelisches Zentralarchiv in Berlin)*

the National Church German Christians hosted a regional meeting of German Christian women in the Berlin area. Held in Potsdam, the event boasted six hundred female participants, a women's choir, and a talk titled "Our Defense against the Jewish and Political-Catholic Spirit in the Church."[67] This gathering was probably the first time that German Christian women met formally to discuss the movement as a whole, not merely a women's branch.

The war created openings for women, too, because the movement depended on them to fill in for men who were absent. When the deputy leader of the German Christian group in East Prussia died in 1943, his wife took over that post in Tilsit.[68] For a short while in 1943 and 1944, a woman headed the German Christian office for Catholic affairs in Eisenach.[69] She was a former Catholic who had been active as a public speaker on women's issues for the National Church wing of the German Christian movement.[70] By February 1944, the director was back and she had left the office.[71] Women officeholders were exceptions in the German Christian movement, but their activities suggest a broad range of possibilities.

## The Liability of Women's Involvement

Women's participation, though crucial, constituted a potential embarrassment to a movement that preached the manly church. A look at specific women illustrates how proponents of the manly image could obstruct and confine the activities of individual women. Guida Diehl offers a useful case to study the treatment of a female leader at the hands of German Christian men. Since the beginning of World War I, Diehl, an unmarried woman originally from Odessa, had headed her own nationalist Protestant organization, the New Land League.[72] Since 1932, she had been active in the National Socialist Women's Organization. She called her New Land group "nothing but a parallel movement to National Socialism," herself "nothing but a National Socialist" who expressed the same desires as Hitler but "in a feminine form and in feminine ways."[73] In 1933, the German Christian publicist Friedrich Wieneke praised Diehl and labeled her New Land League "a fighting group of German Christians."[74]

Diehl had every reason to expect to play an important role in the German Christian movement. Early in 1933, she became head of the subsection on women's issues. But the men in charge had no intention of allowing her into the inner sanctum. At the German Christian Reich Conference in Weimar late that year, key leaders held a special strategy session. They did not inform Guida Diehl. She was furious and appealed to the Reich bishop to "understand the worries of the heart of a woman who is anxious about renewal and about the soul of the people."[75] It was no use; Diehl remained shut out of the top echelons of the German Christian hierarchy.

Bitter at her marginalization, Diehl demonstrated that she too could subvert the movement's interests. In late 1934, she wrote to a prominent leader of the Confessing Church, hinting that she was considering severing her ties to the German Christians.[76] Those overtures came to nothing, and Diehl remained active in the German Christian cause until the end of the war. She continued to earn praise for her devotion to National Socialism: in 1941, party officials in Weimar depicted her "political reliability" as "beyond question."[77] Such endorsements did not prevent the men in the German Christian movement from shunting her aside. More than a decade after the war, when a circle of former German Christians sought to publish biographies of opponents of the Confessing Church, they disqualified Diehl's autobiography, *Christ sein heißt Kämpfer sein. Die Führung meines Lebens* (To be a Christian is to be a fighter: How I lived my life, 1959). One of the men in charge offered an explanation. "Strictly speaking," he insisted, Diehl's account did not belong. The title, he suggested, "does not exactly fit our 'peace line,' even if one thinks of it in terms of the struggle for peace."[78] Presumably, the men concerned found Diehl's image of herself as a fighter too strident for a woman in the manly church.

Diehl was a difficult, outspoken individual who ran into conflicts with women and men inside and outside the German Christian movement. Her admirer and fellow German Christian Karl Wentz suggested that Leffler and Leutheuser, the two Thuringian German Christians leaders, got her into serious trouble with the Nazi party.[79] In 1936, Diehl clashed publicly with Gertrud Scholtz-Klink, leader of the National Socialist Women's Organization; five years later, the Reich Chamber of Culture ejected her, although she was subsequently readmitted.[80] In the early 1940s, Diehl came close to being thrown out of the Nazi party, but in view of her age and ill health, Bormann agreed to drop the case in 1942.[81]

Similar personality traits did not prevent Diehl's male counterparts from playing public roles in the church struggle. Bremen's Bishop Weidemann is an example of someone whose relations with Nazi authorities were more checkered than Diehl's, yet he held a powerful place in the German Christian movement. Diehl's marginalization reflected above all her failure to fit the image of the manly church. Indeed, she represented its antithesis: emotional, sentimental, and assertively female, she was anything but a Christian storm trooper. The male leadership of the German Christians did their best to neutralize her.

The case of a German Christian woman from Berlin-Friedenau illustrates other tensions surrounding women's involvement in a purportedly manly movement. In January 1935, Dörthe Kisting spoke at an educational evening in her parish on the subject of the Ten Commandments.[82] By March, Kisting, an unmarried woman who held the golden party badge as a so-called old fighter, controlled press affairs for the local German Christian group. She was also something of a poet and wrote a set of lyrics to be sung to the tune of a familiar chorale, "Rejoice, Oh My Soul" (*Freue dich sehr, o meine Seele*). Printed on a flyer, those lyrics were distributed in her German Christian parish group in Berlin's Nathanael Church. "Father protect our Hitler, guide his strong hand," the song began.[83] Evidently Kisting and her father, a professor, spearheaded German Christian efforts in a heavy-handed way that drew criticism from within their congregation.[84]

One of Kisting's first tasks as press and propaganda director involved submitting an official account to her German Christian superiors of an event in her congregation. The fate of her report reflects the ambivalence with which the German Christian movement viewed women's efforts. On an evening in March 1935, a Confessing Church leader was to speak at 6:00 P.M. in Berlin's Nathanael Church. Kisting described her group's response.

"Shortly before 5:30 on 3 March," she wrote, " 'German Christians' from Nathanael entered the church together and, to the annoyance of their enemies, also took our places in a group." Their opponents observed them "most distrustfully," she recounted: "a white-haired gentleman in the right balcony continuously stared at us, whereby he shaded his eyes with his hand, although the balcony was dark. The so-called 'Protectors of the Hall,' (young men in black pants and tunic-like white shirts) were posted around us." According to Kisting, one of the "Confession Church" people leaned over to tell a German Christian that "the 'German Christians' intend to disrupt this church service." She did not hear the end of the sermon, Kisting explained, because, with the other German Christians, she "walked out of the church, full of inner rage over the arrogance they had heard." She made sure to emphasize that they "left quietly, accompanied, however, by the loud sigh of relief of one of those 'loyal to the Confession,' and the words, 'Thank God.' "[85]

Kisting's report portrays a stereotypically feminine style of battle. The aggression was passive; the heroic struggle consisted of an exchange of glares and a huffy but quiet departure from the church. Surely this was not what German Christian men envisaged when they trumpeted their manly movement, their church of the brown man. Before sending the report up the German Christian chain of command, Kisting's male superior added one sentence: "Three of our members, women, were grabbed on their way out of the church."[86] It is highly unlikely that a reporter as thorough as Kisting, who included even dirty looks and sighs, would have failed to mention actual physical aggression. Her boss's insertion suggests embarrassment with the unmanly tone of the report and the events it described. Even if women dominated local actions, his comment implied, at least formal accounts of them should reflect the demands of the manly church. Women at best could appear as victims in need of rescue from German Christian men.

## Gender and the Language of Derision

If stressing male participation was a means of implementing the manly church, then pointing at the influence of women and unmanly men provided a way to discredit opponents. In this way, the notion of a manly church provided vocabulary and criteria for derision. When a German Christian group from Neheim (Westphalia) launched complaints against their Confessing Church pastor in 1934, one of their accusations was that mostly women and girls attended his church services.[87] In January 1935, the speaker at a German Christian meeting near Nuremberg used gender stereotypes to belittle the Confessing Church. The "most willing tools" of the Confessing Church pastors, he scoffed, were "old maids and women," who attended only out of love for their pastor.[88] A German Christian speaker in 1935 echoed that assessment. "In the church an hysterical howling has arisen from the old ladies," he jeered. "'We won't let our faith be taken away from us.' On that the Confessing Church was built!"[89]

Deprecation of women's involvement fit with a stereotyped view of women as dupes. That image was part of a polarity that characterized reason as masculine, emotion as feminine. German Christians denounced the Confessing Church by emphasizing the influence of women in the group and then discounting them as manipulable fools. A little dialogue called "In Battle against Mrs. Plischke" develops the theme of women as dupes of the Confessing Church. The author, brother of a leading Westphalian German Christian, personified the Confessing Church in the busybody Mrs. Plischke. Mrs. P., he recounted, detested the Nazi theorist Alfred Rosenberg and was convinced that he wanted to turn Germans into pagans. In the dialogue, the narrator tricks her into condemning quotations from respected German thinkers by claiming they were from Rosenberg and cons her into praising Rosenberg's words, which he tells her stemmed from her intellectual heroes.[90] Two victories intertwined in that little story: German Christian logic triumphed over the fuzzy thinking of the Confessing Church, and male rationality outwitted female emotionality.

German Christian publications described weakness of any kind in feminine terms. They ridiculed the neutrals, the middle group in the church struggle, with the label, "BdM"—*Bund der Mitte* (League of the Center), but also *Bund deutscher Mädel* (League of German Girls).[91] In 1937, German Christians in Frankfurt, disgusted with the "unmanly tone" of calls for conciliation in the church, proclaimed that "in a manly time of struggle, one cannot get by with effeminate and sweet talk of peace."[92]

But the weapons of gender could be turned against German Christians, too. Having created the public image of a masculine movement, German Christians had to keep women in the background or risk becoming the brunt of their own derision of the Confessing Church as the church of maiden aunts and grandmothers and the neutrals as the League of German Girls. Opponents of German Christianity made gleeful use of categories of age and sex to dismiss that movement as well. A 1937 Confessing Church report of a German Christian gathering pointed out that although the seventy people present included about equal numbers of men and women, there were "no youths and no one in uniform."[93] Another Confessing Church report ridiculed a German Christian event in Berlin in 1938, where Hossenfelder was to speak, pointing out that "the room holds about six hundred people—eighty-six were present, mostly elderly—among them ten or eleven men."[94]

Party and state observers used the same categories to describe and discount German Christian audiences. A report prepared for Alfred Rosenberg's office on a German Christian meeting in Berlin in 1934 conceded that 180 to 200 people turned up but mocked the crowd, calling it "a horrifying picture of a racially degenerate *Volk*. Almost all were roundheaded, pot-bellied, slack-jawed—they were matrons, deaconesses, degenerate young men, fanatics."[95] In 1936, a woman from the National Socialist Women's Organization panned Guida Diehl's book, *Heilige Flamme glüh!* (Glow, holy flame!), focusing on its "womanly" style. That tone, she scoffed, would repel the young generation, attracting at most a few "sisters from the Bible circle, or suchlike unoccupied daughters of the upper bourgeoisie, who armed with their fathers' wallets, see the world in 'unspoiled purity.'"[96]

Men in both major camps in the church struggle deplored what they considered the inappropriate, aggressive involvement of women. Their censorious accounts give scanty but provocative glimpses into the scope of activity possible for women, especially in loosely organized crowd actions at the local level. In 1934, for example, Confessing Church sources reported on an event in Nuremberg where a German Christian vicar and a Confessing Church pastor tried to hold services simultaneously in the same church. They introduced competing hymns, a German Christian supporter tried to shove the Confessing Church pastor from the pulpit, and the congregation got into a noisy altercation as to who was in the right. The reporter closed his account with the observation: "It was the women who were the most responsible for increasing the tumult. Indeed some of them knew no limits in their excitement."[97] The German Christians, the account implied, were so morally bankrupt that even their women were little better than thugs.

Their rhetoric of the manly church left German Christians wide open for such derision. Another Confessing Church account is illustrative. In 1934, a Confessing Church pastor was scheduled to preach in the Berlin-Schöneberg Apostle Paul's Church. He arrived to find a small group of German Christians already present. They refused to leave. Competing hymns were sung; the congregation heckled; Confessing Church youths chanted slogans in unison. The German Christian pastor G. Peters called two women up to the altar for support. According to the report, "With hate-filled faces they strengthened him in his scandalous actions. Meanwhile, it was already 11:45 and Peters made no move to break up this shameful performance. The organ continued to be played with all the stops pulled, adding to the chaotic tumult."[98] The image of that German Christian pastor who needed two such women to prop him up was deeply insulting. Not only did the Confessing Church reporter portray German Christians, male and female, as pathetic, he viewed with contempt and horror the apparent reversal of gender roles in their ranks.

The record of a German Christian vicar's speech from 1935 offers additional insight into how women participated in the church struggle at the local level and how men viewed them. When he first arrived in Nuremberg, the young clergyman claimed, the women in his congregation adored him and brought him "forty-three bouquets of flowers, poems, cakes." But when he said he was a German Christian, they turned on him. Once, he said, Confessing Church women "staged a boycott." They occupied the inside seats of the pews and, as he ascended the pulpit, pushed outward, shoving those who did not belong to their group out into the aisles. The women booed and called him a heathen. The vicar was both shocked and resigned to what he considered typical female behavior. "One can apply the words of the poet to this situation," he claimed, quoting Schiller. " 'There women become as hyenas.' They even spat on me three times as I was leaving the church."[99]

When considering the themes of women as dupes and women as religious conscience in relation to each other, one cannot escape the impression that an element of disgust or at best condescension permeated the attitude of German Christians toward their own cause. We might expect the assigned guardians of morality and spirituality to be the most venerated members of a society. Instead, the manly movement left the protection of Christian values to a patronized, even despised group: the women.

CHAPTER 8

The Ecclesiastical Final Solution

*If we National Socialists are ashamed to buy a tie from a Jew, how much more should we be ashamed to accept from the Jew anything that speaks to our soul, to our most intimate religious essence.*
—German Christian Reinhold Krause, 1933

*Because in the course of historical development, corrupting Jewish influence has also been active in Christianity, the* dejudaization of Church and Christianity *has become the inescapable and decisive duty of the church today; it is the requirement for the future of Christianity.*
—*Institute for Research into and Elimination of Jewish Influence in German Church Life, 1941*

Contradictions dogged the German Christian project. Members of the movement sought to revive the church but promoted a self-destructive ecclesiology. They demanded a manly institution, but they associated the church with womanly qualities and roles. German Christian ideas of race presented the most blatant contradiction of all. The movement was committed to preserving Christianity yet demanded total destruction of anything related to Judaism. By trying to tear their religious tradition from its Jewish roots, German Christians took on a boundless task that they could not accomplish without exploding Christianity itself.

Between the movement's inception in the early 1930s and the outbreak of war in 1939, German Christian endeavors to create an Aryan church spiraled into a quest for complete dejudaization of Christianity. The futility of that task spurred on the German Christians' exertions. The more they sensed the centrality of Judaism to Christianity, the more brutally they worked to eradicate its traces. The more Nazi and neopagan critics attacked Christianity as Jewish, the more viciously German Christians fought to prove their religion's antisemitic credentials for the Third Reich. Their efforts reveal the confluence of three factors: Christianity's ambivalent relationship to Judaism; widespread theological ignorance among church people; and devotion to a regime bent on violent antisemitism. Ultimately the German Christians preached Christianity as the polar opposite of Judaism, Jesus as the arch-antisemite, and the cross as the symbol of war against Jews.

This chapter examines efforts to dejudaize Christianity in three key areas: the Old Testament, the New Testament, and church music. For the sake of their racial imperative, German Christians abandoned the Old Testament and revamped the New Testament, jettisoning central teachings of sin and salvation. Only in the area of church music, far from the theological core of Christianity, did their assault on Jewish influence make less significant inroads. It is a testimony to the banality of their understanding of Christianity that, for the German Christians, notions of taste and appropriateness exercised a more effective brake on the project of dejudaization than did doctrinal or theological considerations.

## The Old Testament

*Rejecting Canonicity.* German Christians began their efforts to dejudaize Christianity by denying the canonicity of the Old Testament. Given the movement's opposition to doctrine, it is not surprising that such a radical position constituted the starting point, not the result, of debates about the Old Testament. By rejecting Old Testament canonicity, German Christians perpetuated a tradition within Christianity that extended back, for example, to Marcion in the second century[1] and the Cathari of the twelfth century.[2] Some German Christians knew of such precedents but they rarely mentioned them, preferring to emphasize their uniqueness rather than explore links to developments that predated National Socialism. Liberal theologians like Adolf von Harnack, who died in 1930,[3] had also questioned the Old Testament. They influenced German Christians, even if their motivations did not necessarily correspond with the movement's racialist preoccupations.

Despite affinities and connections, it would be an oversimplification to equate liberal theology and German Christianity. Most German Christians themselves denied ties to theological liberalism, but critics, especially in the Barthian camp, often made a connection as a way of discrediting two opponents at once.[4] From a political point of view, the two schools of thought showed different tendencies. Harnack himself was a rational republican during the Weimar years. Until his death in 1940, the Marburg professor of theology Martin Rade, one of Harnack's most prominent students and founder of the liberal Protestant journal *Christliche Welt* (Christian world), spoke out against chauvinistic nationalism, defended the Weimar Republic, and opposed National Socialism.[5] German Christians owed much to liberal theology, but for instruction on the Old Testament, they generally turned to *völkisch* predecessors who were less scholarly, more accessible, and more explicitly antisemitic.

German Protestant groups had contested the place of the Old Testament well before 1933. Throughout the 1920s and 1930s, the small but vociferous German Church group (*Deutschkirche*) promoted rejection of the Old Testament on antisemitic grounds. In 1931, Protestant church leaders in areas as distant as Austria and Lübeck complained that German Church activists were trying to curtail use of the Old Testament in the schools.[6] Other Protestants joined the fray. A 1932 publication, "Does the Old Testament Still Have Significance for a Christian?," outlined common criticisms: it was a "Jewish book"; it was ethically a poor example for children—"Jacob was a cheat, Abraham a liar, David an adulterer"; it was unscientific; it had been superseded by the New Testament.[7] The 1932 principles of Guida Diehl's Protestant, nationalist New Land Movement sacrificed Old Testament canonicity to national interests. "Our people need a new encounter with Christ," the statement declared, "without a detour through Judaism."[8]

After the Nazi takeover in 1933, German Christians took the lead in denouncing the Old Testament as Jewish. The implications of their position were initially unclear. Adherents of the movement agreed that canonicity per se was untenable but differed as to whether and how portions of the text might be retained. In June 1933, one man warned that unless the Old Testament were dropped from the Christian canon, it would provide "a constantly open door for the infiltration of Jewish matters and liberal degeneracy."[9] In November 1933, the German Christian–dominated church government in Schleswig-Holstein limited use of the Old Testament in religious instruction in schools. The binding of Isaac was the first story axed as "un-German."[10] Perhaps German Christians, devoted as they were to the idea of sacrifice, particularly in war, considered the story of Abraham and Isaac subversive because it rejected human sacrifice.

Reinhold Krause's speech at the Sports Palace rally on 13 November 1933 revealed the extremist potential in the German Christian rejection of Old Testament canonicity. Krause, leader of Berlin's German Christians, based his assault on the Old Testament on the need for a people's church that would encompass all National Socialists. "We must win over the flood of those returning to the church," he urged. "For that to happen, those people need to feel at home in the church. The first step in developing that feeling of belonging is liberation from everything un-German in the worship service and the confessions—liberation from the Old Testament with its cheap Jewish morality of exchange and its stories of cattle traders and pimps." According to the stenographical record, "sustained applause" ensued.[11] Krause's speech precipitated a wave of departures from German Christian ranks, many in protest of his remarks on the Old Testament.[12] Yet Krause was no anomaly. Although his words seemed shocking in 1933, they anticipated what by the late 1930s constituted the definitive German Christian view of the Old Testament.

Throughout the early 1930s, German Christians showed some flexibility in their stance on the Old Testament. In October 1934, Reich leader Kinder argued that the Old Testament need not divide the camps in the church struggle. German Christians, Kinder emphasized, accepted the entire Bible, although "greater significance was due to the New Testament than to the Old."[13] The twenty-eight theses of the German Christians, circulated in 1934, reflected Kinder's conciliatory position. Even that supposedly moderate document did not separate discussion of the Old Testament from considerations of race, however, and described the Old Testament as the story of "the fall of the Jews from God."[14] For German Christians, the canon of blood superseded scriptural canonicity.

Defenders of the Old Testament often praised its merits as an anti-Jewish text, an approach by no means exclusive to German Christians. Sometimes it is impossible to ascertain the church political allegiances of antisemitic champions of the Old Testament. Such is the case with a pamphlet that reasoned, "If the Old Testament were a Jewish book, it would never come into the mind of the Protestant church to use it in religious instruction, because the Jews crucified the Son of God, who brought the gospel."[15] Many German Christians coupled denial of Old Testament canonicity with a commitment to retaining certain "pearls" of special value. In 1935, a German Christian leader in Merseburg identified the psalms, poetic books, and prophets as worthy of preservation. Asked why the prophets, he responded that "the prophets are ... downright antisemitic in their focus."[16]

*Reinhold Krause, Berlin schoolteacher and leader of the German Christians there until the end of 1933. In his speech at the Sports Palace rally in November 1933, Krause called for the radical dejudaization of Christianity in the Third Reich. His crude mockery of the Old Testament "with its stories of cattle traders and pimps" and rejection of the cross and the "Rabbi Paul" shocked many Protestants in 1933 but anticipated the direction that the German Christian movement would take by the end of the decade. (Politisches Archiv des Auswärtigen Amts, Bonn)*

True to their antidoctrinal stance, German Christians never specified the Ten Commandments as among Old Testament segments to be retained. Only one German Christian version of the Bible seems to have attempted to salvage something of the commandments. *Gottes Wort Deutsch, aus Luthers Bibel, nach Luthers Regel, in Luthers Geist* (God's word in German, from Luther's Bible, according to Luther's rules, in Luther's spirit) contained a section titled "The Heart of the Ten Commandments." It did not actually include any of the commandments, only excerpts from Deuteronomy 6:4–10, with the opening call, "Hear, O Israel," altered to "Hear, You People of God."[17]

German Christians salvaged something of the Old Testament in other ways, using the very images and style they derided as Jewish to attack Judaism. For example, the German Christian poet Fritz Veigel, in a poem titled "The People's Atonement 1933," presented "the Jew" as the agent of Germany's destruction. Yet he cast Germany itself in the role of the Children of Israel:

> Us! We are the ones! We strayed from your path!
> We circled around the golden calf!
> We made our bellies, our lust, our money into idols;
> We bartered away our land, our blood, our hearts
> to the eternal Jew, whom you made into a curse!
> And our children cried out: We accuse you![18]

Even if only dimly remembered, the powerful cultural symbols of the Old Testament were important tools that German Christians used to construct their own self-image as figures in a spiritual drama of epic proportions.

Theological illiteracy could also prove an ally of the Old Testament. German Christian clergy might pride themselves on replacing Old Testament confirmation mottoes with words of wisdom from German heroes, but lay adherents did not necessarily notice the difference. A German Christian pastor in Lübeck, who confirmed 161 young people in 1934, boasted that he used confirmation mottoes pairing verses from the New Testament with what he called "Words of the German Prophets."[19] Bella Fromm, a German-Jewish columnist for the liberal *Vossische Zeitung*, recorded the case of a couple who asked their pastor—Martin Niemöller—to omit the usual reading from the Old Testament at their wedding ceremony. Instead they proposed, "As for me and my house, we will serve the Lord" (Joshua 24:15), or "Whither thou goest I will go" (Ruth 1:16)—both Old Testament texts.[20] Such blind spots created space for retention of Old Testament fragments. But for the German Christians, although bits of the

Old Testament might be kept for tradition's sake, a scriptural canon no longer existed.

*From the Nuremberg Laws to the Institute for Dejudaization.* The Nuremberg Laws in the fall of 1935 unleashed a new phase in the Nazi assault by codifying a definition of Jews and depriving them of citizenship. German Christians responded with their own harsher tone against the Old Testament. A German Christian speaker in Bavaria ridiculed the Old Testament as a saga of racial defilement. His remark that "Moses in his old age had married a Negro woman" drew boisterous laughter and enthusiastic applause.[21] The reference is to the Ethiopian wife who was the subject of strife between Moses and his siblings.[22] In the wake of Nuremberg, a Rhenish pastor quit the German Christian movement, appalled by increasing radicalism. The German Christians, he claimed, measured support for National Socialism solely on the basis of "the race question" and denounced anyone who did not reject the Old Testament as "already 'devoured by Jews.'"[23]

Public antisemitism inspired heightened German Christian attacks on the Old Testament; in turn German Christian ideas found resonance in a society that refused membership to those defined as Jews. In late 1936, a Confessing Church pastor described how teenage girls in his confirmation class reacted to a discussion of Jesus' words, "Think not that I am come to destroy the law, or the prophets: I am not come to destroy, but to fulfill" (Matthew 5:17–19). The girls went wild, he said, denouncing "the Old Testament with its filthy stories," the "Jews as a criminal race."[24] It was precisely such attitudes that German Christian pastors and schoolteachers sought to instill in the youth. A German Christian confirmation examination in early 1937 included the following exchange: "Does the church have to address the Jewish question? Answer: Yes. Why? The candidate responded: The Jews are our misfortune. At that, the pastor laughed aloud, adding, 'So it is written in *Der Stürmer.*' A girl then added, 'The curse of God is on the Jews,' and the pastor praised her reply."[25]

Denunciations of the Old Testament by opponents of Christianity brought German Christians scrambling to display ardent antisemitism. At a party meeting in Altdorf (Bavaria) in 1938, the Gau party superintendent blamed the Old Testament for erecting a barrier between National Socialism and Christianity. "If the *pastors* would leave out the Old Testament and refrain from glorifying the old Jews," he proclaimed, "then even now the brown battalions would come back to the church. As it is, the pastors preach against Hitler from the pulpit and pray for him at the altar. What hypocrisy!"[26] In response to such charges, German Christians intensified their assault on the Old Testament in the hope of exonerating Christianity.

The Kristallnacht pogrom of 9 November 1938 signaled new depths of officially sponsored terror against Jews. As Nazi thugs torched synagogues, German Christians rushed to demonstrate their own loyalty to the cause and to ward off criticisms of Christianity as an extension of Judaism. An incident of late 1938 is illustrative. The leader of the National Socialist Teachers' League in Westphalia-South announced that as a result of a Jew's assassination of a German diplomat in Paris, many teachers in the Reich had "spontaneously" abandoned religion classes in an act of anti-semitic solidarity against the Old Testament. But Hermann Werdermann, a German Christian, party member, and professor at the teachers' college in Dortmund, argued for continuing religious instruction. Christianity, he insisted, opposed Judaism, and the Old Testament itself was an antisemitic text. Why, then, he wanted to know, should "the shameful deed of a Jew" cause Christian instruction to cease in German schools?[27] Werdermann deployed antagonism toward the Old Testament in a strategic move to retain some space in Nazi society for Christian education—in its anti-Jewish variant.

By the months following the Kristallnacht pogrom, leading German Christians realized they needed a more formal organization to express their full participation in Nazi antisemitism and develop an effective defense of Christianity. On 4 April 1939, German Christians achieved that structure by founding the Institute for Research into and Elimination of Jewish Influence in German Church Life (Institut zur Erforschung und Beseitigung des jüdischen Einflusses auf das deutsche kirchliche Leben).[28] From then on, the institute led the way in determining the place of the Old Testament and orchestrating the attack on its legacy.

The institute's establishment fulfilled one resolution of the Godesberg Declaration of March 1939. That declaration, signed by representatives of eleven regional churches, propagated the German Christian view of the relationship between Christianity and Judaism with its pronouncement that "the Christian Faith is the unbridgeable religious opposite of Judaism."[29] Details of the institute's establishment are somewhat obscure,[30] but German Christians played the central roles. Headquartered in Eisenach, in the heart of the German Christian stronghold of Thuringia, the institute was directed by Siegfried Leffler, leader of the Thuringian German Christians. Professor Walter Grundmann of Jena led its research division.[31] Funding came from various sources, including individuals and groups in the "circle of supporters," central church organs, and regional church governments.[32]

The institute's cumbersome name bears reflection. The official announcement in a German Christian paper in May 1939 called it the Institute for Research into and Elimination of Jewish Influence in German Church Life,[33] and much of its stationery carried that designation. Over time, however, the term *elimination of* (*Beseitigung*) tended to disappear, apparently eliminated as self-evident. After all, for the institute's German Christian founders, the only reason to delve into Jewish influence was to eradicate it. One would hardly bother to include "elimination of" in the title of an institute created to study cancer. With the word *research* (*Erforschung*), the founders hoped to give their endeavor a scholarly veneer. At the same time, by research they meant more than just study or academic exploration; they intended an investigation such as might be undertaken in a criminal case or in hearings intended to uncover and root out some particular evil.

The institute's dejudaizing mandate determined its stance on the Old Testament. At least one high-ranking supporter of the institute urged retention but on anti-Jewish grounds. By "amputating" the Old Testament, he cautioned, Christians in Germany would ally themselves "with the Jews who have completely destroyed it through the Talmud and rabbinical commentary." He urged the institute to employ "Holy Scripture" as "the sharpest weapon against Rome and Judah."[34] A speech at the meeting of regional representatives in July 1939 was more straightforward. "In the Old Testament," that representative of the institute explained, "we encounter a non-Christian religion and a racially alien *Volk*. Therefore the Old Testament can no longer be the basis for our message."[35]

Attacks on the Old Testament reached a zenith during the war. Even before the formal outbreak of hostilities, notions of dejudaized Christianity gained currency outside the German Christian movement. In August 1939, military authorities issued a new *Evangelisches Feldgesangbuch* (Protestant soldier's songbook). It avoided any explicit reference to the Old Testament but counted on biblical illiteracy among its clientele. Its selection of "famous sayings" included such passages as "The Lord is my shepherd" and "I will lift up mine eyes unto the hills." The editors simply did not specify the source of those Old Testament quotations.[36]

The Institute for Research into and Elimination of Jewish Influence in German Church Life found its niche during the early war years. Deportation of Jews from the Reich and propaganda that presented the war as mortal combat against "international Jewry" gave new meaning and urgency to German Christian efforts to destroy Jewish influence on the religious front. Expanded financial resources allowed the institute to engage

Institut zur Erforschung und Beseitigung des
jüdischen Einflusses auf das deutsche kirchliche Leben

Der Kassenverwalter

Fernsprecher Nr. 1688
Bankkonto: Thür. Staatsbank, Konto Nr. 8033
(Postscheckkonto der Thür. Staatsbank: Erfurt
Nr. 8280)
Postscheckkonto: Erfurt Nr. 5173

Eisenach, den 23.10.42.

deutsche Evang. Kirche
Eing. 27.OKT.1942

An den
Leiter der Finanzabteilung
bei der Deutschen Evangelischen Kirchenkanzlei
m.d.F.d.G.b.
Berlin-Charlottenburg
Marchstr.2

Unterzeichneter dankt ergebenst für den Zuschuss von RM 3.000.--
aus den Mitteln der Deutschen evangelischen Kirche für die
Arbeit unseres Instituts, auch dafür, dass die laufende Ge-
währung dieses Zuschusses in Aussicht genommen ist.

Unterzeichneter erlaubt sich, die Bitte auszusprechen, doch
den laufenden Zuschuss nach Möglichkeit künftig zu erhöhen.

Heil Hitler !

Kassenverwalter.

L 0086 1000 6 41 CKE

In 1939, a group of Protestant church leaders founded the Institute for
Research into and Elimination of Jewish Influence in German Church Life.
This 1942 letter from the institute's director of finances thanks the central
government of the German Protestant church in Berlin for the grant of RM
3,000 and the pledge to continue such support and requests a future increase in
the amount. The institute, under German Christian leadership, coordinated
efforts to eradicate all traces of Judaism from religious practice in Germany.
Both directly and indirectly, its publications and activities underwrote Nazi
efforts to destroy Jews. (Evangelisches Zentralarchiv in Berlin)

in a good deal of self-promotion and to produce a range of anti-Jewish materials, from dejudaized scriptures to liturgical aids. At its wartime meetings and in its publications the institute promoted Nazi racial thought as the fundamental criterion to determine what the new Germany could retain from Christianity.

Typical of the institute's output was a 1940 book of devotions, *Unser Glaube: Wegleite für Deutsche Christen* (Our faith: A guide for German Christians). The editor, Stuttgart pastor Georg Schneider, advocated a smorgasbord approach to Scripture, selecting familiar fragments while discarding material that contravened Nazi ideology. Schneider described the Old Testament as part of a cunning Jewish conspiracy. Clever presentation of its stories made them seem almost appropriate for the *Volk*, he warned, but Germans had to resist temptation for the sake of solidarity in the war against Jews. As Schneider's conclusion revealed, no measures against either the Old Testament or Jews would be too brutal for his taste. "Into the oven," he wrote, "with the part of the Bible that glorifies the Jews, so eternal flames will consume that which threatens our people."[37]

German Christian rhetoric merged with the language of genocide as the attempt to separate Christianity from Judaism became absorbed into a bitter crusade against Jews. In late 1941, the Thuringian German Christian Julius Leutheuser, writing from the eastern front, declared the Old Testament and the religiosity of the past to be foes of German Christianity and Germanness. For Leutheuser, National Socialist war aims promised a chance to realize the anti-Jewish people's church. "We call our people to build a National Church, as this final world struggle breaks out, the struggle against Judaism," he declared. "We now hold the means to strike the weapons from the hands of Judaism for good."[38] From his vantage point on the eastern front, Leutheuser must have known that those means involved extermination of the Jews.

Worried that German Christians would exploit the war to their own ends, Nazi authorities sometimes found even anti-Jewish manipulation of the Old Testament to be suspect. In 1940, an Old Testament specialist in Kiel, responding to the spirit of the times, chose topics for Ph.D. dissertations that included "Blood and Soil in the Old Testament" and "Social Welfare among the Jews: A Comparison with the NSV" (National Socialist welfare organization). He was accused of trying to justify Jewish culture and nature and disciplined by the university rector.[39]

The Institute for Research into and Elimination of Jewish Influence in German Church Life ran into trouble with Nazi authorities as well. In September 1942, Martin Bormann complained that the institute boasted recognition from "important offices of the National Socialist Party," implying it had Rosenberg's backing. But, Bormann insisted, neither Rosenberg nor any party office had ever expressed support of the "German Christian–sponsored Institute" in Eisenach. Bormann ordered the Church Ministry to warn the institute it was forbidden even to refer to the Nazi party.[40] Security Police placed some of the most staunchly pro-Nazi, anti-Jewish members of the German Christian leadership—men such as Wolf Meyer-Erlach and Walter Grundmann—under surveillance.[41] According to an informant, Grundmann, director of research at the anti-Jewish institute at Eisenach, was especially active in trying to abolish the Old Testament and "dejudaize" the New. Instead of praising that anti-Jewish assault on Scripture, the informant claimed it proved German Christians had missed the thrust of National Socialism.[42]

After Stalingrad, shortages of resources and demands for military manpower enabled the state to silence the German Christian–sponsored institute and curtail the movement's activities. Restrictions on paper distribution terminated the institute's newsletter in 1943. Throughout the war, the religious press had encountered restrictive measures of various kinds; the regulations of 1943 sounded the death knell for all but local publications.[43] Leading personalities, among them director of research Walter Grundmann, were called to the front. The institute waned. The last record of its activities dates from spring 1944.

For as long as it could, the Institute for Research into and Elimination of Jewish Influence in German Church Life led German Christians' wartime charge on the Old Testament. Despite bombardment with anti-Jewish tirades in the 1940s, German Christians, attached to their religious traditions, continued to use parts of the maligned text. In 1942, German Christian pastors in Westphalia circulated a list of Bible readings suitable for wedding ceremonies: one-third came from the Old Testament, all of those from the Psalms.[44] Even a 1943 circular from the National Church group, reputedly the most radical German Christians, cherished bits of the Old Testament, although it claimed that the "religious treasures" sprinkled in the Hebrew Scripture stemmed from the "best Aryan tradition."[45] On balance, however, wartime remarks by members of the movement presented a resounding condemnation. Retention of the Old Testament, German Christians suggested, reflected weakness, defeat, and treachery. In May 1943, a pastor in Berlin railed against inclusion of Old Testament materials in catechism classes. In his view, "solidarity with National Socialist Germany, in fact with all of continental Europe" in the "struggle against world Judaism and Bolshevism," forbade use of the Old Testament in religious instruction.[46]

Dominated by a paranoia about ubiquitous Jewish influence that they themselves helped perpetuate, German Christians lost any ability to distinguish between the Old Testament and Germany's enemies in the war. In early 1944, a pastor from Schmolle (Lower Silesia) attacked a way of interpreting the Bible that "confirmed Jewish claims to world dominance." Not only recognition of the Old Testament, he stormed, but any focus on the Bible as the central truth of Christianity played into the hands of a Jewish conspiracy. He closed on an ominous note. "The outcome of the present war," he thundered, "will decide whether this Jewish view of the Bible and the Old Testament is divine truth or if instead the German view holds: 'We will crush and defeat the power of the Jewish world coalition; humanity, which is fighting for its freedom, its life, and its daily bread, will gain the final victory in this struggle.' (Adolf Hitler in his proclamation of 24 February 1943)."[47] For the German Christians, instead of Scripture determining their stance on Nazism and Nazi war goals, war would decide the fate of Scripture.

## The New Testament

Jewish influences were less immediately obvious to the German Christians in the New Testament than in the Old. But once they turned their attention to the second part of their Bibles, German Christians found that it too affirmed the Jewish roots of Christianity. Jesus' Jewish ancestry, his numerous appeals to Old Testament authority, and the background of the Apostle Paul all flew in the face of claims that Christianity was both non-Jewish and explicitly anti-Jewish. Nevertheless, although neither biblical evidence nor logic was on their side, the German Christians remained steadfast on two points: Jesus was not a Jew, they insisted, and the essence of the Gospels' message was hatred toward Jews.

A number of factors enabled the German Christians to dejudaize the New Testament more rapidly than they had the Old. Armed with a denial of scriptural canonicity from experiences with the Old Testament, they began immediately to select from the New Testament those elements that fit their racial vision. In the case of the New Testament, they avoided debates over total rejection versus partial retention. Even the German Christians recognized that their claim to represent true Christianity necessitated preservation of at least some Scripture. Rather than complicating their task, the fact that much of the New Testament concerns the theological foundations of Christianity simplified anti-Jewish revision. Antagonistic as they were to considerations of doctrine, German Christians simply excluded such portions from their field of vision and concentrated on those features that informed their cultural identity: Jesus, the manger, the cross. Finally, with their use of the Gospels, particularly the Gospel of John, German Christians tapped into an existing source and tradition of Christian anti-Jewishness. "Even if all the textbooks were 'corrected,'" Richard L. Rubenstein has pointed out in a sobering passage, "there would still be the Gospels, and they are enough to foster the threat of a murderous hatred of Jews by Christians."[48]

*The Aryan Jesus and the Rabbi Paul.* German Christians resolved the problem posed for them by Jesus' ancestry in a straightforward way: they denied that he was Jewish. In that claim they stood apart from their main opponents within and outside the church; both the Confessing Church and the neopagans accepted the historical fact of Jesus' Jewishness. German Christians used various arguments to substantiate their position. Sometimes they constructed elaborate explanations involving Aryan tribes in Galilee, along the lines that the English racial theorist Houston Stewart Chamberlain and theologians like Emanuel Hirsch popularized. Until his death in 1927, Chamberlain, who became a German citizen, churned out antisemitic tomes from his vantage point in the Bayreuth circle around Richard Wagner.[49] Hirsch, a Göttingen professor affiliated with the German Christians, argued against the Jewish ancestry of Jesus in his 1939 work, *Das Wesen des Christentums* (The nature of Christianity).[50]

At the popular level, German Christian explanations of Jesus' background took various forms. In November 1933, at a meeting of German Christians in Oranienburg (Brandenburg), one speaker called Jesus "a person of Aryan blood from a Viking clan."[51] A 1940 meditation, "Was Jesus a Jew?," claimed Galilee had been home to an "indogermanic population."[52] German Christians explained away or overlooked evidence in the gospel accounts of Jesus' Jewishness. Both Matthew and Luke provide genealogies, but as German Christians noted, they showed the lineage of Joseph, who was, after all, not Jesus' biological father.[53] Luke, however, identifies Elisabeth, the mother of John the Baptist, as a "daughter of Aaron" and the cousin of Mary.[54] And Mary refers to "our father Abraham" in the prayer called the Magnificat.[55] German Christian commentators failed to acknowledge either of those passages.

One line of German Christian argumentation involved removing Jesus from racial categories by denying his genuine humanity. Some contemporaries even accused German Christians of Arianism, a heresy that maintained Jesus was not of one substance with God but represented his "creature and work."[56] An extreme illustration of such tendencies appeared in a letter from a Protestant pastor in South Dakota. The man's letterhead announced him—in German—as "Patriarch of the Holy Gnostic Church." Since 1919, he explained, a "gnostic school" in Südhemmern (Westphalia) had propagated "Aryan religion" through correspondence courses and handwritten textbooks. Now he placed himself "at the disposal of the German Christians."[57] Another German Christian noted that if Jesus were indeed the Son of God, then he existed outside "ethnicity and race."[58]

Most frequently, German Christians based negation of Jesus' Jewishness on their presumption of his antisemitism. Jesus, they asserted, could not have been a Jew because he opposed the Jews. That argument formed the core of their Christology and allowed them to preserve the figure of Jesus in their anti-Jewish Christianity. In late 1933, one German Christian offered citations from the Gospels that, he claimed, revealed Jesus' attitude toward Judaism: "A 'murderer,' a 'liar,' a 'father of lies,'" he quoted. "It is impossible to reject Jehovah and his Old Testament in sharper terms!" In places, he admitted, the Gospels seemed to suggest the opposite. But those were not the words of Christ, he contended; they were "lies," "Jewishness," the "voice of the Old Testament."[59]

A 1940 book of devotions offered the crucifixion as evidence that Jesus was not Jewish, ignoring the fact that crucifixion was a standard Roman means of execution. The struggle between Jesus and the Jews was so intense, the text exclaimed, "that it led to his death on the cross." Jesus, the author concluded, "cannot, therefore, have been a Jew."[60] A German Christian publication advised mothers how to respond when children asked if Jesus were Jewish. They should point out, the author counseled, how "the revolution" opened German eyes to the "great struggle" between God and the devil. Jesus, the piece went on, "was the originator and victor of this gigantic struggle. . . . Because Christ was the 'opponent' of the Jews, it is impossible that he himself could have been of Jewish blood and spirit."[61]

German Christians deemed fraudulent any scriptural evidence that contravened their position. Viewed in this way, indications in the New Testament of Christianity's links to Judaism served not to challenge their arguments but to bolster their conviction of the diabolical powers of Judaism and lend urgency to efforts to cleanse Christianity. Friedrich Tausch, Krause's successor as leader of the Berlin German Christians, demonstrated this conspiracy theory logic in a 1937 speech. "*Christ was no Jew,*" Tausch insisted. "Christ himself was the greatest hater of Jews." Some "clever people," he conceded, might quote Jesus' words that "salvation would come from the Jews." But according to Tausch, "Chamberlain clearly proved that sentence is not authentic. Because people did not accept Christ, from whom salvation came, a pious Jew out of defiance wrote in the margin: But salvation comes from the Jews! A subsequent scribe brought that remark into the text."[62] Such acrobatics of circular logic typified the German Christian approach to the New Testament. Having abandoned canonicity, they edited and selected to create an Aryan, anti-Jewish Jesus, whom they then presented as the justification for discarding any scriptural passages that countered claims of his anti-Jewishness.

Neopagans were quick to point out the absurdity of the German Christian stance. In 1933, Hauer, head of the German Faith Movement, branded German Christians' attempt to fuse a "nature true to the race" with "confessional, doctrinally bound Christianity" a "contradiction in itself." How, he asked, "can they proclaim the Lutheran Confession as an inviolable principle and at the same time talk about a Christ true to our species?"[63] In June 1939, a German neopagan newsletter lambasted the Eisenach Institute for Research into and Elimination of Jewish Influence in German Church Life as an opportunistic ploy and ridiculed notions of an Aryan Jesus. "What kind of belief is it anyway," the author wanted to know, "that can be preached in one way at one time, in another way at other times; that sometimes has a Jewish Jesus and at other times an Aryan Christ being proclaimed through the mouths of its clergy?" An "Aryan Christ," that author concluded, was a crutch for those too weak "for the grand freedom of the Nordic people." Any "upright pastors," the article concluded, long since realizing that Christianity and National Socialism were "irreconcilable," had joined the neopagan ranks.[64]

German Christians devoted less attention to the Apostle Paul. For them he represented both pro-Jewish and anti-Jewish potential. On the one hand, Saul/Paul's Jewish background was incontrovertible. He spoke Hebrew, had studied Jewish law, and consistently identified himself as a Jew.[65] On the other hand, Christianity's break with Judaism hinged on his message to the gentiles. Accordingly, confusion typified German Christian utterances on the place of Paul in their anti-Jewish New Testament. In 1933, one member suggested that although the form of Pauline thinking was foreign to the German experience of God, the church could not eschew the crucial content of Paul's message.[66] Another hazarded the assertion that "Paul was a theologian of struggle. He sought to bear the good news of salvation into the world, through the racial chaos."[67] A sympathetic postwar commentator echoed that stance, pointing out that it had been Paul "who bore the gospel out of the confines of Palestine into the world." That writer referred to Houston Stewart Chamberlain's "most apt" description of Paul as "a soul seized by Christ, bound to the chains of a Jewish rabbinical education."[68]

At the Sports Palace rally in 1933, Reinhold Krause, again in the extremist vanguard, demanded rejection of the "theology of the Rabbi Paul with its scapegoats and inferiority complex."[69] Krause's position emerged dominant in the German Christian movement, more by default than through systematic discussion. Some German Christians contested Paul's Jewishness, like the pastor who claimed, "Paul was so little a Jew as for example a Jew is a German because he lives in Germany and got himself baptized!"[70] But for the most part, German Christians said little about Paul. They spilled much ink to preserve Jesus for anti-Jewish Christianity, but they were less anxious to salvage Paul. After all, his significance for Christianity lay in his theology, not in any key role in the ritual life of the church. In 1942, the German Christian bishop of Bremen concluded that, even given his significance as a transcender of Judaism, Paul was not worth preserving. "Today every German can learn the freedom from the law for example, from Nietzsche; he does not need a Paul for that, and thereby avoids the danger of being infected by dreaded Jewish-rabbinical doctrines."[71]

*The Gospels through an Antisemitic Lens.* The heart of the New Testament message, German Christians insisted, was not the drama of salvation but a racial struggle. On the basis of that belief, they proffered their reinterpretation as a "purification" and "liberation." Krause's 1933 speech at the Sports Palace had demanded removal from the New Testament of an "*exaggerated* emphasis on the crucified Christ."[72] German Christians took up that challenge, attacking the notion of human sinfulness as a Jewish accretion to the true gospel.

In a 1934 declaration, the Protestant faculty of theology in Breslau denounced emphasis on sin as inimical to the needs of the people's church. Blasting Barthian theology, Judaism, and foreign foes in one rancorous breath, the Breslau group announced that Germans could not tolerate a religion based on the concept of sin. "A people," the statement argued, "who, like our own, has a war behind them that they did not want, that they lost, and for which they were declared guilty, cannot bear it, when their sinfulness is constantly pointed out to them in an exaggerated way." The Treaty of Versailles, the Breslauers maintained, made an emphasis on sin untenable. "Our people has suffered so much under the lie of war guilt that it is the task and duty of the church and of theology to use Christianity to give courage to our people, and not to pull them down into political humiliation."[73]

The people's church, German Christians contended, needed a "positive" interpretation of the New Testament. In September 1935, a speaker in Kempten (Bavaria) attacked "Jewish-Semitic additions" that "perverted and encrusted" the gospel. For example, the entire "teaching of sin and grace," he insisted, "was a Jewish attitude and only inserted into the New Testament."[74] German Christians claimed to be answering Richard Wagner's call from the grave to "Redeem the redeemer. Liberate him from everything theologians, Jews, and the church leadership have appended; preach him as he is. . . . Free him from the Jewish spirit."[75] In 1942, a German Christian leader pointed out that only the "Jewish Christian" Matthew included in celebration of the Lord's Supper the words: "For the forgiveness of sins." Concern with sin, he implied, was a Jewish element to be purged from Christianity.[76]

As National Socialist attacks on Jews intensified after 1938, German Christians reduced their assessment of what was genuine in the gospel accounts to those fragments that best served an anti-Jewish agenda. In March 1939, a German Christian confirmation examination asked: "Who was Jesus Christ?" and "against whom did he fight?" "A hero and warrior," candidates responded, who fought against "Jews and Pharisees."[77] Another examination presented Hitler as Jesus, purifier of the "temple of the German *Volk*."[78] German Christians also pointed to the parable of the Good Samaritan as evidence of the Gospels' anti-Jewishness: the hero was the despised Samaritan; the villains were the Jews.[79]

All-out assaults on Judaism and criticism of Christianity during the war led German Christians to insist ever more vehemently on the New Testament's anti-Jewishness. Late in 1939, Minister of Church Affairs Kerrl concluded that antichurch sentiment in the party reflected Christians' failure to heed National Socialism's racial imperative. "Despite the call of Luther in his book *Against the Jews and Their Lies*," he complained, the "further cleansing of Christianity from Judaism did not occur." As a result, Kerrl explained, the party was "practically forced to . . . recognize Christianity as irreconcilable with National Socialism."[80]

German Christians perceived the mood Kerrl described. Their anti-Jewish vituperations in 1939 and beyond represent frantic attempts to prove that Christianity was not only reconcilable with the war against Jews and Judaism but was its most faithful ally. Accordingly, their reading of the Gospels focused on a few key passages. Typical is a textbook lesson from 1940 titled "Jesus' Fight against the Jewish Spirit." It opened with a free "quotation" from the Gospel of John, chapter 8:44–47: "Jesus addresses the Jews: You are of your father the devil and you will do the wishes of your father. He was a murderer from the beginning, and dwelt not in the truth, because there is no truth in him. . . . He that is of God hears God's words: you, therefore, do not hear them, because you are not of God."[81] The book took every negative word Jesus uttered and applied it to Jews. The most convincing evidence of the New Testament's anti-Jewishness, it concluded, was Jesus' message. "Each word of Jesus was directed against the Jew and hit him like the crack of a whip. No one recognized the nature of Judaism more clearly nor fought it more single-mindedly than precisely Jesus the Savior."[82]

That textbook echoed the conspiratorial theory of Scripture and gave revisors a blank check to add or expunge at will. The New Testament, it taught, included "downright forgeries, above all by Jewish Christians who infiltrated the congregations in order to bring the Jewish spirit to dominance there too." It described their supposed falsifications in detail: "Specific words were attributed to Jesus that he never uttered, and sayings of Jesus that clearly revealed the nature of Judaism and in general were directed against the Old Testament and Jewish nature were suppressed." Fortunately, the authors maintained, "it is not difficult to separate these later infiltrations of Jewish thought from the original words of Jesus."[83] The Institute for Research into and Elimination of Jewish Influence in German Church Life promoted precisely such exegesis of the New Testament. Bible studies, it exhorted in 1941, needed to bring out "the opposition of Jesus to Judaism" and to demonstrate that "Christians are called to the troops of Christ against the judaization of religious life."[84]

The German Christian revision of the Gospels culminated in the wartime presentation of the cross as the symbol of anti-Jewish Christianity and the promise of Nazi victory. The cross of Christ, proclaimed the Stuttgart German Christian Schneider, represented "the accusation against Judaism," the "sign of sacrifice, the banner of the struggle against the subhuman, the symbol of God's victory!"[85] A 1943 circular from the National Church group referred to "Jesus of Nazareth, the 'first high-profile antisemite.'" The author explained how the sacrificial cross of Golgotha and the Germanic rune merged in the iron cross; how Baldur and Jesus together constituted the German savior; how the Nordic sunwheel and the rising sun of Easter burned together in the swastika flag, the "symbol of the resurrected, eternal Germany."[86]

Contemporaries and subsequent analysts often focus on fragmentation and dissension within the German Christian movement, using terms like *radical* and *moderate* to differentiate subgroups and factions. But one looks in vain for any significant variation in the anti-Jewish utterances of

German Christian groups in wartime. The National Church wing, also known as the Thuringians, earned a reputation as extremists. Yet purportedly less radical groups made similarly rabid statements about the New Testament message in the war against Jews. For example, in 1941, the Schlachtensee Circle, a group of churchmen publicly dedicated to ending the church struggle and dominated by a handful of putatively moderate German Christians, issued a memorandum on reorganization of the church. It exhorted church leaders to proclaim themselves "completely on Jesus' side in the fight against phariseeism, as the Sermon on the Mount and the Gospel of John clearly indicate," and called for commitment to "Luther's struggle against Christ-hating, exploitative Judaism . . . and thereby also to the struggle of Hitler to defeat the destructive Jewish influence."[87] German Christians struggled to reclaim the Gospels for the Third Reich. The message they preached, however, was not love but hate.

The German Christians followed their anti-Jewish reading of the Gospels with rewriting. The circle around Bishop Weidemann of Bremen published the first new anti-Jewish Scripture.[88] Titled *Das Evangelium Johannes deutsch* (The German Gospel of John), it appeared in 1936.[89] To Weidemann, who wrote the foreword,[90] "true Christianity" was anti-Jewish; anti-Jewish religion was the "ultimate source of power for the National Socialist worldview."[91] Weidemann claimed that fourteen thousand copies of his version of the Gospel of John were printed; "no resounding success," he admitted, but important in stimulating "a translation of the New Testament along such lines."[92] He chose to begin "germanization of the New Testament" with the Gospel of John, he explained, because it constituted "the most sharply anti-Jewish document."[93]

Weidemann's version presented Jesus' entire mission as an onslaught against Judaism.[94] Some passages remained virtually unaltered, most notably those that depicted Jesus' conflicts with certain scribes and Pharisees. In the context of an explicitly anti-Jewish document, however, those accounts took on new meaning. For example, viewed through the lens of Nazi stereotypes of Jewish materialism, the story of Jesus and the money changers in the temple needed little adjustment to fit an antisemitic theme. Weidemann's account, based on John 2:13–16, read as follows: "Soon after, as the highest holiday of the Jews was approaching, Jesus went to Jerusalem. There he found the traders and money changers in the midst of the holy place. He took a whip and chased them out, together with their animals. He scattered the coins of the money changers and overturned their tables. To the traders at the booths he spoke: Away with you and your goods! Do not make God's house into a house of merchandise!"[95]

Weidemann's use of the term *Kaufhaus*, which in contemporary German connotes a department store, follows Luther's translation: "machet nicht meines Vaters haus zum kaufhause." Accounts of the incident in the other three Gospels use the more familiar phrase "a den of thieves."[96]

Weidemann's translation made other changes that showed a propensity to discard as Jewish reminders of human sinfulness and references to atonement. John 1:29, "Behold the Lamb of God who takes away the sins of the world," became "Behold the chosen one of God, who through his sacrifice brings blessing to the world."[97] To Weidemann, the new Scripture reflected the realities of life in Nazi society, where the gospel needed to appeal to a "National Socialist, a storm trooper man, a German child of our day."[98] The new gospel revealed the flexibility of Christian symbols. While preserving many details of the Gospel of John—specific accounts of events, a style of language, even entire passages—Weidemann produced a document that presented a manifesto of hatred toward Jews, not a story of salvation.

Other German Christians tried their hands at revising the gospel accounts. In 1939, Emanuel Hirsch apparently put out a version of the words of Jesus from the Gospels of Matthew, Mark, and Luke, but it is unclear how much circulation that work found.[99] A more ambitious attempt toward an anti-Jewish New Testament emerged from the Institute for Research into and Elimination of Jewish Influence in German Church Life. Indeed, after 1945, one sympathizer labeled that gospel edition the "most important book" to come out of the German Christian movement.[100]

The institute's project was to have three parts: a compilation of the synoptic Gospels, the Gospel of John, and the balance of the New Testament. Title of the complete work would be *Das Volkstestament* (The people's testament). Part 1, *Die Botschaft Gottes* (The message of God), the only portion completed, appeared in December 1939.[101] According to one account, it sold two hundred thousand copies within six months.[102] The institute urged clergy to use the new compilation of the synoptic Gospels in confirmation instruction and pastoral care, suggesting it was "more effective than the New Testament, with its unclear, alien expression of the message of Christ."[103] In March 1942, when the German Protestant church in Romania founded a working group affiliated with the Institute for Research into Jewish Influence in German Church Life, the closing message was read from the institute's version of the Gospels.[104]

The ninety-six-page work took a different tack than Weidemann's earlier project. It drew heavily on the Gospel of Mark. It avoided the word *Jew*, opting instead for a vague depiction of Christianity as a mixture of familiar words and pithy sayings. Rather than narrating the life of Jesus, it limited itself to well-known passages such as Matthew 6:28: "Consider the lilies of the field, how they grow; they toil not, neither do they spin." Jesus appeared in a historical and geographic vacuum; the story of his birth contained nothing about Herod, the flight to Egypt, or Joseph's roots in "the house and lineage of David." Nor did the book mention the resurrec-tion. It closed with the death of Jesus, followed by an account of the Great Commission to Peter and the assembled disciples.[105]

The afterword described the criteria for inclusion. The new Gospels, it explained, aimed to provide a scripture that meshed with its clientele's understanding of Christianity and avoided "frustration with the message, personality, and work of Jesus." Cultural affinities explained the truncated accounts of the Christmas and Easter events: "Legends were excluded. Only the Christmas poetry of the Holy Night and the Wise Men from the East could not be left out because these stories have penetrated so deeply into the people's sensibilities. We have simply freed them of Jewish-Chris-tian accretions."[106] A German Christian who worked on the project noted that the edition purged "individual words that stem from the Palestinian congregation but were wrongly attributed to Jesus, because they are con-tradicted through the behavior of Jesus."[107] An example was Jesus' cry on the cross, "Father forgive them, for they know not what they do" (Luke 23:34). References to the Old Testament were expunged as well.

It is impossible to assess with precision the impact of the new German Christian scriptures. German Christians reached no final consensus on a text of the New Testament. Some used the new versions, but others con-tinued to rely on their old Bibles. Some kept to the Gospels, while others drew from the entire New Testament. In any case, because the new scrip-tures grew out of a denial of canonicity, they could hardly claim to present the definitive message of Christianity. But German Christians did agree on one thing: they all accepted the criterion of anti-Jewishness as a means to decide what to teach from the New Testament and how to understand it. In 1944, a former Catholic priest and prominent German Christian in the Thuringian group released a brochure titled "The Sermon on the Mount as a Declaration of War against Judaism."[108] In the drama of Christianity's redemption from Jewish influence, as German Christians construed it, the Old Testament played the role of the scapegoat that bore away all traces of Jewishness and the New Testament provided marching orders for an anti-Jewish faith.

A look at German Christian revisions of the New Testament raises the issue of opportunism. In 1933, clergy and lay people with ambitions in church politics could expect to benefit from involvement in the movement. Even later, emphasis on Christianity's anti-Jewishness helped German Christians make their activities palatable to National Socialism. But already by 1935, only the naive would have counted on involvement in the German Christian cause to curry favor with Nazi authorities. No high-ranking Nazi asked German Christians to promote the Aryan Jesus; none thanked them for assuming that task. The quest for an Aryan Jesus grew out of more than cynical opportunism; it was the product of a misguided and even pathetic devotion to some vestiges of Christianity. German Christians accepted the Nazi doctrine of race but tried to link it to symbols associated with Christianity. The most important of those was the figure of Jesus. By severing the ties between Jesus and Judaism, German Christians emptied that symbol of its familiar content. Yet they clung to it as an important and empowering part of their identity.

German Christians demonstrated genuine commitment to the fusion of Christianity and Nazism. Their sincerity served not to mitigate but to exacerbate their antisemitism. A telling illustration involves Bremen's Bishop Weidemann. In 1938, he ordered two new churches built: the "Horst Wessel" and "von Hindenburg Memorial" churches. Nazi authorities forbade use of those names and even ejected Weidemann from the party over the issue, although on Hitler's instructions the Reich Chancellery later intervened to readmit him.[109] In response to the uproar, Weidemann rechristened the buildings "Churches of Gratitude" and ordered the following inscription to appear inside each one: "Church of Thanks, out of gratitude to God for the wonderful salvation of our *Volk* from the abyss of Jewish-materialistic Bolshevism through the deed of the Führer, built in the year of our Lord 1938, in the sixth year of the National Socialist revolution."[110] Weidemann played the trump card of antisemitism to make sure that he got his way,[111] a form of opportunism. But his end was not simply advancement of his personal cause; it was the promotion of Christianity, or at least its German Christian version: the anti-Jewish people's church.

## Church Music

Even in their hymnals German Christians discovered echoes of Judaism. On this front, their offensive against Jewish influences was less fierce than in the cases of the Old and New Testaments. It took adherents some time to recognize that racial imperatives impinged here, too, and to overcome force of habit regarding what they sang in the church. Only in the area of church music, far from the theological core of Christianity, did

German Christians show some reluctance to bring their project of dejudaization to its logical conclusions.

*Hallelujah or Hail to Our God: Revising Old Hymns.* Early German
Christian events reflected little concern about Jewish influence in church
music. For example, in June 1933, German Christians met in Dortmund.
The program included congregational singing of three familiar hymns:
"Awake, Awake, Oh German Land," "A Mighty Fortress Is Our God," and
"Oh Come, My Soul with Singing."[112] Two of those hymns contained hebraisms: the second stanza of Luther's "A Mighty Fortress" refers to Jesus as
"Lord Sabaoth," an ancient Israelite title meaning commander of the hosts
of heaven; "Oh Come, My Soul with Singing" mentions "Zion" as well as
the "God of Jacob."[113] The program provided the standard texts of the
hymns, complete with those terms.

Rumblings about Jewish influence in church music throughout 1933
suggested potential for a dejudaizing assault. At the Sports Palace meeting on 13 November 1933, Berlin German Christian leader Krause, whose
proscriptions with regard to the Old and New Testaments proved accurate
predictions of subsequent developments, called for transformation of the
worship service, including attention to church music. "We want to sing
songs that are free from all Israelite elements," he insisted. "We want to
liberate ourselves from the language of Canaan and turn to our German
mother tongue. Only in the German mother tongue can humanity express
its prayers, praise, and thanks in the most profound way." The stenographical record noted "loud applause."[114] At the same meeting, German
Christian leader Hossenfelder announced it was time to break with "un-
German" elements in the liturgy. "Many people," he contended, " would
prefer, instead of the Jewish Hallelujah, to sing the German 'Hail to our
God,' and we will sing it."[115]

Less than a week after the Sports Palace affair, German Christians
announced impending release of their first songbook. It appeared in early
1934 and included fifty-one songs divided into categories of "struggle,"
"work," and "meditation." Most were new texts by German Christian poets set to familiar melodies; they avoided references to the Old Testament
and extolled Germany, the *Volk*, and German soil.[116] The songs were intended to supplement, not to supplant, existing hymnbooks.

In 1934, at least in one local incident, attacks on Jewish influence in
Christian life drew church music into the fray. A professor of music in
Dresden discovered that "anxious choir directors and clergy" advised
against performance of a piece he had composed because it used an old
Hebrew melody. No one seemed to mind that the text itself was a psalm.

*A capacity crowd of twenty thousand at the Berlin Sports Palace on 13 November 1933. The audience responded with enthusiastic applause to the key speaker, Reinhold Krause, and his demands to purge all Jewish elements from Christianity. (Landesbildstelle, Berlin)*

The musician offered his own German Christian–style counteroffense. The popular hymn "Holy God We Praise Thy Name," he pointed out, had Catholic origins while the Netherlander Prayer of Thanks ("We Gather Together to Ask the Lord's Blessing"), beloved by storm troopers, SS, and Stahlhelm men, bore "noticeable melodic similarity to the Jewish tune 'En Kelohena' [*sic*]." And why, he wanted to know, did the "Netherlander Prayer of Thanks" continue "to be sung undisturbed with the text written by the Jew Weyl for Zionistic purposes?"[117]

Later that year, the German Christian organ *Evangelium im Dritten Reich* (The gospel in the Third Reich) tried to rouse its readers on the issue of church music. An article titled *Judeleien* (Jewish nonsense) ridiculed the era when Germans peppered their speech with French phrases and lambasted the Weimar period, when Germans "sang American hits" and "contorted their hips to the Negro beat." Now, the author expostulated, it was church music that provided a gateway for alien influence. Only in the church, he complained, would Germans sing "praise with Abraham's seed, Hallelujah and Hosanna from Zion to the heavenly Jerusalem."[118]

Despite such efforts, German Protestants, including the German Christians, went on singing the familiar hymns, complete with Old Testament references. In November 1934, at a German Christian evening in Münster honoring Reich Bishop Müller and the German Christian bishop of Westphalia, Bruno Adler, the congregation sang "A Mighty Fortress" as well as a stanza of "Praise, Oh Ye People." The program printed Luther's hymn with the original "Lord Sabaoth" in the second stanza; the other hymn closed with a double "Hallelujah."[119]

Only in late 1935 did German Christians begin anything approaching a systematic purge of Christian hymns. The impetus originated high in the movement's ranks, motivated by concern for the church's ability to attract an increasingly antisemitic clientele. And unlike the case of the Old Testament, German Christians expressed a sense of loss in subjecting traditional hymns to considerations of racial purity. Nevertheless, the people's church demanded self-denial; according to Krause's successor as leader of Berlin's German Christians, it was "more Christian to make sacrifice in external forms than through them to kill the spirit and life."[120]

In 1935, German Christians published *Feierstunden Deutschen Christen* (German Christian celebrations), a liturgical guide for all occasions. Its author, Wilhelm Bauer, decried Jewish influence in church music, complaining, for example, about a draggy musical style that he claimed was "borrowed from the synagogue." Bauer saved his most detailed criticism for the texts of hymns. He failed to see how it could "contravene the spirit of the Bible or injure the Confession" if "Lord Sabaoth" were replaced with "lord of the heavenly hosts," the "people of Israel" with the "people of God," the "cedars of Lebanon" with the "firs of the German forest," or "Jerusalem" with the "heavenly abode." Critics might carp, he conceded, but that must not deter from the task of adjusting the language of the church to German "sensitivities."[121] Bauer's willingness to transform church music had its limits, but they were aesthetic rather than moral or doctrinal in nature. It was "in bad taste," he informed his readers, to sing militaristic or folksy music in the church because it "clashed" with the solemn tones of the organ and violated the "hallowed stillness" of the house of God.[122]

As with the Old and New Testaments, German Christian efforts in regard to church music constituted both an anti-Jewish initiative in step with the times and a reaction to attacks on Christianity. In September 1935, the German Christian press denounced a Westphalian pastor who required candidates for confirmation to memorize a hymn that referred to Abraham, Moses, and Elijah.[123] In November, German Christians in the Rhineland praised the resolution of the Berlin Adventist congregation to expunge "Hallelujah" from its liturgy, describing that announcement as an indication that the Adventists understood the "signs of the times."[124]

But the German Christians were fighting a losing battle. In 1936, a Thuringian leader of the anti-Christian German Faith Movement wrote to the Ministry of Church Affairs and the Gestapo. It was offensive, he protested, that at celebrations to honor the war dead, Christians sang hymns to melodies like "Jerusalem Thou City High and Fair."[125] That complaint suggests both the potency of music's link to memory and the impossibility of dejudaizing Christianity to the satisfaction of its critics. Even if the texts were altered to remove so-called hebraisms, the neopagan implied, Jewish influence remained active in the minds of audiences and singers who associated melodies with their old, familiar lyrics. Familiar "Hallelujahs" might resound more loudly in their absence than in their presence.

*"Songs of the Coming Church": The German Christian Alternative.* By the late 1930s, German Christians began to skirt the problem of hebraisms in traditional hymns by relying on new works by their own members. A March 1938 flyer of the National Church wing of German Christians in Berlin included texts of twelve hymns; all except one were recent compositions—the exception was a text by the nineteenth-century nationalist Ernst Moritz Arndt. None of the twelve songs referred to any figures from the Hebrew Bible. For that matter, none mentioned Jesus. The word *German* appeared eight times, *Germany* twelve times in the hymns.[126]

Critics did not fail to notice the non-Christian content of the new German Christian hymns. In 1938, a professor of theology reviewed a new German Christian hymn collection, *Lieder für Gottesfeiern* (Songs for divine celebrations). He conceded that many Germans, annoyed by the "Judaisms" of standard hymns, would rejoice at the "German sound" and "pious, cheerful content" of the new songs. Yet, the reviewer remarked, the forty hymns in the collection mentioned Christ only fourteen times; in thirty-three hymns, he did not appear at all. Nor was the name *Jesus* to be found.[127] With the exception of a handful of Easter and Christmas songs, the hymns focused on nature, daily life, camaraderie, struggle, and the fatherland. Lyrics expressed sentiments such as "God's flame burns eternally"; "God bless our weapons, Germany forevermore!"; "Holy is the day of labor."[128] With these new songs, German Christians hoped to avoid irritating a clientele that resisted any evidence of the Jewish roots of Christianity. The "confessors," one German Christian grumbled in 1939, lampooned the hymns as "Brawling and Boozing Songs of the German Christians." But, he countered, the people's church had its imperative:

"Were we supposed to expect the youth to sing the songs of Zion, Jehovah, and David's son?"[129]

Shortly before the outbreak of war, Bishop Weidemann in Bremen released a new German Christian songbook, *Lieder der kommenden Kirche* (Songs of the coming church);[130] within weeks, it sold ten thousand copies. Weidemann considered his collection "truly German," free of all "Judaisms" and foreign words.[131] More successful than his 1936 edition of the Gospel of John,[132] Weidemann's hymnbook was also far less radical. Most of its contents were familiar Protestant hymns with references to the Old Testament expunged. The new additions, though often more focused on Germany than on Christianity, did not express explicitly anti-Jewish sentiments. Even the firebrand Weidemann, who showed no compunction in rewriting the Gospel of John into a tirade of hatred toward Jews, appeared bound by considerations of what was tasteful and appropriate in church music.

Soon after its establishment in early 1939, the Institute for Research into and Elimination of Jewish Influence in German Church Life got to work on its own new hymnal. A committee examined each of the thirty hymnbooks in use across Germany and reviewed 2,336 songs for "Jewish content, dogmatism, and tastelessness." It recommended 102, less than 5 percent, for unaltered acceptance.[133] The committee's diligence is all the more remarkable when contrasted with the alacrity and haphazardness German Christians showed in discarding scriptural texts. Released in 1941, the product of the institute's labors bore the name of a familiar hymn: "Holy God, We Praise Thy Name!" ("Großer Gott, wir loben Dich!"). It contained 339 hymns, a mixture of old and new German material.

Alterations, revisions, and additions of hymns took various forms in the institute's new hymnal, but all focused on removing references to the Old Testament and its legacy. For example, in "Praise to the Lord, the Almighty, the King of Creation," the reference to "psalters and harps" in the first stanza disappeared in favor of "songs of joy." Luther's "A Mighty Fortress," saw "the Savior in time of need" substituted for "Lord Sabaoth." Reference to "Jesse's lineage" in "Lo How a Rose E'er Blooming" vanished. One Christmas song still mentioned Bethlehem, but the "Hallelujah" in "Silent Night" fell to the editors' scissors.[134] Nevertheless, here too, the result was a self-consciously conventional hymnbook minus Old Testament vocabulary, not a declaration of war on Judaism in general.

German Christian efforts in the area of church music produced some bizarre results. Members of the movement tried to preserve vestiges of Christian tradition, but, unanchored to doctrinal tenets or scriptural authority, those remnants floated freely in competition and conjunction with other cultural affinities. A typical example of what could result is a Christmas cantata that Westphalian German Christians circulated in 1940, titled "The Heliand" (The Savior). The original "Heliand," an anonymous ninth-century, old Saxon epic poem, consists of six thousand lines of alliterative verse that restate the gospel story in Saxon terms.[135] The German Christian cantata continued that syncretic project with a hodgepodge of Christmas carols, New Testament texts, Germanic legends, and Nazi propaganda.

The performance opened with a standard translation of John 1:1: "In the beginning was the Word and the Word was with God, and the Word was God." A narrator followed with doggerel verse on the ancient Germanic tribes: "There dwelt a race in German lands, A strong, upright, and blue-eyed clan; The Germans, whose natural traits combined heroic spirit and gentle mind." Allusions to Valhalla, dragons, blood feuds, and adultery gave way to the Advent hymn "O Savior, Rend the Heavens Wide!" Commentary on the twilight of the gods preceded another hymn, "A Ship Comes Sailing Onward," which retained the original reference to Bethlehem. The choir sang "the people who sat in darkness have seen a great light" (Matthew 4:16), and a narrator told how "the God from Bethlehem became protector of the Germans and awakened the deepest loyalty and love in their hearts and souls." The choir followed again with "Lo, How a Rose E'er Blooming," keeping the original references to Jesse and Isaiah.[136] The "Hallelujah" in the second stanza of "Silent Night" remained as well.

In the cantata, sacred music, like familiar Bible stories, formed just one more element in the cultural melange that constituted a "purely German" Christmas. Instead of rejecting traditional hymns as riddled with "Judaisms," the German Christians who created the cantata embraced the musical past as an integral part of German culture. But that affirmation had nothing to do with theology, nor did retention of those hymns reflect a principled rejection of anti-Jewish Christianity. Instead, use of the Christmas songs in their familiar form expressed a kind of Christmas piety, a vision of Christianity that consisted of a cozy, familiar, magical world of legends and pageantry.

Their efforts at dejudaization notwithstanding, German Christians never made the same transformation in the case of hymns as they did with the Old Testament and New Testament. In treating Scripture, they moved from denial of canonicity to a declaration of war, under the banner of the cross, against Judaism and Jews. With hymns, they never moved beyond attempts to purge what they considered Jewish influences. Indirectly, however, hymns too served the Nazi war effort. In August 1939, shortly before Germany invaded Poland, the military office for pastoral care, in conjunction with the Protestant military bishop, issued a new *Evangelisches Feldgesangbuch* (Protestant soldier's songbook). In addition to patriotic paraphernalia such as the "Oath to the Flag" and "A Prayer for Führer, Volk, and Armed Forces," the book contained fifty-six hymns and twenty-six songs. The hymns were standard Protestant fare: "A Mighty Fortress," "Praise to the Lord, the Almighty," "Silent Night." But they were purified along exactly the lines German Christians advocated. None of the hymns mentioned Old Testament figures by name, nor were Hallelujahs or Hosannas to be found. The sole exception was the second stanza of "Silent Night," which retained the "Hallelujah." That familiar Christmas carol was probably the only religious song in which the average soldier might have noticed omission or alteration of any stanza but the first.[137]

Bremen's Bishop Heinz Weidemann noticed with glee that the new songbook, issued in more than two million copies, followed his lead in purging "Jewish elements" from church music.[138] In his account of the Protestant Wehrmacht chaplaincy during World War II, a former chaplain who was not a German Christian also recognized that the 1939 songbook for soldiers reflected the ideals of that movement.[139] When chaplains distributed the "Protestant Soldier's Songbook" to their men, intentionally or not they handed out a piece of German Christian propaganda and perpetuated the notion that Christianity and Judaism could and indeed must be separated.

Even as they attempted to eradicate Jewish elements from the Old Testament, the New Testament, and church music, German Christians tried to preserve certain cultural artifacts of Christianity. Divorced from theological content and cut adrift from scriptural authority, phenomena such as Old Testament stories, Jesus, the cross, and familiar hymns became hollow symbols, available for infusion with new messages. The German Christian doctrine of race and the context of Nazi antisemitism provided that content. Their forms twisted and their meanings perverted, the symbols and rituals salvaged by the German Christians became incorporated into an anti-Jewish religion that echoed and promoted Nazi genocide.

*The German Christians have thrown a stone into the church. It is drafty now, but fresh air is coming in.*
*—General Superintendent Wilhelm Zöllner (neutral), 1933*

*The German Christians do not know what the church is. They do not know the difference between the people of God and the kingdom of the world. That is why their wish to serve the church is like the bear who saw a fly on his sleeping master—and then killed him with a boulder. Certainly, to a considerable extent, German Christians intend to help the church. They want to make the church big and strong; they want to lead the people back to the church. But, they say, we can only save the church by unconditional incorporation into the kingdom of the world.*
*—Confessing Church Pastor Kurt Frör, 1937*

In 1938, the Thuringian German Christian leader Siegfried Leffler delivered a seventy-five-minute speech in front of ten thousand people. At one point the audience offered enthusiastic applause. When Leffler then attacked the statements he had just made, some of those present realized their mistake. He had been quoting from a neopagan in order to counter that position.[1]

Leffler's experience highlights the pitfalls of the German Christian opposition to doctrine. Members of the movement vowed to promote the cause, but though they knew what they opposed—Jewishness, doctrinal rigidity, effeminate weakness—they lacked clarity as to the positive dimensions of their program. Like their project of purification, the German Christian plan to rejuvenate the church was fundamentally destructive. Existing structures of Protestant tradition provided the context for German Christian activity. But the movement's attack on church doctrine represented an offensive against the very institutions on which German Christians depended for legitimacy and identity. Devoted to religious revival, they spurned belief. Led by pastors, they denounced the clergy. Rooted in the church, they rejected all manifestations of ecclesiastical order.

Throughout the twelve years of Nazi rule, German Christian efforts to reshape the church developed specific nihilistic and anarchic forms. In their quest for a people's church free of doctrine, German Christians promoted three "antis": anti-intellectualism, anticlericalism, and antilegalism. They denounced academic theology as not only useless but harmful and divisive. Their movement showed anticlerical tendencies that both revealed and created conflicts between lay people and pastors. Finally, German Christians launched a frontal assault on the regulations and practices that structured the life of the Protestant church. In all three ways, they attacked not only the core of their own movement but the essence of the church itself.

## Theologians against Theology

In his address to the Sports Palace rally in November 1933, the Berlin German Christian Reinhold Krause sneered at theology as "mental gymnastics."[2] Such anti-intellectualism permeates German Christian statements. After all, if right belief had nothing to do with membership in the church, what purpose could theological reflection serve? German Christian spokesmen contrasted the "courageous spirit of faith of a Dr. Martin Luther" with the spiritual hollowness of "Pharisees and scribes" obsessed with orthodoxy and scriptural texts.[3] According to one German Christian leader, the movement had "nothing to do with theology"; instead, it "grew out of life."[4] When German Christians from Lower Saxony met in October 1935, the conference reporter felt obliged to justify the appearance of an academic theologian among the key speakers. That individual, the reporter assured readers, personified a "new type of professor who stands as a fighting Christian within National Socialism."[5]

Antagonism toward academic theology reflected the inclusive claims of

German Christian ecclesiology. At the same time, it helped the movement rationalize its own failures. In late 1933, after the Sports Palace affair, a number of prominent theologians attracted considerable publicity when they left the German Christian movement. The German Christian weekly *Evangelium im Dritten Reich* (The gospel in the Third Reich) responded with defiance. German Christianity aimed to address the "heart of the people," the paper claimed. On that basis, it was "not of weighty import" that a "group of men who had approached the movement from the point of view of academic thought" had withdrawn their support.[6]

A considerable number of theologians did publicly distance themselves from the movement in late November 1933. The Breslau theologian Friedrich Gogarten, once a champion of the cause, Professor Friedrich Karl Schumann, who had been involved in Reich Bishop Müller's plans to reorganize the Protestant church, the Halle professor of theology Ernst Kohlmeyer, as well as his Tübingen counterpart, Gerhard Kittel, and the Gießen professors Heinrich Bornkamm and Ernst Haehnchen were among the luminaries who announced their dissociation from the movement's Berlin leadership after the Sports Palace affair.[7] In late 1934, six hundred people associated with the theological faculties in Rostock and Erlangen demanded Reich Bishop Müller's resignation. The letter contrasted the "confidence and most sincere will" with which the signatories had supported Müller in the summer of 1933 with the fact that every single one of them had since left the German Christian movement.[8]

A German Christian leader in Mecklenburg urged Müller to keep faith against academic theologians. It was a "good sign," he assured the Reich bishop, that "most professors and most of the upcoming cohort of theologians" had "proclaimed a lack of confidence" in him. After all, he reminded the Reich bishop, "the New Testament illustrates the danger of the caste of scribes."[9] In an explicitly antidoctrinal movement, intellectuals and theologians could be viewed as liabilities. According to a German Christian superintendent, the movement did not need "outstanding minds" but leaders in touch with the "pulse of the average member of the *Volk*!"[10]

German Christians focused their hostility toward academic theology on issues of communication. A people's church, they declared, spoke the people's language, avoiding "hollow or tainted" biblical terms and jargon.[11] Theologians, complained German Christian leader Kinder in 1934, spoke a language "alien to life." Kinder challenged his audience to "ask a simple member of the *Volk* what he understands by redemption, salvation, grace." Such terms, he expostulated, were "bloodless" and "alienating."[12]

A Dortmund German Christian concurred. Theologians since Luther, he lamented, had perverted the Reformer's "powerful, folksy German" into a "secret theological language" incomprehensible to the "man in the street." With that theological jargon, he claimed, preachers "might as well speak Chinese."[13]

By attacking the language of intellectual, religious discourse, German Christians hoped to clear a space for their own message. Reich Bishop Müller, for example, denounced the word *grace* as theological jargon, unusable for German Christians. He drew an analogy with family life to explain. "As a child," he said, "if I ate something up and I went to my father and he forgave me, he did not do so out of 'grace,' but out of goodness and love. The notion of grace is not German. In its place, let us use the greater concepts of goodness and love."[14] Through banal objections about vocabulary, German Christians discarded core tenets of Christianity and exposed their revolutionary transformation of the content of Christian faith. German Christian preachers, Ludwig Müller boasted in 1941, were not "so-called academicians"; they spoke the language of the people, "often coarsely and roughly."[15]

German Christians used anti-intellectualism to disarm and discredit their opponents. More specifically, their opposition to theology per se served to repudiate the theology of one of their most formidable foes: Karl Barth. Barth, professor of theology at Bonn until 1935, directed the Confessing Church offensive against what he considered the heretical nature of German Christianity. Since World War I, Barth had attacked liberal theology, condemned the nationalism of the established Protestant church in Germany, and emphasized the power and mystery of God—the "wholly other." After holding positions at the Universities of Göttingen and Münster, Barth became professor of systematic theology in Bonn. He lost that post in 1935, when he refused to swear an oath of allegiance to Hitler.[16]

Barth dismissed the German Christian movement's theology as "a little collection of prize pieces from the copious theological dustbins of the eighteenth and nineteenth centuries."[17] The facts that Barth, a Swiss citizen, was not a Lutheran but a Calvinist and had been dismissed from his university position by Nazi authorities fueled German Christian denunciations of theology in general, and Barthian theology in particular, as un-German, contrary to the spirit of Luther, and anti–National Socialist. With its insistence on the sole authority of Scripture and its emphasis on the ontological chasm between humanity and God, Barth's thought was anathema to German Christians. Moreover, his dialectical approach and often difficult language and style seemed to confirm the German Christian view that theology was alien to the needs and abilities of the *Volk*.

In 1934, German Christians from the Reformed congregation in Siegen (Westphalia), perhaps anxious to show zeal equal to that of their Lutheran counterparts, produced a lengthy denunciation of Barthian theology. They labeled it "demonic magic" that had ensnared professors, pastors, congregations, and particularly young theologians.[18] Others linked Barthian theology to the stab-in-the-back myth. According to a German Christian article in 1935, "during the war, the church stood bravely at the side of the field-gray armies." But afterward, Barth presided over the emergence of a theology, and with it a form of church practice, "that could not do enough to highlight the chasms that separate the kingdom of God from the state, and humanity from God." That theology, the article complained, bred "passionate devotion to the international connections of the churches."[19]

Even while the German Christian movement waved its anti-intellectual banner, it retained a substantial following among professional theologians. Early in 1935, officials in the movement tried to assemble a list of members with academic training in theology; it is not clear whether the task was completed.[20] But scattered evidence suggests that the numbers were significant. In 1935, Professor of Theology Friedrich Grünagel in Aachen headed a theological working group of German Christians. Grünagel's list of prospective speakers for his organization included fifteen names, all but two of them university professors.[21] Grünagel insisted there were "considerable numbers of serious theologians among the German Christians" and decried the "shameful dilettantism and inferior character of many German Christians."[22]

The years from 1933 to 1936 witnessed a massive turnover in theological faculties. More than half of the positions in faculties of theology in Breslau, Berlin, Königsberg, Göttingen, and Münster were reassigned. Faculty positions in Bonn and Kiel changed hands completely. According to Confessing Church accounts, most of the twenty-odd professors of Protestant theology appointed in that period were German Christians or sympathizers of the movement. No professors known as decisive opponents of German Christianity received posts.[23] In 1938, looking back to the early stages of the church struggle, a spokesman of the Protestant League in Saxony-Anhalt observed that initially the "majority of professors of theology" had joined the German Christian movement.[24]

As of the late 1930s, German Christians kept a firm grip on the universities. According to Confessing Church reports, German Christians occupied twelve out of seventeen deanships in theology; they held as many associate professorships and lecturers' positions as the neutrals and Confessing Church combined. The following list sums up the report's findings:

| | Full Professors | Associate Professors and Lecturers | Deans of Theology | Completed Habilitations |
|---|---|---|---|---|
| German Christians | 14 | 51 | 12 | 2 |
| Neutrals | 36 | 38 | 5 | 2 |
| Confessing Church | 23 | 13 | 0 | 1[25] |

When that report was prepared in 1937, German Christians occupied more than one-third of positions in Protestant faculties of theology.

Numerical realities counter the common impression that academic theologians abandoned the German Christian movement en masse in late 1933. Several prominent theologians did leave the movement in the wake of the Sports Palace affair. Contemporaries and subsequent commentators have often interpreted that wave of departures as an indication that those individuals saw the light. Yet it is important to keep in mind that these theologians explicitly severed their ties with the movement's leadership, at the time under Joachim Hossenfelder. They did not necessarily disavow allegiance to German Christian ideas. In fact, many of them remained loyal advocates of the cause; they just believed the leadership had perverted true German Christianity. As the professor of theology Hanns Rückert explained, his decision to sever ties with the Reich leadership reflected the conviction that he "and the thousands of others who have left the faith movement or will do so" were the "true German Christians."[26]

That so many academic theologians remained in the German Christian movement, despite its explicit rejection of their work, reveals the extent of German Christian nihilism. Often theologians themselves launched the sharpest anti-intellectual attacks. For example, the German Christian professor of theology Emanuel Hirsch summed up his view of church history in one sentence: "Where Church History occurs, there is infamy and sin, violence and misery."[27] His German Christian colleague Erich Winkel, professor of New Testament in Rostock, taught that the entire New Testament represented not only the antithesis of modern theology but redemption from it. " 'Come unto me all ye who labor under the teachings of the theologians and are heavy laden with their ideas and demands under the yoke of the law,' " he wrote. For "it is in this sense that the verse appears in the New Testament."[28] German Christians in the academy were the most articulate troops in the antidoctrinal crusade.

## Pastors against the Clergy

Even more clearly than the movement's anti-intellectualism, German Christian anticlericalism reveals the self-destructive mechanisms inherent in the antidoctrinal church. To a significant extent, pastors themselves created and encouraged antagonism toward the clergy. Within German Christian ranks, they were vastly outnumbered by lay people. The movement never claimed more than one-third of Germany's approximately eighteen thousand Protestant pastors, and the number of clergy involved probably decreased over time. Membership hovered around six hundred thousand, so at the peak of their involvement in 1933, the clergy constituted about 1 percent of the total.[29] But pastors had not only initiated formation of the German Christian movement, they continued to dominate its central organs and to set the tone of its activities.

German Christian pastors encouraged anticlericalism among their lay followers as a weapon against the Confessing Church. At the same time, they used a strident anticlerical rhetoric to try to retain control of the movement while ingratiating themselves with Nazi authorities. Attention to the changing tides of anticlericalism among German Christians suggests three phases: dormant anticlericalism until late 1933; burgeoning anticlerical sentiment between 1933 and 1936; and a reassertion of clerical control beginning around 1936 and bolstered by the experience of war after 1939.

In its earliest stages, the German Christian movement promised to boost the prestige of the clergy. Many Protestant pastors publicly endorsed the National Socialist revolution in the hope that it would inspire renewal in the church. Some individuals even perceived an ecclesiastical calling as a means of participating in the *Volk*'s spiritual rejuvenation. In September 1933, one German Christian explained how he had abandoned a "promising career" in a "Jewish bank" to study theology. As a pastor in the Third Reich, he believed he could promote the "two pillars" on which Germanness rested: "blood and baptism."[30]

Other German Christian pastors floated various schemes intended to exploit the new political situation and expand their control over the Protestant population. In early 1933, one group proposed introducing a passbook to record and enforce church attendance.[31] A rebuttal insisted that German Christians had not in fact suggested the "fantastic scheme" of commandeering Germans to attend church.[32] Nevertheless, the story rings true, and the rejoinder by a prominent German Christian, contrary to its intention, only serves to lend credibility to the initial account. Yet other German Christian pastors advocated examining all officeholders in the church and in the movement to exclude those who "through heresy, violation of rights, and unchurchlike behavior have brought most severe damage to the congregations."[33]

Throughout 1933, German Christians worked not to destroy but to transform the clergy. Members from the Rhineland and Westphalia called for a "healthy, simple and straightforward training of the new cohort of pastors," along with a "fundamental cleansing" of the theological faculties. They planned two new "Protestant academies" to provide advanced training in church outreach (*volksmissionarische Arbeit*).[34] German Christians intended those academies to compensate for perceived deficiencies in academic theology as it existed. It did not build character, they complained, and it neglected the community of the *Volk* as the basis of church life.[35] Beginning in the winter semester of 1933–34, German Christians also planned to open colleges affiliated with the universities in Bonn, Cologne, and Aachen, emphasizing the "*völkisch*, ethical, and religious foundations" of the German people.[36]

In mid-1933, the movement boasted an organization for students of theology, the Fighting League of German Christian Students (Studentenkampfbund Deutsche Christen). Faculties of theology from all of the universities in northern Germany sent representatives to its first Reich conference in August 1933. Dissension prevailed at that meeting. One faction advocated emphasis on church outreach; at the other extreme were those who claimed "National Socialism was already (unconsciously) more Christian than was ecclesiastical Christianity." Nazi authorities later disbanded the students' organization.[37] In 1934, German Christians sponsored a four-week seminar in East Prussia for candidates of theology. The program linked "theological and pastoral training" with the "hard drill of a National Socialist camp"; the routine included parading the flags, military sports, and Nazi indoctrination. Instead of unity, that seminar bred division as well. Six of the nineteen participants, among them two registered German Christians from East Prussia, resisted the nihilistic brand of theology offered by the pastor in charge. Eventually five candidates were expelled, and the seminar director lost his post.[38]

German Christian clergymen themselves fueled the upsurge of anticlericalism among their lay followers that became evident after the Sports Palace affair in November 1933. In the wake of that event, the movement splintered and initiative passed to the local level. Lay people, impatient with the failures, inactivity, and bickering of the pastors who dominated the German Christian organization, used anticlerical rhetoric against their leadership. At the same time, the Pastors' Emergency League and subsequently the Confessing Church began offering increasingly effective resistance to German Christian domination of Protestant life. Clergy in the movement promoted anticlericalism to capitalize on lay energies and denounce their opponents.

According to a 1934 Confessing Church flyer, many lay Protestants considered the church struggle an internal affair among pastors.[39] In response to such views, German Christian leaders rephrased their anti-intellectualism as anticlericalism. Reich Bishop Müller stressed that the church belonged "above all to the congregation, not to the pastors and bishops."[40] In 1934, he announced that the "new Protestant church of Germany" would not be a church of pastors; if the clergy could not find its way to the people, he promised, he would "call the lay people to preach."[41] "Faith in Christ," insisted the German Christian National Youth pastor in 1934, "has always had only one opponent: the clericalism within us and around us."[42]

Lay people took up the challenge. In a letter to Hitler in December 1934, Nuremberg German Christians, emphasizing that they were lay people "joined by a small number of National Socialist pastors," denounced "theology alien to our *Volk*."[43] That same month, German Christians founded a local unit in Siegelsdorf/Veitsbronn (Bavaria). Copies of their telegram to Bavarian governor Franz Ritter von Epp stressed that "lay people" were responsible. The man who signed the telegram gave his occupation as railroad journeyman.[44] In the spring of 1935, German Christians founded a local group in Bevolzheim (Bavaria). The meeting took place in a pub belonging to the local party leader. No clergymen attended, and a retired mailman officiated. In his speech, he lambasted pastors, pausing only briefly to exempt those in the German Christian ranks. He blamed pastors for the fact that storm troopers and the Hitler Youth no longer came to church. The German Christians, he asserted, would see to it that men and young people came back to the church. There was still plenty of space for pastors in Dachau, he concluded.[45]

German Christian clergy tried to manipulate anticlerical sentiments to enhance their own position. In April 1935, Bishop Weidemann of Bremen attempted to convince German Christian Gau leaders to install him as the movement's Reich leader. To that end, he presented himself as the champion of lay interests, failing to mention that he himself was a pastor.[46] In May 1935, a vicar from Nuremberg addressed seventy German Christians in Alersheim (Bavaria). He ridiculed Confessing Church clergy as purveyors of "fossilized" theology and praised German Christian pastors, who "kept the church services short and spoke in a way understandable to everyone." His ninety-minute speech attacked the clergy harshly and handled "humorously" the fact that twenty-one Protestant pastors were incarcerated in concentration camps.[47]

But anticlericalism also rebounded against German Christian churchmen. In 1935, a Berlin pastor, disgusted with Protestant clericalism, left the church altogether and offered his services, not to the German Christian movement, but to the neopagan cause.[48] In October 1935, a longtime lay adherent canceled his membership. A psychologist from Dresden, he expressed contempt for the movement he had hoped would reform the "doctrine of the savior" in a "truly German" way. Instead, he complained, it perpetuated a "church of pastors" and engaged theologians as leaders and speakers.[49]

The creation of the Ministry of Church Affairs in 1935 and its quest to pacify the Protestant church played into the hands of German Christian clergy. To effect a compromise in the church struggle, the ministry needed to identify spokespeople as conversation partners. Clergy were natural candidates for that task. Beginning near the end of 1935, German Christian pastors responded to the anticlericalism they had helped generate by seeking a new image and enhanced role for the clergy. In a meeting with a Church Ministry official in September 1935, two top German Christians, Leffler and Heinrich Oberheid, argued that if the movement were to accomplish anything, it had to be based on "spiritual substance" and "true ecclesiastical education." Tantamount to a bid to reassert clerical control, Leffler's plan involved training "suitable individuals" for building up local German Christian organizations across the Reich. That approach earned approval and a tentative promise of funding from the Church Ministry.[50]

German Christians tried to reassert clerical control and enhance the prestige of the pastoral office by advocating a more aggressive, militant style. Such was the case with a vicar in Bielefeld whom the Westphalian consistory suspended in 1936 for assaulting a Confessing Church clergyman. To justify his behavior, the German Christian argued that his training as a storm trooper had superseded his socialization as a member of the clergy.[51]

The image of the Nazi warrior-pastor helps explain why German Christians continued to seek careers in the clergy, despite their contempt for everything the pastoral office represented. After all, if they reflected an entirely new breed of pastor, the old, negative images did not apply. German Christians used various means to emphasize the anticlericalism of their pastoral style. In 1937, a man from Heppingen wrote to the movement's leadership in the Saar-Palatinate to complain that he had failed his second theological examination. Along with two fellow German Christians, he had appeared for the exam in uniform, complete with party insignia.[52] Among other criticisms, the chief examiner pointed out that the candidate's sermon had not included a single word about sin or guilt. The German Christian was defiant. To his knowledge, he wrote, "the age of pietism" had passed. Church authorities asked him to sever his ties to the party, but that, he protested, would mean "back to sin and guilt, empty churches, contempt for the *Volk*, sabotage of the state." Impossible, he concluded; he was "too good for that. Fight to the knife, that is for sure."[53]

By the late 1930s, anticlericalism, generated and then reappropriated by German Christian pastors, had become part of the movement's identity, a tool in the ongoing struggle for Nazi approval and an expression of German Christian contempt for the church. In May 1938, Berlin German Christian leader Pastor Tausch congratulated the movement that its ranks held no "politicized priests . . . no power-hungry clergyman."[54] Before an audience of ten thousand, Tausch outlined the antidoctrinal and anticlerical odyssey of the German Christian movement. In 1933, he declared, "theological considerations" had inhibited the "spring gusts" of the movement. But now, he boasted, German Christians had formed into a "firm, unbreakable bloc" with "hundreds of thousands" of members and "millions" of sympathizers. Their enemies, in contrast, the "successors of the synagogue and phariseeism," had elevated "theology" to the ruling principle.[55]

German Christians used anticlericalism to deflect and echo Nazi hostility toward the church in general and pastors in particular. That antagonism took many forms. In 1937, many clergy, including German Christians, were expelled from the Nazi party. In 1939, Bormann issued an order from party headquarters that speakers refrain from calling clergy "servants of God" and refer to them instead as "servants of the church."[56]

Despite ambivalence within their own ranks and hostility from Nazi authorities, German Christians reasserted clericalism during the war. Instead of flaunting his lay background, for example, a German Christian active in Bavaria in the 1940s falsely assumed the title of pastor to enhance his authority.[57] In the face of bombing, defeat, bereavement, evacuation, and death, pastors gained prestige as people looked to them to provide some meaning and comfort in suffering. German Christian clergy saw a chance to rejuvenate not only the church but the status of their profession.

Clergy in the National Church group of German Christians organized a German Community of Pastors. In 1944, a spokesman published a plan for the group. With 60 to 70 percent of Protestant clergy under arms, he called on German Christians on the home front to restore the pastorates to their former glory as "cultural centers" of the *Volk*. As models for the role of the clergy in wartime, he pointed to the patriotic preachers of the Wars of Liberation against Napoleon. For him, the "colleagues under arms" represented a new type of pastor: the fighting, praying, spiritual leader who exemplified loyalty and obedience unto death.[58] From their initial attempts to revitalize the clergy, German Christians had eroded the pastoral office until they could conceive of only one meaningful function for an incumbent: to exhort his congregation to follow him into sacrifice for the fatherland.

## Breaking Church Rules

German Christians expressed their opposition to church doctrine in a third negation: they broke church rules. If doctrine and theology were not to be allowed to divide members of the *Volk*, neither, German Christians insisted, would the regulations of the church. Church rules took many forms, but for German Christians the most important were those that defined membership and governed participation in the ritual life of the church. In the established Protestant church of Germany in the 1930s and 1940s, regulations specified to whom services and sacraments could be offered. Regulations did not allow people outside the church to be given a church funeral. They reserved godparenthood and church marriage to members. Only under exceptional circumstances could the children of people outside the church be baptized.[59]

German Christians, at various times and places, violated every such regulation. They performed lay baptisms; their clergy married couples who were outside the faith; they disregarded the fixed boundaries of pastors' jurisdictions. Such incidents of disobedience may appear random and even trivial. The violation of church regulations, however, formed part of the German Christian program of creating a people's church that would include all those defined as true Germans.

In regions where German Christians controlled the organs of church government, they sidestepped issues of disobedience by interpreting the rules to suit themselves. In 1938, the Saxon church government, dominated by German Christians, ordered the church council in Berggießhübel to open the church building for use by a German Christian. The man in question possessed neither theological training nor pastoral experience. Nevertheless, the Saxon church permitted him to deliver sermons, perform confirmations, and administer communion.[60]

In at least one case, German Christians codified their antilegalism. In July 1944, Hugo Rönck, German Christian president of the Protestant church in Thuringia, issued new regulations for that institution. At first glance, Rönck's rules appear conventional because they rely on the standard vocabulary and categories of Protestant church order. But German Christian attitudes pervaded those guidelines. Every distinction the text made on the basis of belief or religious affiliation it dismantled again immediately as inappropriate to the people's church. For example, the regulations permitted a church wedding when "both people involved are members of a Christian religious organization, and at least one of them belongs to a Protestant church." But subsequent points revised that statement so that any members of the German *Volk* could be married in the church as long as they viewed matrimony as a "God-given institution" in keeping with the "pious customs and tradition of the German people" and agreed to have their children baptized. And those who had qualms of conscience regarding "certain confessional practices" could promise instead of having their children baptized to raise them in "the spirit of positive Christianity." In the end, the Thuringian regulations acknowledged only one reason for a pastor to refuse to perform a church wedding: "racial differences."[61]

In the case of baptism as well, the Thuringian regulations reflected German Christian dreams of the church as a spiritual expression of the *Volk*. Any child whose parents agreed to provide a "Protestant upbringing" was eligible to be baptized. Of course, the text specified, "Protestant" was not to be understood in a "confessionally limited" way. In fact, the regulations permitted baptism of any child, provided there were no circumstances that would render it impossible to raise the child in the "spirit of positive Christianity." With regard to funerals, too, the regulations institutionalized an inclusive, antilegalistic vision of the church. Pastors could officiate at funerals of individuals who had left the church "if conditions existed to justify such participation."[62]

The Thuringian church regulations reflect the paradoxical relationship between preservation and destruction that typified German Christian engagement in the church. The form of the regulations is conventional, their purpose familiar: to provide legal contours to the spiritual community. Yet the content of the regulations themselves betrays the essential explosiveness of German Christianity. Instead of defining church membership or delineating the responsibilities of the church and the congregation, the Thuringian regulations functioned as a repudiation of legal parameters in the spiritual community.

German Christians could not legislate their antilegalism in regions where they did not control the organs of church government. Instead, they sniped at church custom and regulation in an attempt to destabilize organized religious life and promote their vision of the inclusive people's church. To examine German Christians' antilegalism in a situation where they constituted a minority, I will focus on one church superintendent and his jurisdiction for which a substantial archival record exists: Adolf Clarenbach in Borgeln/Soest (Westphalia).[63]

Clarenbach was neither a German Christian nor an adherent of the Confessing Church. The number of German Christian clergy under his supervision probably never exceeded four or five at any one time. Their local followings were not large, yet they flooded his files with requests, complaints, and the records of their violations. German Christians had not triumphed in Westphalia in the church elections of 1933, and in the years to follow, they remained a minority within the congregations, on most church councils, and among the clergy. Nevertheless, presbyters, pastors, and church members from the movement found ways to trample convention and defy church regulations. In a minority situation, breaking church rules proved to be an effective tactic.

A sample case from Clarenbach's files illustrates how German Christians could exploit a single violation of church order to harass their opponents, increase their following, and promote their notion of the people's church. In September 1933, a German Christian presbyter from Bad-Sassendorf introduced a motion that would permit wedding ceremonies in the church on any day of the week.[64] The Westphalian consistory and the synod discouraged Saturday weddings on the grounds that pastors and congregations should use Saturday to prepare for Sunday. In the case in question, the groom wanted a Saturday wedding to accommodate relatives from out of town. In fact, the pastor discovered it was actually the cook who found Saturday more convenient. The Bad Sassendorf presbyters, dominated by German Christians, rammed the motion through in a heated session that ended with the pastor, an opponent of German Christianity, storming out of the room.[65]

That simple event constituted a fourfold victory for the German Christians. The grateful bride and groom, and perhaps their families, were likely to look sympathetically on the movement that had championed their cause; the pastor had been discredited; and at least for the moment, the presbyters had asserted their will in the parish. The clash was just one in an ongoing conflict between the presbyters and the pastor in Bad Sassendorf; a year and a half later, the pastor had a new complaint against his presbyters: they refused to pay his salary.[66] Most important, German Christians could portray the incident as a triumph for the people's church. The people's church, they declared, existed to serve its clientele; the pastor "had to be there for his congregation and adjust to its wishes."[67]

Another case in Clarenbach's jurisdiction erupted into a sort of German Christian cause célèbre. In October 1935, a German Christian railroad worker requested permission to have his child baptized by a pastor other than the one in whose jurisdiction he lived. In such a case, the regular pastor had to issue a certificate of release. The pastor in question refused and the Westphalian consistory in Münster upheld that decision.[68] The pastor and the consistory agreed that the railroad worker's grounds for seeking an alternate clergyman were invalid. He based his request on the belief that "children with a German Christian baptism will make better progress in political and economic life."[69]

When they failed to get clearance for a German Christian pastor to baptize the child, local members of the movement staged a lay baptism. A railroad official did the honors, and the parents applied to have the event entered in the church books. The Protestant Church Council of Prussia, the superior authority over the Westphalian consistory, eventually recognized the baptism as an emergency baptism, which was permissible under church regulations only in cases of immediate danger to the life of the child. The occurrence, Prussian church authorities warned, reflected "fanaticism destructive to the church as well as the confession."[70] Westphalian church officials took the event seriously and circulated the statement on lay baptisms to all parishes in its jurisdiction, to be read by the pastor from the pulpit.[71] Nevertheless, neither the parents of the child nor the German Christian who had performed the baptism received more than a rap on the knuckles.[72] Despite numerical weakness, German Christians had managed to disrupt organized church life while winning a symbolic victory for the people's church.

Throughout the 1930s, German Christians who moved in and out of Superintendent Clarenbach's jurisdiction kept him and higher church authorities busy evaluating requests and issuing certificates to bypass the authority of local pastors who opposed them. Only very rarely did non–German Christians in Clarenbach's jurisdiction ask to have regulations waived for matters such as a wedding on Saturday.[73] Church offices in Münster invariably complied with German Christian requests, frequently overturning the superintendent's decisions to do so.[74] In one case, consistorial authorities overruled the superintendent to allow a German Christian curate to perform a baptism. Their reasoning indicates that German Christians struck a responsive chord when they justified violation of church regulations with the need to build the people's church: "We do not want to give grounds that [the baptism] should not occur at all, or should take place in the Catholic church."[75]

Some cases involved so-called mixed marriages between a Protestant and a Catholic or a Protestant and a non–church member, or burial of someone living in the jurisdiction of a non–German Christian pastor. Clarenbach's files are filled with correspondence on such issues, much of it related to one particular German Christian curate.[76] In June 1936, a former Catholic decided to join the Protestant church. He requested instruction from the curate, who was stationed in Soest. The man in question had no baptismal certificate although he claimed to have been baptized.[77] Nevertheless, the German Christian accepted him into the church.[78] He signed the certificate on behalf of the "German Christian pastor's office in Soest." The Westphalian consistory questioned the curate's right to claim to be in charge of a "German Christian pastoral office."[79] But church authorities did not overturn the action.

German Christian violations of church regulations had the effect, as members of the presbyters in Soest observed, of "weakening and crumbling the order of the church."[80] In 1938, a German Christian pastor sponsored a public meeting in Soest. He asked those assembled if they favored replacing the "Hallelujah" in the worship service with "Lord, we praise thee!" When the audience concurred, he announced that he would implement the change, adding that "he was no doubt bound by his ordination oath or some such thing, but he would nevertheless risk this piece of heresy."[81] A pastor who opposed the movement noted that the dissolution of church authority generated a cynical attitude among German Christians themselves. In 1938, he observed that all of the people who had formally left the church in his community in the recent past, with the exception of a handful who converted to Catholicism, had been German Christians.[82]

Funerals provided a useful forum for German Christian pastors. They benefited particularly from cases where the deceased was not entitled to a church burial, but the family wanted Protestant services. In April 1938, a glovemaker in Erlangen died in an accident. He had left the Protestant church shortly after the war, possibly for reasons connected to his membership in the Social Democratic party. The man's family wanted a church burial, but the local vicar and district superintendent refused. The bereaved turned to a German Christian who agreed immediately.[83] In early 1939, a Westphalian German Christian buried a former Catholic who had left the church. At the grave, the pastor preached the message of the people's church: "All members of the *Volk* were God's children," he proclaimed. "God would accept us all in his eternal arms."[84]

German Christians all over the country employed the same tactics that Superintendent Clarenbach witnessed in his jurisdiction. In 1939, a group of German Christians in the movement's National Church wing advertised their willingness to perform church services for people who were technically ineligible. They sent circulars to all Nazi party district leaders informing them that they had designated a pastor for every party district. That pastor would offer church weddings, baptisms, and other services to party members, including those who had left the church. Had it succeeded, the scheme would have been a German Christian coup. It foundered on opposition from the party; Bormann strictly forbade contact between Gauleiters and those German Christians.[85]

As a short-term tactic to disrupt the functioning of the established church and attract attention, German Christian antilegalism had its successes. In 1940, a German Christian pastor in Bavaria attracted ninety-three youngsters to his confirmation instruction by dropping the required examination. In keeping with his antidoctrinal stance, he claimed that "knowledge has nothing to do with faith."[86] But as a standard part of the movement's activities, the violation of church regulations was disastrous. It drew exactly the kind of adherents who undermined the movement: people with only a weak link to some aspect of Christian culture, the intellectually lazy, wastrels, thugs.

The German Christian movement did seem to attract more than its fair share of riffraff. In 1935, a church superintendent wrote to a pastor who had requested information on a particular German Christian. According to the superintendent, that man was a "dazzler," a gambler, embezzler, and troublemaker. "Precisely such people," the superintendent noted, "seek a hiding place these days among the German Christians."[87] Any group of six hundred thousand people is bound to include unsavory elements. But what is significant in the German Christian case is the defiance and even pride with which members acknowledged their movement's rough edges. Critics often pointed to the inappropriate behavior of the movement's adherents in church services and the crude speech and loose lifestyle of some of its clergy. German Christians responded to such charges, not with chagrin but with glee. Instead of denying those accusations or seeking evidence of similar breaches by their opponents, they derided the Confessing Church as a holdout of womanly, weak piety. Their own movement, they boasted, represented vital, aggressive energies. They sought a people's church, and the people, they insisted, had no time for outdated proprieties.

German Christians cultivated a tough image. One pastor described a member he knew well who frequently ended their discussions of religious topics with the remark: "You're too pious; you should get drunk more often; then you would change your ideas."[88] A pastor from Leuthen-

Windorf complained that a German Christian forester on the church council had accosted him in the vestry within earshot of his parishioners and threatened to have him consigned to a concentration camp because his sermon contained material hostile to the state.[89]

A clear illustration of the potential for abuse in the name of the people's church involved one of the pastors in Superintendent Clarenbach's jurisdiction. In 1940, Clarenbach was called to mediate a conflict between that pastor and a presbyter from his congregation. Although not formally a member, the pastor in question worked for the German Christian cause. The dispute involved an exchange of insults between the pastor and the presbyter, culminating in the pastor's charge that the presbyter had told him, "You are shit" ("Sie sind Scheiße"). The presbyter maintained he had not said, "You are shit," but "Oh shit" ("Ach, Scheiße"), implying that something the pastor had said was nonsense. Clarenbach found in favor of the presbyter; people in the area, he pointed out, did not use the phrase, "You are shit." In the process of the investigation, more serious grievances against the pastor emerged: he had used an epidemic of hoof-and-mouth disease in the area as an excuse to cancel church services for two Sundays; he altered the confession of faith, omitting mention of the resurrection of the body and descent into hell. In the previous summer, he had not offered communion even once.[90]

Particularly the pastor's habit of holding church meetings in the pub raised eyebrows among his ecclesiastical superiors. When asked why he engaged in that practice, he responded with a crude version of the argument for a people's church: the presbyters, he claimed, liked to drink while at their task. The pastor again appealed to the imperatives of the people's church when he came under attack for the amount of time he spent in the pub. Sometimes, he told the superintendent, members of the congregation wanted to be able to drink with their pastor.[91] That version of the people's church represented the total defamation of the church as an institution. Teenage boys in the town sensed that fact and serenaded their pastor with a ditty: "We live in a great town, because it no longer has a church! This makes us all very happy, but happiest of all is the pastor!"[92]

Physical force constituted an important part of the German Christian repertoire of disruptive tactics. German Christians cultivated a violent style reflected in the costume some of their clergy affected: black jacket, riding breeches, and knee-high boots. From beginning to end, the story of the German Christian movement is replete with pushing, shoving, whistles, and catcalls in the church. In June 1933, for example, German Christians in the Saar stormed a meeting of their opponents. When organizers

*The church building in Holzwickede (Westphalia), barricaded by German Christians to prevent its use by adherents of the Confessing Church. Conflicts over resources and facilities made up a significant part of the church struggle. German Christians were not averse to using physical force and intimidation against their opponents in the Confessing Church. (Landeskirchenarchiv, Bielefeld)*

refused to permit discussion, the German Christians apparently "went wild." They "screamed, roared, and kicked up a row," hurling insults at the pastor that were "not repeatable," the mildest terms being "traitor, coward, man without a fatherland." He needed a police escort to return home.[93] Similar incidents occurred elsewhere, although they cost the German Christian cause much support.

The movement's antidoctrinal, anarchistic stance attracted people who wanted to retain Christian rituals but considered accepted codes of churchlike behavior too confining. In a society where propriety had been perverted and violence exalted, that combination was explosive. One German Christian curate who played a central role in a series of fisticuffs with Confessing Church people in Bielefeld in 1936 regretted his transfer to another parish because he had grown used to the place, "particularly to the fighting."[94] It was he who had told a Confessing Church clergy: "You claim to be a pastor? It's a good thing I haven't eaten because I would throw up. You belong to the people they forgot on 30 June [1934]."[95] In Saxony during the war, a prominent church leader was known as the "Revolver Bishop" because he drew his gun when he took over the offices of the regional church, "to speed up the process."[96] Once such a style was introduced into church life, it could not be controlled. With a quote from Goethe, a commentator from Berlin summed up a fundamental truth about the German Christian movement: "Die ich rief, die Geister, werd ich nicht mehr los [I can no longer get rid of the spirits I summoned]."[97] It was not just a rock that German Christians threw into the church; it was a bomb.

## CHAPTER 10

# The Bride of Christ at War

*Without the one unified mother soil of the "church," the eternal German wanders without a homeland in foreign places, and in the long run, his soul must atrophy wretchedly.*
—*German Christian Pastor Hans Schmidt, 1943*

Issues of race and church doctrine reveal the nihilism at the core of the German Christian vision of the people's church. The anti-Jewish church was ultimately non-Christian; the church without rules was no church at all. Attention to gender exposes an additional contradiction in German Christian ecclesiology. The people's church, German Christians insisted, would be manly, celebrating hardness and aggression while eschewing compassion and humility. But for most German Christians, indeed, for most Christians in Germany, it was precisely qualities they deemed feminine—nurturing, caring, preserving purity—that defined what a church was and determined what it should do. How could they transform the church into a manly affair when their understanding of it was tied up in a perception of its womanly nature?

War resolved that quandary for the German Christians. Two opposing images—the soldier and the mother—came together in the notion of wartime sacrifice. In war, the church could be both manly and womanly, combative and nurturing, brutal to the enemy yet tender to its own sons, even as it sent them to die. This chapter investigates contradictions inherent in the notion of a manly church. It analyzes the German Christian desire for manliness as a mirror that reflected the gap between ecclesiological ideals and perceptions of the existing church. It explores the movement's gendered dichotomies as a riddle, by which German Christians' own categories precluded realization of their goals until those tensions were subsumed by war.

## The Mother of the *Volk* and the Storm Troopers of the Lord

Whether portrayed as bride, wife, or mother, the church as depicted in German Christian statements and publications was feminine. Feminine metaphors for the religious community are as old as the Bible itself. Both the Old and New Testaments use bride/bridegroom analogies to describe the relationship of God to his people—for example, Isaiah 49:18—and Christ to the faithful—Matthew 25:1–13, John 3:29, Revelation 21:10. But the German Christian version of the bridal metaphor for the church had a crucial twist: the bridegroom was not Christ but the National Socialist state.

That adaptation did not pass unnoticed by the movement's critics. One German pastor observed in 1934 that, just as John saw the "holy city of God descend from heaven prepared as a bride adorned for her husband" (Revelation 21:10), "so the 'German Christian Faith Movement' wants to prepare itself as a bejeweled bride for her husband, German National Socialism."[1] Other non–German Christians were less astute; some even used the marriage analogy themselves to characterize the proper relationship between church and state. In a 1935 pamphlet, Gustav von Bodelschwingh, brother of the onetime Reich bishop-designate and a sympathizer though not a member of the German Christian movement, compared the church to a wife. "Only through cooperation of the spouses can a family flourish," he contended. "Likewise, only in cooperation between state and church can our people prosper."[2]

In German Christian literature, references to the femininity of the church varied from the subtle to the explicit. A 1933 speech by a German Christian in Oberhausen (Rhineland) described the birth of the German Christian movement as the product of "passionate love to church and fatherland."[3] Fritz Engelke, a leading German Christian and vicar to the Reich bishop, used a wife metaphor in his 1933 article "*Volk*, State, Church" to depict the proper relation among those three components of society. Engelke derived his argument from the grammatical gender of the German nouns *Staat* (masculine), *Kirche* (feminine), and *Volk* (neutral).

"Our German language," he announced, "tells us how the three separate poles form a trinity. Father, mother child: that is the trinity granted by creation and the simile for the trinity of state, church, and *Volk*. The *Volk* is the child, the state is the father, the church is the mother."[4]

Engelke's line on church-state relations remained consistent over time, although his rhetoric became more strident. In 1937, at another German Christian event, he again presented the state-church-*Volk* trinity as analogous to father-mother-child. This time he was more specific on the duties of the church/wife and much more critical of that part of the trio: "State and church are created by God as a marriage. God created woman to be the helpmate of the man, to surrender herself as a female completely to the man, and so become completely woman, as he becomes completely man." The successful marriage, he proclaimed, brought "the finest unity of two, the greatest joy, paradise on earth." But now, he admonished, "instead of unity, there was discord," and the reason is that "'she' has the pants on, she tries to henpeck him." In Engelke's analysis the behavior of the wife/church left the husband/state little option: "Because the woman (church), through continuous squabbling, moralistic fighting, and public insulting of the man, severely harms his standing among the other men . . . the man rightfully considers distancing himself, divorcing the woman. The unhappy marriage (pope, emperor, Canossa) must be paid for by the children: the *Volk*!"[5]

A letter of complaint from a Hamburg German Christian woman to the neopagan German Faith Movement in 1938 echoed Engelke's view. The author rested her case for retaining the church in the new Germany on the strength of a gender analogy. "Just as man and woman are both necessary to sustain human life," she wrote, the *"maintenance of the state requires likewise two things: Father State and Mother Church."* She described the qualities state and church must possess before a marriage could occur: "Father must have a healthy mind and manners and be able to provide for a family. Mother must have only one head, and not a crazy one at that, and must be able to fulfill her motherly and housewifely duties well. Mr. 'National Socialist State' is already there and fit for matrimony. Miss 'Christian Church' in one body (Polygamy is taboo in Germany!) has not yet seen the light of day, but seems to be developing." In closing she quoted a poem from her childhood: "The man is king of the house; the wife is the crown. Anyone who bears a crown is not diminished but elevated."[6]

Of the feminine images available, it was those of wife and mother that German Christians most often conflated with the church. German Christian statements posited an almost symbiotic relationship between motherhood and the church and assigned the same functions to both. Both the church and the mother were to offer a sphere for free expression of emotion, to guard virtue, and to protect racial purity.

In a 1933 account of participation in the Lord's Supper, a young storm trooper offered a vivid description of the church as the sphere of emotion. "A festive silence hung over the small room of the vestry," he recounted. "Several older and younger women were present but I was the only male Christian. . . . I've seen a lot at the front that dulls empathy and makes a person coarse and rough, and recently I've experienced a great deal of adversity, which makes the heart hard, but in this festive hour the infinite love of our Lord and Savior overpowered me and I felt like a child."[7] For that man, the comfort of the familiar ritual had a maternal quality; its contrast to the rough world of men outside provided a safe haven for otherwise prohibited feelings. Even his own response did not need to be masculine; he "felt like a child."

A German Christian sermon for Pentecost in 1944 enunciated the connection between the church and the mother as the religious conscience. "The church also belongs to the mothers of our people," the preacher explained. "Like a true mother she has devoted much maternal love to her children. She has sorrowed with them and about them, she has prayed for them like mothers always have, she protected the most holy for them and always wished to tread the blessed path of faith with them."[8]

For German Christians, the most important role attributed both to biological mothers and to the mother church was the preservation of racial purity. German Christians presented the true people's church not only as the loyal wife of the German fatherland and the virtuous mother of all true Germans but as the guardian of racial purity, committed to the enforcement and legitimation of the National Socialist racial worldview. One of the movement's pamphlets instructed mothers as to how to answer "growing children" with difficult questions like, " 'Mother, we were told that Jesus was a Jew. Christianity doesn't fit with our National Socialist thought.' " "Isn't it best," the tract advised, "simply to answer: Through the revolution . . . the eyes of us old people too were opened to many things. . . . Because Christ was the 'opponent' of the Jew, it is impossible that he himself could have come from Jewish blood and a Jewish spirit."[9] Just as the mother assumed the task of explaining and preserving racial purity in the home, the church would perform those tasks in public, raising her children in the racial spirit. German Christians fondly and frequently cited Hitler's speech of 23 March 1933, in which he praised the Protestant and Catholic churches as the "most important factors in the preservation of our *Volkstum*."[10]

In concrete ways, the German Christians sought to ensure that the church performed its prime motherly function. In 1935, under the director-ship of the German Christians Friedrich Werner and Karl Themel, the Chancellery of the German Evangelical church promoted a course for pas-tors on genetics and racial hygiene. Scheduled lectures included "Prevent-ing genetically ill progeny," "Marriage Counseling," "Racial divisions," and "Race and Culture."[11] In 1938, a group of German Christian students and pastoral candidates further developed and propagated the link between the church and the mother as protectors of the *Volk*. They toured West-phalia with a program including a talk by one of the candidates titled "Peo-ple—Church—People's Church!" (*"Volk—Kirche—Volkskirche!"*). The fight for racial purity, he stressed, was willed by God. God had placed each German into that particular community of blood, he emphasized; "not just any mother but the German mother has given birth to us into this home-land." It was therefore the duty of every German Christian not only to respect the new laws of "blood and honor" but to live them. And the church was to spread the word, as this group was doing.[12]

Like a mother, the German Christian people's church would provide a homeland for the German *Volk*. Nazi authorities believed that the preser-vation of Germanness outside the boundaries of Germany depended above all on women. In a 1942 reflection on the matter, one German newspaper claimed that in "mixed marriages," unions between ethnic Germans and others, "the decisive thing is always which partner's character and life-style prevails." In many cases where the German blood won out, the article maintained, "it has been established that the woman held especially firmly to her Germanness."[13] In much the same way, German Christians argued, the church, the spiritual community of Germans, was responsible for pre-serving the bond among Germanic peoples beyond the boundaries of Ger-many. Discussions of ethnic Germans often referred to Germany as the "motherland of the Reformation," an image that intertwined mother, church, and the spiritual essence of the German nation. For example, an anonymous German Christian reporter in 1936 described a visit to Den-mark and Norway with a focus on "the relationship between Germany as the motherland of the Reformation and the two Nordic states."[14]

Eagerly German Christians took up the theme of the church's maternal role among ethnic Germans in what they liked to call the diaspora. In the period before the Saar referendum in January 1935, German Christians made impassioned use of the image of Germany as the spiritual mother of all true Germans. In 1934, for example, an article in the *Evangelium im Dritten Reich* derided as the "purest insanity" and "a disturbance of God's divine order" the fact a people was to vote where it belonged. That, the article expostulated, was tantamount to children voting "whether their mother should remain their mother." In case that comparison was not clear enough, the article offered a bridal metaphor as well, pointing out how apt the words of Jesus were to the situation: "What God has joined together let no one put asunder."[15] The "Saar Hymn," sung frequently at German Christian events in 1934 and early 1935, presented the spiritual Germany as a mother who drew her children toward herself. After several stanzas stressing the "eternally German" nature of the Saar, the song closed with these lines: "Reach out your hand, tie up the band; Around a young *Volk* that calls itself German, in whom the flaming passion burns; Toward you, oh mother, toward you!"[16]

The tendency to portray the church as mother and, more specifically, the German mother-church as spiritual homeland, is especially evident in Christian literature stemming from ethnic German groups outside the Reich. Often such publications refer to Germany not as the fatherland but as the motherland. For example, in 1938, Bishop Viktor Glondys of the German church in Romania pledged the German-speaking church to the preservation and promotion of German culture in eastern and southeastern Europe. He praised the practice of educating ethnic German teachers and pastors from those areas in Germany so that "they could deepen their relationship with the motherland."[17] Glondys was not a German Christian, but his successor Wilhelm Staedel was. Staedel consistently referred to Germany as the "motherland,"[18] the spiritual homeland for him and other ethnic Germans. Ties of sentiment and piety bound people like Staedel to the German church, the German mother, which in turn gave spiritual expression to the nation. Even after 1945, Staedel explained in a talk that the "warm word 'motherland'" expressed the "close, indeed intimate, way" that the old German settlement in Transylvania was bound to the German Reich.[19]

But if German Christians perceived the spiritual community through the metaphor of a woman, negative stereotypes of womanhood carried over onto the church as well. The traits that made women good mothers and guardians of piety and virtue, those characteristics that, in the words of the Thuringian German Christian Cläre Quambusch, bound "the woman's heart" intimately "to that which we call the church and church life,"[20] were the emotionality and irrationality that also branded women as dupes. The image of weeping women in contrast to fighting men recurs in the songs and jokes of the storm troopers and soldiers of Nazi Germany, and the "storm troopers of Christ," the manly men of the German Christian movement, shared that gendered model. Many German Christian men hoped to emulate the gender roles conveyed in songs like the National Socialist ditty "Assault troops!": "Once there was a young storm trooper, Ah, and it was determined that he must leave his wife, that he must leave his child, and leave without delay. Old women cry terribly, and young girls are still much worse; So farewell my dear child, we'll never see each other again."[21]

The link between feminine qualities in women and the femininity of the church led German Christians to warn against the special danger of "fanaticism" in religious life. One German Christian article, after decrying "certain overexcited women who collect cigarette butts from famous personalities," went on to denounce religious excess: "The sphere of religion is very closely located to the life of the feelings and it may be for that reason that over and over again overexcited feelings are mistaken for faith, speaking in tongues for the Holy Spirit, and the foam of human emotion for the underlying wave."[22] Association of feminine traits with the church led some German Christians to regard that institution with contempt. In the late 1930s, Fritz Engelke, the same prominent German Christian who had urged the marital union of mother-church and father-state, denounced the church as a "soft, effeminate, tottering affair." It aimed, he charged, to "make man, child, state and *Volk* womanish—our hymns are songs for sheep, our sermons are effeminate, griping, whining and complaining." In Engelke's opinion, the youth, who "strongly reject the church and spend Sunday forenoon playing sports, are a sign of the awakening health of our *Volk*, for which we must thank God."[23]

Even in its much-extolled role of protector of the *Volk*, German Christians feared that the church shared the weakness of women. Like womanhood, the church was both a bulwark against racial disintegration and the prime suspect for admitting undesirable elements into the national bloodstream. German Christian literature—like National Socialist accounts—frequently depicted women as the weak link, the group that had to be prevented from permitting debasement of the race. A song in the *Little Nazi Songbook* made this pledge: "On the dishonored bodies of blond, blue-eyed German women, the vermin of thieves shall not set up a stock exchange."[24] Hitler used a similar image of woman as the dupe of racially destructive forces in *Mein Kampf*. His theory of how "the Jew" would attempt to destroy Aryan culture presented women as passive objects of a strategy of defilement. The Jew, Hitler wrote, "systematically spoils the women and girls of our people by mixing the blood. Only the racialist [*völkische*] state will rescue marriage from the level of ongoing racial desecration [*Rassenschande*] in order to consecrate it as the institution called to produce people in the Lord's image and not miscarriages that are half human and half ape."[25]

In the German Christian view, the church, by allowing "baptized Jews" to enter the national spiritual community and by promoting and preserving elements such as the Old Testament in German cultural life, threatened in a similar way to further the destruction of German purity. An incident in 1935 captures the double fear of women and of the church as floodgates to racial destruction and shows how German Christians propagated that paranoid view. A Confessing Church flyer tells the story of a Jewish man in Magdeburg who ran a private business school. In late 1934, he asked a Confessing Church pastor to baptize him. Convinced of the man's sincerity, the pastor agreed and, after instruction, the man was received into the church.

Just weeks later, a Nazi court convicted the man of sexual offenses. The Confessing Church's report was apologetic and pointed out that even the man's friends and family had no idea that "his relationship to the girls in the school was anything other than that between teacher and students." The antisemitic paper *Der Stürmer* went wild with the case, even putting out a special issue. On the cover was a photograph of the Confessing Church pastor with the caption: "Confessing Church Pastor Z on 17 March baptized the race-desecrator H-, who was then arrested on 20 April 1935. As is visible on the photo, the pastor looks almost more Jewish than does the Jew he baptized."[26]

The German Christian bishop Friedrich Peter in Magdeburg publicly counseled the pastors in his jurisdiction to distance themselves from the Confessing Church clergyman involved.[27] German Christians wanted nothing to do with an image of the church as the weak link in the fight against racial impurity. To the contrary, with their rallying cry of the manly church, German Christians sought to present themselves as the heroes who would rescue German womanhood from dishonor and save German blood from degeneration, the manly champions who would make sure that what they considered the feminine, vulnerable church did not become the portal through which non-Aryan elements, thinly disguised by baptism, undermined the German *Volk*. While they trumpeted the manly church, German Christians' feminine ecclesiology reflected condescension and contempt for the very institution that their movement sought to revive and reform.

## War and Fulfillment of the Manly Ideal

German Christians tended to propound the manly slogan less often after the early stages of their movement's development. After 1933, although few people rejected the manly motif outright, some German Christians at least recognized that, if carried to extremes, it could be dysfunctional. One publicist claimed that precisely the "unmanly" nature of Christianity made it an ideal religion for the people as a whole. The old Germanic religion, he conceded, was suitable for the "man at arms" and the "hero." But, he contended, it was not "adequate" for "the women, the children, the weak." Only under the banner of a unifying religion, he announced, could the Germans "march behind the Führer with closed ranks, the entire *Volk* together."[28]

If German Christians were going to build a people's church they could not afford to antagonize women. It was not simply that German Christians believed woman, in the words of a female member, "by nature tends more to belief than does man."[29] Empirical evidence also indicated that women were more loyal to the church than men. From 1925 to 1933, the number of individuals outside the established religions in Germany more than doubled, but the percentage of women in that category actually dropped by 39.5 percent.[30] Local reports confirm the view that women were more reluctant than men to leave the church. In 1936, a Lippstadt pastor sent his superintendent a list of twenty-one individuals who had left the church that year; only three were women.[31] In 1938, another Westphalian pastor reported that six of the thirteen people who left the church in Neheim that year were women, but of those, five were the wives of men who had taken the step long before and one led the local League of German Girls.[32]

Anecdotal information reveals a widespread perception that women's attachment to the church was more intense than men's. In 1938, a German Christian from Minden reported irately that a non–German Christian pastor had made it clear at the funeral of a young man that the deceased had quit the church. According to the account, the dead man's "sister got heart spasms"; fortunately, the "old mother," who also had "a bad heart," was not present.[33] In 1940, a Viennese theologian who was close to the German Christians produced a list of complaints about the treatment of loyal Nazi Christians in Austria. He portrayed women as the backbone of the church, pointing, for example, to a local party leader who had left the church for political reasons but whose wife remained Protestant, even though her choice meant that "harmony between the spouses has been severely disrupted."[34] He also recounted the story of a "peasant woman" who wept bitterly in his presence "because her daughter could not have a church wedding"; the groom had been told that he would receive the new farmers' certificate only if he was not married in church.[35] The dominance of women in religious life meant that women's cooperation was crucial in achieving German Christian goals. Even the dream of a manly church could not be allowed to jeopardize that.

The form the church struggle took also meant that the tasks performed and the skills required were to a large extent those associated with women. Verbal skills of persuasion and denunciation and a convincing show of piety and religious respectability were needed to gain followers and legitimize the cause. Coarse and heavy-handed tactics, even when rationalized as manly, alienated many people who felt close to the German Christian ideas but would not tolerate violence and disruption in church life. For example, in October 1933, a deaconess in Berlin wrote to the Reich bishop complaining that German Christians had insisted she be dismissed from her nursing position. The only reason, she wrote, was an assumption on the part of German Christians in her congregation that she could not be one of them. In fact, she contended, she had nothing against the movement; she simply refused to accept the aggressive local leadership.[36] A woman from Bielefeld described herself as a nonmember of the German Christian movement but an "old cofighter" of the prominent Westphalian German Christian Karl Wentz. In 1934, she complained that at a recent German Christian event in Bielefeld, the leaders had worn storm trooper uniforms. For her and, she contended, for many others, that form of dress in a religious context was "alienating."[37]

In practical ways, the manly church brought negative returns for the German Christian movement because it blocked women and "unmanly" men from full participation and alienated potential supporters. Even before the war began, German Christians had grown more aware of the value of women's involvement, and the language of the manly church appeared less often as they expanded their outreach to women. Gripes about women's overrepresentation petered out in the mid-1930s as the movement became more dependent on and grateful for women's participation and indeed for lay participation from both sexes.

At first glance, the war itself might appear to render the notion of a manly church obsolete. Once the "manly men," that is, the soldiers, were at the front, the church at home could hardly claim to be manly in the sense that it housed a lot of males. To the contrary, the true manliness of a German Christian congregation, given their own criteria, would be measured in exactly the opposite terms: by the number of men who were absent, serving at the front. And indeed, during the war years German

Christian men increasingly passed the torch into women's hands. An article by a German Christian Women's Service leader in the early 1940s celebrated the willingness of women to do essential work in the parishes. The author, describing an encounter in Pomerania, postulated a kind of German Christian superwoman: "I will never forget the parsonage where seven little Germans lay in their little white beds and the diligent pastor's wife toiled to continue the parish work in the new way and in the new spirit for her husband who was at the front."[38]

By midway through the war, some German Christian publications had begun to recognize women, or at least mothers, as independent members of the movement and to acknowledge in print the bereavement of those who had lost sons or husbands. In March 1943, for example, the newsletter of the National Church group of German Christians mentioned in its list of fallen two women group members whose sons died in the war.[39] A 1944 bulletin of the German Christians in Thuringia reported that church president Rönck was organizing pastors' wives to take a larger role in the "orphaned congregations." Fifteen times annually they were to receive German Christian materials to help them hold devotions, celebrations, and other services. Four seminars for pastors' wives had already been planned.[40]

But rather than heralding the end of the manly church, the war brought new viability to that notion. German Christians had preached the need for enhanced manliness in the religious sphere in the first place as an expedient to address the needs of a country defeated at war. So it is no surprise that the manly church as a soldierly church for people of both sexes came into its own precisely in wartime. The two images that dominated the gendered vision of the church—the weeping woman-mother and the fighting warrior-man—could be reconciled in the notion of sacrifice. In wartime, the love of the mother and the love of the church, viewed through the prism of sacrifice, were no longer sentimental, weak, or emasculating but constituted the source of inner strength for an assertion of masculine values on the battlefield.

Reich Bishop Müller took up the theme of women and sacrifice in his 1939 publication *Der deutsche Volkssoldat* (The German people's soldier). For Müller the demand for sacrifice would weld together the feminine and the masculine in the community devoted to victory: "The homeland is the source of power for the fighting soldier. The source of victory for the homeland is the brave German mother who continuously steels the courage of her fighting son."[41] In wartime, motherly love, for the German Christians, found its highest expression in sacrifice. And the feminine, irrational qualities of that love need no longer elicit embarrassment or contempt from the spokesmen of the German Christian movement because the mother and the soldier were mutually dependent, supportive, and reinforcing.

According to an article by a Westphalian German Christian pastor in the early months of the war, women's wartime sacrifice reconciled them with the true people's church. It was the camaraderie of the world war, the author explained, that had produced "the new structure of *völkisch* life in the Greater German territory." And now, in the age of total war, he continued, women too experienced a togetherness "worthy of the camaraderie of men at the front." Through the "sacrifice of blood" and their service to the *Volk*, he proclaimed, a "new type of German woman" was emerging: "a loyal and grateful cofighter and comrade in the one church in the Reich of Peace."[42]

Christianity too revolves around a sacrifice, and the vocabulary of the crucifixion became the language used to describe, legitimize, and sanctify mothers' sacrifice. A Mother's Day sermon for 1942 distributed to German Christians in Westphalia illustrates the German Christian view of motherly love as fulfilled in wartime. For the author, the love of a mother was not just analogous to the love of God for his people, it was identical to that love: "Love is red and red is the sacrifice of love, both unified in the mother. . . . Love is only whole where it becomes sacrifice. The Savior's love is crowned in the sacrifice on the cross. Motherly love too encompasses sacrifice from beginning to end. . . . Motherly love means to die oneself more and more. . . . Motherly love is sacrifice." The author called "motherly love" the "invisible bridge between the homeland and the front." In quiet moments,  he wrote, it was to "the peace at the mother's breast" that the thoughts of the soldier sped. With the "army of the sons," he wrote, "the army of the mothers advances in proud anxiety; and where a soldier's heart breaks and life is crowned by a sacrifice, there a sword pierces a mother's heart and a crown of thorns sinks onto a mother's head."[43]

Sacrifice connected mothers and soldiers and, by extension, the church and the fighting man, but it also constituted the link between heroism and manly love. German Christians had always attached religious significance to the soldier's death, but in wartime that notion gained vital relevance. Until 1939, the movement's publications had looked back to the world war as the scene of holy sacrifice. In 1934, for example, a leading German Christian from Hamburg addressed the question of heroism and sacrifice. He discussed the despair among the bereaved by the end of the war and the urgency with which people questioned the meaning of so much sorrow. It was the Christian understanding of sacrifice, he insisted, that gave death meaning and dignity. "Greater love hath no man than this," he reminded his audience, "that he lay down his life for his brother."[44]

In the years before war began again, German Christian preoccupation with soldierly sacrifice had seemed somehow contrived. Neopagans had attacked the movement with jeers such as, "There is nothing more demeaning for a soldier than to kneel in front of a cross."[45] But war resolved the problem of reconciling the image of the soldier and the image of sacrifice bound up in the cross: every soldier lived on the verge of the grave, and every grave was symbolized by a cross. How could the cross be unmanly?

For German Christians, the heroic soldier and the long-suffering mother had always provided the standards against which they measured religious experience. But only war could resolve the tension between those polarized images; only the church of a people at war would provide a spiritual refuge for both the soldier and the mother, reflect the virtues of both, and strengthen the resolve of both to fulfill their respective roles. A funeral blessing, published in a German Christian guide to religious celebrations, expresses this reconciliation:

> Pastor: This is the voice of the dead: Do not complain!
> Bear the fate of the earth! Love our death!
> (The bell rings. The wreath is lowered silently.)
> Where men stand and pass through the fire,
> There it is finished. The flag flies.
> He who has faith will triumph,
> in your power, Lord God.
> Where mothers pass and stand still in sacrifice,
> There you are, God. The fire burns.
> Whoever professes faith in you,
> Lord God, conquers need.
> Lord, lay your hand over *Volk* and land
> in this war.
> The joyous hour is yet to come;
> Lord God, you give the victory.[46]

Far from abandoning the manly church, German Christians codified it in wartime in a form intended to draw in both men and women. In 1944, in an open letter from the front, the German Christian theologian Walter Grundmann explored the mother/soldier polarity and its relationship to the German Christian vision. For Grundmann, the German Reich was a "parable for the Kingdom of God." The symbols of "faith in the Reich" that he identified echoed the solution to the riddle of the manly church: the merging of the mother and the soldier in sacrifice. "One symbol is the mother with child," Grundmann explained, "the image of burgeoning life that is born out of love. It is precisely we soldiers who do not experience the fighting man as the focal point of life . . . rather the mother with her child. It is she who gives our struggle meaning and content."

Grundmann developed Christian dimensions to his symbolism: "In every mother with her child the madonna is present; she is the rendering into poetry of this scene." For Grundmann it was the notion of sacrifice that linked the manly church of the Reich with the ultimate symbol of Christianity—the cross:

> In the center of the earth stands the cross. It stands on our heroes' graves. . . . [It] is . . . the revelation of the life that sacrifices itself, that even in death and through death is triumphant. Again all of the crosses on all of the graves become poetry in the sacrificial cross of Golgotha, which proclaims to the world the victory of life in a sacrifice that overcomes death. In the future, each German who is born, each marriage that takes place shall know: We thank the sacrifice of our brothers for our lives. That is why the madonna and the cross are the symbols of faith in the Reich! In both images, however, Christianity is submerged in the Reich. . . . The faith in the Reich is the German form of Christianity in the twentieth century.[47]

So the symbols were inverted, the metaphors reversed. For Grundmann, the Christian madonna and the cross became poetic forms of the German mother and the soldier killed in war. In his view, the manly church, a church of and for soldiers, was already there. It was the "faith in the Reich," the "definitive German form of Christianity in the twentieth century." Only in the destructive, brutalizing experience of war could German Christian ecclesiology reach its full realization.

*We confess our guilt before those who, innocent, had to suffer,—before those who, unwarned, trampled God's commandments with perverted will, and before those who today, more than we ourselves, bear the terrible burden of the results of our collective path of error.*
*—Anti-Nazi pastor Hermann Diem, 1946*

*I still believe . . . that everything would have turned out differently if the entire* Volk *had truly stood by the Führer. . . . In our hearts, are we any freer today? Are we today a Christian people?*
*—Eleanor Liebe-Harkort, former German Christian, 1956*

In May 1945, two days after American troops occupied the Bavarian town of Eibach, the leader of the Franconian German Christians met with a local clergyman from the Confessing Church there. Only three years earlier, in 1942, Franconian German Christians had endorsed Bremen bishop Weidemann's establishment of an officially anti-Jewish church, outside the Protestant church of Germany. Now, the German Christian explained, he considered his task ended. He asked that his group be received back into the regional church. He himself planned to enter overseas missions in China.

The Confessing Church pastor assured the German Christian that he and his followers were welcome but asked whether they could accept the authority of a church that recognized the Old Testament as the word of God. The German Christian hastened to deny that he had ever preached dejudaized Christianity. For a long time already, he protested, he had granted the Old Testament prophets a place in his sermons; recently he had introduced the Psalms as well. He had withheld the first five books of the Hebrew Bible from his congregation, he admitted, but read them for his personal edification.

Even as he tried to distance himself from an anti-Jewish position, the Franconian German Christian leader betrayed his inability to conceive of Jews as anything other than the enemies of Christianity. They had "once been the chosen people," he maintained, but with their rejection of Christ had "come under a curse." Vicissitudes of postwar life cut short that man's dubious religious reversal. Less than a month after his attempt to recant, he died suddenly, a victim of tainted canned meat.[1] His departure eased reincorporation of his former flock into the Bavarian Protestant church.

With defeat and collapse of the Nazi regime in 1945, the German Christian movement came to an end.[2] But its members and their ideas did not simply disappear. In some cases, as the story of the Franconian leader might suggest, the past seemed conveniently to dissolve into irrelevance. German Christians and others in the church encouraged that view, anxious to avoid attention and recrimination. On closer reading, however, even the brief account from Eibach reveals significant ways that the German Christian legacy persisted. Most members desired and achieved full reintegration into the German Protestant community. With them they brought ideas and habits of thought from their German Christian past.

This concluding chapter examines the postwar fate of the German Christians by addressing four questions. What part did the movement and its adherents play in the denazification of the Protestant church? How did German Christians justify or rationalize their attitudes and behavior when called upon publicly to do so? What were their private responses? And finally, are there ways in which German Christian ideas lingered on into the postwar period? Answers to these questions reveal significant change but exhibit some important continuities as well. For the German Protestant church and former German Christians, 1945 brought much that was new. But it was no zero hour.

## The German Christians as Alibi

The job of rebuilding the Protestant church after the war ended fell to the German Christians' former opponents: neutral and Confessing Church clergy. They faced two major challenges. First, they had to prove the church's value to a defeated and disillusioned German populace. That task necessitated a rapid return to business as usual, with a minimum of disruption. Second, to achieve credibility in the eyes of occupying authorities, they needed to establish the church's credentials as an opponent of National Socialism. Efforts to please either one of those audiences tended to alienate the other.

At the local level, pastors and their flocks showed little interest in obstructing German Christian desires to rejoin the Protestant mainstream. Preoccupied with efforts to restore normalcy in the postwar confusion, most of them preferred to close the book on old church political struggles. Any investigation of church members' activities and attitudes during the previous twelve years was also likely to reveal German Christian propensities on the part of individuals who had never formally joined the movement. And no one seemed enthusiastic about instituting some test of orthodoxy to determine, as one pastor put it, "who still had a Christian basis of faith at all among those who wanted to come back to the church."[3]

At the national level, the Protestant church faced pressures in the opposite direction. American occupation authorities in particular urged the church to purge its leadership or risk imposed denazification.[4] They were especially interested in action against German Christian clergy, and members of the movement complained bitterly of victimization. According to Walter Fiebig, former German Christian leader in Westphalia, the British military government showed much more lenience, even permitting German Christians to hold public lectures as long as they were not political.[5] Prominent churchmen—Martin Niemöller, Bishops Meiser and Wurm in Bavaria and Württemberg—argued that secular powers had no business determining who was or was not fit to serve the church. That decision, they insisted, had to be based on loyalty to Scripture and the confession of faith.[6] Their efforts paid off; autonomous church boards won control of denazification of the clergy. But the problem of balancing internal and external demands remained.

For the German Protestant church, the Stuttgart Declaration of Guilt of October 1945 constituted an important step toward regaining international credibility. That statement, signed by church leaders on behalf of German Protestantism, acknowledged a "great solidarity of guilt" between the Protestant church and the German people. At the same time, it reminded its audience that the church had "struggled for many years" against the "National Socialist regime of violence." It expressed repentance "for not witnessing more courageously, for not praying more faithfully, for not believing more joyously, and for not loving more ardently."[7] Yet while the Stuttgart Declaration bought goodwill abroad, it alienated some of the clientele at home. Even though it avoided any reference to specific crimes, it sparked resentment from many Protestants who denounced it as an admission of "war guilt" tantamount to a "second Versailles."[8]

In this context, the German Christians provided an ideal target for ecclesiastical denazification efforts. Thanks to foreign press coverage of the church struggle, they were notorious outside Germany as the Nazi Protestants par excellence. The American Occupation Forces' questionnaire even identified their movement specifically as a Nazi organization.[9] Censure of the German Christians seemed likely to satisfy occupation authorities as an adequate expression of denazifying zeal. At the same time, focus on the movement promised not to disturb most Protestants. In the summer of 1945, a former German Christian estimated that the movement had about fifty thousand adherents in Bavaria and eight thousand in Baden.[10] Clergy made up only a small percentage of those totals. Once identified as the sole Protestant collaborators, a few German Christian pastors could be removed from their positions and the rest of the church could consider its hands clean. In that way, the torturous prospect of denazifying the church could be recast as the much simpler task of "de-German-Christianizing" the clergy. The stakes were high; the war had enhanced the prestige of the Protestant church, and American military occupation authorities' recognition of the Confessing Church as a resistance organization further increased its status.[11] By limiting public disclosure of Protestant collusion in Nazism to the German Christian movement, church leaders hoped to preserve that sheen. Few people were likely to complain about denazification that targeted German Christian clergy. Who wanted to be reminded that lay people too had helped muster Protestant energies in the service of Nazism? Who would choose to recall that many non–German Christian pastors had joined the Nazi party, praised Hitler from the pulpit, and contributed to the appearance of legitimacy on which the regime had depended? Only German Christians themselves were likely to protest that their opinions had been common currency in Protestant circles.

Accordingly, efforts to denazify the Protestant church zeroed in on the German Christian movement. In September 1945, church leaders from Westphalia and the Rhine Province passed a regulation to discipline clergy compromised by Nazism. They set up a committee to hear cases of pastors who had shown themselves unworthy of their calling or violated Scripture and the confession of the faith.[12] But no general investigation of orthodoxy followed. Instead, the committee summoned only German Christian pastors for hearings. Attempts to address Nazi influence among lay church members targeted German Christians as well. In November 1945, the Westphalian German Christian Fiebig complained that the synodal administration in Münster had dismissed from office those members of church representative bodies who had been German Christians.[13] No one asked whether other presbyters had been Nazis.

Church authorities pointed to measures taken against the German Christian movement to prove that denazification was complete and further purges unnecessary. In May 1946, Protestant spokesmen in Württemberg announced that they had already removed Nazi elements from their ranks during the war and therefore saw no need for additional denazification. As evidence, they pointed to actions against German Christians. On grounds of "Nazi ideology," they claimed, the Württemberg church had dismissed several consistory councillors, seventy pastors, and almost eight hundred parish representatives.[14] In 1937, it had even denied validity to baptisms performed by the People's Church Movement of German Christians (Volkskirchenbewegung DC).[15]

In late 1947, the central office of the Protestant church in Germany declared the German Christian threat eradicated. Even in Thuringia, the statement announced, once a stronghold of the movement, the new regional church organization had cleansed its jurisdiction of "German Christian heresies" and removed "all German Christians of the National Church Union" from pastoral office. In Saxony, another former German Christian bastion, the proclamation observed, the movement was defunct as well, and the church government in Magdeburg had "spiritually subdued" German Christian leaders through theological retreats and individual hearings. With the disappearance of the German Christian movement, the report implied, denazification of the Protestant church was now complete.[16]

Some observers regarded the postwar focus on the German Christian movement as a smoke screen. In October 1945, the German Christian pastor Friedrich Buschtöns protested that the regulation to cleanse the church in Westphalia and the Rhineland aimed not at denazification but at removal of German Christians. "Why does the 'regulation' not mention *party membership?*," he wanted to know. Why did it not "raise the question about special *political* engagement to the benefit of the party?" And most important, Buschtöns insisted, "Why were questionnaires about membership in the party and its organizations not sent to *all* pastors in Westphalia, for example, with the embarrassing questions: who had been contact men of the Security Service, who had dedicated party flags, held speeches at party events, and baptized under the war flag?" Buschtöns, who had never joined the Nazi party, called the postwar measures against the German Christians a "political alibi."[17]

The theologian Hermann Diem, an outspoken opponent of National Socialism, had occupied a position at the opposite end of the church struggle from Buschtöns. But he too saw ways in which exclusive focus on the German Christians made a sham of ecclesiastical denazification.[18] Diem called Württemberg church leaders to task for misrepresenting the past with their assertion that they had already purged the ranks. Many of the pastors the church claimed it had dismissed had left voluntarily, he pointed out, or had been removed for disciplinary problems unrelated to the church struggle. Still others had been redeployed as teachers of religion, hardly a harmless position. Church officials were equally fraudulent, Diem maintained, in trying to present their dismissal of eight hundred parish representatives as evidence of an anti-Nazi purge. It was Nazi authorities, he reminded his readers, not the Protestant church, who had forced party members to surrender their church offices.[19]

In Diem's view, genuine denazification had to go beyond German Christian ranks. All pastors who had supported National Socialism were guilty of misleading their congregations, he charged, even if they had later reversed that position. Although Diem echoed some sense of the injustice that Buschtöns expressed, the two men's motivations differed entirely. Buschtöns hoped to blackmail Protestant authorities into more forbearance toward former German Christians by reminding them of the glass house from which they threw their stones. Diem sought an authentic new beginning in the Protestant church based on honest acknowledgment of guilt. Buschtöns, a pugnacious German Christian, stood alone. But Diem, whose record as an opponent of National Socialism was spotless, found just as little support.[20]

In April 1946, Diem and four others signed the "Declaration of the Church-Theological Society in Württemberg." That statement stood in contrast to the cautious denazification efforts of the official Protestant church. It began with an explicit confession of guilt, which pointed specifically to the church's failure with regard to Jews and non-Aryans. "We stood back in a cowardly, inactive way as the members of the people of Israel among us were dishonored, robbed, tormented, and killed," Diem wrote. "We allowed fellow Christians, who physically descended from Israel, to be excluded from church offices; indeed, the church even refused baptism to converts from Judaism." Diem pointed to specific, painful failings: "We did not speak out against the prohibition of the mission to the Jews. We did not defend against militaristic falsification of love of the fatherland. Indirectly we aided the racist conceit by preparing countless certificates of Aryan ancestry. In doing so, we injured the preaching of the good news of the gospel for the entire world."[21] Cursory denazification that targeted a few German Christian clergy was an easy way out for the Protestant church. But Diem's statement bears witness to the fact that it was not the only alternative.

## The People's Church as Rationalization

Protestant denazification efforts targeted the German Christian movement as if it had been the only repository of Nazism in the church. Church authorities showed less stringency, however, in dealing with individual members. Lay adherents encountered few barriers to reintegration. And despite some initial disciplinary actions, generally complete with pensions for those removed from their posts,[22] by 1949, almost all German Christian clergy had reentered the service of the church or were in the process of doing so.[23] When German Christians sought to defend themselves in public or justify their beliefs and behavior during the Nazi years, they found that some of the very arguments they had posited in support of their people's church served as effective postwar rationalizations.

In the Third Reich, German Christians had rationalized the dejudaization of Christianity by pointing to their desire to build a church that met the needs of the *Volk*. After the war, they returned to that same line of argumentation to justify their involvement in the cause. In a 1954 account, a retired German Christian pastor from Hanover reduced the movement's entire anti-Jewish program to a quest for viable Christianity. "The German Christians," he wrote, "reached down to roots in the deepest longing of the Western, Germanic circle of life, for a Christian piety that was genuine and that was their own. When the Apostle, in reference to his preaching said: 'to the Jew a Jew, to the Greek a Greek,' in the same way they believed they were able to demand rightly 'to the Germans a German.' "[24]

In the 1970s, another sympathizer of the movement described its revised liturgy, hymns, and scriptures as its greatest achievement, with no reference to the murderous antisemitism that had motivated and accompanied those innovations. Echoing the vocabulary of the 1930s and 1940s, he decried the continued use of the "language of Canaan" in the church. It had been the "passionate goal" of German Christians, he declared, to get rid of "incomprehensible expressions" like "Hallelujah," "Hosanna," and "Jehovah." By refusing to acknowledge any link between German Christian anti-Jewishness and Nazi antisemitism, that commentator was able to present the movement's work as nothing but a natural, necessary update of the language of Christianity. The church has always had to adapt its preaching, he argued, pointing to the example of "the mission to the Eskimo." Eskimos, he explained, could not understand the term "lamb of God." Missionaries substituted the "seal of God," an ethnic adaptation tantamount to "Greenlander Christianity."[25] German Christianity, he concluded, had been no different.

During the twelve years of Nazi rule, German Christians had worked to transform Christian symbols and rituals into weapons in the assault on Jews and Judaism. After the war, they pointed to their retention of those same cultural artifacts as proof that they had resisted nazification. In August 1945, a German Christian pastor emphasized in his statement to the ecclesiastical hearings board at Bethel that he had never used anything but the Westphalian hymnal.[26] With that trite remark he intended to demonstrate that he had not partaken in German Christian anti-Jewish excesses. Congregants of another German Christian pastor, in Schwelm (Westphalia), wrote twenty-two letters of support to the denazification tribunal, pointing out that he had held to Scripture and used both the Old and New Testaments for his sermons.[27] They did not disclose what he actually had said about those biblical texts. A third pastor admitted to his denazification board that he had replaced the "Hallelujah" in the liturgy with "Amen" because he "could not find a German text that also fit the melody of 'Hallelujah.'" But, he insisted, he had effected such an alteration solely to avoid attacks from "antichurch propaganda."[28]

Emphasis on the cultural rather than doctrinal or ethical dimensions of Christianity tended to fit the needs of the postwar Protestant church as a whole. As church authorities sought to assert moral authority, they tried to downplay Christian complicity in Nazi crimes.[29] As a result, accusations against those who had pushed anti-Jewish Christianity tended to address symbolic acts and violations of church custom instead of addressing directly the ways pastors had contributed to antisemitism and legitimized genocide. An example is the case of a Rhenish German Christian called to task, not for preaching the anti-Jewish church but for removing the name "Yahweh" from the church seal.[30]

Until the spring of 1945, German Christians had preached the antidoctrinal people's church. After the war, that antidoctrinal stance served both to discredit the movement as a whole and to help rehabilitate individual members. Through its aggressive repudiation of right belief, German Christianity had created a space for a multitude of offensive and outrageous views; the movement as a whole could be implicated in each of those heresies. But when it came to the fate of individuals, the movement's doctrinal nihilism eased reintegration of adherents, most significantly clergy, into the life and service of the church. After all, they had joined a group that not only refused to endorse specific religious beliefs but denied that right belief played any role in the church. Thanks to that antidoctrinal stance, each former German Christian who faced a church board of inquiry had to justify only his own comportment. Demonstration of isolated incidents of orthodoxy often sufficed.

Former members emphasized diversity within the movement to counter charges that involvement implicated them in heresy. The vast majority of German Christians, Bruno Adler, the former bishop of Westphalia, contended in 1949, had been "neither un-Christian" nor "anti-Christian." Membership in the group had been purely a matter of church politics, he maintained. "Persecution" of German Christians, Adler concluded, was "a matter of reprisals, not an issue of the purity of doctrine."[31] German Christians could not have been heretics, another former member wrote after the war, because their "first and only concern at the time lay totally outside questions of 'doctrine and confession.'" They had been "*exclusively* interested" in the "arousal of an active people's church," he declared, "that would not be laden with any rigid dogmas."[32]

German Christians fell back on familiar sources of unity to reestablish themselves in the postwar church. The former German Christian bishop Staedel offered ethnic identity as evidence of Christian orthodoxy. The "*genuine concern*" of the "best German Christians," he contended, had been to prevent alienation of the Protestant church from a "great movement of the *Volk*." How, he asked, could anyone label the Saxon Germans of Transylvania heretics when they merely followed "the tendencies of their forefathers" in longing for a "church of God of the German nation?"[33] A military chaplain reported that in an American prisoner of war camp in Colorado, German clergy built a community. "We were together in harmony," he wrote, "a German Christian bishop, a Baptist preacher, a Reformed churchwarden and elder."[34] In that setting, reintegration of the German Christian was eased as belief retreated in importance behind national fellowship.

Throughout the Nazi years, German Christians had eschewed discussion of theological matters as useless and divisive. Later their very silence on doctrinal issues helped counter accusations of false belief. In late 1945, Superintendent Clarenbach of Westphalia, a neutral, testified on behalf of a German Christian in his jurisdiction. That pastor, Clarenbach observed, possessed a "manly, aggressive attitude." His activities had engendered a "number of conflicts regarding the worship services, ringing of church bells, payment of salaries, and so on." As far as Clarenbach could recall, however, the many complaints had not been about the pastor's teachings but about the "aforementioned external things." Clarenbach accordingly withheld judgment on the orthodoxy of that pastor's religious beliefs, recommending that he be transferred but not dismissed. "In these times," he maintained, the church could not do without "upright men," especially those who possessed "special talents to preach the Lord Jesus to people estranged from the church."[35]

In early 1946, the Westphalian German Christian Buschtöns predicted that the movement's antidoctrinal stance would produce a wave of reversals. In denazification hearings, he feared, the young German Christians especially would "talk nonsense."[36] Buschtöns was right. Many former German Christian clergy quickly abandoned the old party line, "begging and whimpering," as he put it, for readmittance into church jobs. In Westphalia, Buschtöns lamented, a number of former adherents had "lowered the flag"; in the Rhineland only one clergyman he knew of had defended himself.[37] By 1950, Buschtöns noted that almost all former German Christian clergy had chosen the path of retreat. "It is eternally regrettable," he wrote, "and it shows how little they knew about what the real issue was when they became German Christians."[38]

Indeed, those German Christians who had most thoroughly internalized the antidoctrinal stance found it easiest to adapt to postwar demands. In 1947, the church hearings board in Bethel (Westphalia) was stymied by the inability of a former German Christian pastor to grasp basic theological distinctions. The pastor, the committee's decision stated, evidently lacked "a genuine insight into the heresy of the German Christians and a real understanding for the message of the Confessing Church." He had expressed his willingness to serve a church "that is oriented to the Barmen theological declaration," the decision continued, "but he does not recognize that this would entail a fundamental reversal from his old ways."[39] Even the former "spiritual leader" of German Christians in Westphalia, Fiebig, maintained there had been only a relative difference between the Confessing Church and the German Christians; to the former he conceded a "prophetic task," to the latter, one of "pastoral care and outreach to the *Volk*."[40]

German Christians like Buschtöns, Staedel, and Heinrich Meyer, who had turned their German Christian views into rigid doctrines, found it much more difficult to seek reintegration on any terms but their own. Meyer, German Christian pastor and leader of the Reformed church in Aurich, had been involved in efforts to organize National Socialist clergy in the Hanover area since as early as 1931.[41] More than twenty years later, in 1953, he announced that he was not prepared to issue a "one-sided and insecure declaration of guilt."[42] Buschtöns boasted that he had continued to "go his way without compromise."[43] Staedel had "serious misgivings" about reentering the service of the church. For example, he would want to know before accepting a position whether it was necessary to pray the Lord's Prayer and recite the Apostles' Creed.[44] These men posed a different threat to the church than did their more thoroughly antidoctrinal, and therefore malleable, German Christian colleagues. As one witness testified: "The others were not so much teachers of false doctrine as no teachers at all."[45]

Like the German Christians' antidoctrinal stance, the notion of the manly church survived the debacle of defeat and collapse to reappear as a rationalization in the postwar period. In this case, too, the old German Christian ideas helped stigmatize the movement as a whole while exonerating individual members. Perhaps the movement had gone too far in promoting an aggressive manliness, the former German Christian bishop of Westphalia conceded in 1954. But such excesses, Adler contended, demonstrated devotion to the people's church. The movement's only crime, he insisted, had been to incorporate into its ritual a "storm trooper tone" and a style of celebration that "did not reflect the church 'space' and church 'customs.'"[46] By emphasizing the manly nature of German Christianity, Adler managed to portray individual German Christians not as heretics or Nazi collaborators but at worst as violators of a Christian aesthetic.

After the war, some German Christians found refuge in the very image of neutral, passive femininity that they had combated in their movement. German Christian women were the main beneficiaries of this stereotype. There is no evidence to suggest that women in positions of leadership within German Christian ranks underwent hearings at the hands of the church authorities. No doubt some individuals encountered problems within their communities, like the wife of a German Christian pastor who came under criticism for her role as leader of the local women's organization.[47] But she was not called to public account.

In fact, the most prominent female German Christian, Guida Diehl, reestablished her New Land League, first in Thuringia, and subsequently, with the support of none other than Martin Niemöller, in Hesse. While some of her male counterparts were censured, Diehl propagated her unreconstructed ideas under the sponsorship of the man who had headed the Confessing Church.[48] Willingness to excuse German Christian women seems to have extended to men who worked primarily with women's groups as well. Niemöller also reemployed Pastor Hans Hermenau, the

German Christian who had led the Women's Service under Reich Bishop Müller.[49] In 1960, Hermenau intimated to the circle of former German Christians in Minden that his views had not changed but said he owed self-restraint in church affairs to his mentor Niemöller, who had treated him "fairly" and "kindly" despite their "different outlooks."[50]

In postwar retrospect, one widow attributed her support of the German Christian movement solely to her husband. If not for him, she suggested, she likely would have "ended up with the Confessing Church (like most 'educated people') perhaps even in the political resistance."[51] Freed from old habits of thought by her husband's death, by 1960, that particular German Christian wife had articulated an independent position. It had become clear to her, she wrote, that the German Christian ideals, pure as they may have seemed at the time, were illusions, branded as such by "euthanasia, concentration camps, persecutions of Jews." She no longer believed Hitler had been a Christian, she admitted, and could not "represent the old position publicly." In fact, she confessed, she had been wrong. "I find now that my naïveté at the time, my ignorance, my trust that was too open . . . bear a certain guilt." This woman's candid confession stands out as exceptional in postwar German Christian correspondence. But she too retreated to the protection of women's private sphere. "I am of the opinion," she wrote, "that one should deal with this guilt with God, and not somehow confess it publicly, like the church did after 1945." For her, she concluded, nothing remained but "silence."[52] Like her earlier, womanly involvement in the German Christian movement, her renunciation of its ideas was practically invisible.

Statements by former German Christians after 1945 often referred to the movement's outreach to men as the core of its program and used that aspect of the manly church slogan to justify their own involvement. In his postwar account, former bishop Staedel described the revival represented by the German Christians as an outreach to the people, but especially to the "new men" of the National Socialist era. "The German Christian goal was to seek out the German people and especially the German men there where they stood, marched, and fought," Staedel wrote, "in order to make a great breakthrough with the message of good news and offer them a homeland of the heart."[53] Another after-the-fact account decried the movement's failure to attract men to the church but echoed the view that somehow that task had been the essence of German Christianity. "Seen as a whole, our work was in vain," that man lamented. "Precisely the internally most valuable goal was not achieved: the *völkisch*-oriented world of men, largely due to the Party and to the Confessing Church . . . ended up exactly where we did not want it to be." Still today, he wrote in 1954, "this group is innerly cold toward the church and for the most part toward Christianity as well."[54]

German Christians had not been alone in their concern to bring the men into the church. But as some postwar observers noted, they had gone farther than their rivals. In a 1949 conversation, the chair of the Braunschweig denazification committee noted that many members of the movement "claim that they only altered their message for reasons having to do with their attempt to bring the church to all the people. But it then has to be investigated whether something of the 'substance' was sacrificed in this process." At this point, he suggested, the Confessing Church and the German Christians parted ways: "They too, the Confessing Church people, no doubt saw that the churches were empty, and that for the most part only a few little old grandmothers were coming. The Confessing Church people too, would have wished that the youth and the broad masses would find their way back to the church. But they did not wish so 'at any price.'"[55]

## Amnesia, Defiance, Repentance

The Protestant church used the German Christian movement to avoid thorough denazification; German Christians used the image of the people's church to deflect charges of heresy or complicity in Nazi crimes. But how did former members of the group themselves come to terms with their involvement in the movement? It is difficult to answer this question on the basis of scattered archival records. Existing evidence indicates a spectrum of responses—forgetting or revising the past, clinging defiantly to German Christian ideas, recanting halfheartedly. All of those possibilities reveal a sobering degree of continuity and reflect the acute challenge of genuine contrition.

The German Christian movement's frenzied activities up until collapse of the Third Reich stand in stark contrast to members' postwar silence. Most of them showed particular reticence about the very issues that had been at the heart of their agenda: their stance on Judaism, Jews, and non-Aryan Christians. It was as if they had forgotten their efforts to purge Jewish elements from Christianity, as if they had never read, heard, or uttered the scathing denunciations of Jews and Judaism that had made up the core of their agitation. In December 1945, a former German Christian pastor penned the following pious remarks: "The entire Old Testament is full of 'German Christianity,' that is, full of that which I have always considered the greatest goal of the German Christians: an intimate bond of the people ... with religious faith, a bond to which the Jewish people owes its power into the present day. I see the peak of this development in the Old Testament prophets."[56] To believe that individual, Jews had come full circle, from pariah to paragon. But even that conciliatory effort echoed German Christian praise of the Old Testament prophets as leaders and legitimizers of antisemitism. After the demise of National Socialism, German Christians did not necessarily abandon their old ideas, but they restated those notions in the forms of self-justification and denial.

Some former adherents of the movement declared complete ignorance of Nazi crimes or German Christian collaboration. Guida Diehl, in memoirs she wrote in the 1950s, described aggression against Jews as an inexplicable quirk of Hitler's; it was Hitler's "divided soul," she claimed, that deemed Jews "rabble of the lowest sort," forced them to emigrate, and aimed to eradicate them. But, she claimed, the public did not learn of such things. Diehl described the Kristallnacht pogrom of 9 November 1938 as "the blackest day in the history of National Socialism." She was in Frankfurt/Main at the time, where she claimed to have "good acquaintances" among the Jews, "even friends among the half-Jews." On that day, she asserted, she did not see "one single face in Frankfurt that approved of this cruel corruption."[57] Not only did Diehl deny any knowledge of the implications of National Socialism for Jews, she failed to remember that at least since the 1920s, she herself had been an active proponent of dejudaized and anti-Jewish Christianity.

For some of Diehl's counterparts, denial took more blatant forms, as they refused even to pretend to abandon German Christian ideas. One German Christian broke the religious "truce" established among the Germans in a prisoner of war camp by giving a lecture attacking the "calcified, medieval dogmas of the church."[58] In 1948, a Ludwigsburg man complained about a pastor who had once "preached the ideas of Rosenberg and the party with fiery zeal and rejected Christ as a Jew." Now, unharmed by denazification measures, he was again stirring up those ideas among church groups.[59] A clergyman from the Rhineland admitted to a denazification tribunal that he had been a committed antisemite before National Socialism and remained so after its collapse. He claimed always to have held "to the word of Jesus" in his preaching and defended his stance by referring to Luther's hostility toward Jews. He skirted the question of the Old Testament. The board then produced an antisemitic poem he had written in 1937 for the birth announcement of his daughter. When asked if he had not, with such sentiments, entered the ranks of those guilty of murdering millions of Jews, he dismissed the poem as a "harmless private joke."[60]

*"Mother Guida" Diehl, founder of the nationalist, Protestant New Land League and an early supporter of both National Socialism and the German Christian movement. An influential women's leader, Diehl promoted religious revival and national strength, continuing her work in the postwar period with the support of Martin Niemöller. (Courtesy of Brunnen Verlag)*

Self-interest ensured that German Christians who took such a public stand after 1945 were exceptions rather than the rule. But in more private contexts, many expressed defiance of developments that had discredited their movement. In 1953, Buschtöns denounced denazification efforts, especially those in the church, with the words, "and if the Nazis burned the Jews, so the others have not shown any less hatefulness."[61] Even a former German Christian who was critical of the movement after 1945 complained about "Catholicizing and Judaizing tendencies" in the postwar German church.[62]

In at least some cases, German Christians developed defiance to the point of denying that the Holocaust had occurred. Despite their own eager participation in efforts to expunge Jewish influences from Christianity, after the war, leading Westphalian German Christians Fiebig and Buschtöns resisted suggestions of Christian complicity in assault on the Jews and agreed that they had not even known of the concentration camps.[63] Buschtöns discounted the murder of the Jews as a rumor, one more indication of the "injustice" Germans now suffered. Early in 1958, Staedel, the former bishop of the German Protestant church in Romania, showed how he had processed his anti-Jewishness into an anti-Holocaust position. Staedel took issue with remarks that the theologian Karl Heim had made on the "Hitler era." He attacked Heim's reference to the murder of six million Jews, "as if it had to do with firmly established facts—especially with regard to the high number of victims cited." Citing revisionist literature from France and the United States, Staedel labeled such statistics "conscious exaggerations from enemy propaganda."[64] Moreover, he fulminated, it was unbearable "to watch how our former enemies tried, and continued to try, to magnify and coarsen 'German crimes' beyond all measure, while silencing or explaining as necessities of war their own actions (terror bombing, Dresden!—expulsion from the homeland, cruelty toward the Germans who became fair game after the collapse)."[65]

For twelve years, German Christians had dreamed of delivering to triumphant National Socialism a version of Christianity from which all vestiges of Judaism had been excised; they had offered the anti-Jewish people's church as an ally in the war against Jews and Judaism. Even after collapse of the Third Reich, they refused to recognize the magnitude of the destruction they had attempted and the atrocity of the anti-Jewish assault to which they had pledged their support.

Most German Christians opted for silence or some form of repentance rather than open defiance. Often their apologias reveal the intense difficulties surrounding denazification efforts. In 1947, the maverick German

Christian Heinz Weidemann, former bishop of Bremen, came before a denazification tribunal. He had gained notoriety in certain Protestant circles for his anti-Jewish version of the Gospel of John, his hymnbooks, and his plans to christen two new church buildings the Horst Wessel and von Hindenburg churches. Weidemann appeared before a secular not an ecclesiastical board whose members had little familiarity with developments in German Protestantism. In that initial hearing, by pointing to his engagement in church affairs and his repeated conflicts with National Socialist authorities, Weidemann managed to convince his judges that he had not been a collaborator but a victim of Nazi persecution.[66]

Like Weidemann, some other German Christians found they could present the very evidence of their crimes as proof of their innocence. After the war, at least one German Christian offered as evidence of his resistance to Nazism the fact that he had defended the right of the African pastor Kwami to speak in Oldenburg.[67] At the time, German Christians had promoted Kwami's appearance in an attempt to build support for the idea of racially specific Christianity. In 1953, a former German Christian seeking a church post boasted that the denazification commission of West Berlin had rehabilitated him. He possessed a certificate from the Protestant Consistory testifying that through his "efforts for positive Christianity and for a just treatment of the Jews," he had been active as an "antifascist," ejected from the Nazi party, and called to account by the Gestapo.[68] Eleven years earlier that same man had sought to extricate himself from the very party criticism he later presented as evidence of resistance by sending Nazi authorities a copy of an anti-Jewish confirmation sermon he had delivered.[69]

Some German Christian apologias reveal how deeply entrenched their ideas remained. One of the most explicit recantations came from Siegfried Leffler, former leader of Thuringian German Christians and director of the Institute for Research into and Elimination of Jewish Influence in German Church Life. In 1947, Leffler, incarcerated in Ludwigsburg (Württemberg), performed public penance in a widely circulated letter. He had sincerely believed in a "synthesis between National Socialism and Christianity," he professed, but the quest for it became "an ominously false path." Since soon after the war began, he claimed, he had been "haunted" by guilt that his actions and words, as well as those of his friends, had "harmed" the "Christian church, and the German as well as the Jewish people."[70]

Leffler's letter was unique in its public renunciation of the German Christian agenda. But the subtext of his mea culpa expressed an adamant refusal to accept responsibility for the implications of German Christianity and its anti-Jewish teachings. It was not the case, Leffler insisted, that he had "personally hated or stirred up hatred!" In his view, the blame for atrocities lay elsewhere. "Everyone who knows and knew me, knows that I have always stood for genuine tolerance and reconciliation and personally have never denied any human being in need, whether a German or a Jew."[71] Leffler's efforts paid off; Protestant publications, like the congregational bulletin for Augsburg and area, printed his letter with sympathetic commentary.[72] By 1949, he was back in the service of the church.[73]

As they tried to retain or regain church posts, German Christian clergy dredged their memories for evidence of compassion they had shown Jews. Such attempts too tend to highlight the extent to which individual German Christians had internalized racialist thinking. Lübeck bishop Balzer, for example, explained that he had joined the Nazi party because he thought it would bring about a "genuine community of the German *Volk*." In this goal, he claimed, he did not see a "negative" attack on specific people, "like the Jewish group," but rather a "positive" will to "protect and consciously preserve German ethnicity." He recalled that once he had officiated at a church service in the Berlin mission to the Jews, and later, while pastor on Helgoland, "despite some misgivings," had performed the burial ceremony for an individual "of the Jewish race." To support his representation of that deed toward a fellow Christian as an act of resistance, Balzer indicated that he had already joined the party by that time.[74]

In July 1948, a former leading German Christian wrote to church authorities requesting employment in the church. To document his tolerance toward Jews, that man told of an encounter with a non-Aryan pastor. He described how he had tried to comfort that individual in the face of his "difficult situation in the Third Reich." The non-Aryan had rebuffed his overtures, "on the basis that he was not Jewish." The astonished German Christian informed his colleague that because "he had been baptized into Christianity as a Jewish child," he remained, "purely physically, according to race, Jewish."[75]

Instead of recognizing such notions of the biological immutability of Jewishness as a central assumption of Nazi racial thought, the German Christian displayed continued faith in the rectitude of race as the fundamental spiritual truth. "I . . . tried to encourage him to open up an entirely new kind of large and intensive mission to the Jews. . . . I explained that every person must love his *Volk*, and in someone who had found the savior, that love for the *Volk* must be multiplied many times." The German Christian closed with a rhetorical question that revealed his utter failure to grasp the disastrous implications of anti-Jewish Christianity in the context of a genocidal state. "I ask you, respected Bishop, to consider whether my attitude toward the Jewish problem reflected the spirit of the National Socialist state, or whether this equally complicated position served the final solution of the Jewish question."[76] Using the very racist ideas he sought to refute, that German Christian offered his own engagement in the anti-Jewish cause as evidence of his compassion for Jews.

## Continuity

Not surprisingly, some German Christian ideas carried over into the postwar church. Their views had originated in the society around them in the first place, and, after defeat of Nazi Germany, many of them folded back in with barely a ripple. Of all the dimensions of their program, it was issues of gender that had attracted least attention and criticism. Accordingly, after the war, German Christians experienced no need to revise their thinking on that score. The cult of motherhood they had propagated in the Nazi era remained a common motif in postwar church literature, and former German Christians helped perpetuate it. In her 1959 autobiography, Guida Diehl reduced the Nazi years to a few pages and emphasized her conflicts with state, party, and German Christian authorities, most of them related to the fact she had opposed SS promotion of childbearing out of wedlock. In summing up the significance of her life and struggle, Diehl reached for the familiar rhetoric of motherhood. "It is a difficult and weighty task," she wrote, "to be a soldier of Christ." For women, she continued, that duty "has to be complemented by service out of maternal love." "The most beautiful and profound aspect of my life's work," she concluded, "is that I was able to be Mother for so many."[77] That Diehl had used her maternal authority to promote the Nazi cause did not disturb her; to her, the motherly role existed outside moral scrutiny.

Wolf Meyer-Erlach, a strident German Christian who had been prominent in the Institute for Research into and Elimination of Jewish Influence in German Church Life, made his postwar reappearance in public life as a proponent of the cult of motherhood as well. In 1962, Meyer-Erlach published an article in the *Idsteiner Zeitung* called "For Mother's Day" (*Zum Muttertag*). "Nothing," he effused in that sentimental piece, "can replace the love of a loyal mother, a loyal grandmother."[78] In the postwar climate, Meyer-Erlach could no longer publish the kind of anti-African, anti-Jewish tirades he had produced in the 1920s, 1930s, and 1940s. But he did not need to adjust anything in his view of motherhood. The 1962 article could have appeared in an identical form twenty years earlier.

With regard to their views on church doctrine, former German Christians found they could blend adaptation to the new circumstances with retention of old habits of thought. Many German Christian clergy discovered that their postwar parishioners shared their hostility or at least indifference toward the concept of right belief. In 1947, one former adherent of the movement wrote proudly from his new pastoral post that he had held three worship services so far, all well received. He had not, he emphasized, altered his message.[79]

In 1948, when church authorities decided to dismiss the Westphalian German Christian Fiebig from his post in Münster, they noted that his congregation supported him, despite the destructive role he had played in the church struggle. As one observer concluded, "We cannot expect that each member of the congregation will be in a situation to judge the theological attitude of the pastor and his activities in church politics."[80] Even a pastoral colleague who testified on Fiebig's behalf expressed doctrinal indifference. That Fiebig's theology did not reflect "all aspects of the confession" had not bothered him, he claimed; Fiebig "had preached the message of Jesus."[81] The former German Christian bishop Walther Schultz, by 1956 ensconced in a church post, wrote that he had settled down "beyond all dogmatism, also that of the German Christian variety," yet remained firm on the course he had always tread.[82] German Christian clergy might not have adapted their beliefs after 1945, but their congregations did not necessarily notice or care.

Antidoctrinal Christianity persisted in even more concrete forms. In September 1946, when an opponent of the postwar Protestant church order set out to find allies, he discovered "here and there" groups of the type he planned to form: the August-Hermann-Francke Circle in Halle, the Provincial Association of Protestant-Lutherans; the League of the Protestant People's church in Berlin and Brandenburg. It was "completely false," he decided, "to assume that political collapse in 1945 also constituted a collapse of the Protestant people's church."[83] According to another former German Christian, 1951 brought a rash of communications, correspondences, meetings, and reunions among old adherents of the movement. All of those initiatives, he claimed, reflected dissatisfaction with the postwar church's emphasis on doctrine, or what he called its "defection from the Lutheran understanding of the 'church' to a pre-Constantinian 'Ghetto-'ideal of the Confessing Church." The German Christians, he contended, had always sought "the people's church, demythologization of the gospel, and Christ alone." In 1951, he argued, those concerns were more vital than ever.[84]

The following year, the People's Church Movement of Free Christians (Volkskirchenbewegung Freie Christen) under Heinz Sting in Hanover advertised two series of publications, both edited by former German Christians. Sting's group also echoed German Christian antagonism to doctrine. It pledged to make the "powers of God" accessible to people of the day, recognizing that those "powers are not limited to one source in the form of a holy book."[85] In March 1959, a publication of the group defined its goal as "creation of a people's church that is in tune with the present, that can fulfill the longing of all who truly seek God." It explicitly rejected "all dogma and all confessions as unnecessary for faith." Its clergy offered to perform baptisms and confirmations, "without implying any obligation to a confessional church or the Bible or a confession of faith."[86]

None of the new antidoctrinal groups was large. By May 1959, the Free Christian People's Church counted thirty-eight pastors, three professors, and seven nontheologians as speakers in its ranks. It printed only four hundred copies of its monthly papers. Between 1949 and 1959, the group centered in Stuttgart performed 312 baptisms, 74 weddings, 862 funerals, 114 confirmations, and 32 silver and golden anniversaries.[87] But the continued existence of such associations more than a decade after the collapse of the Nazi regime, and the number of former German Christians who played a leading role in them, suggests the persistence of an antidoctrinal vision of Christianity.

After 1945, German Christians and their sympathizers could no longer fulminate openly against Jews. But even in this area, the new situation provided its own possibilities for continuity. Cut off from the Nazi context, German Christians could present their anti-Jewish thoughts as harmless theological or pedagogical considerations. In early 1960, a former German Christian described the new schoolbook he was writing for religious instruction and posed a question that plagued him: "How should a religion teacher handle it properly when he has to treat the Old Testament with pupils in the upper classes? Or when it has to be discussed, because someone asks and it is not possible to evade the question?"[88] Another former German Christian, recording his experiences in 1954, admitted that he had accepted the anti-Jewish campaign in the church. Having grown up in Frankfurt/Main, the author explained, a city he called "New Jerusalem," he was "no friend of the Jewish mode of thought." But as a Christian, he added, he "opposed violent measures." Nevertheless, even after the war, he announced, his goal was not to convert anyone to the "God of Jacob," but rather to Christ.[89]

One of the most chilling illustrations of German Christian racial thought years after World War II comes from the former bishop in Romania, Wilhelm Staedel. Staedel's postwar comments on what he called the "race issue" revealed continued endorsement of biological determinism. In a telling sleight of hand, however, he adjusted the old Nazi dichotomy of "Aryan—non-Aryan" to a polarization he expected would find more resonance in the postwar world: "white—nonwhite." "It would have been good for all of us," he contended in 1958, "if the statesmen representing the peoples of the West had taken Hitler's ideas on this question more seriously than they did." To Staedel, it was "an unprecedented tragedy of world history that the white people of the world called forth the two last wars with each other and thereby weakened each other and themselves." Hitler's involvement in the "race question," he theorized, reflected an assumption he presumed his reader shared as well, that, "contrary to the well-known enlightenment idea, and despite a basic similarity of structure, people are not all the same, but are different." Were that the case, he argued, then "preservation of one's own *Volk*, of one's own race," became a "serious duty"; the "mixing of races," in contrast, was to be "checked." To validate his stance, Staedel quoted an African American pastor's remarks to the Stockholm World Conference of Churches in 1925: "Christian powers have helped the Negro to advance and shall continue to do so. *However, we do not want any mixing of the races.* Like the five fingers on the hand, so shall the different races in God's plan remain standing next to one another." Was that so wrong, Staedel asked?

In Staedel's view, National Socialism represented the "fundamental truth" of racial difference. There had been excesses, he admitted, even genocide, but, he parried, "has there been no hatred, no disdain, no oppression, even genocide, toward our people, although our former enemies supposedly entered the fight for the sake of true humanity? Which lofty and great cause ever was and remained free of misuse?!" Staedel closed his diatribe by citing none other than Martin Niemöller, then president of the Protestant church in Germany, on the subject of race: "According to a report of the American newspaper *The Virginian* in October 1957, Niemöller said: 'The crucial issue was not whether the USA or the USSR would win the next war. The big question rather was whether there would still be a white race in thirty or forty years.'"[90]

It is tempting to dismiss Staedel's analysis as the bitter rantings of a disillusioned old man. Yet his comments show how the social construct of race itself provided some German Christians with a vehicle to normalize and legitimize their anti-Jewishness, casting it as part of a cosmic struggle for white, Western, Christian purity. At the same time, Staedel's diatribe suggests how easily old Nazi Christian ways of thinking could blend into revised strands of racism.

## Conclusion

In 1945, the German Christian movement ceased to exist. But its influence, its ideas, and its former members did not simply disappear. Indeed, there are people in Germany today who were baptized, confirmed, or married by German Christian pastors. Whenever I have met such people, I have been taken aback by the way they respond when they discover the subject of my research. Invariably they ask, with a mixture of irony and embarrassment, whether their church membership or marriage vows are in fact valid. Somehow, one legacy of the German Christian movement has been a vague sense of discomfort in the minds of people who themselves may not have endorsed German Christian ideas.

But this half-serious questioning of the German Christians and the authority of the sacraments they administered raises an important question. How could a movement, which now seems so illegitimate, have gained the currency it did and have persisted for so long? The German Christians rose to prominence in the summer of 1933 when they won two-thirds of the votes cast in Protestant church elections in Germany. They managed to weather the storms of late 1933, as the Nazi party withdrew its support and fragmentation beset their movement, as well as to make something of a comeback around the mid-1930s. Despite many obstacles, the war years witnessed intense German Christian activity, as representatives of their group remained in top church positions and their dejudaized hymns even found their way into the hands of Protestant soldiers. After 1945, former German Christians were integrated into the church with little difficulty, and even some of the most prominent spokespeople of the movement discovered they could reenter the service of the church without significantly changing their views.

The German Christian movement persisted, I have suggested, because it was embedded in the culture around it. German Christians did not invent the core ideas of their movement. The ideal of a people's church, Christian anti-Jewishness, racial antisemitism, an antidoctrinal, romantic understanding of religion, glorification of the masculine—those were all familiar themes to Germans of the 1920s and 1930s. German Christians pulled them together into a movement dedicated to creation of a church that would provide spiritual expression to the racially pure nation.

The war and the debacle of the Third Reich discredited some German Christian ideas, particularly their vehement anti-Jewishness. But other aspects of their program, most notably their romanticized notion of church doctrine and gendered vision of the church, flowed easily back into the mainstream of the society around them. And even their ideas about race needed only a little tinkering to make them again appear rather respectable. In some ways, the differences between the German Christians and their fellow Protestants had never been so great after all.

The persistence of the German Christian movement may also reflect a more general crisis of Christianity in modern Germany. The German Christians' retention of certain aspects of Christian practice and tradition meant that the movement appeared both revolutionary and familiar to fellow Protestants. In that way, it offered a welcome compromise for Germans who embraced the new Nazi ideology yet were unwilling to abandon completely their Christian heritage. German Christians jettisoned everything theological and moral about Christianity and reduced it to a handful of cultural symbols and practices from their childhoods. Yet they clung to those with a tenacity that suggested both genuine dedication and profound spiritual confusion.

It would be a mistake, however, to emphasize only the successes of German Christianity. After all, in many ways the movement was a dismal failure. Despite early triumphs and a high profile, it never achieved a membership of more than about six hundred thousand people—not even 2 percent of Germany's Protestant population. The theological and moral bankruptcy of German Christianity was glaringly obvious, not only to Jews, non-Aryans, and sincere Christians, but even to cynics in the neo-pagan camp. With their antisemitic savaging of biblical texts, German Christians elicited only disdain from their Nazi heroes and despair from true Christians. For committed National Socialists, German Christian obsession with preserving vestiges of Christianity revealed a hopeless inability to comprehend the total demands of Nazi ideology and an outdated loyalty to alien authorities. For genuine Christians, German Christian abuse and distortion of Scripture represented heresy of the worst sort.

German Christians, caught between enthusiasm for an all-or-nothing ideology and piety toward their religious heritage, held desperately onto both, struggling to reconcile the two incompatible systems of belief. As a result, they created a cult based on blood membership and dressed it in the ritual clothing of their Christian tradition. One of the few statements from the Apostle Paul that German Christians frequently quoted—in fact, misquoted—was the description of how he adapted to the minds and ways of different peoples, being "to the Greeks a Greek, to the Jews a Jew." Ironically, in the end, the German Christians represented exactly the opposite. To Nazi "true believers," they were never Nazi enough. To Christians, at least to those who took seriously the Gospels' message of universal love, they were virtually unrecognizable as members of the same faith.

# Notes

## Abbreviations

| | |
|---|---|
| AA Bonn | Politisches Archiv des Auswärtigen Amts, Bonn |
| AEKR Düsseldorf | Archiv der Evangelischen Kirche im Rheinland, Düsseldorf |
| BA Koblenz | Bundesarchiv Koblenz |
| BA Potsdam | Bundesarchiv Potsdam (formerly Zentrales Staatsarchiv, Potsdam) |
| BA-MA Freiburg | Bundesarchiv-Militärarchiv, Freiburg im Breisgau |
| BDC | Berlin Document Center |
| BHStA Munich | Bayerisches Hauptstaatsarchiv, München |
| DAF | Deutsche Arbeitsfront Zeitungsausschnitte |
| DC | Deutsche Christen |
| DG | Deutsche Glaubensbewegung |
| EB Bensheim | Evangelischer Bund, Konfessionskundliches Institut, Bensheim |
| EZA Berlin | Evangelisches Zentralarchiv in Berlin |
| KA Lübeck | Nordelbische Evangelisch-Lutherische Kirche, Nordelbisches Kirchenamt, Archiv Lübeck |
| KAG Minden | Kirchengeschichtliche Arbeitsgemeinschaft, Kommunalarchiv Minden |
| LKA Bielefeld | Archiv der Evangelischen Kirche in Westfalen, Bielefeld |
| LKA Nuremberg | Evangelisch-Lutherische Kirche in Bayern, Landeskirchliches Archiv, Nürnberg |
| NL | Nachlaß |
| NSDAP | Nationalsozialistische Deutsche Arbeiterpartei |
| OKH | Oberkommando des Heeres |
| RGBl | Reichsgesetzblatt |
| RLB | Reichlandbund Pressearchiv |
| T-175 | Captured German Documents, National Archives Microfilm Publication, Series T-175, Records of the Reich Leader SS and Chief of German Police |

## Chapter One

1. Bonhoeffer to Erwin Sutz, 18 Apr. 1934, Bonhoeffer, *Gesammelte Schriften*, 1:39–40. All translations from the German are mine unless otherwise noted.

2. The most thorough study of the German Christian organization is Meier, *Die Deutschen Christen*. Meier covers the period up to 1939 but concentrates on the early years. On the war years, see vol. 3 of Meier's *Der Evangelische Kirchenkampf*. Works that address German Christian ideas include Buchheim, *Glaubenskrise im Dritten Reich*; Götte, "Die Propaganda der Glaubensbewegung 'Deutsche Christen'"; Zabel, *Nazism and the Pastors*; and Sonne, *Die politische Theologie der Deutschen Christen*. For regional studies, see Baier, *Die Deutschen Christen Bayerns*; and Heinonen, *Anpassung und Identität*.

3. For example, Johannes Brosseder has analyzed the German Christian movement in terms of accommodation rather than collaboration. See "Kirche für die Menschen," pp. 403–14.

4. In my use of *Protestant* as a translation of *evangelisch*, I follow the English version of Scholder's standard work, *The Churches and the Third Reich*, 1:vii (glossary of terms).

5. Meier provides an overview of the early work of Leffler and Leutheuser and their involvement with the Berlin circle of German Christians in *Die Deutschen Christen*, pp. 1–16.

6. Arnold Dannenmann, an adherent of the German Christian movement, describes the group's naming in his 1933 work, *Kirche im Dritten Reich*, pp. 10, 48. Apparently Dannenmann, later repenting of his German Christian stance, bought all remaining copies of his book and had them destroyed. See Günther Siegel to Wilhelm Niemöller, 31 Mar. 1947, Schwäbisch Gmünd, LKA Bielefeld 5,1/293.

7. See Walter Grundmann, "Ein klarendes Wort der Landesleitung der 'Deutschen Christen in Sachsen' an unsere Kameraden!," in *Deutsche Christen in Sachsen—Aufklärungsblatt Nr. 3* (Dresden, 10 June 1936), pp. 1–3, KAG Minden, folder V.

8. For an outside view of the relationship between the German Christian movement and some predecessor groups, see Chef des Sicherheitsamtes, "Lagebericht, Mai/Juni 1934," T-175/415/2940752. A German Christian view of "Pathfinders and Precursors" is found in Grossmann, *Deutsche Christen*, pp. 17–25.

9. On the church elections, see Conway, *Nazi Persecution of the Churches*, p. 41; Meier, *Der Evangelische Kirchenkampf*, 1:103–9; and Baranowski, "The German Protestant Church Elections."

10. The text of Hitler's radio address before the church election of July 1933 appears in Nicolaisen, *Dokumente zur Kirchenpolitik*, 1:119–22.

11. See pamphlet labeled "GB 148," news item under column "Deutsche Christen," with subheading 18 June, Baden, [1934], p. 233, LKA Bielefeld 5,1/554,2.

12. See circular from German Christian regional office, Dresden, signed Martin Beier, 9 July 1934, "An alle Mitarbeiter der DC!," including a copy of telegram from German Christian Reich Leader Christian Kinder to Hitler, 1 July 1934, referring to six hundred thousand members of his organization "and millions of supporters," LKA Bielefeld 5,1/290,2. That same year, General Superintendent Otto Dibelius in Berlin, an adherent of the Confessing Church and no friend of the German Christians, accepted the figure of five to six hundred thousand as a valid assessment; see "Evangelische Kirche im Kampf unserer Tage. D. Dibelius beendete seine Vortragsreihe über die Germanisierung der Kirche," in *Reichsbote*, 28 Oct. 1934, clipping in BA Potsdam, RLB 1862, p. 31. State offices also accepted the figure of six hundred thousand; see Reichskanzlei, "Vermerk. Betrifft: Fragen der evang. Kirche," initialed by Wienstein, 26 Oct. 1934, p. 2, BA Koblenz R 43 II/163/fiche 2, p. 54.

13. See, for example, "Versuche der 'Deutsche Christen' sich mit dem National Sozialismus zu identifizieren," 1941, in Boberach, *Meldungen aus dem Reich*, 7:2634.

14. See "Personnel Questionnaire" [English-language version], in Friedmann, *Allied Military Government of Germany*, pp. 326–31.

15. See *Evangelisches Feldgesangbuch*, throughout, and comments in Weidemann, "Mein Kampf," p. 7. The "Protestant Soldier's Songbook" is discussed in detail in Chapter 8.

16. Rhodes, *Hitler Movement*; Pois, *National Socialism*, esp. pp. 24–31.

17. Rubenstein, *Cunning of History*, p. 31.

18. As Jonathan Steinberg puts it, "The standard image of Fascism has been sketched for us by secular historians and sociologists." See "The Roman Catholic Church and Genocide in Croatia, 1941–1945," in Wood, *Christianity and Judaism*, p. 464.

19. Katz quoted in Liz McMillen, "The Uniqueness of the Holocaust," *Chronicle of Higher Education*, 22 June 1994, A 13.

20. Donald Niewyk, "Solving the 'Jewish Problem'—Continuity and Change in German Antisemitism, 1871–1945," *Leo Baeck Yearbook* 35 (1990): 369.

21. Baum and Coleman, *The Church and Racism*, p. vii.

22. For some discussion of links between Christian sermons and Nazi antisemitism and genocide, see Bacharach, *Anti-Jewish Prejudices*.

23. Steinberg, "The Roman Catholic Church and Genocide in Croatia, 1941–1945," in Wood, *Christianity and Judaism*, p. 465.

24. Browning, *Ordinary Men*.

25. For a discussion of the historical development of the *Volkskirche*, see Meier, *Volkskirche*, p. 7.

26. For a history of the term *Volkskirche*, see Mahling, *Der Wille zur Volkskirche*, esp. pp. 76–88.

27. On the identity crisis specifically in the Prussian Protestant church after 1918, see Elliger, *Die Evangelische Kirche der Union,* pp. 125–37; Jacke, *Kirche zwischen Monarchie und Republik*; and Borg, *The Old Prussian Church and the Weimar Republic.* On Württemberg in the same period, see Diephouse, *Pastors and Pluralism in Württemberg.* A view across Germany is offered by Dahm, *Pfarrer und Politik*; and Wright, *"Above Parties."*

28. For example, Acts 2:38–47, 1 Cor. 1:2, Eph. 2:11–22 and 4:1–6, and Heb. 10:23–25.

29. For a thoughtful assessment of the concept of the church struggle, see Georg Kretschmar, "Die Auseinandersetzung der Bekennenden Kirche mit den Deutschen Christen," in Rieger and Strauss, *Kirche und Nationalsozialismus,* pp. 117–21. A critical analysis of the use and misuse of the entire notion of the church struggle is reflected throughout Prolingheuer, *Wir sind in die Irre gegangen.*

30. One need only glance at a few titles as an illustration: Hermelink, *Kirche im Kampf*; Zipfel, *Kirchenkampf in Deutschland*; and *Arbeiten zur Geschichte des Kirchenkampfes,* 30 vols.

31. Baumgärtel, *Wider die Kirchenkampf-Legenden.*

32. Conway, *Nazi Persecution of the Churches,* p. xx.

33. On Bonhoeffer and his involvement in the Confessing Church and political resistance, see Bethge, *Dietrich Bonhoeffer.*

34. On Karl Barth's role in the church struggle, see *Karl Barth zum Kirchenkampf*; Moltmann, *Anfänge der dialektischen Theologie*; and Busch, *Karl Barths Lebenslauf.*

35. The overwhelming neutrality of German church people is discussed in numerous places, e.g., Meier, *Volkskirche,* p. 61. Ericksen's *Theologians under Hitler* addresses many of the complex issues surrounding what passed for neutrality in the church struggle.

36. See "Kanzelabkundigung Wilhelm Niemöller in Bielefeld—Jakobuskirche, 2.7.1933," carbon copy of typed paragraph with handwritten label, LKA Bielefeld 5,1/358,2.

37. See material from interviews with Wilhelm Niemöller in Barnett, *For the Soul of the People,* e.g., pp. 41–42, 251.

38. Buschtöns to Karl Wentz, 10 Nov. 1958, 26, 31 Jan. 1959, KAG Minden, file no. 15, Schriftwechsel Prof. Wentz–F. Buschtöns.

39. Bonhoeffer to Sutz, 18 Apr. 1934, Bonhoeffer, *Gesammelte Schriften,* 1:39–40.

40. An overview of these and other *völkisch* groups is available in Cancik, "'Neuheiden' und totaler Staat. Völkische Religion am Ende der Weimarer Republik," in Cancik, *Religions- und Geistesgeschichte,* pp. 176–212.

41. See Dierks, *Jakob Wilhelm Hauer*, for insight into Hauer's education, philosophy, and scholarly activities. His neopagan organization gets surprisingly little attention.

42. "Vermerk," signed Haugg, 18 Jan. 1937, BA Potsdam, DG II, 1936–37, p. 415.

43. Confusion between the German Christians and the German Faith Movement continues today. When I requested files on the German Christian Faith Movement from the staff at the (then) Central State Archive in Potsdam, I also received folders labeled *Deutsche Glaubensbewegung*. That error was in my interest because items on German Christians had been filed with materials from the neopagan group.

44. See Meier, *Die Deutschen Christen*. An example of a successful recent regional study is Lächele, *Ein Volk, ein Reich, ein Glaube*.

45. On this stage of development, see Miller, "National Socialism and the Glaubensbewegung." Also useful is van Norden, *Der deutsche Protestantismus*.

46. On Müller's rise to Reich bishop, see Schneider, *Reichsbischof Ludwig Müller*, esp. pp. 103–52.

47. On Hess's statement and its background, see Scholder, *The Churches and the Third Reich*, 1:572.

48. Krause, *Rede des Gauobmannes der Glaubensbewegung*, pamphlet in LKA Bielefeld 5,1/289,2.

49. One Security Service report claimed 250 pastors quit the movement in Württemberg alone: "Lagebericht Mai/Juni 1934," T-175/415/2940753. The *Allgemeine Evangelisch-Lutherische Kirchenzeitung* maintained that 800 Württemberg pastors withdrew their membership: "Kirchliche Nachrichten—Deutschland," AELKZ (24 Nov. 1933): 1108.

50. See the SS and SD reports: "Lagebericht Mai/Juni 1934," T-175/415/2940752-3; "Sonderbericht: Die Lage in der protestantischen Kirche und in den verschiedenen Sekten und deren staatsfeindlichen Auswirkung," Feb./Mar. 1935, T-175/409/2932647; and "Gegnerbekämpfung," 25 June 1942, T-175/285/2780127.

51. On Hossenfelder, see party records in BDC, Hossenfelder materials. He joined the party in 1929 and held membership number 124881.

52. For Kinder's own account of his disputes with Hossenfelder and his role as German Christian leader, see his memoir, *Neue Beiträge*.

53. See Kessel to Heinrich Stüven, 6 Nov. 1953, Osterode/Harz, pp. 1–2, KAG Minden, file labeled "Freie Volkskirche 2."

54. Wieneke offers a sympathetic outline of some of the difficulties that faced the German Christian movement from late 1933 on in "Zehn Jahre Deutsche Christen," pp. 11–14.

55. On Kerrl and his appointment, see Meier, *Der Evangelische Kirchenkampf*, 2:66–78; and Siegele-Wenschkewitz, *Nationalsozialismus und Kirche*. For an insider's description of the Ministry of Church Affairs and its functions, see Haugg, *Das Reichsministerium*.

56. Typed report, [Wilhelm Niemöller?], "Sitzung mit Herrn Reichsminister Kerrl," 29 Oct. 1935, Münster, LKA Bielefeld 5,1/358,1.

57. Wieneke, "Zehn Jahre Deutsche Christen," p. 15; Meier, *Die Deutschen Christen*, pp. 147–51.

58. See Kessel to Stüven, 6 Nov. 1954, p. 2, KAG Minden, file labeled "Freie Volkskirche 2."

59. On Leffler and Leutheuser, see Scholder, *The Churches and the Third Reich*, 1:esp. pp. 194–95.

60. On the Godesberg Declaration, see Meier, *Deutsche Christen*, pp. 267–78; and Boyen, *Kirchenkampf und Ökumene*, pp. 256–57.

61. Some particularly useful exceptions are Baier, *Kirche in Not*; Meier, *Kirchenkampf*, vol. 3; and Brakelmann, *Kirche im Krieg*.

62. On developments in the Protestant church after collapse of the National Socialist regime, see Boyens, Greschat, von Thadden, and Pombeni, *Kirchen in der Nachkriegszeit*; Besier, *"Selbstreinigung"*; Vollnhalls, *Evangelische Kirche und Entnazifizierung*.

## Chapter Two

1. "Bericht über den Verlauf der am 12. Feb. 1934 im Orpheumssaal, Hasenheide 32–38 . . . Versammlung der 'Deutschen Christen,'" sent from Geheimes Staatspolizei Berlin to Prussian Ministry of Science, Art, and Education, 17 Feb. 1934, pp. 1–2, BA Potsdam DC I, 1933–35, pp. 187–88.

2. Flyer, signed Hossenfelder, *Richtlinien der Glaubensbewegung "Deutsche Christen,"* [1932], LKA Bielefeld 5,1/294,1.

3. Flyer, signed Müller, Hossenfelder, Weichert, *Die neuen Richtlinien der "Deutschen Christen." Wehrkreispfarrer Müller übernimmt die Oberleitung,* 16 May 1933, in *Die Kirchenfrage*, no. 56, *Austauschdienst des Evangelischen Preßverbandes für Deutschland*, Berlin-Steglitz, LKA Bielefeld 5,1/550,1.

4. Flyer, signed Hossenfelder, *Richtlinien der Glaubensbewegung "Deutsche Christen,"* [1932], p. 2, LKA Bielefeld 5,1/294,1.

5. Flyer, *Ist das Führerprinzip in der evangelischen Kirche gegen Gottes Wort? Dr. Martin Luther sagt: Nein!*, [Mar. 1934], LKA Bielefeld 5,1/289,1.

6. "Rundschreiben Nr. 2, Kampf- und Glaubensbewegung 'Deutsche Christen' (Hossenfelder Bewegung)," [1935], pp. 4, 6, EZA Berlin 1/A4/93.

7. Heinrich Detel to Hossenfelder, 16 Sept. 1935, Breslau, BA Potsdam,

DC-I, 1933–35, p. 333. In 1933, Detel was assistant to the state commissioner for the Protestant churches in Silesia.

8. Point 11 in "Die Deutschen Christen in Abwehr und Aufbau. Grundsätzliche Erklärungen zu den kirchlichen Aufgaben unserer Zeit, erarbeitet auf der ersten westfälischen Gautagung in Bochum am 31. März und 1. April 1936," p. 20, KAG Minden, unlabeled black book.

9. Pamphlet, *Eine heilige, allgemeine, christliche Kirche*, Confessing Church material containing documents regarding the Godesberg Declaration, [1939], pp. 2–3, LKA Bielefeld 5,1/293. The eleven regional churches represented by the declaration's signers were Prussia, Saxony, Nassau-Hesse, Schleswig-Holstein, Thuringia, Mecklenburg, Palatinate, Anhalt, Oldenburg, Lübeck, and Austria. An additional nine signatures appeared on the declaration. See Wilhelm Niemöller to Leffler, 28 May 1958, Bielefeld, LKA Bielefeld 5,1/297. After the fact, at least two of the twenty signatories—Walter Fiebig and Gerhard Kittel—denied having actually signed the declaration. See Fiebig to Wentz, 7 Mar. 1946, Münster, p. 2, KAG Minden, file V Fiebig.

10. "Grundsätze für eine den Erfordernissen der Gegenwart entsprechende Neuordnung der Deutschen Evangelischen Kirche," signed Happich, Marahrens, Johnsen, Hollweg, 24 May 1939, p. 1, LKA Bielefeld 5,1/297. This file also contains a copy of the note Marahrens attached to qualify his signature (p. 3). The Hanoverian bishop attempted to soften the stance toward Jewish influences in Christianity without, however, refuting the basic view.

11. Hilberg discusses the decree of 1 September 1941 and its implications, including reference to developments in the Protestant church, in *Destruction of the European Jews*, 1:178–80.

12. "Nr. 102 Kirchengesetz über den Ausschluss rassejüdischer Christen aus der Kirche," signed Klotsche, Protestant Lutheran Consistorial Office, Dresden, 28 Dec. 1941, EZA Berlin 50/576, p. 40.

13. "Bekanntmachung über die kirchliche Stellung der evangelischen Juden vom 17 Dez. 1941," no. 101, signed Klotsche (Saxony), Kipper (Nassau-Hesse), Kinder (Schleswig-Holstein), Volk (Thuringia), Schultz (Mecklenburg), Willkendorf (Anhalt), and Sievers (Lübeck), in *Kirchliches Gesetz- und Verordnungsblatt*, no. 17, 29 Dec. 1941, pp. 117–18, EZA Berlin 50/576, p. 40.

14. A wealth of information regarding Weidemann and his checkered relations with Nazi authorities is found in BA Koblenz R 43II/165, fiches 1–4.

15. Copy, German Christian General Congregation of Franconia, signed Lottes and E. Weidemüller, to Reich Church Ministry, c/o Undersecretary Dr. Muhs, 7 Feb. 1942, Nuremberg-Eibach, EZA Berlin 50/576, p. 39.

16. "Wesen und Entstehung der Judenfrage—Auszug aus einem Vortrag von K. F. Euler," Deutsche Christen Nationalkirchliche Einung *Informationsdienst*, no. 4, 29 Apr. 1944, p. 6, EZA Berlin 1/A4/566.

17. See excerpt from Hitler's speech and discussion of its significance in Hilberg, *Destruction of the European Jews*, 2:393–94.

18. "Gaukirchentag der 'Deutschen Christen,'" *Saarbrücker Zeitung*, no. 117, 30 Apr. 1933, clipping in AA Bonn, Besetzte Gebiete, vol. 3, Saargebiet.

19. "Grundsätze für die Glaubenserneuerung," in *Was ist der Eisenacker Arbeitsring?*, flyer of the New Land Movement, Eisenach, [1934], p. 2, KAG Minden, file Neulandbewegung.

20. On Diehl's background, the founding of the New Land group, and her early support of National Socialism and the German Christian movement, see her memoir, *Christ sein heißt Kämpfer sein*, esp. pp. 152–61, 237–45.

21. Copy of "Bericht über eine 'Konfirmandenprüfung' der Thüringer Deutschen Christen in Berlin-Siemensstadt am 22. März 1939," Confessing Church material, p. 4, LKA Bielefeld 5,1/293.

22. "Gespräche mit Katholiken. Nationalkirche auch in anderen Ländern?," *Die Nationalkirche—Briefe an Deutsche Christen*, no. 28/29 (9 July 1939): 311.

23. "Luther's 'deutsches Christentum,'" in Fliedner, *Glaube und Tat*, p. 122.

24. Schenke, "Luther: *Wider die Jüden und ihre Lügen*," in DC-National-kirchliche Einung *Informationsdienst*, no. 2/43 (25 Jan. 1943): 4–5, EZA Berlin 1/A4/565.

25. Memo from the Protestant Consistory Berlin, signed Kapler, to German Protestant Church committee (*Kirchenaussschuß*), 18 Apr. 1931, pp. 1–4, EZA Berlin 1/A2/493.

26. Kessler, Protestant Consistory of the Palatinate, to German Protestant Church committee, Office of the Church League (*Kirchenbundesamt*) Berlin-Charlottenburg, Speyer, 12 Mar. 1931, no. 932/31, EZA Berlin 1/A2/493, p. 92. The same file contains a copy of the original questionnaire of 17 Dec. 1930 (p. 115).

27. See Franzen, "Protesterklärung des Bundes für Deutsche Kirche gegen den Erlaß des Landeskirchenausschusses in Schleswig-Holstein an die Geistlichen der Landeskirche vom 11. März 1936," Kiel, 7 May 1936, pp. 1–4, EZA Berlin 1/C3/307.

28. Petri, *Zu Jesu Füßen*, p. 19.

29. Wieneke, *Die Glaubensbewegung "Deutsche Christen,"* p. 8.

30. See Wieneke, "Zehn Jahre Deutsche Christen."

31. Pauli, *Die Kirche im Dritten Reich*, pp. 4, 6, 9.

32. Pastor Ankermann, "Der deutsche Christ und die Heidenmission," *Mitteilungen der Glaubensgemeinschaft Deutsche Christen*, no. 21 (21 May 1933): 2, LKA Bielefeld 5,1/289,2.

33. Ludwig Weichert, "Kwami," *Evangelium im Dritten Reich*, no. 1 (16 Oct. 1932): 6–7, ibid.

34. See Marks, "Black Watch," pp. 297–334.

35. Meyer-Erlach, *Das deutsche Leid.*" A copy is in BDC, Partei Kanzlei Correspondence, Wolf Meyer-Erlach materials.

36. Report on Meyer-Erlach, from office of the Chief of the Security Police and Security Service to Foreign Office, 1 Oct. 1942, Berlin, AA Bonn, Inland I-D, Kirche 2, 3/4.

37. "Fragekasten," *Evangelium im Dritten Reich,* no. 1 (16 Oct. 1932): 7.

38. "Richtlinien der Liste 'Deutsche Christen,'" signed Hossenfelder, Berlin, 26 May 1932, LKA Bielefeld 5,1/550,1.

39. "Tagungsplan zur Ersten Reichstagung des Studentenkampfbundes Deutsche Christen in der Friedrich-Wilhelms Universität zu Berlin vom 7.–10. August 1933," attached invitation signed Kurt Werner, Reich Organization Leader of the Student Combat League of German Christians, July 1933, EZA Berlin 50/631.

40. See two unidentified clippings, "Heidenmission und Kirchenverfassung" and "'Hakenkreuz und Christenkreuz vereint!,'" [1933], LKA Bielefeld 5,1/697,2.

41. Knak, *Kirchenstreit und Kirchenfriede,* pp. 12–13, 22.

42. "Die Erklärung der Frankfurter Pfarrerschaft und der Kampf gegen die Gottlosigkeit," *Frankfurter Zeitung,* no. 157/159 (28 Feb. 1933): 2, BA Potsdam, DC-I, 1933–35, p. 11. That pastor closed his antisocialist, anti-Jewish speech with an unusual call for moderation: "We shouldn't allow hatred against individuals to grow out of this fact."

43. Ilse von Rabenau to Reich Bishop Müller, 16 Nov. 1933, Berlin-Lankwitz, EZA Berlin 1/A4/101.

44. "Vortrag des Landesbischofs Schultz, Mitglied des Geistlichen Vertrauensrats, bei der Versammlung der Thüringer Deutschen Christen in Stuttgart am 13.7.1940 über 'Mit Deutschem Christentum in Deutschlands Zukunft!,'" Confessing Church report, LKA Bielefeld 5,1/561,1.

45. Account of speech by church vice-president Hahn of Hanover in "Reichskirchentagung für Niederdeutschland," *Bremer Nachrichten,* no. 264, 24 Sept. 1935, clipping in LKA Bielefeld 5,1/291,2.

46. Friedrich Kapferer, *Die dem heutigen Denken möglichen Aussagen über den Urgrund des Seins,* circular of German Christian National Church group, Schwein, 8/9 Jan. 1943, EZA Berlin 1/A4/565.

47. "Was Deutsche Christen zu verkünden haben," *Rundbrief der Württembergischen Bekenntnisgemeinschaft,* no. 9 (Stuttgart, 20 June 1935): 13, LKA Bielefeld 5,1/554,2.

48. Manuscript by Immanuel B. Schairer, "Die Weltenglocke tönt. Worte vom Warten der Deutschen Christen," LKA Nuremberg, KKU 6/IV.

49. German Christian circular, *Antwort auf den Artikel im lokalen Teil des Nachbar vom 25.7.37*, German Christian National Church Movement, local group Rahmede, p. 1, LKA Bielefeld 5,1/294,1.

50. "Mitgliederversammlung der Deutschen Christen, Ortsgruppe Augsburg im Stockhausbräukeller, den 4. Mai 1935, 8 Uhr," Confessing Church account, p. 2, LKA Nuremberg, KKU 6/IV.

51. "Bericht über die Gründungsversammlung der Ortsgruppe Reichelsdorf der Deutschen Christen am 5. Jan. 1935—Nebenzimmer Restauration Rührer," LKA Nuremberg, KKU 6/IV.

52. Theophil Krawielitzki to Birnbaum, 25 Aug. 1934, Marburg/Lahn, pp. 2–3, EZA Berlin 1/A4/55. A report on that pastor and his experiences in North America was sent to the Foreign Office. See "Abschrift aus einem Brief des deutschen Pastors C. F. H., z. Zt. auf Reisen in Nordamerika vom 19. Nov. 1934," attached to Birnbaum to Foreign Office, 7 Dec. 1934, AA Bonn VI A, Evang. Ang. 2: Verfassung der ev. Kirche, vol. 2.

53. Georg Schneider, "Viele Konfessionskirchen oder Eine Volkskirche?," special reprint from *Deutscher Sonntag*, nos. 38, 39, 40 (20, 27 Sept., 4 Oct. 1936), LKA Bielefeld 5,1/291,1.

54. Sommerer's remarks are quoted in copy of Schieder, Protestant Lutheran district superintendent to Protestant-Lutheran Consistory, Munich, 30 Nov. 1935, Nuremberg, p. 1, LKA Nuremberg, KKU 6/IV.

55. Herbert Propp, "Niemöller im Dienste der Einkreisung!," [Sept. 1939], EZA Berlin 50/600, p. 4.

56. Lörcher, Wittkopp, "Vor den Kirchenwahlen," in *Mitteilungen aus dem Bund für evangelische Freiheit (Bund Freie Volkskirche) in der Provinz Sachsen*, no. 3 (Halle/Saale, May/June 1932): 14–17, KAG Minden, loose materials.

57. See Buchholtz to Reich Bishop Müller, 13 Oct. 1933, Berlin-Templehof, p. 1, EZA Berlin 1/A4/251.

58. Wieneke, *Die Kampf- und Glaubensbewegung "Deutsche Christen,"* pp. 5–6.

59. For a contemporary discussion of the debate over the Aryan Clause in the church, see Duhm, *Der Kampf um die deutsche Kirche*, pp. 117–18. For a secondary interpretation, see Gutteridge, *Open Thy Mouth*.

60. Tal, "On Modern Lutheranism," p. 204.

61. Quoted in ibid., pp. 208–9.

62. Buchheim, "Ein NS-Funktionär zum Niemöller-Prozess."

63. Haug, "Die Glaubensbewegung 'Deutsche Christen,'" *Beilage zum Wochenblatt des Christlich-sozialen Volksdienstes*, no. 16 (1933), LKA Bielefeld 5,1/289,1.

64. "Brief an einen Berliner Pfarrer vom 2. Juni 1933," LKA Bielefeld 5,1/289,2.

65. Ehrenberg, "72 Leitsätze zur judenchristlichen Frage im Namen des Vaters Jesu Christi, des Gottes Abrahams, Isaaks und Jakobs," Bochum, July–Aug. 1933, pp. 2–4, LKA Bielefeld 5,1/550,1.

66. Loewe, *Das A.B.C. des Deutschen Heiden!*, p. 1.

67. Mayor Ettwein to Hauer, 22 July 1935, Stuttgart, BA Koblenz, NL 131/88, pp. 52–53.

68. Poster, "Öffentliche Kundgebung des Merseburger Kirchenvolkes. Antwort auf die 'Deutsche Glaubensbewegung' . . . Deutsche Christen und Bekenntnisfront in Merseburg einigen sich in der Abwehr des Neuheidentums!," [1935], BA Potsdam, DG I, 1934–36, p. 329.

69. Friedrich Oberschilp, "Meine Antwort an Herrn Pfarrer Brökelschen," *Drehscheibe. Das Blatt der denkenden Menschen*, no. 42 (13. Gilbhard [September] 1935): 165–67, AEKR Düsseldorf, NL Schmidt/17, pp. 50–52.

70. Brökelschen, "Offener Brief des Pfarrers Brökelschen an die Drehscheibe, 'Das Blatt der denkenden Menschen,'" *Nachrichten-Blatt der Ev. Gemeinde Oberhausen I*, no. 42 (20 Oct. 1935): 1–2, AEKR Düsseldorf, NL Schmidt/18.

71. See Pastor Kittmann to Public Prosecutor, Tilsit, 1 Apr. 1937, Tilsit, p. 1, BA Potsdam DG III, 1937–39, p. 345. Information on the charge against the German Faith Movement speaker for blasphemy is also in the same file (pp. 351–53). See Public Prosecutor to Reich Minister of Justice, 5 June 1937, Bochum, and Reich Minister of Justice to Reich Minister for Church Affairs, 18 June 1937.

72. Lecture by German Faith Movement speaker Oettel, 19 Jan. 1938, in Frankfurt a. M., quoted in President of the Consistory, Protestant Church of Nassau-Hessen, to Reich- and Prussian Minister of Church Affairs, 28 Mar. 1938, BA Potsdam, DG IV, 1938–43, pp. 43–44.

73. Schultz to Hitler, 30 Apr. 1941, Charlottenburg, and attached report, relevant subsections titled "Bekämpfung und Verächtlichmachung des Christentums und der Kirche," and "Angriffe auf Geistliche," pp. 4–5, BA Koblenz R 43 II/172/fiche 1, pp. 3–6. Confessing Church circles also complained about the storm trooper song because of its lyrics about the preacher who "robs the *Volk* of its soul, and whether he does it in a Roman or Lutheran way, teaches the Jewish faith." See circular, *Einem SA-Sturm in Rostock wurde das Singen des Liedes "Der Herbst weht ueber das Stoppelfeld befohlen,"* [1937?], p. 2, LKA Bielefeld 5,1/559.

74. Copy of letter by Erich Bechtholdt, "Ein Pastor aus dem Ruhrgebiet," *Der Stürmer* [1935], AEKR Düsseldorf, NL Schmidt/2, p. 90.

75. Wohlert, *Frauendienst am deutschen Volke*, p. 12.

76. Klüppel, in his study of euthanasia policies in two Hessian institutions, points out that the Jewish patients were the first to be removed and murdered; see *"Euthanasie" und Lebensvernichtung*, p. 15.

77. See Klee, *"Euthanasie" im NS-Staat*, pp. 36–38.

78. See Nowak, *"Euthanasie" und Sterilisierung*, for reactions of the Protestant and Catholic churches with regard to Nazi initiatives in this area. German Christians receive little attention.

79. Henry Friedlander, "Step by Step," p. 497.

80. Mimeographed report, "Vortragsabend des Reichsvikars Dr. Engelke, veranstaltet von der Akademie Münster in Verbindung mit der Ortsgruppe der Deutschen Christen, Münster i. W.," [1935?], p. 1, LKA Bielefeld 5,1/294,1.

81. Arno Wegrant [name unclear] to Müller, 9 July 1935, p. 2, EZA Berlin 1/C3/101.

82. O. Kleinschmidt, "Der Deutsche Christ und die Rassenfrage," in Kinder, *Die Deutschen Christen Reichskalender 1935*, pp. 44–45.

83. Slawinsky, *Blut und Rasse*, pp. 4, 6.

84. "Im Kampf gegen Materialismus und Gottlosenbewegung," in Neumann et al., *Licht und Leben*, pp. 175–76.

85. Stroothenke, *Erbpflege und Christentum*, p. 26.

86. See Klee, *"Euthanasie" im NS-Staat*, p. 280.

87. For extracts of Galen's sermon, see Noakes and Pridham, *Nazism*, 2:1036–39.

88. See duplicated sheet, "An alle deutsch-christliche Gemeinden," signed Horstmann, Münster, 20 Dec. 1941, KAG Minden, DCS.O. Also see "DC Westfalen—Der Landesleiter, Münster—Rundschreiben an alle Gemeinden," signed Horstmann (31 Oct. 1941), KAG Minden, file V Fiebig.

89. Franz Bergmann to Deputy Chief Command of the Sixth Military District, Chief of Staff Division, Münster, 8 Sept. 1941, Neheim-Ruhr, BA-MA Freiburg, RH 14/46, p. 47.

90. Cover letter from Military Subdistrict VI to Chef H Rüst u. Bd E., Staff IC Berlin, 23 Sept. 1941, Münster, ibid.

91. Hilberg discusses development of a definition of "Jews" in Nazi Germany in *Destruction of the European Jews*, 1:65–80. A first step was the Interior Ministry regulation of 11 April 1933 that defined as of "non-Aryan descent" anyone with a parent or grandparent of the Jewish religion. As Hilberg points out, that definition was "in no sense based on racial criteria." A definition of Jews followed over two years later, in the First Regulation to the Reich Citizenship Law, 14 November 1935. The basis of distinction remained the religious status of the grandparents.

## Chapter Three

1. Report by Confessing Church observer, "Versammlung der 'Deutschen Christen' im Saal des Schützenhofes" [Herford, 18 Nov. 1934], LKA Bielefeld 5,1/294,2. The report does not specify the number of people present; my estimate of the attendance is based on many similar accounts. The translation of "A Mighty Fortress" is by Frederick H. Hedge (1805–90).

2. "Bericht über die Rede des Reichsbischofs Ludwig Müller am Sonntag 21.2.37 im Saale Gehle in Gütersloh [Westphalia]," p. 3, LKA Bielefeld 5,1/292,2.

3. "Neues Kirchenlied," to tune of "Valet will ich dir geben," quoted in "Schnellbrief für Glieder der Bekennenden Kirche," no. 36 (Berlin-Dahlem, 15 Nov. 1935), LKA Bielefeld 5,1/555,1.

4. "Sitzung des Geistlichen Ministeriums am 21. April 1933," Pastor Jensen reporting on trip to Berlin, KA Lübeck, Protokollbuch 3:203.

5. "Die Sendung der Deutschen Christen," Speech by Kinder, 28 Feb. 1934, Berlin, in *Evangelium im Dritten Reich* (4 Mar. 1934): 101–6, LKA Bielefeld 5,1/289,1.

6. See reference to a speech by Kerrl on 27 Nov. 1935, in "Die Irrlehre Lebt!" in *Aus der Kirche*, Confessing Church circular, [1936], pp. 1–4, LKA Bielefeld 5,1/556,1.

7. "Zur Unterrichtung," report of meeting of German Christians in Oberhausen (Rhineland), *Deutsches Pfarrerblatt*, no. 14 (1937): 240, clipping in LKA Bielefeld 5,1/292,1.

8. Bauer, *Feierstunden Deutscher Christen*, p. 49.

9. For an example and some brief discussion of German Christian celebratory style, see "Arbeitstagung der Kirchenbewegung 'Deutsche Christen,'" *Allgemeine Thüringische Landeszeitung, Deutschland*, no. 124 (Weimar, 6 May 1935), LKA Bielefeld 5,1/290,1.

10. "Evang. Feierstunden im Advent 1935 in der evangelischen-Kirche zu Berlin-Tegel," Pastor Günther Minia, EZA Berlin 50/210 I.

11. "Feierstunde am 3. Jahrestage der nationalen Erhebung," in "Schulungsbrief der Reichsbewegung Deutsche Christen," no. 3 (Jan. 1936), Pastor Georg Hauck, Berlin, responsible, KAG Minden, no. 27. The opening hymn was "Ist Gott für mich, so trete gleich alles wider mich."

12. Dr. Thom, "Ostern," *Des Deutschen Volkes Kirche*, no. 1 (12 Apr. 1936): 2, LKA Bielefeld 5,1/291,2.

13. "Die Irrlehre der Thüringer Deutschen Christen, die neue Grundlage der Kirche?," in report, "Wie die Ausbildung unserer zukünftigen Pastoren aussieht wenn Thüringer Deutsche Christen Theologie Professoren werden," [1937], p. 3, LKA Bielefeld 5,1/291,1.

14. Report of baptism performed by Schneider, in "Nationalkirche," Confessing Church materials, [1937?], p. 3, LKA Bielefeld 5,1/292,1.

15. Schneider, "Die Taufe," in *Unser Glaube*, pp. 77–80.

16. "Spendformal einer Abendmahlsfeier der Thüringer Richtung verwendent von Probst Breso [name unclear] unter Assistenz von Pastor Harloff von Dom zu Güstrow in der Adventszeit 1936 in Krakow, Mecklenburg," in report, "Wie die Ausbildung unserer zukünftigen Pastoren aussieht wenn Thüringer Deutsche Christen Theologie Professoren werden," [1937], p. 2, LKA Bielefeld 5,1/291,1.

17. Schneider, quoted in "Die Irrlehre der Thüringer Deutschen Christen, die neue Grundlage der Kirche?," ibid., p. 4.

18. Schneider, quoted in "Eintopf und Abendmahl!," in *Nachrichtenblatt für Deutsche Christen*, nos. 4 and 5 (Frankfurt/Main, Mar. and Apr. 1937): 2, LKA Bielefeld 5,1/292,2.

19. Bauer, "Vorschlag zu einer Sonnenwendfeier," EZA Berlin 1/A4/45.

20. "Bericht über die Gedenkfeier für Leutheuser, den Führer der Thüringer Deutschen Christen, am 2.1.1943 in der Georgenkirche zu Eisenach," LKA Bielefeld 5,1/293.

21. Paul Schwadtke, "Weihenacht," in *Deutsche Christen Nationalkirchliche Einung. Liedblätter*, p. 37.

22. "Auszug aus einem Brief vom 15. Mai 1942 [signed Jul Leutheuser]," p. 4, LKA Bielefeld 5,1/293.

23. "Auf, auf, mit grünen Maien," words by Hermann Ohland, no. 205 in *Großer Gott, wir loben Dich!*, p. 294.

24. "Pfingstsonntag," sermon on Romans 8:9, for 24 May 1942, in "Theologischer Arbeitsbrief" (Münster, 1 May 1942): 1–3, LKA Bielefeld 5,1/295,1.

25. Hagemann, "Pfingsten. Thema: Feuer Gottes auf Erden," text Luke 12:49, in "Theologischer Arbeitsbrief" (1 May 1944): 6–8, LKA Bielefeld 5,1/295,2.

26. Pastor Berckenhagen, "Evangelisches Deutschtum in der Türkei," *Evangelium im Dritten Reich*, no. 44 (29 Oct. 1933): 450, LKA Bielefeld 5,1/289,1.

27. Will Ulmenried (pseudonym), "Der deutsche Auslandspfarrer," in Kinder, *Der Deutschen Christen Reichs-Kalendar, 1935*, pp. 102–3.

28. Presentation by Pastor Polednik, in "Bericht über die 50. Jahreshauptversammlung des Evangelischen Bundes Sachsen-Anhalt in Naumburg (Saale), 12.–14. Juni 1938," p. 7, EB Bensheim 3.05.19.

29. Staedel, "Die Volkskirche der Siebenbürger Sachsen. Vortrag, gehalten im Rahmen der 'Kulturwoche,' welche im Herbst 1960 von der Landsmannschaft der Siebenbürger Sachsen in Zusammenarbeit mit ihrem Patenland Nordrhein-Westfalen veranstaltet worden ist," p. 1, BA Koblenz, NL 252/18.

30. For evidence of Staedel's worldview, both during and after the Nazi era, see his own writings and the notebooks he maintained of excerpts from the works of others, BA Koblenz, NL 252.

31. E. Graenz (spelling of name unclear), "Lagebericht erstattet in der Dechantenkonferenz in Heltau im Mai 1941," 26 May 1941, Heltau, p. 2, BA Koblenz, NL 252/20, p. 2.

32. Staedel to Beyer, 23 Apr. 1963, p. 3, BA Koblenz, NL 252/13.

33. "Deutsche Auslandspfarrer grüßen die Glaubensbewegung," *Evangelium im Dritten Reich*, no. 50 (10 Dec. 1933): 528, LKA Bielefeld 5,1/289,1.

34. Balzer to Karl Richter, 5 Oct. 1936, Lübeck, pp. 2–4, KAG Minden, file Lübeck.

35. See, for example, German Protestant Church, Ecclesiastical Foreign Office, to Foreign Office, 22 Feb. 1935, Berlin-Charlottenburg, thanking Foreign Office for RM 2,000 to help fund a theological working group for ethnic German theologians of Central Europe, AA Bonn VI A, Evang. Ang. 2: Verfassung der Evang. Kirche, Bd. 10. On Heckel's German Christian sympathies, see Bonhoeffer to Rößler, 20 Nov. 1934, London, pp. 1–4, BA Koblenz, NL 308/A42/fiche 3/41,9; and Heydrich to von Ribbentrop, 13 Apr. 1942, Berlin, pp. 1–4, AA Bonn, Inland I-D, Kirche 2, 3/5.

36. Lammers, Chief of Reich Chancellery, to Governors of Sudentengau, Warthegau, Danzig-West-Prussia, Vienna, Lower Danube, Upper Danube, Steiermark, Kärnten, Tirol and Vorarlberg, and Salzburg, 25 Sept. 1941, BA Koblenz R 43II/152/fiche 3, pp. 103–4.

37. Heydrich to von Ribbentrop, 13 Apr. 1942, Berlin, pp. 1–4, AA Bonn, Inland I-D, Kirche 2, 3/5.

38. See, for example, unsigned, undated carbon copy of "Welche Forderungen stellen wir an die 'Bekennenden Gemeinden'?," essay by member of a "Jungreformatorischer Kreis," AEKR Düsseldorf, NL Schmidt/1, pp. 15–18.

39. Rößler to "Verehrte Kollegen! Liebe Brüder!," 16 Nov. 1934, Heerlen-Holland, copy sent to Dietrich Bonhoeffer in London, BA Koblenz, NL 308/A41/fiche 3/item 41(9).

40. Bonhoeffer to Rößler, 20 Nov. 1934, London, pp. 1–4, BA Koblenz, NL 308/A42/fiche 3/41,9.

41. F. Schmitz to Hitler, 20 Nov. 1934, Oberhausen-Alstaden, BA Koblenz R 43 II/171, fiche 1/pp. 38–39.

42. Pamphlet with foreword by Martin Niemöller, *Die Staatskirche ist da!*, pp. 5–7, KAG Minden, no. 26.

43. Typed statement, signed "Die Laienvertretung der Deutschen Christen Westfalens: Irle and Salzbrunn," 31 Oct. 1936, KAG Minden, no. 26.

44. Report signed by Wentz, "Betr. DC," 31 Oct. 1936, Minden, pp. 1–2, KAG Minden, no. 24.

45. "Richtlinien für die Neugestaltung der Evangelischen Kirche," [in pencil, "Dibelius Plan"], "(von D. Dibelius am 30.9.1940 aufgestellt)," KAG Minden, no. 8.

46. Wentz, "Beurteilung des Dibelius-Plans zur Bereinigung der Kirchenfrage von Prof. Wentz," 30 Nov. 1940, pp. 1–4, ibid.

47. In fact, Wentz scoffed at the fact that Dibelius bothered to mention exclusion of "non-Aryans." Ibid.

48. G. A. Wilhelm Meyer, "Im Dritten Reich zur Dritten Kirche, Predigt am 2. Pfingstfeiertag 1933 über Epheser 4, 3–6," *Die deutsche Wende*, pp. 23–27.

49. Quoted in Winkel, *Jesu ursprüngliche Verkündigung*, p. 6.

50. For example, German Lutheran pastor Alexander Wolfram to Superintendent Zöllner and to the Protestant Military Bishop of the German Reich, 16 Mar. 1935, Luseland, Saskatchewan, EZA Berlin 1/A2/498, pp. 79–81.

51. Otto Jäger to Müller, 6 May 1935, also J. Bendrat to District Party Leader Uschdraweit, 11 Aug. 1935, Pillkallen, both in EZA Berlin 1/A2/498, p. 27.

52. See Order from the War Minister, signed Semler, to Protestant Military Bishop Franz Dohrmann, 30 Apr. 1935, Berlin, regarding the promotion as of 1 April 1935 of base chaplain Lonicer to army pastor, BA-MA Freiburg, RW 12 I/2, p. 18. In 1939, Heinrich Lonicer (born 1888) advanced to superintendent in the chaplaincy (*Wehrmachtdekan*), BA-MA Freiburg, N282/v. 16, "Pers. Akten." He was a member of the NSDAP. See memo War Ministry to Dohrmann, 12 July 1935, BA-MA Freiburg, RW 12 I/2.

53. In February 1939, Goebbels announced at a press conference that Protestant Military Bishop Dohrmann had resigned and Lonicer would succeed him. No notices of Goebbels's statement appeared in the press and Dohrmann remained in office, thanks probably to power struggles between Brauchitsch, who wanted Lonicer in the bishop's seat, and Admiral Raeder, who had his own candidate, Naval Chaplain Friedrich Ronneberger, a man who was also known to be sympathetic to the German Christian cause. Dohrmann's notes, BA-MA Freiburg, N282/1, p. 62.

54. See Baedeker, *Das Volk das im Finsternis wandelt*, p. 64.

55. Lonicer to Colonel Radtke, OKH, [Apr. 1942], BA-MA Freiburg, N282/2. A copy of the program for Lonicer's service is also in the file, "Feldgottesdienst," 19 Apr. 1942, Poltawa, BA-MA Freiburg, N282/2. Lonicer notes that he ran the service three times with a total participation of 2,800 men.

56. Duplicated letter, Pastor Fiebig to "dear comrades," including excerpts from a soldier's letter of 9 October 1939, attached to "Feldanschriften," 19 Oct. 1939, LKA Bielefeld 4,55/A/61.

57. The 1944 complaint about the German Christian pastor Emil Engelhardt

and his activities in the Lake Constance area generated considerable correspondence. See, for example, Pastor Waßmer to Superintendent of Chaplains, c/o Deputy Chief Command V A.K., Stuttgart, 28 Mar. 1944, and clipping regarding Engelhardt and his lecture series, from *Bodensee-Rundschau* 13 (217) (Constance, 27 Mar. 1944): 3, BA-MA Freiburg, RW 12 I/4, pp. 111–14.

58. "Verzeichnis der von den zuständigen amtlichen Stellen zur Verbreitung innerhalb der Wehrmacht freigegebenen Schriften," 19 Sept. 1940, ed. Evang. Presseverband für Deutschland, BA-MA Freiburg, RW 12 I/14.

59. See, for example, the 1 April 1943 issue in LKA Bielefeld 5,1/295,2, or special ten-page issue for the front, "Die geistliche Leitung Pfarrer Fiebig grüßt Euch Soldaten," 15 Jan. 1940, Münster, LKA Bielefeld 5,1/295,1.

60. See, for example, no. 4 (30 Mar. 1943), EZA Berlin 1/A4/565.

61. Pastor Niemann, Hagen, "Christentum und Deutschtum. Predigt im Reformationsmonat, Römer 8, 31," in "Theologischer Arbeitsbrief," 1 Oct. 1942, pp. 10–13, LKA Bielefeld 5,1/295,2.

62. "Gottesfeier am 23.2.1941" (Confessing Church material), LKA Bielefeld 5,1/293.

63. Ernst Bertram, born 1894, "Aber erst Gräber schaffen uns Heimat," no. 219 in *Großer Gott, wir loben Dich!*

64. Fiebig and Wentz, "Die kirchlichen Verhältnisse Westfalens zu Beginn des 5. Kriegsjahrs," submitted to Council of the Regional Court of Appeal (Oberlandesgerichtsrat), 22 Oct. 1943, p. 2, KAG Minden, file V, Fiebig.

65. See Messerschmidt, "Aspekte der Militärseelsorgepolitik in national-sozialistischer Zeit," *Militärgeschichtliche Mitteilungen* (1/1968), and "Zur Militärseelsorgepolitik im Zweiten Weltkrieg," *Militärgeschichtliche Mitteilungen* (1/1969). See also Schübel, *300 Jahre Evangelische Soldatenseelsorge.*

66. Hempel, *Die Aufgabe von Theologie und Kirche*, pp. 15–16.

## Chapter Four

1. Denzer, Lanzenstiel, and Schindelbauer, "Bericht über Gründungsversammlung der D.C. Gau Oberbayern," Munich, 20 Jan. 1935, LKA Nuremberg, KKU 6/IV.

2. Typescript, Pastor Dr. Wendel, "Aufklärungs-Veranstaltung des Landesbischofs Dr. Dietrich nach dem Himmelfahrtsgottesdienst in Kirtorf, Kreis Alsfeld (Hessen)," [1935?], p. 9, LKA Bielefeld 5,1/289,1.

3. Declaration signed by nine German Christians, "Aufruf der Kirchengemeinde Dinslaken-Hiesfeld," 7 Dec. 1933, pp. 2–3, EZA Berlin 1/A4/249.

4. "Mit Gottes Hilfe Vorwärts und Hindurch," *Unsere Sendung: Mitteilungsblatt der Deutschen Christen in der Provinz Sachsen und in Anhalt*, no.

3 (Brachet [June], 1934): 1–2, AEKR Düsseldorf, Pfarrer Walter Wilm Collection, folder 8.

5. Hossenfelder, "Der Sonntag des Hausvaters," *Evangelium im Dritten Reich*, no. 49 (3 Dec. 1933): 516, clipping in LKA Bielefeld 5,1/289,1.

6. See Ernst Lohmeyer, "Gnade und Männlichkeit," in *Gnade und Männlichkeit*, esp. p. 8, LKA Bielefeld 5,1/289,2.

7. H. J. König, "Entwurf eines volksmissionarischen Vortrages über Gnade und Männlichkeit für jungen Männern," ibid., pp. 14–15.

8. Account of Müller's speech in Oberbarmen, 4 Dec. 1936, in "Sinngemässe Nachschrift," LKA Bielefeld 5,1/291,1.

9. Hossenfelder, "Kämpferisches Christentum," *Neue Badische Landeszeitung* (Mannheim, 20 July 1933), clipping in BA Potsdam DC-I, 1933–35, p. 81.

10. "Bischof Kessel in Breslau," in *Irrlehren der "Deutschen Christen,"* Confessing Church circular, [1934?], LKA Bielefeld 5,1/290,1.

11. Klara Lönnies, "Die deutsche evangelische Frau und ihre Kirche," in Kinder, *Der Deutschen Christen Reichskalendar 1935*, p. 80. A copy of Lönnies's 1936 *Lebenslauf*, prepared for the Reich Chamber of Writing, appears in Kaiser, *Frauen in der Kirche*, pp. 196–97.

12. Müller, *Der deutsche Volkssoldat*, p. 56.

13. The biblical reference here is to 1 Corinthians 14:34.

14. Stapel, "Kampf um die evangelische Kirche," in *Deutsches Volkstum*, reprinted as "Worum kämpft der Pfarrer'not'bund," in *Evangelium im Dritten Reich*, no. 2 (14 Jan. 1934): 20, LKA Bielefeld 5,1/289,1. A letter to the *Deutsches Pfarrerblatt*, not a German Christian paper, struggled with the same analogy. See "Zur Arierfrage in der D.E.K.," signed Quehl, Kassel-Wilhelmshöhe, in *Deutsches Pfarrerblatt*, no. 46, clipping in LKA Bielefeld 5,1/294,3.

15. Circular issued by "Deutsche Christen," Leitung der Reichsbewegung, *Die angebliche Irrlehre der "Deutschen Christen"* (31 May 1935): 6, LKA Bielefeld 5,1/290,1.

16. Bonhoeffer, "Der Arierparagraph in der Kirche," in "Entwurfen in Vorbereitung auf die Wittenberger Nationalsynode vom 27 September 1933" (Aug. 1933): 3, BA Koblenz, NL 308/A38/fiche 1/item 38,5.

17. See "Niederschrift über die vorbereitende Sitzung zur Bildung einer volksmissionarischen Kammer am 3. November 1933 im Evangelischen Oberkirchenrat," EZA Berlin 1/A4/41.

18. Report of Peter's speech included in "Weimar," *Evangelium im Dritten Reich*, no. 49 (3 Dec. 1933): 512, LKA Bielefeld 5,1/289,1. Emphasis in the original.

19. For Coch's speech, see "Bericht über die Mitgliederversammlung der Kirchenbewegung Deutscher Christen e.v. (Nationalkirchliche Bewegung) Dresden," 20 Oct. 1936, p. 7, LKA Bielefeld 5,1/291,1.

20. Hans Schweiger, ". . . wie wir vergeben unseren Schuldigern!," *Evangelium im Dritten Reich*, no. 47 (19 Nov. 1933): 489–90, LKA Bielefeld 5,1/289,2.

21. "Aus dem Gemeindeblatt der Deutschen Christen für Wetten-Ruhr" (26 Jan. 1936), LKA Bielefeld 5,1/294,1.

22. Pastor Schindelin, Duisburg-Wedau, "Mann und Kirche. Leitsätze zum Monatsthema der kirchlichen Männerarbeit," 1937, p. 1, AEKR Düsseldorf, DEK, 1937.

23. Fritz Duvernoy to Hauer, 6 Dec. 1932, Stuttgart, p. 2, BA Koblenz, NL 131/70, p. 59.

24. Hauer to Duvernoy, 22 Dec. 1932, BA Koblenz, NL 131/70, p. 57.

25. Staedel identifies the phrase "commandeered Christianity" as originating with Count Ernst von Reventlow. See Staedel to Karl Heim, 7 June 1958, Holzhausen an der Porta (Westphalia), p. 8, BA Koblenz, NL 252/13.

26. See, for example, remarks by Hamburg bishop Franz Tügel from 1942–43, in *Mein Weg. 1888–1946*, p. 242, and postwar reflections of Staedel in letter to Heim, 17 June 1958, BA Koblenz, NL 252/13.

27. For some discussion, see Conway, *Nazi Persecution of the Churches*, p. 50, and Scholder, *The Churches and the Third Reich*, 1:450.

28. Conway, *Nazi Persecution of the Churches*, p. 160.

29. Order of 15 Oct. 1934, cited in "SS-Befehl," 20 Sept. 1935, T-175/149/2677453. The 1935 regulation appears in the September order as well.

30. Himmler to SS Division Leaders, 26 Aug. 1936, T-175/149/2677448.

31. Hossenfelder, "Der Sonntag des Hausvaters," *Evangelium im Dritten Reich*, no. 49 (3 Dec. 1933): 516, clipping in LKA Bielefeld 5,1/289,1.

32. Pastor Hitzer to Müller, 1 Dec. 1933, Rösnitz (Upper Silesia), EZA Berlin 1/A4/249.

33. Reported in Frederking to Lücking, 25 Apr. 1935, Neheim/Ruhr, pp. 3–4, LKA Bielefeld 4,55/B/17,3.

34. See columns on news from the church districts of Westphalia, "Nachrichten aus den Kirchenkreisen," in *Evangelische Nachrichten*, various dates, LKA Bielefeld 5,1/294,1.

35. See, for example, the report, "Über eine Versammlung der Amtswalter der 'Glaubensbewegung Deutsche Christen' Gau Groß-Berlin, am 28. Sept. 1936, im Kriegervereinshaus, Chausseestrasse," LKA Bielefeld 5,1/291,1.

36. In fact, until I began to do archival research on the German Christian movement, I was not even certain that women could be card-carrying members.

37. Photo of first Reich Conference of German Christians, Berlin, 3–5 Apr. 1933, in BDC, Partei Kanzlei Correspondence file, Joachim Hossenfelder materials. The numbers I have given here exclude the two sections of seating labeled "guests of honor from the state" and "guests of honor from the church" because those areas by definition would be very unlikely to send women to the conference.

38. Report, "Einführung des D.C. Pfarrers K. Grams in Fürth am 9.4.1939," LKA Nuremberg, KD Nbg 118.

39. Report regarding meeting of German Christian parish group "Heilig Kreuz," 1 Mar. 1934, in the "Kleine Festsäle," Blücherstr., from Stapo Ad. III, signed Criminal Secretary Lemke, Berlin, 2 Mar. 1934, sent from Geheimes Staatspolizei to Prussian Minister for Science, Art, and Education, 9 Mar. 1934, II E 2-244/3/14, BA Potsdam, DC I, 1933–37, pp. 194–95.

40. "Bericht über die Versammlung des Bundes für Deutsches Christentum—Landesleitung Hannover," 17 Mar. 1937, Bethlehemskirche Hannover-Linden, p. 1, LKA Bielefeld 5,1/294,1.

41. "Nachrichten aus den Kirchenkreisen, Dortmund-Pauluskirche," *Evangelische Nachrichten* (17 Oct. 1937): 14, ibid.

42. Hertzberg, *Der Deutsche und das Alte Testament*, p. 57.

43. Ernst Lange, "Dinge, die ich verstehe, und Dinge, die ich night verstehe," offprint from Lange's book, *Der Ausweg* (Diesdorf-Breslau: Schwert and Schild, [1936?]), pp. 1 and 7, LKA Bielefeld 5,1/664,1.

44. See, for example, untitled flyer from Deutsche Christen Braunschweig, 18 Apr. 1934, in LKA Bielefeld 5,1/290,1.

45. C. Kohs, "Aufsatz betr. 'Glaubensbewegung Deutsche Christen,'" 18 Aug. 1933, Lüdinghausen, p. 6 (copy sent by the author to Hitler, 28 Sept. 1933), EZA Berlin 1/A4/248.

46. Martin Sasse, "Die Stellung des Thüringischen Landeskirchenrats zur deutschen Erziehungs- und Schulfrage," 28 July 1936, reproduced from *Thüringer Kirchenblatt und kirchlicher Anzeiger, B: Kirchliche Anzeigen*, no. 146 (1936): 3, LKA Bielefeld 5,1/291,1.

47. Fritz Engelke, "Luthers Ehe," in *Der Ruf an die Frau* (Potsdam: Blätter für den Frauendienst*, Oct. 1937), p. 2, LKA Bielefeld 5,1/292,1.

48. von der Heydt, *Die Kirche Luthers zwischen Rom und Mythus*, pp. 153–54.

49. The canon of manly heroes also provided content for religious instruction in the spirit of German Christianity. See Linder, String, and Grunow, "Die Parole 'Gnade und Männlichkeit' und der evangelische Religionsunterricht," in *Gnade und Männlichkeit*, pp. 19–20, LKA Bielefeld 5,1/289,2.

50. Ingeborg Wessel, "Vom Glauben meines Bruders Horst," *Evangelium im Dritten Reich*, no. 9 (4 Mar. 1934): 99, clipping in LKA Bielefeld 5,1/289,1.

51. See, for example, telegram signed Pressel and Weber on behalf of 380 Württemberg pastors half of whom until shortly before had been in the German Christian Faith Movement, to Reich Bishop Müller, 16 Nov. 1933, Stuttgart, EZA Berlin 1/A4/99. The same file contains many similar messages.

52. See report on Church Leaders' Conference, 29 Nov. 1934, in *Rundschreiben Deutsche Christen*, 13 Jan. 1935, p. 2, LKA Bielefeld 5,1/290,2.

53. "Bericht über den Besuch des Reichsbischofs Ludwig Müller am 24. April 1935 in Bad Oeynhausen," pp. 7, 26, LKA Bielefeld 5,1/305,1.

54. Elisabeth Bresser to Müller, 7 May 1936, Schopfheim (Baden), EZA Berlin 1/A4/25.

55. "Die Führer der 'Deutschen Christen,'" in *Beilage des "Reichsboten,"* no. 173 (2 Aug. 1933), clipping in BA Potsdam, DC-I, 1933–35, p. 86.

56. Quoted in listener's notes, "Kundgebung der Deutschen Christen in der Westfalenhalle, Dortmund am 24. März 1934," p. 8, LKA Bielefeld 5,1/289,1.

57. Quoted in "Sinngemässe Nachschrift: Feierstunde der DC im Rheinland (Gauobmann Pack), Kreis Barmen, 4.12.1936 im Kirchsaal Higelstr.-Oberbarmen," p. 3, LKA Bielefeld 5,1/291,1.

58. Listener's notes, "Kundgebung der Deutschen Christen in der Westfalenhalle, Dortmund am 24. März 1934," p. 8, LKA Bielefeld 5,1/289,1.

59. "Bauernfeldgottesdienste bürgern sich ein," *Evangelischer Beobachter* (8 June 1934): 12, clipping in LKA Bielefeld 5,1/290,1.

60. "Tod du bist der bleiche Kamerad," hymn no. 831 in *Lieder für Gottesfeiern*.

61. "Aufruf der Reichsleitung zur Schaffung eines deutsch-christlichen Laienspiels," *Evangelium im Dritten Reich*, no. 26 (1 July 1934): 335, clipping in LKA Bielefeld 5,1/290,2.

62. "Deutsches Volk feiert Advent," *Rundschreiben, "Deutsche Christen" Schleswig-Holstein*, supplement to Nov. 1934 issue, ibid.

63. Heinz Dungs, "Ewiges Reich wollen wir bauen! Die 4. Reichstagung der deutschen Christen, nationalkirchliche Bewegung," *Die Nationalkirche. Briefe an deutsche Christen*, no. 42/43 (Weimar, 24 Oct. 1937): 332.

64. See, for example, "Marschlied (Geeignet für die Saalfeier)," lyrics by Hermann Ohland, music by Herbert Barbi. The first two lines of this hymn are as follows: "Comrade at my side, do you see the dawn? The drum is calling to combat." *Deutsche Christen Nationalkirchliche Einung—Liedblätter*, p. 47, in KAG Minden. See also "Heil'ger Gott wir treten an," lyrics by Hermann Ohland, music by Adolf Daum; no. 818, in *Lieder für Gottesfeiern*, with mention of "deines Geistes Sturmgeschlecht."

65. "Wir brauchen Männer," lyrics by Fritz Woike, music by Paul Schwadtke, in *Liedblätter der Deutschen Christen Nationalkirchliche Einung*, p. 14. These song sheets have been collected in KAG Minden, no file number.

66. "Christlich-nationalsozialistische Lieder aus dem Jahre 1933," words and music by Paul Friebel, sent by him to Reich Bishop Müller, 22 June 1935, EZA Berlin 1/A4/93.

67. *Großer Gott, wir loben Dich!*, 1941.

68. See, for example, "Macht das Christentum untüchtig zum Dienst für Vaterland?," in *Kraft und Licht* (Berlin) no. 31 (1 Aug. 1937): 1, LKA Bielefeld 5,1/664,2. The authors of this article specified that their information came from the *Deutsches Pfarrerblatt*, 1937.

69. In German: "Wachet! Stehet im Glauben! Seid männlich und seid stark!" See flyer put out by Wahldienst der Evangelischen Bekenntnissynode im Rheinland, *Entweder—Oder!*, [1937], LKA Bielefeld 5,1/292,1.

70. For the German text and musical setting of this poem by Arndt (1769–1860), see *Gesangbuch der kommenden Kirche*, no. 98.

## Chapter Five

1. Walter Schmidt-Henrici to Müller, 15 Oct. 1933, Erfurt, EZA Berlin 1/C4/17. See also account in Scholder, *The Churches and the Third Reich*, 1:530–31.

2. Professor H. M. Müller to Walter Schmidt-Henrici, 3 Nov. 1933, Jena, EZA Berlin 1/C4/17.

3. Schmidt-Henrici to H. M. Müller, 21 Nov. 1933, Erfurt, ibid.

4. "Wieviel Juden gibt es in der Welt?," *Unsere Sendung. Mitteilungsblatt der Deutschen Christen in der Provinz Sachsen und in Anhalt*, no. 3 (Brachet [June] 1934): 23, AEKR Düsseldorf, NL Wilm/8. See also statistics from the Statistisches Reichsamt quoted in "Die Religionsgliederung in Deutschland," *Berliner Börsenzeitung*, no. 543 (18 Nov. 1934), BA Potsdam RLB 1862, p. 72; and "Das konfessionelle Bild des deutschen Volkes," *Basler Nachrichten*, no. 317 (19 Nov. 1934): 2, LKA Bielefeld 5,1/305,1.

5. Memo signed Pfundtner from Reich- and Prussian Minister of the Interior to Military Adjutant, c/o Major Hoßbach, 3 Apr. 1935, p. 2, BA Koblenz, R 43 II/595/fiche 1, pp. 20–21.

6. "Rassische und kirchliche Mischehen," in *Blätter für kirchliche Mischehenarbeit*, ed. von der Heydt, no. 1 (Mar. 1937): 1–4, EB Bensheim, EB 5.04.8a.

7. "Übersicht über die in der Deutschen Evangelischen Kirche in den Jahren 1934–1939 vorgekommenen Übertritte vom Judentum zur evangelischen Kirche," initialed and dated by Karl Wentz, 30 Aug. 1941, KAG Minden, unlabeled file.

8. The Ministry of Church Affairs collected these data and was probably the

source for the German Christian statistics cited above. See "Übertritte von Juden zur evangelischen Kirche," in "Zusammenstellung über Kirchenaustritte und Kirchenrücktritte bezw. Übertritte, ermittelt nach den von den Kirchen veröffentlichten Zusammenstellungen," [1940], BA Koblenz R 79/19.

9. Oskar Karbach, "Judenfrage, unpathetisch betrachtet," *Deutsches Volkstum*, no. 1 (1 Jan. 1933): 23–24, 27.

10. Wieneke, *Die Glaubensbewegung "Deutsche Christen,"* p. 14.

11. Quoted in "Propaganda an der Chaussee," in "Schnellbrief für Glieder der Bekennenden Kirche," no. 31 (2 Oct. 1935): 120, LKA Bielefeld 5,1/555,1.

12. Heinrich Detel to editors of the *Völkischer Beobachter*, 10 Sept. 1935, Breslau, BA Potsdam DC-I, 1933–35, pp. 334–36. In the summer of 1933, Detel was deputy state commissioner for church affairs in Silesia.

13. "Deutsche Christen Gemeindekirchenräte," in Confessing Church Berlin-Brandenburg, "Rundbrief Nr. 12" (17 Oct. 1935): 11, LKA Bielefeld 5,1/664,1.

14. See Gülzow, *Kirchenkampf in Danzig*, p. 19.

15. Pamphlet by German Christian District Group, Siegen, *Um was geht es? Eine Erklärung zur Kirchenwahl* (Münster: Balve, [1937]), pp. 13–14.

16. Declaration of 1941 quoted in Fiebig, "Theologischer Arbeitsbrief" (1 Apr. 1942): 1, LKA Bielefeld 5,1/295,2.

17. On the "seesaw" fate of Aryan Paragraph legislation in the church, see Gutteridge, *The German Evangelical Church and the Jews*, pp. 94–96, 119–22.

18. "Die evangelische Kirche in des Volkes Schicksalsstunde," *Dortmunder Anzeiger* (21 July 1933), clipping in LKA Bielefeld 5,1/294,3.

19. Margarete Koch to Müller, 6 Oct. 1933, Berlin, EZA Berlin 1/A4/251.

20. Handwritten notes by Lohmeyer, "Aussprache mit den 'Deutschen Christen,' Sonntag, den 29. Okt. 1933 in Hamm," pp. 4–9, LKA Bielefeld 5,1/836,1. Wilhelm Niemöller's remark was recorded in another set of notes on the same meeting. See untitled notes of meeting between Gospel and Church group and German Christians on 29 Oct. 1933 in Hamm (Westphalia), pp. 5–7, LKA Bielefeld 5,1/836,1.

21. According to Bonhoeffer's report to a pastoral conference in Bradford (England), the Aryan Paragraph had not been negotiated at the National Synod in September 1933 because "the Foreign Office had intervened." See "Pfarrkonferenz in Bradford (27.–29.11 1933)," p. 2, BA Koblenz, NL 308/fiche 2/A 41, item 41,4.

22. Untitled memo beginning, "Die Auswirkung der Friedenskundgebung des Herrn Reichsbischofs ist in Berlin z. T. geradezu katastrophal gewesen," [Sept. 1933], EZA Berlin 1/A4/95.

23. Copy, "Folgende Entschließung wurde in der Mitgliederversammlung

des Gaues Groß-Berlin der Glaubensbewegung 'Deutsche Christen' im Berliner Sportpalast am 13. Nov. 1933 von ca. 20 000 Anwesenden einstimmig angenommen," LKA Bielefeld 5,1/289,2.

24. See, for example, Nikodemeus (pseudonym), "Der Sturm im Wasserglase! Betrachtungen zur kirchlichen Lage," *Unsere Volkskirche*, no. 8 (26 Nov. 1933): 115, BA Potsdam DC-I, 1933–35, p. 163. Scholder suggests that Nikodemeus was the pen name for Johannes Schmiedchen, one of Reinhold Krause's Berlin associates. Scholder, *The Churches and the Third Reich*, 1:551.

25. "Volksmission?," in press release, "Nachrichten aus der Glaubensbewegung 'Deutsche Christen,'" 15 Nov. 1933, p. 1, LKA Bielefeld 5,1/289,2.

26. Letter to the editor signed Quehl, Kassel-Wilhelmshöhe, "Zur Arierfrage in der D. E. K.," *Deutsches Pfarrerblatt*, no. 46, undated clipping in LKA Bielefeld 5,1/294,3.

27. Philipps, "'Die kirchliche Wollen der Deutschen Christen,'" *Deutsches Pfarrerblatt*, no. 3 (16 Jan. 1934): 30, LKA Bielefeld 5,1/289,1.

28. Martin Niemöller, "Sätze zur Arierfrage in der Kirche," *Deutsches Pfarrerblatt*, no. 4 (23 Jan. 1934): 46, LKA Bielefeld 5,1/289,1.

29. Bonhoeffer, "Entwurfen in Vorbereitung auf die Wittenberger Nationalsynode vom 27.9.1933," in "Der Arierparagraph in der Kirche," Aug. 1933, pp. 2–5, BA Koblenz, NL 308/A 38/fiche 1.

30. Heinz Brunotte, "Vermerk zu KK III 1475," 17 June 1936, EZA Berlin 1/A4/220.

31. "Arierparagraph in theologischen Prüfungsbestimmungen," *Mitteilungsblatt Deutscher Christen*, no. 11 (15 Oct. 1935): 4, LKA Bielefeld 5,1/291,2.

32. Flyer produced by Liebe-Harkort, Women's Service of Westphalia, *Praktische Aufgaben der Frauendienstfrau!* (6 June 1937), LKA Bielefeld 5,1/294,1.

33. Manuscript by Liebe-Harkort, "Aus meinen Lebenserinnerungen (1884–1936!)," pp. 1–4, KAG Minden, Liebe-Harkort folder.

34. Chair of Financial Division of Protestant-Lutheran Consistory, signed Hoffmeister, to Bishop Dr. Johnsen in Wolfenbüttel, 10 Nov. 1938, Wolfenbüttel (Braunschweig), EZA Berlin 1/A4/220. In the same file is Johnsen to Reich Minister for Church Affairs, 17 Dec. 1938, Wolfenbüttel, on the same subject.

35. Memo, Protestant Consistory of the Province Grenzmark Posen–West Prussia, signed Graupe, to Protestant Upper Consistory, Berlin-Charlottenburg, 18 Mar. 1939, Schneidemühl, EZA Berlin 7/1960.

36. Memo signed Dr. Werner, to the Protestant Consistories of the internal area of jurisdiction, 12 May 1939, ibid.

37. See Leader of the Reich Office for Genealogical Research to Protestant Upper Consistory, 7 July 1939, Berlin, ibid. Dr. Werner, the president of the

Upper Consistory of the Church of the Old Prussian Union, was also the head of the chancellery of the German Protestant church.

38. Order signed Dr. Werner, Protestant Upper Consistory, to Protestant Consistories in the internal area of jurisdiction, 4 July 1939, ibid. Attached are copies of the questionnaires no. 64 IIa for clergy and 65 IIa for spouses. Each is two pages long. The order was linked to the Reich Civil Servants Law of January 1937 (RG Bl. I S.39). The questionnaire asked if the individual had Jewish parents or grandparents and requested information on previous religion, if any, of parents or grandparents. Documentary proof was to be appended.

39. Protestant Consistory of the Church Province of Silesia to Upper Consistory, 5 Aug. 1939, Breslau, ibid.

40. See Protestant Consistory of the Church Province of Silesia to Theological Education and Examinations Office of the Protestant Upper Consistory Berlin, 4 Mar. 1940, ibid., and subsequent correspondence in the same file. The decision permitting the individual in question to work for the church was initialed by, among others, Buschtöns and Freitag.

41. Weidemann, President and Bishop of the Protestant Church of Bremen, to Werner, 29 Aug. 1939, EZA Berlin 1/A4/220.

42. Protestant Consistory of the Church Province Grenzmark Posen–West Prussia, signed von Renesse, to Upper Consistory, Berlin-Charlottenburg, 16 Sept. 1939, Schneidemühl, EZA Berlin 7/1960.

43. Protestant-Lutheran Consistory of Saxony, to Head of the Chancellery of the German Protestant Church, 16 Oct. 1939, Dresden, EZA Berlin 1/A4/220.

44. File copy of Protestant Upper Consistory, signed Hymmen, for the President, to Protestant Consistories in the Jurisdiction, 22 Dec. 1939, marked sent 3 Jan. 1940, EZA Berlin 7/1960.

45. The completed questionnaire and attachments are in EZA Berlin 7/1960. See also Protestant Consistory of the Province of Saxony to Protestant Upper Consistory, 20 Feb. 1940, ibid. The petition to retain the pastor in question was based on age, which would have exempted him from the German Civil Servants law. (He was sixty-six years old.) One of the Upper Consistorial Councillors remarked that the entire petition was incomprehensible because the Civil Servants Law did not apply to pastors in any case. See marginal notes by Scheller on letter from Protestant Consistory of the Province of Saxony to Protestant Upper Consistory, 20 Feb. 1940, ibid.

46. Protestant Consistory of the Mark Brandenburg, reported by Dr. Kegel, to Upper Consistory, 7 Feb. 1941, Berlin, ibid.

47. Hymmen of Upper Consistory to Protestant Consistory of the Mark Brandenburg, 3 Mar. 1941, ibid.

48. Protestant Upper Consistory, signed Heyer, for the President, to Protestant Consistories in the sphere of jurisdiction, 8 Aug. 1944, ibid.

49. For measures adopted by the Ministry of Interior on 20 September 1943, see RM Bl IV. 1943, sp. 1505.

50. See Niemöller, *Wort und Tat im Kirchenkampf*, p. 363.

51. See Edelmann, Gruppe S, "Anstellungs- und Beförderungsbestimmungen für Wehrmachtpfarrer," [1940], p. 1, BA-MA Freiburg, N 282, v. 8. The first point of the document reads in full: "Appointment to a position as military pastor can only occur when an authorized post is vacant and the individual in question, and his wife if he is married, is of German or kindred blood."

52. Flyer, "Juden als evangelische Pfarrer," *Evangelisch-kirchlicher Anzeiger* (16 Nov. 1933): 2, LKA Bielefeld 5,1/289,1.

53. Streng to Müller, 13 Oct. 1933, Waldwimmersbach-Heidelberg, EZA Berlin 1/A4/251.

54. Reich bishop, signed Dr. Benn, to Streng, 18 Oct. 1933, ibid.

55. Gerhard Steinberg to Müller, 22 Dec. 1933, Stuttgart, EZA Berlin 1/A4/252.

56. Seidenstücker to Clarenbach, 25 May 1935, Soest, LKA Bielefeld 4,55/B/26,5.

57. This impression is conveyed in Wilhelm Hengst to Clarenbach, 11 June 1935, Hattrop (Westphalia), LKA Bielefeld 4,55/B/26,5.

58. See Clarenbach to unknown, 16 June 1935, Borgeln-Soest, ibid.

59. When pushed for evidence, the churchwarden produced passages from the periodical *Der Roland* and from the *Deutsches Pfarrerblatt* "supposedly" referring to the Jewish ancestry of Mrs. Seidenstücker. One of the articles had appeared in 1929, the other in 1933; neither mentioned Mrs. Seidenstücker specifically. The other "evidence" he offered was that another presbyter had said she was of Jewish ancestry. See copy of minutes of meeting of presbytery, St. Peter's parish, secretary Dr. Schwartz, certified correct by Seidenstücker, "Sitzung des Presbyteriums am 11. Juni 1935," Soest, 16 Aug. 1935, ibid.

60. Seidenstücker's response to the second accusation is excerpted in copy of Protestant Consistory, signed Kupsch, to Wallrabe, Pieper, Plagemann, Nölle, Presbyters of St. Peter's, 8 Aug. 1935, Münster, ibid. See also letter signed Wallrabe, Pieper, Nölle, Plagemann, "the National Socialist Presbyters of the St. Peter's Parish," to the Protestant Consistory in Münster, 6 July 1935, Soest, ibid.

61. See copy of minutes signed Nölle, Plagemann, Bauerhenne, "Sitzung der grösseren Gemeindevertretung am 2.8.35," Soest, ibid. Also Pastor Seidenstücker to Superintendent Clarenbach, 12 Aug. 1935, Soest, and Berta Seidenstücker to Presbytery of St. Peter's congregation, 12 Aug. 1935, Soest, both in LKA Bielefeld 4,55/D/7,1.

62. Goosmann to NSDAP Office for Cultural Reconciliation [Kulturelle Befriedungsstelle], 25 Feb. 1936, Berlin-Adlershof, EZA Berlin 50/210/II.

63. Goosmann to Commissioner of the City of Berlin, 20 Feb. 1936, Berlin-Adlershof, ibid.

64. Chair of Parish Church Committee, Berlin-Adlershof [H. Sievers], to Chair of Provincial Church Committee, Berlin, 14 July 1936, EZA Berlin 50/4, item 54.

65. Alfried Bobsin to Chair of Provincial Church Committee, Berlin, 6 July 1936, Berlin-Adlershof, EZA Berlin 50/4, item 52.

66. See statement prepared for Goosmann, signed H. Sievers, Chair of Parish Church Committee, "Kirchengemeinde Berlin-Adlershof," 2 June 1936, EZA Berlin 50/210/III. See also flyer signed Lotzer, Bethe, Bobsin, "Deutsche Christen—Gemeinde Adlershof," [18 Sept. 1936], quoted in Goosmann to unknown, 21 Sept. 1936, Berlin-Adlershof, EZA Berlin 50/4, item 33.

67. On the church committees see Helmreich, *German Churches under Hitler*, pp. 189–205.

68. Bishop Tügel to German Protestant Church Chancellery, 8 July 1936, Hamburg, and response, Brunotte, Reich Church Committee to Tügel, 19 Aug. 1936, both in EZA Berlin 1/A4/220.

69. Applications for membership required a pledge of Aryan descent. See coupon attached to flyer, *Ist das Führerprinzip in der evangelischen Kirche gegen Gottes Wort? Dr. Martin Luther sagt: Nein!*, [Mar. 1934], LKA Bielefeld 5,1/289,1; and pledge of Aryan descent on membership application for the "Combat and Faith Movement of 'German Christians,'" in "Rundschreiben Nr. 2, "Kampf- und Glaubensbewegung 'Deutsche Christen' (Hossenfelder Bewegung)," [1935], pp. 4, 6, EZA Berlin 1/A4/93.

70. On Schlossmann-Lönnies, see Kaiser, *Frauen in der Kirche*, pp. 196–97; Phayer, *Protestant and Catholic Women*, esp. p. 85; and Koonz, *Mothers*, p. 240.

71. See report from "Ausschuß 15 des Hauptausschusses für Sozialpolitik in der Reichsleitung," titled "Stellungnahme und Antrag, betreffend Vortrag von Frau Schlossmann-Lönnies . . . zur Frage 'Mutter und Volk!,'" 5 Jan. 1933, Berlin, attached to letter from Deutscher Evangelischer Kirchenausschuss (Kirchenbundesamt), signed Hosemann, to Evangelische Reichs-Frauenhilfe, Potsdam, 5 Jan. 1933, LKA Bielefeld 5,1/550,1.

72. Account 133a of unnamed woman born in 1905, living in Neuss, transcript of recorded conversation, in Kauffels, *Die nationalsozialistische Zeit*, p. 194.

73. Doris Reiprich and Erika Ngambi ul Kuo, "Our Father Was Cameroonian, Our Mother, East Prussian, We Are Mulattoes," in Opitz, *Showing Our Colors*, p. 62.

74. NSDAP Reich Leadership, USchlA R. L., the President, signed Walter Buch, to Reich Bishop Müller, 14 Oct. 1933, Munich, EZA Berlin 1/C4/17.

75. Mayor Schulz, Berlin-Schöneberg, to Pastor Pfeiffer, 16 Mar. 1936, EZA Berlin 50/4, item 70.

76. "Satzung des Thür. Landesvereins des Evang. Bundes e.V.," 1 Jan. 1937, in *Der Evangelische Bund in Thüringen*, 1938, pp. 76–80, EB Bensheim, EB 3.05.16.

77. Parish council, St. Gertrud parish Lübeck, to the Consistory in Lübeck, 14 Feb. 1939, pp. 1–2, AEK Lübeck, NL Julius Jensen, no. II.12.

78. Speech by Heinrich Himmler to SS leaders on 4 October 1943 in Posen, excerpted in Noakes and Pridham, *Nazism*, 2:1199.

79. "Thüringens evangelische Kirche schließt Juden aus," no author, *Deutsche Allgemeine Zeitung*, no. 100 (28 Feb. 1939), BA Potsdam, RLB 1864, p. 145.

80. See reference to these pieces of church legislation in untitled Confessing Church response to the Godesberg Declaration, [May 1939], EZA Berlin 50/600, p. 30.

81. Reich Chamber of Music, Office of the President, signed Karrasch, to German Protestant Church, 22 Oct. 1934, EZA Berlin 1/C3/131. See also Reich Chamber of Music, signed Karrasch, to German Protestant Church, 15 Nov. 1934, ibid. The comments of the parish council are quoted in Bishop Coch of Saxony, signed Adolf Müller, Consistory Councillor, to the Reich Chamber of Music, special group B: Reich Musicians, 25 Oct. 1934, Dresden, p. 2, ibid.

82. "Liste der nichtarischen Organisten," sent from Reich Musicians of the Reich Music Chamber: Specialty V—Protestant Church Musicians, to the Organizational Director of the Reich Association for Protestant Church Music, 2 Sept. 1935, ibid.

83. Excerpt from speech of Hans Hinkel in Wedding, "Vollblutjuden an der Orgel," in *Schnellbrief für Glieder der Bekennenden Kirche*, no. 28 (10 Sept. 1935): 110, LKA Bielefeld 5,1/555,1. For more on Hinkel and his activities to eliminate Jews from German culture, see Alan E. Steinweis, "Hans Hinkel and German Jewry, 1933–1941," *Leo Baeck Institute Year Book*, no. 38 (1993): 209–19.

84. President of the Bremen Protestant Church to the Reich Church Committee, 7 Dec. 1935, Bremen, EZA Berlin 1/C3/131.

85. Reich Church Committee, initialed by Söhngen and Mahrenholz, to Bremen Protestant Church, 17 Jan. 1936, pp. 1–3, ibid.

86. Protestant Upper Consistory to President of Reich Chamber of Music, 3 July 1936, pp. 1–6, ibid. A copy was sent to the Chancellery of the German Protestant church as well as to all of the regional churches.

87. "Vermerk," signed Söhngen, 5 Feb. 1941, Berlin-Charlottenburg, ibid.

88. See file copies of letters from the Protestant Church Chancellery to

Consistories in Darmstadt, Vienna, Hamburg, Dresden, Danzig, Sudenten-
land, Bohemia, and Moravia, [1941], ibid.

89. Chancellery of the German Protestant Church to the Minister of Church
Affairs, copy to President of Reich Music Chamber, 4 Nov. 1941, ibid. On the
organist in Königsberg and the loss of his position in August 1936, see Protestant Upper Consistory to Reich- and Prussian Minister for Church Affairs,
25 Aug. 1936, ibid. The impetus for dismissal seems to have come from the
ministry.

## Chapter Six

1. Theobald Lehbrink to Wentz, 19 Feb. 1958, Kassel, KAG Minden, folder
Lehbrink.

2. 1933 German population: 69,460,000; Catholics: 23,167,000 (32.4 percent);
Protestants: 42,105,000 (62.7 percent); Jews: 499,000 (0.8 percent); Other:
2,682,000 (4.1 percent). Source: Gotto and Repgen, *Kirche, Katholiken und
Nationalsozialismus*, p. 121.

3. The group of German Christians generally known as the Thuringians
used different names for themselves over time, from Kirchenbewegung
Deutsche Christen to Deutsche Christen—Nationalkirchliche Einung. Sometimes those alterations reflected the leadership's attempts to draw attention to
one or the other aspect of the group's identity; other changes resulted from
National Socialist prohibitions on particular words, for example, *Bewegung*
(movement).

4. "Feierstunde bei den 'Deutschen Christen,'" in *Geraer Zeitung, 1. Bei-
blatt* (30 Nov. 1933), EZA Berlin 1/A4/100.

5. Krause, "Rede des Gauobmannes der Glaubensbewegung 'Deutsche
Christen,'" p. 1, LKA Bielefeld 5,1/289,2.

6. "Kirchenkreis Kölln-Land II," announcements, in *Unsere Volkskirche—
Sonntägliches Nachrichtenblatt aus den Berliner Kirchengemeinden*, no. 7
(19 Nov. 1933): 112, BA Potsdam DC-I, 1933–35, pp. 154–69.

7. Rössler to Bonhoeffer, 6 Dec. 1934, pp. 1–2, in "Bonhoeffers Briefwechsel
als Pfarrer in London," item 21, BA Koblenz, NL 308/A 41/fiche 3.

8. German Christians, Gau Rhineland, "Rundschreiben Nr. 10/36," signed
Pastor Brökelschen, deputy Gau leader, 20 July 1936, Oberhausen, p. 2, AEKR
Düsseldorf, NL Schmidt/17, pp. 55–63.

9. Leutheuser's statement quoted in "Von der Toleranz in der neuen
deutschen Kirche," in "Glaubensbekenntnisse Deutscher Christen," typescript assembled by critics of the German Christians, [1937?], p. 11, LKA
Bielefeld 5,1/289,1.

10. Julius Leutheuser, "Die Grundlage für die religiöse Einigung des deutschen Volkes!," *Die Nationalkirche. Briefe an Deutsche Christen*, no. 45 (7 Nov. 1937): 353–54, LKA Bielefeld 5,1/292,1.

11. [Karl Wentz], "Programm des Schlachtenseekreises (Entwurf vom 23. Juli 1941)," p. 1, KAG Minden, file Schlachtensee 1944.

12. This point is made explicitly in von Alvensleben, "Denkschrift—Volksgemeinschaft trotz Religionsverschiedenheit," [31 Oct. 1941], p. 10, BA Koblenz R 43 II/151/fiche 1, p. 9. Other variations in the wording appear, such as on a German Christian flyer: "One Führer, One Reich, One *Volk*, One positive-Christian church!" Flyer, "In diesem Zeichen siegen wir!," *Des Deutschen Volkes Kirche*, no. 1 (12 Apr. 1936): 3, LKA Bielefeld 5,1/291,2.

13. Fr. de Fries, Dortmund, "Aus der Bewegung," *Briefe an Deutsche Christen*, no. 17 (1 Sept. 1936): 195, LKA Bielefeld 5,1/291,1. The biblical reference is to Matthew 6:9–13.

14. See "Weihungsgottesdienst der Frauenkirche (Dom) [Dresden] durch Reichsbischof Müller und Landesbischof Coch, am 29 Nov. 1942," sent from Regional Council of Brethren of the Confessing Protestant Lutheran Church of Saxony to Provisional Leadership of the German Protestant Church, c/o Pastor Dr. Böhm, Berlin-Zehlendorf, 9 Dec. 1942, Dresden, EZA Berlin 50/576, pp. 22–23.

15. Fr. de Fries, Dortmund, "Aus der Bewegung," *Briefe an Deutsche Christen*, no. 17 (1 Sept. 1936): 195, LKA Bielefeld 5,1/291,1.

16. "Eine bedeutsame Kulturelle Tat der Thüringer evangelischen Kirche," *Die Nationalkirche*, no. 45 (7 Nov. 1937): 358–59.

17. Confessing Church report, "Versammlung der 'Deutschen Christen' im Saal des Schützenhofes," [Herford, 18 Nov. 1934], LKA Bielefeld 5,1/294,2.

18. Excerpts from a lecture by Professor Dr. Schmidt-Japing, Bonn, on 4 Nov. 1933, in "Die Bibel und wir Deutschen," *Nachrichten Blatt der Evangelischen Gemeinde Oberhausen I*, no. 21 (11 Nov. 1934), AEKR Düsseldorf, NL Schmidt/18.

19. *Irrlehre? Unsere Antwort an den Reichskirchenausschuß*, p. 19, LKA Bielefeld 5,1/291,1.

20. von Loewenfeld, "Wenn Luther heute lebte!," *Glaube und Heimat*, no. 9 (Sept. 1933): 102, LKA Bielefeld 5,1/289,2.

21. Pastor Dr. Gahr (name unclear) to Frick, 20 Dec. 1936, Herbishofen, p. 2, attached is pamphlet by Gahr, *Die Deutschen Christen und ihre Geschichte vor Bonifatius*, 1935, (references above to pp. 10ff.), BA Koblenz R 18/5057, pp. 153–62.

22. Wilhelm Kotzde-Kottenrodt, "Der heilige Berg des Elsaß," [1941], pp. 4, 8, cover letter from Kotzde-Kottenrodt to Wolfram Sievers, 6 Scheiding (Sep-

tember) 1941, Ebnet/Freiburg Br., BDC Wilhelm Kotzde-Kottenrodt materials.

23. Kotzde-Kottenrodt, "Um die Deutschwerdung am Oberrhein. Gedanken und Vorschläge," Erntemond (October) 1941, Ebnet Amt Freiburg (Breisgau), pp. 1, 5–6, ibid. See also Kotzde-Kottenrodt to SS-Obersturmbannführer W. Sievers, 12 Mar. 1942, Weimar, p. 1, ibid.

24. "Nach der Einigung zwischen Kinder und Leffler. Die interkonfessionelle Nationalkirche im Marsch," in *Schnellbrief für Glieder der Bekennenden Kirche*, no. 21 (Berlin-Dahlem: 1 Aug. 1935): 1, LKA Bielefeld 5,1/554,2.

25. Leffler, "Denkschrift," written after meeting with Ministerialrat Stahn in Kerrl's office, and cover letter Leffler to Stahn, 28 Aug. 1935, Weimar, pp. 3–4, BA Potsdam DC-I, 1933–35, pp. 345–48.

26. Pastor Krüger, Gera, speech quoted in "'Ein Volk—eine Kirche'—Versammlung der Deutschen Christen im 'Central-Hotel,'" *Göttinger Tageblatt*, no. 222 (22 Sept. 1936): 4, LKA Bielefeld 5,1/291,1.

27. Müller, *Der deutsche Volkssoldat*, pp. 114–15.

28. Edelmann, "Wesen und Aufgabe der Feldseelsorge," 1941, BA-MA Freiburg, RH 15/282, pp. 22–36. "Richtlinien für die Durchführung der Feldseelsorge," signed Keitel, Oberkommando der Wehrmacht, 24 May 1942, Berlin, BA-MA Freiburg, RM 26/7.

29. Alberti, *Als Kriegspfarrer in Polen*, pp. 17, 29.

30. "Aufruf des stellvertretenden Leiters der Nationalkirchlichen Einung Deutschen Christen," *Die Nationalkirche*, no. 38/1939 (17 Sept. 1939), clipping in EZA Berlin 1/A4/468.

31. "'Glaubensfreiheit' in Oesterreich," *Der Weckruf*, no. 29 (Cologne, 22 July 1934): 397, LKA Bielefeld 5,1/290,2. The *Völkischer Beobachter* reported gains of 9,581 in 1936, bringing the total number of Austrian Protestants to 327,468. "Kirchenbewegung in Österreich," *Völkischer Beobachter*, no. 87/88 (28/29 Mar. 1937), BA Potsdam RLB 1864, p. 63. See also "Uebertrittsbewegung in Oesterreich," *Deutsch-Evangelische Korrespondenz* (12 Apr. 1939), LKA Bielefeld 5,1/297. That account gives the total number of Protestants in Austria as 342,308 in 1939, over 10,000 more than in the previous year.

32. See, for example, remarks in "Verhandlungsnachweise der Sitzung des Zentralvorstandes des Evangelischen Bundes am 2. und 3. August 1933 in Saalfeld (Thüringen)," p. 18, EB Bensheim S 500.9.140.

33. Jörg Thierfelder, "Ökumene der Bedrängten—Die Jahre 1933 bis 1945," in Maron, *Evangelisch und ökumenisch*, p. 194. Micklem refers to the "abortive *Katholisch-nationalkirchliche Bewegung*" founded at the end of 1935 by Pastor Hütwohl. Micklem, *National Socialism and the Roman Catholic Church*, p. 137.

34. See *Nationalkirche?*, flyer of the Protestant League, 1937, EB Bensheim S 500.9.136.

35. Neuhäusler, *Kreuz und Hakenkreuz*, pp. 286, 330. Guenter Lewy mentions that Kuno Brombacher, once in Papen's entourage and a member of the Nazi party since 1931, sought to "further the union of cross and swastika" by joining the Old Catholic church. According to Lewy, the Nazis distrusted the Old Catholics and they played no significant role in the Third Reich. Lewy, *The Catholic Church and Nazi Germany*, p. 162.

36. "Die katholisch-Nationalkirchliche Bewegung," *Mitteilungsblatt der Glaubensbewegung Deutscher Christen Mecklenburg*, no. 5/6 (June 1937): 50, LKA Bielefeld 5,1/292,1.

37. Micklem, *National Socialism and the Roman Catholic Church*, pp. 209–10.

38. Excerpt from *Die Nationalkirche in Sachsen, Bezirks-Ausgabe Dresden* (Mar. 1938) in "Nationalkirchliche Einung Deutsche Christen bestimmt *nicht* mehr Landeskirche," Confessing Church report, 19 May 1938, LKA Bielefeld 5,1/296.

39. See Wenner, "Monatsbericht der Regierung (September 1934)," 8 Oct. 1934, Speyer, in Prantl, *Die kirchliche Lage in Bayern*, p. 44.

40. Ziegler, "Monatsbericht der Regierung (Okt. 1937)," 9 Nov. 1937, ibid., p. 212.

41. Excerpts from Archbishop Hauck's speech with commentary are provided in Dippold, "Monatsbericht der Regierung (Dez. 1934)," 9 Jan. 1935, Ansbach, in Witetschek, *Die kirchliche Lage in Bayern*, vol. 2, *Regierungsbezirk Ober- und Mittelfranken*, p. 45.

42. Wenner, "Monatsbericht der Regierung (Oktober 1934)," 9 Nov. 1934, Speyer, in Prantl, *Die kirchliche Lage in Bayern*, p. 52.

43. "Hirtenbrief des deutschen Episkopates, Fulda, 20 August 1935," in Stasiewski, *Akten Deutscher Bischöfe*, 2:332.

44. Ludwig Biehl, *Deutsche Nationalkirche? Ein aufklärendes Wort an die deutschen Katholiken* (Speyer: Bischöfl. Ordinariat, [1937]). See also Wenner, "Monatsbericht der Regierung (January 1938)," 8 Feb. 1938, Speyer, in Prantl, *Die kirchliche Lage in Bayern*, p. 226.

45. Bertram, Archbishop of Breslau, to Cardinal Pacelli, 5 Jan. 1938, Breslau, in Volk, *Akten deutscher Bischöfe*, 4:415. See also, in same volume, "Aufzeichnungen Sebastians von der Plenarkonferenz des deutschen Episkopats," 17–19 Aug., 1938, Fulda, p. 541.

46. Protestant Consistory Westphalia, signed Kupsch, to Karl Leben in Bad Sassendorf, 23 Jan. 1937, Münster, LKA Bielefeld 4,55/A/34.

47. Pastor Scheuermann, "Die nationalkirchlichen Deutschen Christen," in

*Der Stand der völkischreligiös-kirchlichen Auseinandersetzung*, [Stuttgart, 1938], p. 7, KAG Minden, unlabeled folder.

48. *Deutsches Christentum* (8 May 1938), quoted in Scheuermann, *Der Stand der völkischreligiös-kirchlichen Auseinandersetzung*, p. 8, ibid.

49. Special edition of *Deutsches Christentum* (4 Sept. 1938), quoted in Scheuermann, *Der Stand der völkischreligiös-kirchlichen Auseinandersetzung*, p. 9, ibid. See also flyer from Deutsche Christen (Nationalkirchliche Einung), advertising upcoming address of Pastor Friedrich Kapferer, 14 Nov. 1938, BA Potsdam DG IV 1938–43, p. 208. Until February 1938, the flyer confirms, Kapferer was active as a Catholic priest.

50. "Aus der Arbeit der Einung," *Informationsdienst*, 3/44 (5 Apr. 1944): 11, EZA Berlin 1/A4/566.

51. "Aufruf," signed Adolf Daum, 8 May 1941, Bayreuth, EZA Berlin 50/576, p. 45, with attached questionnaire regarding church taxes.

52. Report from Bezzel, Protestant-Lutheran District Superintendent Bayreuth, to Protestant Lutheran Regional Church Council, Munich, 22 Sept. 1941, LKA Nuremberg, LKR II 246/Bd. 9.

53. Ziegler, "Monatsbericht der Regierung," 9 Nov. 1937, in Prantl, *Die kirchliche Lage in Bayern*, p. 212.

54. Memo from German Christians, Congregation of Franconia, with three signatures, including Karl Matthauer, to Bavarian Ministry for Education and Cultural Affairs, 23 July 1942, Nuremberg-Eibach, BHStA Munich MK 36986. The memo noted that the statistics did not include members of the National Church wing of German Christians because they had separate groups in Franconia.

55. Report of Riedel to Protestant Lutheran Superintendent Kulmbach, 27 Mar. 1944, Kulmbach, "Betreff: Bericht über DC-Gemeinde in Kulmbach," p. 1, LKA Nuremberg, LKR II 246/Bd. 9.

56. "Einladung zur Ersten Reichstagung des Studentenkampfbundes Deutsche Christen in der Friedrich-Wilhelms Universität zu Berlin vom 7.–10. August 1933," Studentenkampfbund Deutsche Christen, signed Kurt Werner, July 1933, Berlin, LKA Bielefeld 5,1/687,2. Gögginger's speech on "Katholizismus und deutsche Gegenwartsfragen" is quoted in "Studententagung 'Deutsche Christen,'—Volkskirche im Werden," *Kirche im Kampf—Beilage zum "Reichsboten*," no. 180 (10 Aug. 1933): 2, LKA Bielefeld 5,1/687,2.

57. "Rundschreiben Nr. 17, signed Hildebrandt, Deutsche Christen Mecklenburg-Schwerin, to all German Christians of Mecklenburg, 25 June 1935," p. 1, EZA Berlin 1/A4/96.

58. "Dr. Konrad Möckel in einem Kronstädter Vortrag über 'Kirche und Gemeinschaft,'" *Kirchliche Blätter*, no. 2 (12 Jan. 1937): 17, BA Koblenz, NL 252/22.

59. Engelland, *Drei Wege zu Gott?*, pp. 11–12.

60. For example, Glaubensbewegung 'Deutsche Christen,' Evangelische Nationalsozialistischen und Freunde der Glaubensbewegung, "Was ist seit Wittenberg geschehen?," offprint from *Evangelium im Dritten Reich*, [late 1933], LKA Bielefeld 5,1/289,1.

61. "Bericht des Gemeindekirchenrats der Apostel-Paulus-Gemeinde Berlin-Schöneberg," signed Pastor Peters, H. Schmidt, Franz Steller (elders), Dr. Bergmann, lawyer, 3 Dec. 1934, Berlin, p. 3, EZA Berlin 1/A4/55.

62. Leffler, "Leiter der Deutschen Pfarrergemeinde," to members of the Congregation of German Pastors, 18 July 1935, Weimar, pp. 1–2, LKA Nuremberg, KKU 6/IV.

63. Pastor Ehrenfried Haufe to Birnbaum, 18 Oct. 1934, Dresden-Briesnitz, EZA Berlin 1/A4/54.

64. Pastor Hermann Burcksturtz (name unclear) to Protestant-Lutheran Regional Church Council, Munich, 16 Feb. 1942, Mühldorf, "Betreff: DC und Reichsbischof in Mühldorf," pp. 1–2, LKA Nuremberg, LKR II 246, Bd. 9.

65. For example, see letters to Reich Bishop Müller from Pastor Eberlein, Editor of the Association for Silesian Church History, 16 Nov. 1933, Strehlen (Silesia), p. 1, EZA Berlin 1/A4/100, and Superintendent Heise, 19 Nov. 1933, Burg b. M., EZA Berlin 1/A4/98.

66. Pastors Dieckmann and Dahlkötter to Bishop Adler, 22 Nov. 1933, Lippstadt (Westphalia), pp. 1–2, LKA Bielefeld 5,1/836,2.

67. "Die Irrlehre der Thüringer Deutschen Christen, die neue Grundlage der Kirche?," in report, "Wie die Ausbildung unserer zukünftigen Pastoren aussieht wenn Thüringer Deutschen Christen Theologie Professoren werden," [1937], p. 3, LKA Bielefeld 5,1/291,1.

68. Martin Maier-Hugendubel to Hitler, 10 Oct. 1934, Tübingen, p. 2, BA Koblenz R 43 II/171/fiche 1/p. 6.

69. "Pfingstgeist in der Marahrenskirche," in German Christian newsletter, "Deutsche Christen—Kirchenkreis Iserlohn," (1 Aug. 1935): 6–7, LKA Bielefeld 5,1/294,2.

70. Untitled flyer, LKA Bielefeld 5,1/290,1.

71. "Bayern—Die Deutschen Christen in Bayern," in "Westdeutsche Eilkorrespondenz," no. 16 (25 Feb. 1935): 2–3, LKA Bielefeld 5,1/553,2.

72. *Deutscher Sonntag* (15 Sept. 1935), quoted in Protestant Senior Church Council, Württemberg, signed Wurm, to Reich Church Committee Berlin-Charlottenburg, 12 Nov. 1935, pp. 3–4, EZA Berlin 1/A4/471.

73. Meiser to Brunotte, 9 Feb. 1940, quoted in Baier, *Kirche in Not*, p. 266.

74. "Erklärung aus Westfalen zur Zentralvorstandssitzung des Ev. Bundes," attachment to "Verhandlungsbericht über die Zentralvorstandssitzung des

Evang. Bundes am 5. Okt. 1934 in Breslau," EB Bensheim S.500.9.140. On the early years of the league, see Heiner Grote, "Der 'Evangelische Bund zur Wahrung der deutsch-protestantischen Interessen' (1886–1918)," in Fleischmann-Bisten and Grote, *Protestanten auf dem Wege*, pp. 9–84.

75. "Aufruf zur Gründung des Evangelischen Bundes zur Wahrung der deutsch-protestantischen Interessen," 15 Jan. 1887, in Kupisch, *Quellen zur Geschichte des deutschen Protestantismus (1871–1945)*, pp. 52–54.

76. Quoted in "Protestantismus und völkische Bewegung," in *Germania* (5 Sept. 1924), clipping in BA Potsdam RLB 1836, p. 42.

77. On the history of the Protestant League itself during the Third Reich, see Fleischmann-Bisten, "Der Evangelische Bund in der Weimarer Republik und im sog. Dritten Reich (1918–1945)," in Fleischmann-Bisten and Grote, *Protestanten auf dem Wege*, pp. 85–163.

78. Report on address by Pastor Niemann, "Der Deutsche Sieg und die Zukunft des Protestantismus," *Neue Westfälische Zeitung* (6 Mar. 1918), BA Potsdam RLB 1836, pp. 6–7.

79. On the German Christian activities of Pastor Niemann the son, see Wilhelm Niemöller files throughout. For example, he is mentioned in W. Stuckmann, "Kurzer Bericht über eine Deutsch-Christliche Versammlung am 12.1.1935 im Saale Jansen, Hasslinghausen," LKA Bielefeld 5,1/294,2.

80. See clipping from *Bayerischer Kurier*, no. 243 (3 Sept. 1924), BA Potsdam RLB 1836, p. 37. On Fahrenhorst's subsequent involvement with the German Christian movement, see Fleischmann-Bisten, "Der Evangelische Bund," p. 121.

81. "Die Wächter auf der Zinne," *Reichsbote*, no. 144 (17 June 1930), BA Potsdam RLB 1836, p. 102.

82. See "Verhandlungsnachweise der Sitzung des Zentralvorstandes des Evangelischen Bundes am 2. und 3. August 1933 in Saalfeld (Thüringen)," pp. 2, 6–11, 18, and "Verhandlungsbericht über die Zentralvorstandssitzung des Evang. Bundes am 5. Okt. 1934 in Breslau," pp. 3, 5, with attachment, "Erklärung aus Westfalen zur Zentralvorstandssitzung des Ev. Bundes," both in EB Bensheim S.500.9.140.

83. "Sitzung des Präsidiums . . . 23. Jan. 1933 . . . im Bundesheim," p. 8, EB Bensheim S.500.9.133.

84. Waitz, *Nationalkirche*, pp. 15–17.

85. "Nationalkirche?," Protestant League, 1937, EB Bensheim S 500.9.136, pp. 1–2.

86. Schmuhl, *Rassenhygiene*, pp. 154–60; on the response of the churches, pp. 305–12. Nowak, *"Euthanasie,"* provides an overview on pp. 64–68, specific information on the Protestant response, pp. 91–106, and on the Catholic position, pp. 106–19. Also see Klee, *"Euthanasie,"* pp. 36–38.

87. On the response of Germany's Catholic bishops to the Sterilization Law, see Stasiewski, *Akten Deutscher Bischöfe*, 1:223–24, 357–65, 392–93.

88. Denzler, *Widerstand oder Anpassung?*, p. 107; Lewy, *Catholic Church and Nazi Germany*, p. 261.

89. "Nationalkirche?," Protestant League, 1937, EB Bensheim S 500.0.136, p. 2.

90. Pastor Dr. Wilhelm Bergér, Darmstadt, "Der Evangelische Bund in der Landeskirche Nassau-Hessen, 1934–1937," in *Der evangelische Bund in Nassau und Hessen, 1887–1937* (Berlin: Verlag des Evang. Bundes, 1937), p. 99.

91. Report of address by Pastor Hoensch—Halle i. W., "Gottes Walten in der Kirchengeschichte der Gegenwart," 12 Apr. 1934, p. 1, LKA Bielefeld 5,1/294,2.

92. See, for example, Spotts, *The Churches and Politics*, pp. 6–7.

93. Geheime Staatspolizei, signed Heydrich, to Reich Congregation of German Christians (National Church Movement), c/o Leffler, 21 Dec. 1937, BA Koblenz R 43 II/150/fiche 2, p. 96.

94. Office of the Chief of Security Police, signed Best, to Chief of Reich Chancellery Lammers, 23 Mar. 1938, BA Koblenz R 43 II/150/fiche 3/pp. 98–99, and in same file, Reich Chancellery "Vermerk zu RK. 6032 B," dated 4 Apr. 1938.

95. Kerrl to Führer's Deputy, Munich, 19 Feb. 1938, ibid., p. 102.

96. Stahn, "'Wesen und Aufgabe der Feldseelsorge,' Vortrag am 9 Dec. 1940 beim Kriegspfarrerlehrgang im OKH," BA-MA Freiburg, N282/11. See also May, *Interkonfessionalismus*, esp. p. 342.

97. Ronneberger, "Denkschrift über die Wehrmachtseelsorge," [1941?], pp. 1–2, 4, BA-MA Freiburg, RM 26/6.

98. von Alvensleben, "Denkschrift—Volksgemeinschaft trotz Religionsverschiedenheit," [31 Oct. 1941], passed on by Senior Consistorial Councillor Wieneke to Reich Chancellery, 24 Feb. 1942, pp. 1–2, 5, 10, 12–19, 22, BA Koblenz R 43 II/151/fiche 1, pp. 2–15.

99. Excerpted copy, Rönck, President of the Thuringian Protestant Church, to Muhs, State Secretary, Ministry of Church Affairs, 30 Dec. 1943, Eisenach, sent to Lammers's office, 2 Dec. 1944, BA Koblenz R 43 II/172, fiche 5/pp. 210–12.

100. Leffler, "Weltkirche oder Nationalkirche? Volk—Staat—Kirche," in *Vom Werden deutscher Volkskirche*, p. 41.

## Chapter Seven

1. See report (*Gutachten*) by Finance Councillor Dr. Max von Bahrfeldt, "Entwicklung und gegenwärtige wirtschaftliche und finanzielle Lage des 'Evangelium im Dritten Reich,'" 27 Mar. 1935, pp. 7–8, EZA Berlin 1/A4/166.

2. Kinder, "An alle Gau-Obmänner," in "Deutsche Christen" Reichsleitung, *Rundschreiben Nr. 17*, Berlin (10 Apr. 1935), EZA Berlin 1/A4/96.

3. Curt R. Dietz, untitled graveside reading "(bei einer Mutter)," in *Stärker als das Schicksal*, p. 20.

4. Hans Robert Schröter, "Halte Fest," in *Wir sind tausend und sind eins*, p. 63.

5. See, for example, "Ehre den Müttern (14 May)," in "Ordnung für die Gottesfeier der Kinder," no. 16, *Die Gottesfeier*, p. 4. One hymnbook of the German Christians, *Großer Gott, wir loben Dich!*, featured drawings of mothers and children on pages opposite hymns dealing with family themes.

6. "Das sind die Stillen im Lande," lyrics by Friedrich Lienhard, tune adapted by Fritz Schwadtke, no. 806 in Schwadtke, *Lieder für Gottesfeiern*.

7. Koonz, *Mothers*, p. 17.

8. Hans Christoph Kaergel, "Der Dank des Dichters," *Der Weckruf, Evangelisches Gemeindeblatt der Westmark*, no. 19, Bonn (12 May 1935): 291, LKA Bielefeld 5,1/290,1.

9. Item in Confessing Church flyer, *Zur Wahl*, in "Material für Vorträge und Schulungen," Stuttgart, [1937], p. 3, LKA Bielefeld 5,1/292,2.

10. See, for example, the report of the celebration of Diehl's birthday, the New Land Festival Day (*Neulandfesttag*): Lisbeth Geerdes, Lena Matthies, et al., "Bericht über unsre Freizeit vom 27.7.–3.8.1960," KAG Minden, no. 13.

11. See account by the German Christian teacher Menzer, "Bericht über die Reichstagung," (3–5 Apr. 1933 in Berlin), in *Glaubensbewegung "Deutsche Christen," Nachrichten des Gaues "Industrie,"* Witten [Apr. 1933], p. 2, LKA Bielefeld 5,1/289,2.

12. Else Hasse, "Vom Ganzheitscharakter der Frau," *Neulandblatt*, no. 21 (1 Nov. 1934): 258, LKA Bielefeld 5,1/290,2.

13. Klara Lönnies, "Denkschrift über die Notwendigkeit einer besonderen symbolischen Tat der DEK im Auftrage des Staates und der Nation!," and attached cover letter from Lönnies to Birnbaum, 13 Sept. 1934, on letterhead of "Mutter und Volk—Verlagsgesellschaft m.b.H. Berlin," pp. 1–6, EZA Berlin 1/A4/55.

14. "Die Führer der Deutschen Christen," in supplement to the *Reichsboten*, no. 173 (2 Aug. 1933), clipping in BA Potsdam, DC-I, 1933–35, p. 86.

15. E. Neumüller, "An alle Mitglieder der Reichsgruppe," *Rundschreiben*, no. 35/8 (30 Oct. 1935), EZA Berlin 1/A4/93.

16. Superintendent [Krause?] and E. Rutkowsky, Director, to Mrs. (Reich Bishop) Müller, 15 Nov. 1934, Wanne-Eickel (Westphalia), EZA Berlin 1/A4/55.

17. According to a newspaper account, Mrs. Paula Müller, Cuxhaven, contended that the former Reich bishop, her deceased husband, did not commit

suicide but died of a heart attack. See clipping from *Welt am Sonntag*, 5 July 1953, LKA Bielefeld 5,1/305,1. Ludwig Müller's sister shared his widow's stance on the cause of his death. Sophie Dehls to Wentz, 11 Mar. 1960, Berlin-Templehof, KAG Minden, no. 1.

18. Irma Rehm to Reich Bishop Müller, 17 Feb. 1935, EZA Berlin 1/A4/95.

19. This was the female vicar Ehmann, later the wife of Pastor Jihr in Waldeckerland. See pamphlet from *Frau und Kirche* series, Potsdam. Ehmann is mentioned in the report of Helene Vogel regarding her trip for the Women's Service through the Reich, p. 8, KAG Minden, loose materials.

20. Leni Schroeter, Cläre Höse, and Gertrud Weißnew to Müller, 14 Nov. 1933, Hermannswerder-Potsdam, EZA Berlin 1/A4/248.

21. Elisabeth Jacob (name unclear) née Müller-Buchhof to Müller, 15 Nov. 1933, Berlin-Wilmersdorf, EZA Berlin 1/A4/101. The benediction comes from Numbers 6:25–26.

22. Marie Lammersietz (name unclear) to Müller, 17 Nov. 1933, Pr. Oldendorf (Westphalia), ibid.

23. Ilse von Rabenau to Müller, 16 Nov. 1933, Berlin-Lankwitz, ibid.

24. Charlotte Pinski to Müller, [Nov. 1933], ibid.

25. Elisabeth Janssen to Müller, 18 Nov. 1933, Holtland (Ostfriesland), pp. 1–3, ibid.

26. Alice Aßmus-Ohlweig (name unclear) to Mrs. Schulze-Naumburg (Frick's secretary), 17 Feb. 1937, Droskau N.L., BA Koblenz R 18/5057, pp. 165–66.

27. Alice Aßmus-Ohlweig (name unclear) to Frick, 13 Feb. 1937, Droskau N.L., p. 2, BA Koblenz R 18/5057, p. 169.

28. Gertrud Wendel to Reich Minister of Foreign Affairs, 27 Aug. 1935, Berlin, AA Bonn, VI A, Evang. Ang 2: Verfassung der ev. Kirche, vol. 12.

29. Liebe-Harkort, *Frau und Kirche*, pp. 10, 13.

30. Account of Liebe-Harkort's talk in "Aus dem Frauendienst. Bezirksfrauenschulung des Frauendienstes," *Evangelische Nachrichten: Gemeindeblatt für Westfalen*, no. 26 (28 June 1936): 9, EZA Berlin 1/A4/467.

31. These groups are mentioned, for example, in the column "Aus unsern Gemeinden," *Der Sonntagsfreund*, no. 6 (Wattenscheid, 9 Feb. 1936): 9, LKA Bielefeld 5,1/291,2.

32. *Rundschreiben, DC Landesleiter Oldenburg*, no. 4 (5 June 1935): 4, LKA Bielefeld 5,1/291,2. In November 1935, the person in charge of Women's Service groups for the Rhineland was also a German Christian pastor. See "Aus Kirche und Gemeinde," no author, *Nachrichten-Blatt der Evangelischen Gemeinde Oberhausen I*, no. 45 (10 Nov. 1935): 3, AEKR Düsseldorf, NL Schmidt/18.

33. See "Die reichskirchliche Frauenhilfe," in *Sondernummer vom Nach-*

*richtenblatt der Ev. Gemeinde Oberhausen I*, ed. Pastor Brökelschen, Oberhausen (Rhineland), [1935], AEKR Düsseldorf, NL Schmidt/18. On Hermenau, see "Frauenwerk DEK: Anlage zum Mitgliederbrief der DC, Gau Rheinland," no. 3, LKA Bielefeld 5,1/290,2. Also see Koonz, *Mothers in the Fatherland*, pp. 247–51.

34. Report, "Betr.: 'Evangelischer Frauendienst' im Deutschen Frauenwerk. Besprechung am 6. März 1935 in Anwesenheit des Führers des Frauendienstes Pfarrer Lic. Hermenau-Potsdam," LKA Bielefeld 5,1/290,1.

35. See flyer advertising Krummacher's book *Weltwirtschaftskrise und
Christentum* and offering biographical information on him, in BDC, Partei
Kanzlei Correspondence, Hossenfelder material; see also Stephenson, *Nazi
Organisation of Women*, pp. 99, 102–5.

36. Pastor Brandes to Pastor Lücking, 4 Aug. 1933, Lengerich (Westphalia),
LKA Bielefeld 5,1/836,1.

37. Circular, signed Kinder, *Rundschreiben, DC Reichsleitung*, no. 25
(Berlin-Charlottenburg, [June 1934]), LKA Bielefeld 5,1/290,1.

38. Pastor (sig. illegible) to unknown, 23 Jan. 1935, Schwelm (Westphalia), p.
2, LKA Bielefeld 5,1/294,2.

39. "Anlage zum Mitgliederbrief der Deutschen Christen, Gau Rheinland,
Nr. 3—'Frauenwerk DEK,'" LKA Bielefeld 5,1/290,2.

40. Beckemeier to unknown, 15 Dec. 1934, Lübeck, KA Lübeck, KA, KK 48,
p. 8.

41. Minny Wimmers to Hitler, 12 Nov. 1934, Bielefeld (copy sent by NSDAP
Division for Cultural Harmony to the Prases of the Confessing Synod in Bad
Oeynhausen, then on to Wilhelm Niemöller, Bielefeld, "zur Kenntnis,"), LKA
Bielefeld 5,1/358,2.

42. Mr. Wimmers sent the reply his wife received from the NSDAP's Division for Cultural Harmony, dated 15 January 1935, to Wentz in Minden and
expressed his outrage that the response quoted none other than Wilhelm Niemöller himself in refuting Mrs. Wimmer's charges. Walter Wimmers to Wentz,
18 Feb. 1935, Bielefeld, with attachments, including copy of letter from
NSDAP Division for Cultural Harmony to Mrs. Wimmers, 15 Jan. 1935, KAG
Minden, folder of unorganized Wentz correspondence.

43. A representative from the central office of the Westphalian Women's Aid
in Soest was on hand and prepared a report. See Lutterjohann, "Bericht über
die Feier des 25 jährigen Bestehens des 'Frauenvereins' in Lohne am 15. Dez.
1936. (Der 'Frauenverein' ist Mitglied des Westf. Frauenhilfe)," LKA Bielefeld 4,55/B/12,3.

44. See Lutterjohann's report, pp. 1–3, ibid.

45. Protestant Women's Association, Lohne, signed Elisabeth Sander, Mrs.

Pastor Graffunder, Pastor Graffunder, and ten others, to the Westphalian Women's Aid in Soest, 17 Dec. 1936, ibid.

46. "Kölln-Land I: Gemeindegruppe Zehlendorf," *Evangelium im Dritten Reich für Groß-Berlin*, no. 47 (19 Nov. 1933): 206, LKA Bielefeld 5,1/289,2.

47. Unlabeled clipping, "Einführung des Pfarrers Vetter in sein Amt" (8 July 1934), LKA Bielefeld 5,1/552,1.

48. See Helene Vogel's report on a trip through the Reich for the Women's Service, in pamphlet, no title, in series "Frau und Kirche" (Potsdam), p. 8, KAG Minden, loose materials.

49. See list of names headed "Ich persönlich kenne als 'Betroffene,'" no signature but included in file of items from Pastor Otto Koch, Wattenscheid, [1947?], KAG Minden, no. 17.

50. Flyer and attached list of candidates, "Pfarrer-Kirche oder Volks-Kirche?," [July 1933], LKA Bielefeld 5,1/294,3.

51. Dr. Krummacher, H. Lauterbach, "Wahlordnung für die Glaubensbewegung 'Deutsche Christen' Landesgruppe West (Rheinland und Westfalen)," [July 1933], LKA Bielefeld 5,1/289,2.

52. See booklet, "Nr. 1–10. Generalsynode Tagung 1933, Verzeichnis der Mitglieder," ibid.

53. See letter from four German Christian elders of the Friedens- und Erlöser Gemeinde, Potsdam, to the Upper Church Council in Berlin, c/o Consistory Councillor Dr. Freytag, 18 Nov. 1933, copy to the Reich bishop, EZA Berlin 1/A4/251. A woman was one of the signers of the above letter.

54. Helene Wiesejahn to Müller, 8 Feb. 1934, Berlin, EZA Berlin 1/A4/252.

55. Mimeograph, signed Hellweg, Meise, Mrs. Rullkötter, and Neuhaus, "An die Gemeindeglieder der Petri-Gemeinde: Erklärung und Bitte!," Bielefeld, 24 Feb. 1935, KAG Minden, unorganized folder of Wentz's correspondence.

56. "Aus der Bewegung," *Evangelium im Dritten Reich, Groß-Berliner Beilage*, no. 8 (24 Feb. 1935): 59–60, LKA Bielefeld 5,1/588.

57. Report from the Protestant parish of Münster, "Betrifft: Presbyterium der Kirchengemeinde Münster," 27 Nov. 1935, copy sent by Pastor Dr. Flemming, Münster, to Superintendent Dr. Schmidt, Oberhausen, 29 Nov. 1935, AEKR Düsseldorf, NL Schmidt/2, pp. 130–34.

58. "Kirchenkreis Kölln-Stadt, Gemeindegruppe Treptow," *Unsere Volkskirche: Sonntägliches Nachrichtenblatt aus den Berliner Kirchengemeinden*, no. 7 (19 Nov. 1933): 107, BA Potsdam, DC I, 1933–35, pp. 154–69.

59. "Aus der Bewegung," *Evangelium im Dritten Reich, Groß-Berliner Beilage*, no. 5 (3 Feb. 1935): 35, LKA Bielefeld 5,1/588.

60. See EZA Berlin 1/A4/54 throughout.

61. Birnbaum to Schröder, 9 July 1934, ibid., p. 204.

62. Grundmann to Birnbaum, 11 July 1934, Dresden, ibid., p. 213.

63. German Christian Gau Gross-Berlin, parish group Bartholomäus, signed G. Hagen, leader of the fraction, and K. Witte, group leader, to Reich Bishop Müller, 22 Feb. 1934, Berlin, EZA Berlin 1/A4/252, p. 2.

64. Senior Public Prosecutor (*Oberstattsanwalt*), signed Dresler, to Reich and Prussian Minister of Justice, 7 Nov. 1934, Bochum, EZA Berlin 1/A4/25.

65. Account of lecture by Ida Hermann, "Die deutsche Frau und das Christentum," in *Die Nationalkirche* (Hesse-Nassau edition: Worms), no. 6 (5 Feb. 1939): 61.

66. Photo in "Aus unserer deutsch-christlichen Arbeit," with the caption "Tagung der Landeskassenwarte der Nationalkirchlichen Einung in Eisenach," in *Die Nationalkirche*, no. 28/29 (9 July 1939): 312, EZA Berlin 1/C3/174.

67. "Aus unserer deutsch-christlichen Arbeit," ibid.

68. See announcements, *Informationsdienst, DC Nationalkirchliche Einung*, no. 3/43 (10 Mar. 1943): 14, EZA Berlin 1/A4/565.

69. Announcements in *Informationsdienst: DC Nationalkirchliche Einung*, no. 2/43 (25 Jan. 1943): 13, ibid.

70. See Kapferer, "Von der Fachabteilung katholische Kirche," ibid., p. 9.

71. [Kapferer], "Aus der Arbeit der Fachabteilung katholische Kirche," *Informationsdienst, DC Nationalkirchliche Einung*, no. 2/44 (28 Feb. 1944): 9, EZA Berlin 1/A4/566.

72. Background on Diehl and her establishment of the New Land League is provided in her autobiography, *Christ sein heißt Kämpfer sein*.

73. Diehl to Reich Organization Leader Gregor Strasser, 3 Oct. 1932, Eisenach, and Diehl to Hitler, 8 Nov. 1932, in BDC, Reichskulturkammer, Guida Diehl materials.

74. Wieneke, *Die Glaubensbewegung "Deutsche Christen,"* p. 10.

75. Diehl to Müller, 1 Dec. 1933, Eisenach, EZA Berlin 1/A4/249.

76. Diehl to Koch, 6 Nov. 1934, Eisenach, LKA Bielefeld 5,1/290,2.

77. Gau Personnel Director, NSDAP Gau Thuringia, Weimar, to President of the Reich Chamber of Writing, 1941, BDC, Reichsschrifttumskammer, Guida Diehl materials.

78. Staedel to Wentz, 31 Dec. 1959, Marburg, KAG Minden, no. 22.

79. Wentz, "Wie ich den Kirchenkampf erlebte," p. 31, KAG Minden, no. 4.

80. Information on Diehl's conflict with Scholtz-Klink—including a *Gutachten* of 20 March 1936 by Scholtz-Klink—Diehl's ejection from the Reich Chamber of Culture in 1941, and her subsequent readmission in the BDC, Reichskulturkammer, Guida Diehl materials.

81. Bormann to the Supreme Court of the NSDAP, 10 May 1942, BDC, Partei Kanzlei Correspondence, ibid.

82. "Aus der Bewegung," *Evangelium im Dritten Reich, Groß-Berliner Beilage*, no. 5 (3 Feb. 1935): 35, LKA Bielefeld 5,1/588.

83. See flyer from Deutsche Christen Gemeindegruppe Nathanael, EZA Berlin 1/A4/95. Dörthe Kisting's song to melody of "Freue dich sehr, o meine Seele" was titled "Vater, schirme unsern Hitler."

84. Anonymous, "Denkschriften an Herrn Prof. Kisting nebst Tochter!," 3 Mar. 1935, Berlin-Friedenau, EZA Berlin 1/A4/95.

85. Kisting, "Bericht unserer Pressereferentin Pgn. Kisting über den Verlauf des Gottesdienstes am 3.3. cr," 4 Mar. 1935, and anonymous letter, "Denkschreiben an Herrn Prof. Kisting nebst Tochter," Friedenau, 3 Mar. 1935, ibid.

86. Spinola, German Christian parish group leader in the Nathanael Church, Friedenau, to Engelke, Vicar of the German Protestant Church (DEK), 9 Mar. 1935, and Spinola, "Anmerkung des Gruppenleiters," 4 Mar. 1935, both attached to Kisting, "Bericht unserer Pressereferentin Pgn. Kisting über den Verlauf des Gottesdienstes am 3.3. cr," [Mar. 1935], ibid.

87. Consistory of the Church Province of Westphalia, signed Jung, to Inspector Kleine, 1 Nov. 1934, Münster, LKA Bielefeld 4,55/B/17,3.

88. "Bericht über die Gründungsversammlung der Ortsgruppe Reichelsdorf der Deutschen Christen am 5. Jan. 1935—Nebenzimmer Restauration Rührer," p. 1, LKA Nuremberg, KKU 6/IV.

89. Report, "Sprechabend der 'Reichskirchenbewegung Deutsche Christen' in Augsburg," 19 Jan. 1935, p. 3, ibid.

90. Typescript, Dietrich Wentz, "Im Kampf gegen Frau Plischke (Ein paar Zitate), Erzählung von Dietrich Wentz," [1944?], pp. 1–3, KAG Minden, unlabeled file.

91. See, for example, reference to the neutrals as the "ecclesiastical BDM—Bund der Mitte" in report, "DC-Versammlung in Bad Münster am Stain am 11.3.37," p. 1, LKA Bielefeld 5,1/292,2. In postwar retrospect, the widow of a German Christian leader discussed this label for the neutrals but added that a man she knew who used to describe himself that way was, in fact, a military pastor. Ilse Werdermann to Wentz, 4 Sept. 1956, Bad Soden, KAG Minden, file Werdermann.

92. "Über die Tätigkeit des LKAs Nassau-Hessen: a) Propstei Frankfurt a.M.," in *Informationsdienst*, no. 4, DC Landesleitung Nassau-Hesse, Frankfurt a/M (30 Jan. 1937): 4, LKA Bielefeld 5,1/292,2.

93. "Bericht über eine Versammlung der Volkskirchenbewegung DC mit 'Reichsvikar' D. Engelke am 31. Jan. 1937" (prepared by Confessing Church people), p. 1, ibid.

94. "Nachrichten: Hossenfelder spricht im Gemeindehaus der Immanuel Gemeinde zu Berlin, 5. März 1938," LKA Bielefeld 5,1/296.

95. Report prepared by staff of the Reich Farmers' Leader, Berlin, "Mitgliederversammlung . . . der Deutschen Christen, Ortsgruppe Marburg am 12.4.34," Marburg-Lahn, 14 Apr. 1934, sent to Alfred Rosenberg, 30 Ostermond [Apr.] 1934, BA Koblenz NS 8/257, p. 4.

96. Erika Semmler, Publications Office of the N.S. Women's Organization, *Gutachten*, on Guida Diehl's *Heilige Flamme glüh!* (1928), 9 Apr. 1936, BDC, Reichskulturkammer, Guida Diehl materials.

97. "Gottesdienst in Nürnberg. Tumult und Wortwechsel in der Kirche," 5 Nov. 1934 (copy sent to the Foreign Office by Prases Koch of the Confessing Church), AA Bonn VI A Evang. Ang. 2: Verfassung der ev. Kirche, vol. 8.

98. Pastor Dühring, "Bericht über die skandalösen Vorgänge in der Apostel-Paulus-Kirche in Berlin am I. Advent, den 2. Dez. 1934," AA Bonn VI A Evang. Ang. 2: Verfassung der ev. Kirche, vol. 9.

99. See "2. Bericht. Mitgliederversammlung der Deutschen Christen, Gemeindegruppe Augsburg, im Stockhausbräukeller, den 4. Mai 1935, abends 8 Uhr" (Confessing Church report), p. 1, LKA Nuremberg, KKU 6/IV. The quotation comes from Schiller's poem "Das Lied von der Glocke" (1799).

## Chapter Eight

1. Marcion, who died around 150 C.E., taught that the God of Jesus and the New Testament was pure goodness and had nothing to do with what he considered the imperfect creator God of the Hebrew scriptures. See Adolf von Harnack, *Marcion: The Gospel of the Alien God*, trans. John E. Steely and Lyle D. Bierma (Durham, N.C.: Labyrinth, 1990).

2. Catharism, a dualist heresy with gnostic roots, made its most dramatic western European appearance in the twelfth century. Also known as Albigensians, Cathari rejected the Old Testament as the account of the tyrannical reign of the evil creator. See Arno Borst, *Die Katharer*, vol. 12, *Schriften der Monumenta Germaniae historica* (Stuttgart: Hersemann, 1953).

3. Adolf von (since 1914) Harnack, (1851–1930) professor of theology in Leipzig, Gießen, Marburg, and Berlin, was the most influential proponent of liberal theology in Germany. He questioned retention of the Old Testament in the Protestant canon, characterizing it at as archaic and outmoded. See Agnes von Zahn-Harnack, *Adolf von Harnack* (Berlin-Templehof: Hans Bott, 1936).

4. See, for example, Sprank, Protestant Garrison Pastor in Berlin, "Denkschrift," [1937], p. 6, BA-MA Freiburg, RH 15/262, p. 93.

5. See Scholder, *The Churches and the Third Reich*, 1:49–50, 130–31, 143.

6. In 1931, the German Protestant Church Committee in Berlin surveyed regional churches regarding the activities of the German Church group. See

responses from Austria and Lübeck: Protestant Consistory A. and H.B. to German Protestant Church Committee Berlin, 5 Feb. 1931, EZA Berlin 1/A4/493, item 111; Consistory of the Protestant Lutheran Church in Lübeck, signed Evers, to German Protestant Church Committee, 27 Feb. 1931, EZA Berlin 1/A2/493, item 104.

7. Kalle, *Hat das Alte Testament noch Bedeutung*, p. 3. Kalle himself defended the Old Testament.

8. Diehl, "Grundsätze für die Erneuerungsarbeit," in flyer, *Einladung zu einer Neulandtagung des Eisenacher Arbeitsringes*, 19–22 Sept. 1932, LKA Bielefeld 5,1/550,1.

9. A. Bernhardi, "Gedanken zur Glaubensbewegung," sent by author to Prussian Minister for Science, Art, and Education, 27 June 1933, pp. 4–5, BA Potsdam DC-I, 1933–35, p. 62.

10. "Das Alte Testament im Unterricht," unlabeled clipping (4 Nov. 1933), LKA Bielefeld 5,1/289,1.

11. Krause, *Rede des Gauobmannes*, pp. 6–7.

12. Typical was the response of a Mecklenburg pastor who withdrew his application for membership in the German Christian movement because he refused to give up the Old Testament. See Schreiber to Müller, 20 Nov. 1933, Brunshaupten (Mecklenburg), EZA Berlin 1/A4/249.

13. See account of meeting between Interior Ministry official Wienstein and Christian Kinder, 25 Oct. 1934, in "Vermerk—Betrifft: Fragen der evang. Kirche," initialed by Wienstein, 26 Oct. 1934, p. 2, BA Koblenz R 43II/163/fiche 2/p. 54.

14. Flyer signed Kinder, *Die 28 Thesen der Deutschen Christen*, [1934], LKA Bielefeld 5,1/289,1.

15. Pamphlet, *Das Alte Testament ein "Judenbuch"?*, Ev. Gemeindedienst für Württemberg, Landesstelle Stuttgart, p. 1, Rudolf Fischer pamphlets.

16. Pastor Ziehen, "Wir Deutschen Christen und das Alte Testament," *Kirche im Aufbruch. Mitteilungsblatt der Deutschen Christen im Gau Halle-Merseburg*, no. 11/12 (July 1935): 7–8, LKA Bielefeld 5,1/291,2.

17. Schöttler, *Gottes Wort Deutsch*, p. 27.

18. Veigel, "Volkes Buße 1933," in Veigel, *Deutsche Gebete*, pp. 7–9.

19. Gerhard Meyer, "Aus der Gemeinde," *Ein feste Burg—Kirchenblatt der Luthergemeinde*, Lübeck, no. 4 (15 Apr. 1934): 4; Meyer, "Aus der Gemeinde," no. 7 (15 Aug. 1934): 5, KAG Minden, file V.

20. Fromm, *Blood and Banquets*, entry of 2 July 1937, p. 247.

21. Report signed "Evang.-Luth. Stadtpfarramt, St. Mang.-Kempten," 20 Sept. 1935, p. 2, LKA Nuremberg, KKU 6/IV.

22. Num. 12:1–15.

23. Copy, "Was wollen die rheinischen Deutschen Christen?," includes letter announcing decision to leave the German Christian ranks, AEKR Düsseldorf, NL Schmidt/17. A copy elsewhere reveals the identities of the correspondents: see excerpts from letter, Loy to Johannes Pack, 9 Nov. 1936, Duisburg-Hamborn, ibid., pp. 68–69.

24. Pastor Weber to Praeses and Members of the Berlin Fraternal Council (Bruderrat), 9 Nov. 1936, Berlin, reproduced in "Beschwerden persönlicher Anliegen und Mitteilungen seitens des Berliner Bruderrates und seiner Mitglieder, Jan. 1936–Dez. 1936," p. 8, EZA Berlin 50/4.

25. "Konfirmandenprufung in . . . Fürth durch Pfarrer [Hans] Baumgärtner am 14.3.37," LKA Nuremberg, KD Nbg 118.

26. Protestant Lutheran Superintendent, Altdorf, to Protestant Lutheran Consistory Munich, 3 Nov. 1938, LKA Nuremberg, KD Nbg 121.

27. See decision of Supreme Party Court with regard to Dr. Hermann Werdermann, in file "Akten des Obersten Parteigerichts, I. Kammer, Pg. Dr. Werdermann—Gau Westfalen-Süd—Ortsgruppe Dortmund," BDC, Werdermann materials.

28. My understanding of the Institute for Research into and Elimination of Jewish Influence on German Church Life has benefited from conversations with Professor Susannah Heschel. See her essay, "Making Nazism a Christian Movement," in Rubenstein, *Reflections*.

29. Text of the Godesberg Declaration from meeting on 25–26 March 1939 with names of twenty-one signatories in *Sonntag im Volk*, no. 1 (15 Apr. 1939), LKA Bielefeld 5,1/560,1.

30. Even some members of the institute were unclear about its origins. In 1948, a former member and German Christian, Wilhelm Staedel, wrote to another clergyman requesting information on the institute's foundation. Staedel to "Herr Amtsbruder," 26 Jan. 1948, BA Koblenz, NL 252/3.

31. Copy of "Eröffnung des 'Institutes zur Erforschung und Beseitigung des jüdischen Einflusses auf das deutsche kirchliche Leben,'" *Die National-kirche*, no. 19 (7 May 1939): 213, EZA Berlin 1/C3/174. On Grundmann, see Heschel, "Nazifying Christian Theology," pp. 587–605.

32. See flyer with application to join circle of supporters, *Das Institut zur Erforschung des jüdischen Einflusses auf das deutsche kirchliche Leben*, Apr. 1941, Eisenach, signed Leffler, AEKR Düsseldorf, Provinzialsynodalrat der Rheinprovinz, A VI,2. Also see Finance Division of the Chancellery of the German Protestant Church, signed Fürle, to members of the Finance Committee, regarding funding for the institute, 27 June 1942, EZA 1/C3/174; and memo, "An die Provinzialsynodalkasse Düsseldorf," 18 Mar. 1941, regarding annual pledge of funds from the Rhenish Consistory to the institute, AEKR Düsseldorf, Provinzialsynodalrat der Rheinprovinz, A VI,2.

33. "Eröffnung des 'Institutes zur Erforschung und Beseitigung des jüdischen Einflusses auf das deutsche kirchliche Leben,'" *Die Nationalkirche*, no. 19 (7 May 1939): 213, EZA Berlin 1/C3/174.

34. File copy, President of the Provincial Synodal Council of the Rhine Province Horn to Leffler, 2 May 1939, Duisburg-Ruhrort, AEKR Düsseldorf, Provinzialsynodalrat der Rheinprovinz, A VI,2.

35. Report on talk by Prof. Eisenhuth, "Die Bedeutung der Bibel für den Glauben," in "Bericht über die Tagung des landeskirchlichen Referenten zum 'Institut zur Erforschung und Beseitigung des jüdischen Einflusses auf das deutsche kirchliche Leben', an 6. und 7. Juli 1939 in Eisenach," signed Pich, p. 2, EZA Berlin 1/C3/174.

36. See *Evangelisches Feldgesangbuch*, BA-MA Freiburg, N 282. The biblical passages quoted above come from Psalms 23 and 121.

37. Georg Schneider, "Wir und die Bibel," in Schneider, *Unser Glaube*, p. 36.

38. Julius Leutheuser, "Liebe Kameraden in der Heimat und im Felde!," 20 Dec. 1941, Russia, duplicated and circulated, presumably by German Christian National Church Union "Informationsdienst," p. 3, LKA Bielefeld 5,1,293.

39. "Meldungen aus dem Reich," 4 Mar. 1940, "Kulturelle Gebiete: Die Theologischen Fakultäten im 1. Trimester 1940," p. 6, T-175/258/2750964.

40. Martin Bormann, NSDAP Party Chancellery, to Minister for Church Affairs, Attention State Secretary Hermann Muhs, 25 Sept. 1942, Munich, BA Koblenz R 43 II/151/fiche 1, pp. 44–46.

41. Report on Professor Dr. Meyer-Erlach, from office of the Chief of the Security Police and Security Service to Foreign Office, 1 Oct. 1942, Berlin, AA Bonn, Inland I-D, Kirche 2, 3/4.

42. "Bericht der 1. V.-Person,—Weißenfelser Tagung der Arbeitsgemeinschaft 'Germanentum und Christentum', 7.–13. Okt. 1942," sent to Foreign Office by Office of Chief of Security Police and Security Service, 2 Dec. 1942, Berlin, p. 2, AA Bonn, Inland I-D, Kirche 2, 3/4.

43. Stöver provides some information on the situation in *Protestantische Kultur*, pp. 170–72.

44. German Christian Pastors Association, Bielefeld, "Die Trauung," in "Theologischer Arbeitsbrief," (1 May 1942): 2. See also list of texts, p. 4, LKA Bielefeld 5,1/295,1.22.

45. Hans Schmidt, "Die Nationalkirche als religiöse Erbe und überkommene Verpflichtung für die nach uns Kommenden," circular of the DC Nationalkirchliche Einung Theol. Arbeitskreis (Saarburg/Trier, 20 Jan. 1943): 17, EZA Berlin 1/A4/565.

46. The pastor spoke on behalf of the German Pastoral Community of Greater Berlin German Christians, National Church Union. Pfeiffer, "Konfir-

mandenunterricht heute," DC Natkirchl. Einung, "Informationsdienst," no. 6/43 (31 May 1943): 8, ibid.

47. Dr. Zimmermann, "Die biblische Grundlage der jüdischen Weltherrschaftserwartung," DC Nationalkirchliche Einung, "Informationsdienst," no. 2/44 (28 Feb. 1944): 8, EZA Berlin 1/A4/566.

48. Rubenstein, *After Auschwitz*, p. 12.

49. On Chamberlain, see Field, *Evangelist of Race*. Best known of Chamberlain's works was *Die Grundlagen des neunzehnten Jahrhunderts* (Munich: F. Bruckmann, 1899), in English, *The Foundations of the Nineteenth Century*, trans. John Lees (New York: H. Fertig, 1968). A laudatory synopsis of Chamberlain's *Grundlagen* from 1939 and a bibliography of his works appears in Meyer, *Houston Stewart Chamberlain*.

50. For a summary and analysis of Hirsch's life and work, see Ericksen, *Theologians under Hitler*, esp. pp. 164–65.

51. Account of Dr. Lüdtke's speech in "Reformationsfeier der Deutschen Christen," untitled clipping (Oranienburg, 2 Nov. 1933), EZA Berlin 1/A4/101.

52. Dollberger, "War Jesus Jude?," in Schneider, *Unser Glaube*, p. 40.

53. See Matt. 1:1–25 and Luke 3:23–38.

54. Luke 1:5 and 36.

55. Luke 1:46–55.

56. Stahn, "Vermerk," Feb. 1940, pp. 2–3, 4–5, BA-MA Freiburg, N282/11.

57. Ernst Christian Heinrich Peithman to Müller, 12 Julmond [July] 1933, Webster, South Dakota, EZA Berlin 1/C4/17.

58. Wilhelm Stapel, *Sechs Kapitel Christentum und Nationalsozialismus*, 1931, p. 15, quoted in Grundmann, *Gott und Nation*, p. 88.

59. Wilhelm Schielmeyer to Müller, 1 Dec. 1933, EZA Berlin 1/C4/17. Schielmeyer referred to Luke 17:20–21, John 18:36–37, and John 8:44.

60. "Der Heiland der Deutschen," in *Deutsche mit Gott*, p. 46. *Deutsche mit Gott* was the new "catechism" produced by the Institute for Research into and Elimination of Jewish Influence in German Church Life.

61. H. Vogel, "Du Mutter heranwachsender Kinder," in Reich Office for Women's Service, Potsdam, *Die deutsche Mutter*, p. 7, KAG Minden, loose materials.

62. "Aus einer Rede von Pfarrer [Friedrich] Tausch, gehalten bei einer Versammlung der Deutschen Christen in Berlin-Lankwitz," in Confessing Church report, "Deutsche Christen im Wahlkampf," 1937, p. 4, LKA Bielefeld 5,1/292,2. The biblical reference is to John 4:22, "for salvation is of the Jews."

63. Hauer, *Unser Kampf*, p. 13, LKA Bielefeld 5,1/296.

64. "Entjudung der Kirche," from a speech by Willi Greiner, *Der gottgläubige Deutsche, Nachrichtenblatt des Reichsringes der gottgläubigen Deutschen*, series 6 (June 1939): 1–2, BA Potsdam DG IV, 1938–43, pp. 294 and reverse.

65. The Book of Acts makes frequent reference to Saul/Paul's Jewish background and identity. See, for example, Acts 16:3, 16:20, 21:39, 22:3, and 26:5.

66. Grundmann, *Gott und Nation*, pp. 64–65.

67. "Niederschrift über die vorbereitende Sitzung zur Bildung einer Volksmissionarischen Kammer am 3. Nov. 1933 im Evang. Oberkirchenrat," p. 3, EZA Berlin 1/A4/41.

68. Eichenberg, "Sie waren anders als ihr Ruf," p. 22.

69. Krause, *Rede des Gauobmannes*, p. 7.

70. "Aus einer Rede von Pfarrer Tausch, gehalten bei einer Versammlung der Deutschen Christen in Berlin-Lankwitz," in Confessing Church report, "Deutsche Christen im Wahlkampf," 1937, p. 4, LKA Bielefeld 5,1/292,2.

71. Weidemann, "Mein Kampf um die Erneuerung des religiösen Lebens in der Kirche: ein Rechenschaftsbericht," [1942], pp. 5–6, BA Koblenz R 43 II/165, fiche 4, p. 323.

72. Krause, *Rede des Gauobmannes*, p. 9.

73. "An die evangelischen Theologen!," signed "Die Fachschaft der evangelisch-theologischen Fakultät Breslau," 7 May 1934, p. 3, LKA Bielefeld 5,1/289,1.

74. Report signed "Evang.-Luth. Stadtpfarramt, St. Mang.-Kempten," 20 Sept. 1935, p. 2, LKA Nuremberg, KKU 6/IV.

75. "Großversammlung der Thüringer Deutschen Christen in Künstlerhaus zu Nürnberg am 2.6.1938," p. 1, LKA Nuremberg, KD Nbg 117.

76. Duplicated excerpt from presentation by Hans Hermenau, "Unsere Seelsorge am deutschen Volke," in "Bericht über die Tagung des Frauendienstes Gr. Berlin in Spandau am 27. II. 1942," EZA Berlin 50/600, p. 2.

77. "Eine Konfirmandenprüfung abgehalten in der Friedenskirche zu Düsseldorf am 12. März 1939," Confessing Church materials, p. 1, LKA Bielefeld 5,1/812.

78. "Bericht über eine 'Konfirmandenprüfung' der Thüringer Deutsche Christen in Berlin-Siemensstadt am 22. III. 1939," p. 2, LKA Bielefeld 5,1/588.

79. See, for example, sermon reproduced in the "Theologischer Arbeitsbrief" (1 Aug. 1942): 3–6, LKA Bielefeld 5,1/295,1. The parable of the Good Samaritan is found in Luke 10:30–37.

80. Kerrl, "Die praktisch-politische Lösung der religiösen Frage im Dritten Reich," 25 Oct. 1939, pp. 3–4, BA Koblenz, R 79/26, pp. 29–30.

81. "Jesu Kampf gegen den jüdischen Geist," in Fliedner, *Glaube und Tat*, p. 30.

82. "Jesu Rasse," in Fliedner, ibid., p. 241.

83. "Entwicklung und Entartung des frühen Christentums," ibid., p. 64.

84. Pich to Clergy in the Circle of Supporters, 2 Jan. 1941, Eisenach, AEKR Düsseldorf, Provinzialsynodalrat der Rheinprovinz, A VI, 2.

85. Schneider, "Vom Sinn des Kreuzes," in Schneider, *Unser Glaube*, p. 58.

86. Hans Schmidt, "Die Nationalkirche als religiöse Erbe und überkommene Verpflichtung für die nach uns Kommenden," circular of the DC Nationalkirchliche Einung theol. Arbeitskreis (Saarburg/Trier, 20 Jan. 1943): 7–8, EZA Berlin 1/A4/565.

87. "Schlachtensee Kreis," [Karl Wentz], "Grundgedanken zur Neuordnung der Kirche," Nov. 1941, p. 3, KAG Minden, no. 7.

88. Schöttler had released his *Gottes Wort Deutsch* in 1934 but that work represented a collection of excerpts from the Luther Bible rather than an entirely new version of the New Testament. It was still available in 1938. See advertisement in "Mitteilungsblatt," no. 4, Deutsche Christen in Westfalen, Iserlohn (23 Nov. 1938), KAG Minden, no. 14.

89. See Weidemann, "Mein Kampf um die Erneuerung des religiösen Lebens in der Kirche: ein Rechenschaftsbericht," [1942], pp. 4–5, BA Koblenz R 43 II/165, fiche 4, pp. 322–23.

90. *Das Evangelium Johannes deutsch*, p. i.

91. Weidemann to Franz Ritter von Epp, Dec. 1936, BHStA Munich, RSth 636/7.

92. Weidemann, "Mein Kampf um die Erneuerung des religiösen Lebens in der Kirche: ein Rechenschaftsbericht," [1942], pp. 4–5, BA Koblenz R 43 II/165, fiche 4, pp. 322–23.

93. Weidemann to Franz Ritter von Epp, Dec. 1936, BHStA Munich, RSth 636/7.

94. *Das Evangelium Johannes deutsch*, for example, pp. 5, 12, 29. The passages referred to come from John 1:40, 3:31–36, and 7:1.

95. *Das Evangelium Johannes deutsch*, p. 7.

96. Matt. 21:12–13, Mark 11:15–17, Luke 19:45–46.

97. See quotations in K. G. Steck, "Eine neue Uebersetzung des Johannes-Evangeliums," clipping from *Frankfurter Zeitung*, [1936], LKA Bielefeld 5,1/291,1.

98. Weidemann, "Mein Kampf um die Erneuerung des religiösen Lebens in der Kirche: ein Rechenschaftsbericht," [1942], p. 4, BA Koblenz R 43 II/165, fiche 4, p. 321.

99. Emanuel Hirsch, *Jesus, Wort und Geschichte Jesu nach dem ersten drei Evangelien* (Bremen: Kommende Kirche, 1939). This text appears to have been produced in very limited numbers. I located only one copy, in the collection of Druckschriften at LKA Bielefeld.

100. Eichenberg, "Sie waren anders als ihr Ruf," p. 19.

101. There is some unclarity as to the fate of the other projected segments of the *Volkstestament*. Some accounts refer to an edition of the New Testament

called the *Volkstestament*, but presumably they were using the collective title for the first part only. In any case, no copies of anything but *Die Botschaft Gottes* could be located.

102. Eichenberg, "Sie waren anders als ihr Ruf," p. 22.

103. Pich to Clergy in the Circle of Supporters, 2 Jan. 1941, Eisenach, p. 2, AEKR Düsseldorf, Provinzialsynodalrat der Rheinprovinz, A VI, 2.

104. Andreas Scheiner, "Bericht über die gründende Tagung der Arbeitsgemeinschaft des Institutes zur Erforschung des jüdischen Einflusses auf das deutsche kirchliche Leben in der evangelischen Landeskirche A. B. in Rumänien am 4. und 5. März 1942 in Hermannstadt," p. 7, BA Koblenz, NL 252/20.

105. See *Die Botschaft Gottes*, pp. 95–96.

106. The afterword was apparently not included in all editions of the text, but excerpts appear in the Confessing Church circular *Die Behandlung des biblischen Textes im "Volkstestament,"* [1940], LKA Bielefeld 5,1/561,1.

107. See quotations from German Christians who had worked on the project, ibid., p. 1.

108. See announcement of Arbeitsmaterialien including Kapferer's *Die Bergpredigt als Kampfansage gegen das Judentum*, in flyer, *Nationalkirchliche Einung Deutsche Christen, Fachabteilung Kirchenpolitik*, no. 4, ed. Karl Dungs (Essen-Kupferdreh, 13 Jan. 1944), EZA Berlin 1/A4/566.

109. For this correspondence, see Mayor of Bremen, signed Böhmcker, to NSDAP Chancellery of the Gauleiter, Gau Weser-Ems (Oldenburg), 12 Apr. 1938, Bremen; Head of Reich Chancellery Lammers to Bishop Weidemann, 3 June 1938; and Lammers to Heß, marked sent 3 June 1938, all in BA Koblenz R 43 II/165, fiche 1, pp. 35, 47–50.

110. Weidemann to Lammers, 11 Nov. 1938, Bremen, BA Koblenz R 43 II/165, fiche 2, p. 137.

111. Weidemann wrote to party and state authorities to ensure that the dedication ceremony for the churches would not encounter any snags. Everything went as planned. Telegram, Weidemann to Lammers, 28 Nov. 1938, Bremen, BA Koblenz R 43 II/165, fiche 2, p. 143.

112. "Wach auf, wach auf, du deutsches Land," Johann Walter, 1561, no English equivalent located; "Ein feste Burg ist unser Gott," inspired by Psalm 46, Martin Luther, 1529, standard translation by Frederick H. Hedge, 1852; "Du meine Seele singe," based on Psalm 144, translated by Miss Burlingham, 1866. In discussing hymns, I have given titles or first lines of English-language versions when available.

113. See "Wach auf, wach auf, du deutsches Land, du hast genug geschlafen," program for meeting of the German Christian Faith Movement in Dortmund, 22–24 June 1933, LKA Bielefeld 5,1/294,3.

114. Krause, *Rede des Gauobmannes*, p. 9.

115. "Begrüssungsworte des Bischof Hossenfelder anlässlich der öffentlichen Generalmitgliederversammlung der Deutschen Christen, Gau Gross-Berlin," 13 Nov. 1933, p. 2, LKA Bielefeld 5,1/289,2.

116. Protz, *So singen deutsche Christen*. See also Protz, "Neues Liederbuch der 'Deutschen Christen,'" *Evangelium im Dritten Reich*, no. 47 (19 Nov. 1933): 492, LKA Bielefeld 5,1/289,2.

117. Otto Richter, Dresden, "Ich bitte ums Wort," *Deutsches Pfarrerblatt*, no. 3 (16 Jan. 1934): 37, LKA Bielefeld 5,1/289,1. The German text to the "Netherlander Prayer of Thanks" ("Wir treten zum beten") is by Josef Weyl (1821–95). Ignaz Franz (1719–90) wrote "Holy God, We Praise Thy Name!" ("Großer Gott, wir loben Dich!").

118. Ernst Lot, "Judeleien," *Evangelium im Dritten Reich*, no. 40 (7 Oct. 1934): 24, BA Potsdam DC-I, 1933–35.

119. Flyer, "Evangelische Kundgebung für den Herrn Reichsbischof Ludwig Müller," 11 Nov. 1934, Münster, KAG Minden, unlabeled file.

120. Tausch, "Entwurf zu einem Propagandadienst der Reichskirchenregierung," 8 May 1935, p. 3, EZA Berlin 1/A4/93.

121. Bauer, *Feierstunden Deutscher Christen*, pp. 47–48.

122. Ibid., p. 44.

123. Pastor Knebel to Gauleiter and Reichsstatthalter Dr. Meyer, Münster, 11 Sept. 1935, Ibbenbüren (Westphalia), "Betrifft 'Nationalzeitung' vom 10.9.35," LKA Bielefeld 5,1/555,1. The reference is to "Geist des Glaubens, Geist der Stärke" ("Spirit of Faith, Spirit of Strength"), a hymn by Spitta, presumably Carl Johann Philipp, 1801–59. I have not located either a German or English text for this hymn.

124. "Gesangbuchnot," in *Nachrichten-Blatt der Ev. Gemeinde Oberhausen I*, no. 45 (10 Nov. 1935): 1, AEKR Düsseldorf, NL Schmidt/18.

125. Report from German Faith Movement, Organizational Leader Thuringian Regional Congregation, 18 Lenzing [March]/III (1936) to Office of the Leader of the German Faith Movement in Tübingen. Copies sent to Reich Ministry for Church Affairs and Gestapo Office, 24 Oster [April] 1936 by Wilhelm Hessberg, Chief Organizational Leader, German Faith Movement, BA Potsdam DG II 1936–37, pp. 73–74. "Jerusalem, du hochgebaute Stadt," by J. M. Meyfart, 1590–1642, translated by Catherine Winkworth.

126. German Christian song sheet, "Liederblatt Nr. 1," with twelve hymns, attached to flyer, *Wille und Ziel der "Deutschen Christen" (Nationalkirchliche Bewegung) e.V.*, Berlin, Mar. 1938, LKA Bielefeld 5,1/293.

127. Ernst Barnikol, "Lieder für Gottesfeiern, Verlag Deutsche Christen, Weimar 1938," from *Theologische Jahrbücher*, no. 4 (1938), ed. Barnikol

and Erfurth, p. 162, LKA Bielefeld 5,1/293. A copy of the hymnbook itself, Schwadtke, *Lieder für Gottesfeiern*, is in the same file.

128. Schwadtke, *Lieder für Gottesfeiern*, ibid. See songs numbered 814, 816, and 819, texts all by Hermann Ohland, and 822 by Fritz Wolke. The hymns are numbered 800 to 839.

129. "Versammlung bei den 'Thüringern,'" report of speech of the German Christian Pastor Dr. Wippermann, (Saar-Palatinate), in Nuremberg, 27 Apr. 1939; 250 to 280 people were present. LKA Nuremberg, KD Nbg 118.

130. *Lieder der kommenden Kirche*, foreword by Weidemann, contains 112 hymns. An expanded version with 186 hymns appeared subsequently: *Gesangbuch der kommenden Kirche*.

131. Advertisement from *Evangelische Nachrichten* (23 Apr. 1939) for "*Die Lieder der kommenden Kirche*, hrsg. von Landesbischof Lic. Dr. Weidemann," including quotations from Weidemann's foreword, LKA Bielefeld 5,1/293.

132. Weidemann, "Mein Kampf um die Erneuerung des religiösen Lebens in der Kirche: ein Rechenschaftsbericht," [1942], pp. 6–7, BA Koblenz R 43 II/165, fiche 4, pp. 325–27.

133. "Bericht über die Tagung der landeskirchlichen Referenten zum 'Institut zur Erforschung und Beseitigung des jüdischen Einflusses auf das deutsche kirchliche Leben' am 6. und 7. July 1939 in Eisenach," signed Pich, with the report of the schoolteacher Gimpel, head of the Committee for Revision of the Hymnbook, p. 1, EZA Berlin 1/C3/174.

134. "Psalter und Harfe wacht auf!" became "Lieder der Freude, klingt auf" in "Lobe den Herren, den mächtigen König der Ehren" (no. 17). See reference to "Der Retter in Not" in "Ein feste Burg" (no. 26), "Es ist ein Ros' entsprungen" (no. 145), "Zu Bethlehem geboren" (no. 155), "Stille Nacht" (no. 295), all in *Großer Gott, wir loben Dich!*

135. See C. Ronald Murphy, *The Saxon Savior: The Germanic Transformation of the Gospel in the Ninth-Century Heliand* (Oxford: Oxford, 1989), p. vii. The standard text of the "Heliand" is Otto Behagel, ed., *Heliand* (Halle: Max Niemeyer, 1882). Behagel's edition has been reprinted many times, including in 1933, and, most recently, in 1984.

136. "Der Heliand. Eine Sprechkantate für die Advents- u. Weihnachtszeit," in "Theologischer Arbeitsbrief" (25 Nov. 1940): 21–27, LKA Bielefeld 5,1/295,1. The following hymns appeared in the cantata: "O Heiland reiß den Himmel auf," anonymous, seventeenth century, "Es kommt ein Schiff geladen bis an den höchsten bord," by J. Tauler, ca. 1300–1361, revised by Daniel Sudermann, 1550–1631, translated by Catherine Winkworth, "Es ist ein Rose entsprungen," anonymous, fifteenth century, "Stille Nacht, Heilige Nacht," Joseph Mohr (1792–1848).

137. "Stille Nacht," *Evangelisches Feldgesangbuch*, p. 59.

138. Weidemann, "Mein Kampf um die Erneuerung des religiösen Lebens in der Kirche: ein Rechenschaftsbericht," [1942], p. 7, BA Koblenz R 43 II/165, fiche 4, p. 327.

139. Schübel, *300 Jahre Evangelische Soldatenseelsorge*, pp. 90–92.

## Chapter Nine

1. Recorded in Karl Kleinschmidt, "Bericht über die Kundgebung der Deutschen Christen (Nationalkirchliche Einung) 'Volk im Herzen einig vor Gott,'" 28 May 1938, pp. 4–5, LKA Bielefeld 5,1/289,2.

2. Eyewitness account by Johannes Korb, Spandau, present at the rally as a member of the brass ensemble, 17 Nov. 1933, sent to Reich Bishop Müller by Martin Niemöller, EZA Berlin 1/A4/252.

3. Krummacher, "Staat und Kirche," 8 July 1933, in campaign material, "Dokumente für Deutsche Christen die denken können und die Wahrheit wissen wollen," put out by electoral list, "Evangelische Kirche," Berlin, LKA Bielefeld 5,1/289,1.

4. Gestapo report, "Bericht über den Verlauf der am 12. Februar 1934 im Orpheumsaal, Hasenheide 32–38 stattgefundenen öffentlichen Versammlung der 'Deutschen Christen,'" BA Koblenz, R43 II/162/fiche 1/p. 46.

5. "Bremen—was es uns hielt und was es uns verspricht. (Die erste Reichs-kirchentagung für Niederdeutschland)," *Mitteilungsblatt Deutsche Christen, Niedersachsen*, no. 10 (Bremen, 1 Oct. 1935): 2, LKA Bielefeld 5,1/291,2.

6. Gotthard Rachner, "Gerüchte und Tatsachen," *Evangelium im Dritten Reich*, no. 50 (10 Dec. 1933): 524, LKA Bielefeld 5,1/289,1.

7. "Austritte bei den Deutschen Christen," *Der Montag*, no. 46 (27 Nov. 1933), clipping in BA Potsdam DC-I, 1933–35, p. 125.

8. Copy, theological communities of the Universities of Rostock and Erlan-gen, signed candidates of theology Gerstenmeier and Seyferth, with 610 addi-tional signatures, 23 Nov. 1934, EZA Berlin 1/A4/25.

9. Walter Wendorf to Müller, 5 Jan. 1935, Boizenburg/Elbe, EZA Berlin 1/A4/95.

10. "Die Aufgabe der 'Deutschen Christen' (von einem Superintendenten der Deutscher Christ ist," [1933?], LKA Bielefeld 5,1/289,2.

11. For an early expression of concerns with the language of the church by a man who later became a prominent German Christian, see Birnbaum, *Die neue Sprache*, esp. pp. 11, 14.

12. Typescript including listener's notes from speech by Kinder, "Kundge-bung der Deutschen Christen in der Westfalenhalle, Dortmund, am 24. März 1934," p. 3, LKA Bielefeld 5,1/289,1.

13. "Eindrücke eines Dortmunders von der Reichstagung der Deutschen Christen und der Einführung des Reichsbischofs," *National-Zeitung*, no. 265 (Dortmund, 26 Sept. 1934), LKA Bielefeld 5,1/290,2.

14. Müller quoted in Confessing Church report, "Nationalkirche," [1937?], p. 3, LKA Bielefeld 5,1/292,1.

15. Quoted in "Gottesfeier am 23.2.1941," Confessing Church report, LKA Bielefeld 5,1/293.

16. For more on Karl Barth (1886–1968), see Busch, *Karl Barth*.

17. Quoted in Julius-Ruprecht von Loewenfeld, "Grundsätzliches zur heutigen Kirchenfrage," *Glaube und Heimat—kirchlich-positives Monatsblatt für die Osnabrücker Lutherischen Gemeinden*, no. 9 (Sept. 1933): 100.

18. "Eine Erklärung der Siegener Deutsche Christen gegen Barth und Bekenntnissynode, ihre verkehrte Bibel- und Bekenntnisauffassung und ihre Irreführung unserer Gemeinden," German Christian congregational group, Siegen (Westphalia) [1934?], Minden no. 8172.

19. Herbert Propp, "Vaterländische Gottesdienste," *Evangelium im Dritten Reich*, no. 5 (3 Feb. 1935): 38, LKA Bielefeld 5,1/588.

20. See request from Friedrich Engelke, Vicar of the German Protestant Church, to Reich Leadership of German Christians, 21 Feb. 1935, Berlin-Charlottenburg, EZA Berlin 1/A4/95.

21. Grünagel's circular, 27 Apr. 1935, LKA Bielefeld 5,1/290,1.

22. Grünagel to Superintendent Schmidt, 8 Jan. 1936, Aachen, AEKR Düsseldorf, NL Schmidt/11, p. 7.

23. "Von den theologischen Fakultäten," in circular, *Nachrichten. Aus der Bekennenden Kirche*, [fall 1936]: 3, statistics evidently from Hermann Molert in *Christliche Welt*, LKA Bielefeld 5,1/291,1.

24. Mantey, "Der Hauptverein Sachsen-Anhalt, 1933–1938," in v. Schweinitz, *"Mit Luther für Kirche und Volk,"* p. 27, EB Bensheim 3.05.20.

25. Report by Heinrich Schlier on training of theologians summarized in Karl Immer, "Bericht über die Freizeit in N. am 27./28. Feb. 1937," pp. 1–2, LKA Bielefeld 5,1/358,1.

26. "Die Austritte aus der Glaubensbewegung: Tübinger Professoren geben die Begründung ihres Schrittes," *Tübinger Chronik und Steinlachbote*, no. 273 (28 Nov. 1933), LKA Bielefeld 5,1/289,1. For more on Hanns Rückert, see Siegele-Wenschkewitz, "Geschichtsverständnis angesichts des Nationalsozialismus," pp. 113–44.

27. Hirsch quoted in German Christian circular, *Kirchlicher Rundbrief Nr. 2: um die rechte Haltung der kirchlichen Presse*, German Christians Gau Rhineland, 15 Oct. 1934, Cologne, p. 1, LKA Bielefeld 5,1/290,2.

28. Winkel, *Jesu ursprüngliche Verkündigung*, p. 6. Winkel's remarks paraphrase and comment on Matthew 11:28.

29. In June 1934, Reich leader Kinder conceded that many pastors had dropped out of the movement but claimed membership was still expanding rapidly and approached the one million mark. See "Vortrag der Deutschen Christen am 25. Juni 1934 in Gustav-Sieble-Haus. Redner: Dr. Kinder, Pf. Langmann," LKA Bielefeld 5,1/290,1.

30. Sauer to [Hossenfelder?], 30 Sept. 1933, Frankfurt/Main, EZA Berlin 1/A4/40.

31. A.F., "Wird ein Kirchenpaß eingeführt? Kirchenreformegedanken der 'Deutschen Christen,'" *Tägliche Rundschau*, no. 58 (9 Mar. 1933), clipping in BA Potsdam DC-I, 1933–35, p. 14.

32. See Beyer, "Staat erzwingt Kirchenbesuch?," *Kreuz-Zeitung* (10 Mar. 1933), clipping in ibid., p. 13.

33. "Erklärung" sent to Müller, cover letter from Preiser, Görlitz, identifies declaration as work of German Christian pastors there, EZA Berlin 1/A4/250.

34. Flyer, *Aufruf der Deutschen Christen*, [1933] responsible: Glaubensbewegung Deutsche Christen, Landesgruppe West (Rheinland und Westfalen), p. 2, LKA Bielefeld 5,1/289,1.

35. Pamphlet, *Evangelische Akademie Düsseldorf*, 15 Oct. 1933, Düsseldorf, LKA Bielefeld 5,1/289,2.

36. Heinrich Forsthoff, "Evangelische Akademien im Rheinland," clipping, July 1933, ibid.

37. Werner Wiesner, "Bericht über die erste Reichstagung des Studentenkampfbundes 'Deutsche Christen' in Berlin vom 7.–10. August 1933," p. 1, ibid.

38. "Aus dem Versuchskursus des Herrn Reichsbischofs Ludwig Müller im Predigerseminar Klein Neuhof bei Rastenburg, Ostpr.," four signatures, 9 July 1934, Gütersloh, LKA Bielefeld 5,1/552,1. See also copy of counterreport by Friedrich Schotte and Georg Schrem, "An die 'Freie evangelische Synode im Rheinland,'" 8 Aug. 1934, Alberfeld, pp. 1–11, LKA Bielefeld 5,1/812.

39. Flyer, Ludwig Schneller, Pastors' Emergency League, Cologne, *Wie der Kirchenstreit entstand*, 1934, LKA Bielefeld 5,1/290,2.

40. Müller, "Grußwort des Reichsbischofs an die deutschen evangelischen Gemeinden vom 3. Oktober 1933," EZA Berlin 1/A4/25.

41. Müller in Kiel, 7 Jan. 1934, quoted from *Völkischer Beobachter* (9 Jan. 1934), in "Glaubensbekenntnisse Deutscher Christen," [1937], p. 9, LKA Bielefeld 5,1/289,1.

42. Karl Friedrich Zahn on "Pfaffentum," quoted from *Wille und Tat, Führerblatt der nationalsozialistischen Jugend*, cited in "Aus anderen Blättern," *Evangelischer Beobachter* (8 June 1934): 14, LKA Bielefeld 5,1/290,1.

43. Reich Church movement of German Christians, District Leadership

Nuremberg, signed Georg Stadlinger, in the name of twenty local groups, 31 Dec. 1934, Nuremberg, BA Koblenz R 43 II/163/fiche 2, pp. 124–25.

44. Carbon copies to Ritter von Epp (Munich) of telegrams signed Fritz Tiefel to Reich Bishop Müller, 6 Dec. 1934, Siegelsdorf/Veitsbronn (Bavaria), and Tiefel to Meiser, same date, both in BHStA Munich, RSth 636/3.

45. "Der Einbruch der 'Deutschen Christen' in Markt Bevolzheim," [Pastor Haffner], [May 1935], pp. 1–5, LKA Nuremberg, KKU 6/IV. The pastor who wrote the report was not present; a party member took notes.

46. Weidemann, "Erklärung auf der Gauobmännertagung der 'Deutschen Christen' am 12. April 1935 in Berlin," EZA Berlin 1/A4/96.

47. "Bericht über die Versammlung der Deutschen Christen in Alersheim am 28. Mai 1935," Confessing Church materials, LKA Nuremberg, KKU 6/IV.

48. Franz Blumberg to Hauer, 4 Sept. 1935, Berlin, BA Koblenz, NL 131/87, pp. 211–12.

49. C. J. Rudolf Berge, "Denkschrift an die Deutsch-Christen Bewegung," 5 Oct. 1935, Dresden, pp. 1–6, EZA Berlin 1/A4/93.

50. "Vermerk," signed [Julius] Stahn, 2 Sept. 1935, BA Potsdam DC I, 1933–35, p. 337.

51. Willfried Hahn to Wentz, 2 July 1936, Bielefeld, KAG Minden, no. 28.

52. It is unclear which uniform the men were wearing, whether military, storm trooper, or the so-called uniform of German Christian pastors that came into use: black tunic, riding trousers, and high boots.

53. Copy of Fritz Thöne to Weinmann, 29 Sept. 1937, Heppingen, copy sent by Carl Wippermann, German Christian National Church Movement, Gau Saar-Palatinate and Koblenz-Trier to Werner, President of Protestant Church Council, 20 Oct. 1937, EZA Berlin 1/A4/167.

54. Flyer, signed Tausch, *Auf in den Sportpalast*, [1938], LKA Bielefeld 5,1/293.

55. For an account of Tausch's speech, see Karl Kleinschmidt (Confessing Church), "Bericht über die Kundgebung der Deutschen Christen (National-kirchliche Einung) 'Volk im Herzen einig vor Gott,'" 28 May 1938, p. 2, LKA Bielefeld 5,1/289,2.

56. Circular, signed Bormann, *Rundschreiben Nr. 31/39*, 2 Feb. 1939, Munich, pp. 1–2, BA Koblenz R 79/25/pp. 7–8.

57. The man in question had been dismissed as a deacon and had not taken the theological examinations required for ordination. See Pastors' Association of the German Protestant Church of Bavaria East of the Rhine, signed Klingler, to Protestant Lutheran Regional Church Council, Munich, 15 Nov. 1943, Nuremberg, LKA Nuremberg, LKR II 246/Bd.IX.

58. A. Körner, "Die Arbeit der Deutschen Pfarrergemeinde. Rückblick und

Ausblick," DC Natkirchl. Einung Informationsdienst, 1/44 (22 Jan. 1944): 3–6, EZA Berlin 1/A4/566.

59. See memo from the Reich Church Committee, "Betrifft: Kirchenaustritte," to senior church officials of the regional German Protestant churches, 5 Jan. 1937, sent on to superintendents by the Protestant Consistory of Westphalia, 4 Feb. 1937, LKA Bielefeld 4,55/A/34.

60. "Nationalkirchliche Einung Deutsche Christen zerstört evang.-luth. Kirchenordnung," item labeled "Berggießhübel," in Confessing Church report [1938], pp. 1–2, LKA Bielefeld 5,1/296.

61. See sections II.3 and 6, "Trauung," III.11, in *Thüringer Kirchenordnung vom 15.Juli 1944*, introduction by Hugo Rönck, pp. 7–9, 15, KAG Minden, loose materials.

62. See sections III.11, "Taufe, religiöse Erziehung und Konfirmation," and IV.28 and 29, "Kirchliche Bestattung," ibid.

63. A rich collection of material from Superintendent Clarenbach is located in LKA Bielefeld 4,55/various files.

64. Heinrich Krampe, "An das Presbyterium der Evangelischen Kirchengemeinde Bad-Sassendorf," 21 Sept. 1933, Bad-Sassendorf (Westphalia), LKA Bielefeld 4,55/A/90.

65. Certified copy of report of meeting of presbyters in Bad Sassendorf, 22 Sept. 1933, signed Pastor Johannsen and chair, Andreas Schröer, ibid.

66. For more on problems between the presbyters and the pastor in Bad Sassendorf, see report of meetings of presbyters on 5 and 31 Jan. 1934, signed Johannsen, sent to Clarenbach, 14 Feb. 1934, Bad Sassendorf, ibid. On the salary issue, see Johannsen to Clarenbach, 7 Mar. 1935, Bad Sassendorf, LKA Bielefeld 4,55/B/22,4.

67. Johannsen, "Bericht zu dem von dem Unterzeichneten gegen den Beschluß des Presbyteriums vom 22.9.1933 erhobenen Einspruch," 16 Oct. 1933, Bad Sassendorf, pp. 1–2, LKA Bielefeld 4,55/A/90. The same file contains copies of the resolutions of the Provincial Synod advising presbyteries to forego Saturday weddings in the interest of maintaining the sanctity of Sunday: "Beschluss 299 der 20. Provinzialsynode," "Beschluss 88 der 23. Pr. Synode," and "Beschluss 183 der 23. Synode."

68. Schürmann, member of the District Synodal Board to Protestant Consistory (Münster), 11 Oct. 1935, Soest, and response, Protestant Consistory, signed Heyer, to Schürmann, 12 Oct. 1935, ibid.

69. See Protestant Consistory of Westphalia, signed Heyer, "Betr. Beschwerde über Studiendirektor Lic. Winter-Soest, Zur Eingabe vom 11. Oktober," 15 Oct. 1935, Münster, quoting response to Schürmann in Soest, providing the reasons behind request for a certificate enabling baptism of the Bielefeld railroad worker's child by a German Christian, LKA Bielefeld 4,55/A/35.

70. Protestant Upper Church Council to Protestant Consistory of the Church Province of Westphalia, 29 Jan. 1936, Berlin-Charlottenburg, LKA Bielefeld 4,55/A/90.

71. Form letter, Protestant Consistory of the Church Province of Westphalia, signed Heyer, to presbyters of Protestant congregation in [place name left blank], 6 Feb. 1936, Münster, ibid.

72. Protestant Consistory of the Church Province of Westphalia, signed Heyer, to Mr. Bielefeld, railroad worker in Schwefe, 6 Feb. 1936, Münster, ibid. See also in same file correspondence of same date from Heyer to Milger, Reich Railroad senior clerk in Soest.

73. At least one non–German Christian pastor did request permission to perform a Saturday wedding in late 1937, but he expressed considerable reluctance. See Frederking to Clarenbach, 1 Dec. 1937, Neheim, ibid.

74. See, for example, Protestant Consistory Westphalia, signed Kupsch, to Curate Drewer in Soest, 12 June 1936, Münster, with regard to request for a certificate of permission for a tax inspector to have the German Christian Drewer baptize his child, ibid.

75. Protestant Consistory in Westphalia to Clarenbach, 14 May 1937, with copies included of Consistory to Viktor Turchich in Soest, to Drewer in Soest, and telegram from Clarenbach to Drewer and Mrs. Turchich of 16 May 1937, ibid.

76. For example, see Clarenbach to Kamen, 14 July 1936, Borgeln, giving Kamen permission to have his son buried by the German Christian curate Drewer, and Protestant Consistory Westphalia, signed Krieg, to Drewer, 22 Sept. 1936, giving Drewer permission to perform marriage ceremony for a Hiddingsen woman, ibid.

77. Ludwig Amann, locksmith, to Clarenbach, 25 June 1936, Soest, and Drewer to Clarenbach, 12 Nov. 1936, Soest, LKA Bielefeld 4,55/A/34.

78. Announcement of Amann's acceptance into the Protestant church, signed K. Drewer, Ludwig Amann, and two witnesses, 11 Oct. 1936, Soest, ibid.

79. Protestant Consistory of Westphalia, signed Kupsch, to Clarenbach, 26 Oct. 1936, ibid.

80. Protestant-Lutheran St. Peter's Church Congregation Soest, signed by Pastor Gottfried Freytag on behalf of the presbyters, to Clarenbach, 3 June 1938, LKA Bielefeld 4,55/A/90.

81. Report from the presbyters of the Protestant-Lutheran Church of St. Peter in Soest, signed Freytag, to Protestant Consistory Münster, 3 Dec. 1938, "Betr.: Tätigkeit des Herrn Hilfspredigers Drewer in Soest," pp. 1–3, LKA Bielefeld 4,55/B/26,5.

82. Frederking to Protestant Consistory in Münster, 22 Mar. 1938 (postscript dated 28 Mar.), Neheim, pp. 1–4, LKA Bielefeld 4,55/B/17,3.

83. Report from Protestant-Lutheran Superintendent, Erlangen, to District Superintendent in Nuremberg, 29 Apr. 1938, "Betreff: kirchliche Beerdigung durch einem D.C.-Pfarrer," LKA Nuremberg, KD Nbg 117.

84. Circular of Westphalian Confessing Church, "1939: Nr. 2—Februar," 18 Feb. 1939, p. 5, LKA Bielefeld 5,1/560,2.

85. Bormann, "Anordnung Nr. 125/39 (Nicht zur Veröffentlichung), 'Betrifft Propaganda der Deutschen Christen (Nationalkirchliche Einung D.C.),'" 13 June 1939, Munich, this copy sent to Gau office leaders and district leaders of the Gau Munich–Upper Bavaria from Gauamtsleiter Munich, signed Hackl, 22 June 1939, Munich, BDC Research, File 244, p. 108.

86. Schieder, Protestant-Lutheran Superintendent in Nuremberg, to Regional Church Council in Munich, 10 Mar. 1940, LKA Nuremberg, LKR II 246/Bd. IX.

87. Kramm to Seidenstücker, 8 Mar. 1935, Recklinghausen, pp. 1–3, LKA Bielefeld 5,1/294,2.

88. Klingbeil to Kertz, 14 Oct. 1933, Essen-Borbeck, AEKR Düsseldorf, NL Schmidt/1, pp. 11–12.

89. Hans Georg Düring to Reich Minister of the Interior, copy to Müller, 28 Nov. 1933, Leuthen-Windorf, pp. 1–6, and Düring to Müller, 4 Dec. 1933, EZA Berlin 1/A4/252.

90. Clarenbach to [no addressee], 22 Jan. 1940, and Report from Clarenbach to Protestant Consistory in Münster, 22 Feb. 1940, including excerpt from minutes of the District Synodal board in Soest from 20 Feb. 1940, with Graffunder's statement, Presbyter Heinert's statement, signed by Clarenbach, von Werthern, Koopmann, and Schürmann, and additional comments from Clarenbach, pp. 1–4, all in LKA Bielefeld 4,55/B/12,2.

91. Fragment of report by Clarenbach to Protestant Consistory Westphalia, 7 May 1940, LKA Bielefeld 4,55/B/12,3.

92. Clarenbach to Protestant Consistory in Westphalia, 22 Feb. 1940, "Zur Konsistorial-Verfügung vom 8.2.1940 Nr. 1246/Personal. Graffunder," LKA Bielefeld 4,55/B/12,2.

93. "Die neuesten Landesverräter! Ueberfallkommando muß die Kirche schützen!," in *Volksstimme*, no. 148 (29 June 1933), clipping from AA Bonn Bes. Geb. Bd. 3, Saargebiet.

94. Hahn to Wentz, 25 June 1936, Bielefeld, pp. 1–4, KAG Minden, no. 28. The other side of the story of this conflict appears in a copy of Council of Brethren of the Westphalian Confessing Synod, signed Lücking, to Superintendents of the Westphalian Confessing Synod, 26 June 1936, Dortmund, pp. 1–4, KAG Minden, no. 28.

95. Hahn to Wentz, 4 June 1936, Bielefeld, pp. 1–2, and Hahn to Wentz, 12

Oct. 1936, Münster, p. 1, ibid. Also copy of decision regarding Hahn's case, Protestant Consistory of Westphalia, signed Dr. Thümmel, 15 Sept. 1936, Münster, pp. 1–2, ibid. The consistory dismissed complaints against Hahn with a warning to him to mend his ways.

96. Note added to copy of letter from President of the Protestant Lutheran Regional Church Office, Saxony, signed Klotsche, to Senior Church Councillor Wäntig, 20 Mar. 1941, Dresden.

97. Paul Fuhrmann to Müller, 15 Nov. 1933, Berlin-Grunewald, pp. 1–2, EZA Berlin 1/A4/101. The quotation is from Goethe's "Der Zauberlehrling" (1797).

## Chapter Ten

1. Joseph Gauger, "Aus Gottes Reich," in *Licht und Leben: Evangelisches Wochenblatt*, no. 1 (7 Jan. 1934): 4, LKA Bielefeld 5,1/358,2.

2. von Bodelschwingh, *Unsere kleine Arbeit*, p. 15, in KAG Minden, no. 28.

3. Report from Parish Group Oberhausen I, "Versammlung der DC," Dec. 1933, p. 2, AEKR Düsseldorf, NL Schmidt/17, p. 21.

4. Fritz Engelke, "Volk, Staat, Kirche," in *Aus Gottes Garten, Monatsblätter aus dem Rauhen Haus*, no. 1/2 (1934): 8.

5. Report by vicar and SA senior warrant office J. Schellenberg, "Bericht über eine Versammlung der Volkskirchenbewegung DC mit 'Reichsvikar' D. Engelke am 31. Jan. 1937," pp. 1–2, LKA Bielefeld 5,1/292,2.

6. Emmi Lange to German Faith Movement, 16 Jan. 1938, Hamburg, pp. 4–6, BA Potsdam, DG IV, 1938–43, pp. 64–66.

7. A.A., "Die Macht des Wortes," in "Zwei junge SA-Leute über 'Wort und Sakrament,'" *Evangelium im Dritten Reich*, no. 47 (19 Nov. 1933): 488, LKA Bielefeld 5,1/289,2.

8. Pastor Schaefer, Hennen (Westphalia), "Lesepredigt zu Pfingsten," *Theologischer Arbeitsbrief* (1 May 1944): 14, LKA Bielefeld 5,1/295,2.

9. H. Vogel, in *Die Deutsche Mutter* (Potsdam: Reichsstelle für Frauendienst), p. 7, KAG Minden, loose materials.

10. See Scholder, *The Churches and the Third Reich*, 1:226, and Conway, *Nazi Persecution of the Churches*, p. 20.

11. Circular signed Themel from DEK Kirchenkanzlei, 3 Jan. 1935, *An die obersten Behörden der deutschen evangelischen Landeskirchen und an die Evangelischen Konsistorien des inländischen Aufsichtsbereichs der evangelischen Kirche der altpreußischen Union*, EZA Berlin 1/C3/101.

12. Text of presentation by Schreyer in *Theologischer Arbeitsbrief*, undated fragment, LKA Bielefeld 5,1/295,1.

13. Heinz Henckel, "Herr Szulc aus Zichenau—Grenzfälle der Deutschen Volksliste," *Das Reich*, no. 18 (3 May 1942), clipping in EZA Berlin 1/A2/620.

14. Dr. L., "Nach Dänemark und Norwegen: Eindrücke von einer Spätherbstfahrt 1936," *Evangelium im Dritten Reich*, no. 48 (29 Nov. 1936): 3, LKA Bielefeld 5,1/291,1.

15. Pastor Peschke, Niederullersdorf, Kr. Sorau, "Zur Saarabstimmung!," *Evangelium im Dritten Reich*, no. 26 (1 July 1934): 330, LKA Bielefeld 5,1/290,2.

16. Stanzas 1, 2, and 4 of "Saarlied" by Hanns Maria Lux, quoted here from "Liedertexte für die Reichstagung," *Evangelium im Dritten Reich*, no. 38 (23 Sept. 1934): 459, ibid.

17. Zielinski, "'DAZ'—Unterredung mit Bischof Glondys—Über die Arbeit der Evangelischen Kirche in Osteuropa," *Deutsche Allgemeine Zeitung*, no. 551 (25 Nov. 1938), clipping in BA Potsdam, RLB, 1864, p. 140.

18. See, for example, the excerpt Staedel copied into his journal from the German-language paper *Kirchliche Blätter*, no. 12 (22 Mar. 1934): 124, BA Koblenz, NL 252/22.

19. Staedel, "Ansprache bei der behördlichen Vorfeier anläßlich der Einweihung der 'Siebenbürger Altersheims' in Osterode v. d. Harz am 7.11.1964 Vormittags," BA Koblenz, NL 252/19.

20. See text of speech by Cläre Quambusch at the fourth Reich Conference of German Christians in Eisenach, Oct. 1937, "Die Aufgabe der deutschen Frau in Glaubensfragen der Gegenwart," in *Die Nationalkirche: Briefe an Deutsche Christen*, no. 42/43 (24 Oct. 1937): 338, LKA Bielefeld 5,1/292,1.

21. "Sturmsoldaten!," in *Das kleine Nazi-Liederbuch*, song no. 2, pp. 2–3, Rudolf Fischer collection.

22. "Schwarmgeister," in *Nachrichten-Blatt der Ev. Gemeinde Oberhausen*, no. 12 (24 Mar. 1935): 1, AEKR Düsseldorf, NL Schmidt/18.

23. Confessing Church report of Fritz Engelke's "Vortrag in Neckarsulm, 31.01," [1937], p. 4, LKA Bielefeld 5,1/292,1.

24. "Sturmlied," no. 12 in *Das kleine Nazi-Liederbuch*, p. 9.

25. Here pp. 357 and 444–45 of *Mein Kampf* are quoted, partly paraphrased, and criticized by Strathmann, *Nationalsozialistische Weltanschauung?*, p. 11.

26. Confessing Church flyer signed by the provincial brotherhood of the Province of Saxony, *Evangelium und Taufe! Bericht zu den Angriffen gegen Pfarer Zuckschwerdt, Magdeburg*, EZA Berlin 50/3a, pp. 72–74.

27. See ibid.

28. Confessing Church report, "DC Theologie: Der Deutschglaube für die Helden und das Christentum für die Frauen, Kinder, Schwachen und Hilflosen—Kundgebung der GDC, 28 February 1935 in Göttingen," pp. 1–2, LKA Bielefeld 5,1/290,1.

29. Liebe-Harkort, *Frau und Kirche*, p. 2.

30. "Die Religionsgliederung in Deutschland," *Berliner Börsenzeitung*, no. 543 (18 Nov. 1934), clipping, BA Potsdam RLB, 1862, p. 72.

31. Dahlkotter to Clarenbach, Borgeln, 23 Dec. 1936, Lippstadt (Westphalia), LKA Bielefeld 4,55/A/34.

32. Frederking to the Protestant Consistory in Münster, 18 May 1938, Neheim, p. 2, LKA Bielefeld 4,55/B/17,3.

33. "Bericht über die deutsch-christlichen Gemeinden Minden, Hausberge und Holzhausen II vom 7. Juli 1938," p. 3, subtitled "Bericht über Pfarrer Dr. Hahn, Minden i. W.," KAG Minden, no. 14.

34. Entz to Deputy Gau Leader Scharizer, Vienna, 28 May 1940, Vienna, p. 12, BA Koblenz R 43 II/155, fiche 2, p. 50.

35. Ibid., p. 17, BA Koblenz R 43 II/155, fiche 2, p. 55.

36. Marie Krause, deaconess at the Paul Gerhardt Foundation in Berlin, to Müller, 15 Oct. 1933, EZA Berlin 1/A4/251, pp. 1–2.

37. Helene Landgraf to Wentz, 3 May 1934, Bethel (Westphalia), KAG Minden, unorganized folder of Wentz correspondence.

38. Hildegard Schultze, "Auf Frauendienst-Fahrt durchs Reich," in untitled pamphlet (Potsdam, [1941 or 1942]), p. 6, KAG Minden, loose materials.

39. DC Nationalkirchliche Einung *Informationsdienst*, no. 3/43 (Weimar, 10 Mar. 1943): 1, EZA Berlin 1/A4/565.

40. Cläre Quambusch, "Auszug aus dem Jahresbericht 1943 über die Frauenarbeit der Thüringer Kirche in Verbindung mit der Fachabteilung XI der Nationalkirchlichen Einung Deutsche Christen," Deutsche Christen Nationalkirchliche Einung, *Informationsdienst*, 1/44 (22 Jan. 1944): 10, EZA Berlin 1/A4/566.

41. Müller, *Der deutsche Volkssoldat*, p. 125.

42. P. Alberts, Waltrop (Westphalia), "Die deutsche Frau im Kriege," *Theologischer Arbeitsbrief*, [1939 or 1940]: 17–20, LKA Bielefeld 5,1/295,1.

43. "Exaudi, den 17. Mai 1942 (Muttertag), Text: I. Kor. 13, V. 8: Die Liebe höret nimmer auf," *Theologischer Arbeitsbrief*, Münster, (1 May 1942): 4–6, ibid.

44. Langmann-Hamburg, "Heldentum und Opfertat," *Evangelium im Dritten Reich*, no. 8 (25 Feb. 1934): 87–88, LKA Bielefeld 5,1/289,1.

45. See complaint about Deutsche Glaubensbewegung speaker Kniggendorf: Pastor Kittmann, on behalf of the Tilsit parish council, to Senior Public Prosecutor, 1 Apr. 1937. Copy sent by the Reich Minister of Justice to Minister Kerrl, 10 May 1937, BA Potsdam, DG III, 1937–39, p. 345.

46. "Gedächtnisfeier," no. 31 in *Die Gottesfeier*.

47. Grundmann to Kottenrodt, 10 Feb. 1944, printed in DC Nationalkirch-

liche Einung, *Informationsdienst*, no. 3/44 (5 Apr. 1944): 6–7, EZA Berlin 1/A4/566.

## Chapter Eleven

1. The account of the Franconian German Christian leader appears in a Confessing Church report, "Das Ende der 'Deutschen Christen' in Eibach," 22 May 1945, pp. 1–2, LKA Nuremberg, LKR II 246, Bd. IX.

2. See survey of the demise of German Christian church governments in Bremen, Lübeck, and Thuringia, in Herman, *Rebirth of the German Church*, pp. 3–9.

3. Pastor Heilsbronn to Protestant Lutheran Regional Church Council, Nasbach, 1 June 1945, Heilsbronn, "Betreff: Rückführung der D.C. in die Kirche," LKA Nuremberg, LKR II 246, Bd. IX. Heilsbronn recounted his reflections when the local German Christian leader, a schoolteacher, asked that his followers be reabsorbed into the congregation.

4. See complaints by Lieutenant-Colonel Marshall M. Knappen, head of the Religious Affairs Section in the Office of Military Government for Germany, United States (OMGUS), of reluctance on the part of Protestant organizations to denazify adequately, in report from Knappen to Lucius Clay, "Stewart W. Herman: Interview with Major-General Clay at Berlin on December 5th, 1945," in Vollnhalls, *Die evangelische Kirche nach dem Zusammenbruch*, p. 305.

5. Fiebig to Wentz, 8 Nov. 1945, KAG Minden, file V Fiebig. Besier refers to tensions between the American and British occupation authorities and their varying policies on German Christians in *"Selbstreinigung,"* esp. pp. 53–62.

6. See, for example, "Marshall M. Knappen. Report on Interview with Bishop Wurm of Württemberg (leading Protestant ecclesiastic of Germany), 22 June 1945," p. 26, and Niemöller to Barth, 15 June 1946, pp. 135–36, both in Vollnhalls, *Die evangelische Kirche nach dem Zusammenbruch*.

7. See English translation of the Stuttgart Declaration and discussion of its reception in Germany and abroad in Herman, *Rebirth of the German Church*, pp. 140–46, and Herman, "Report on German Reactions to the Stuttgart Declaration. [14 Dec. 1945]," in Vollnhalls, *Die evangelische Kirche nach dem Zusammenbruch*, pp. 309–14.

8. For the German text of the declaration and commentary from a Swiss delegate to the meeting between German church leaders and representatives of the World Council of Churches where it was presented, see "Alphons Koechlin: Ökumenische Mission nach Deutschland vom 15. bis 21. Oktober 1945," in Vollnhalls, *Die evangelische Kirche nach dem Zusammenbruch*, pp. 212–13.

Besier and Sauter provide related documents and analysis in *Wie Christen ihre Schuld bekennen.*

9. "Personnel Questionnaire" (English-language version), in Friedmann, *Allied Military Government of Germany*, pp. 326–31.

10. Gotthardt Goertz's figures are included in a report commissioned by the Religious Affairs Branch of the British Occupation Authority, in Besier, "*Selbstreinigung*," p. 61. Statistics of denazification of clergy in the American zone (Protestant churches in Bavaria, Württemberg, Hesse, Bremen, and Baden) in Vollnhalls, *Evangelische Kirche und Entnazifizierung.*

11. See Prolingheuer, *Wir sind in die Irre gegangen*, p. 166. For commentary on the effect of the declaration of the Protestant church in Württemberg as an "antifascist institution," see Karl Haldenwang, "Die württ. evangelische Kirche und der Nazismus: Die kirchlich-theologische Sozietät," *Schwäbisches Tagblatt*, no. 67 (23 Aug. 1946), LKA Bielefeld 5,1/686,1.

12. "Ordnung für das Verfahren bei Verletzung von Amtspflichten der Geistlichen," signed by the leadership of the Protestant church of Westphalia—Koch, Brandes, Hardt, Kleßmann, Lücking, Nockemann, Philipps, and Schlink, and by the leadership of the Protestant Church of the Rhine Province—Beckmann, Harney, Held, Mensing, Rössler, Schlingensiepen, from Stoltenhoff, Bielefeld, and Düsseldorf, 1 Sept. 1945, LKA Bielefeld 4,55/B/26,6.

13. Fiebig to Wentz, 8 Nov. 1945, KAG Minden, file V Fiebig.

14. The Württemberg church leadership's proclamation over Radio Stuttgart on 5 May 1946 was subsequently printed in the "Nachrichten und Verordnungsblatt der EKiD" (Protestant Church in Germany) for May 1946 as *Erlaß des Oberkirchenrats* Nr. A 10864, 28 Oct. 1935.

15. Protestant Senior Church Council, signed Haug, to Protestant Superintendent's Office, Göppingen, "Betr. 'Kirche und Entnazifizierung'—Denkschrift der kirchl.-theol. Sozietät," 20 Aug. 1946, Stuttgart, pp. 5–8, LKA Bielefeld 5,1/686,1.

16. "Neue Wirksamkeit der früheren DC," in circular from the Chancellery of the Protestant Church in Germany, signed Asmussen, 3 Dec. 1947, Schwäbisch Gmünd, pp. 2–3, LKA Nuremberg, LKR II 246, Bd. IX.

17. Buschtöns to Koch, 14 Oct. 1945, Ilsenburg, pp. 4–7, KAG Minden, no. 15.

18. For a summary of the work of Hermann Diem and his "Ecclesiastical-theological society" see [Karl Haldenwang], "Die württ. evangelische Kirche und der Nazismus: Die kirchlich-theologische Sozietät," *Schwäbisches Tagblatt*, no. 67 (23 Aug. 1946): 6, LKA Bielefeld 5,1/686,1.

19. See manuscript (draft of pamphlet later released by "kirchlich-theologische Sozietät"), Hermann Diem, "Die Entnazifizierung in der Kirche," pp. 5–7, ibid.

20. Diem was denounced for using "German Christian methods" and publishing in "Communist" papers. See Georg Schmidgall to Haldenwang, 26 Aug. 1946, Tübingen, pp. 1–4, and Hanns Rückert to Diem, 26 Aug. 1946, Tübingen, ibid.

21. "Erklärung der kirchlich-theologische Sozietät in Württemberg vom 9. April 1946," signed Diem, Christian Berg, Heinrich Fausel, Kurt Müller, Paul Schempp, p. 1, ibid.

22. See "Stewart W. Herman: General German Church Situation [September 1945]," in Vollnhalls, *Die evangelische Kirche nach dem Zusammenbruch*, esp. pp. 160–61, on the purge of "Nazi church governments."

23. Circular by Pastor Wilhelm Oberlies, *Liebe Freunde und Kameraden*, Nov. 1949, KAG Minden, no. 17. Pastor Oberlies requested donations to help needy pastors, presumably German Christians.

24. Mimeograph, Heinrich Bergholter, "Die Deutschen Christen Hannovers in den Jahren 1933–35," [1954], p. 31, KAG Minden, no. 21.

25. Karl Eichenberg, "Sie waren anders als ihr Ruf," [1970s], pp. 14–17, KAG Minden, no. 6410.

26. Carbon copy, [Christiansen] to Pastor Frick (Bethel), 30 Aug. 1945, Enger (Westphalia), p. 2, KAG Minden, no. 33.

27. See copies of letters from congregational members testifying, dated August and September 1945, attached to "An die Spruchkammer," Pastor Rohlfing, [fall 1945], Gevelsberg-Haufe, ibid.

28. Karl Graffunder, "Betr.: Stellung des Pfarrers Graffunder zum Bekenntnis und zu den Deutschen Christen," 4 Sept. 1945, Lohne (Westphalia), sent to "den Vorsitzenden des Ausschusses zur Wiederherstellung eines an Schrift und Bekenntnis gebundenen Pfarrerstandes, Herrn Pfr. Lic. Frick in Bethel durch Herrn Superintendenten Clarenbach," p. 3, LKA Bielefeld 4,55/B/12,3.

29. See Siegfried Hermle on the legacy of anti-Jewish Christianity in "Die Evangelische Kirche und das Judentum nach 1945," in Bergmann and Erb, *Antisemitismus*.

30. See Hans Meyer to Sachsse, 16 June 1946, Neuwied, AEKR Düsseldorf, Bevollmächtigteramt d. franz. Zone, Bf. 17 B. M-Wied.

31. Draft, Bruno Adler to Hanns Lilje, 6 June 1949, Minden, KAG Minden, no. 17.

32. Kessel to Stüven, 6 Nov. 1953, Osterode/Harz, KAG Minden, FVK 2.

33. Staedel, "Zusammenfassende Thesen zum Vortrag des Bischofs a. D. Wilhelm Staedel über das Thema 'Der siebenbürgische und der deutsche Kirchenkampf,'" [1950s]: 6, BA Koblenz, NL 252/20.

34. Baedeker, *Das Volk das im Finsternis wandelt*, p. 87.

35. Clarenbach, "Stellungnahme des Superintendenten des Kirchenkreises

Soest in Sachen Drewer (St. Petri II, Soest)," 21 Dec. 1945, Borgeln über Soest, pp. 1–2, LKA Bielefeld 4,55/B/26,6.

36. Buschtöns to Wentz, 31 Jan. 1946, Ilsenburg, pp. 2–4, KAG Minden no. 15.

37. Buschtöns to Wentz, 15 Feb. 1947, Ilsenburg, pp. 1, 3, ibid.

38. Buschtöns to Wentz, 15 July 1950, Klein-Machnow, ibid.

39. "Beschluss," signed Frick, Barnstein, Geibel, 15 Nov. 1946, Bethel, penciled in "Drewer," implemented 11 Jan. 1947, pp. 1–2, KAG Minden, no. 17.

40. "Beschluß," Ausschuss zur Wiederherstellung eines an Schrift und Bekenntnis gebundenen Pfarrerstandes, signed Frick, Münter, Geibel, implemented 4 June 1946, dated 17 May 1946, Bethel, KAG Minden, no. 15.

41. Scholder, *The Churches and the Third Reich*, 1:193.

42. Heinrich Meyer, "Mein Einsatz für Deutsches Christentum," 28 Sept. 1953, KAG Minden, no. 2.

43. Buschtöns to Wentz, 26 Feb. 1949, Ilsenburg, KAG Minden, file V Fiebig. In July 1949, the church leadership determined it would do nothing to obstruct further engagement in church work on Buschtöns's part, even though he refused to recognize the Barmen confession. Buschtöns to Wentz, 19 July 1949, Ilsenburg, ibid.

44. Staedel to Willi Roth, 18 May 1948, BA Koblenz, NL 252/3.

45. "Urteilsbegründung," [Fiebig–Münster], 23 June 1948, Münster, signed Philippi, Brandes, and Franke, p. 7, KAG Minden, file V Fiebig.

46. Adler to Staedel, 13 Apr. 1954, Minden, pp. 1–2, KAG Minden, no. 17.

47. See Johannes Endler, curriculum vitae of sorts, p. 3, KAG Minden, no. 29, labeled "Pfarrer a. D. Endler, Joh. (1953–56)."

48. On Diehl's postwar fate, see her newsletter, "Liebe Neuländer und Neulandfreunde," 20 June 1960, Laurenburg an der Lahn (Hesse), KAG Minden, no. 1.

49. Hermenau to Wentz, 2 June 1960, Wiesbaden-Biebrich, ibid.

50. Hermenau to Wentz, 14 Oct. 1960, Wiesbaden-Biebrich, KAG Minden, folder Hermenau.

51. Ilse Werdermann to Wentz, 28 Feb. 1960, Bad Kreuznach, KAG Minden, file Werdermann.

52. Ilse Werdermann to Wentz, 12 Mar. 1960, Bad Kreuznach, ibid. See also Werdermann to Wentz, 6 May 1960, Bad Kreuznach, KAG Minden, no. 1.

53. [Staedel], "Zusammenfassende Thesen zum Vortrag des Bischofs a.D. Wilhelm Staedel über das Thema 'Der Siebenbürgische und der deutsche Kirchenkampf,'" p. 2, KAG Minden, no. 2.

54. Bergholter, "Die Deutschen Christen Hannovers in den Jahren 1933–35," [1954], p. 33, KAG Minden, no. 21.

55. See report by former bishop of Lübeck Erwin Balzer, of his conversation with Buttler on 12 Dec. 1949, "Niederschriften über die Versuche des Bischof Balzer, nach seiner 'Verurteilung' durch den neuen Lübecker Kirchenrat (Entscheidung von 1948), die von der Lübecker Kirche vor ihm verlangte 'staatliche' Entnazifizierung zu erreichen und irgend wieder ins Amt zu kommen," p. 10, KAG Minden, file Lübeck.

56. Schleuning to Lilje, 14 Dec. 1945, Helmstedt (Braunschweig), p. 1, KAG Minden, no. 17.

57. Diehl, *Christ sein heißt Kämpfer sein,* pp. 252–54.

58. Paul Bauer, "Praktische Grundsätze zur Seelsorge an Kriegsgefangenen," [1946?], BA-MA Freiburg, N282/4.

59. Mägerle [name unclear] to Diem, 3 Mar. 1948, Ludwigsburg, LKA Bielefeld 5,1/686/2.

60. Minutes of hearing of Hans Schmidt before justice committee, signed Consistory Councillor Rößler, 22 Oct. 1947, Düsseldorf, pp. 2–3, AEKR Düsseldorf, Bevollmächtigteramt d. franz. Zone, Bf 10, CD-Konsistorium KL.

61. Buschtöns to Wentz, 27 Nov. 1953, KAG Minden, no. 15.

62. Werdermann to Wentz, 6 May 1960, Bad Kreuznach, p. 2, KAG Minden, no. 1.

63. Fiebig to Buschtöns, 27 Feb. 1946, Münster, p. 1, KAG Minden, V, Fiebig. Fiebig's exact words were as follows: "Der Vorwurf, daß wir uns nicht über die Konzentrationslager geäussert hätten, wird immer wieder einmal auch hier erhoben. Sie erinnern mit Recht daran, daß wir nichts davon gewußt haben und auch nichts wissen konnten, weil die uns zugänglichen Nachrichten anders lauteten."

64. Staedel to Heim, 17 June 1958, BA Koblenz, NL 252/13, p. 2. Staedel cited the French historian Maurice Bardèche, author of *Nürnberg oder Die Falschmünzer,* Peter Kleist's *Auch Du warst dabei,* and a 1952 American paper, the *Broom,* in which "the Jew Dr. Listojewski, lawyer and statistician" claimed that the number of dead or missing Jews could not exceed 350,000 to 500,000.

65. Staedel to Heim, 24 Jan. 1958, Holzhausen a. d. Porta (Westphalia), p. 4, BA Koblenz, NL 252/13.

66. Dr. Stoevesandt, "Zur Rechtfertigungsschrift Weidemann von 1960," 30 May 1960, Bremen, LKA Bielefeld 5,1/288,2.

67. "Fall Kwami," in "Drei Dokumente zum Fall Meyer-Aurich. Bericht von Pastor a.D. Heinrich Meyer in Aurich (Ostfriesland), 28 July 1958," KAG Minden, file labeled Duhm.

68. Gustav Endler to all Protestant Regional and Provincial Churches in the Federal Republic of Germany, 5 May 1953, Berlin-Hermsdorf, KAG Minden, no. 29.

69. Gustav Endler, "Konfirmationsansprache gehalten im Kriegsjahr 1942 von Pfarrer Endler, I. Kor. 3,11," attached to Endler to Supreme Party Court (Munich) 11 Mar. 1942, Berlin, BDC, Endler Material, Oberstes Parteigericht file.

70. Siegfried Leffler to Dr. Hutten, 24 Sept. 1947, Ludwigsburg, pp. 1–2, LKA Nuremberg, LKR II 246, Bd. IX.

71. Ibid.

72. "Siegfried Lefflers Widerruf," in "Kirchliche Nachrichten," *Evangelisches Gemeindeblatt für Augsburg und Umgebung*, no. 5 (1 Feb. 1948): 21, KAG Minden, no. 2.

73. See Vollnhalls, *Evangelische Kirche und Entnazifizierung*, p. 287, also notation by Wentz, dated July 1960, on copy "Siegfried Lefflers Widerruf," ibid.

74. Report by Erwin Balzer, 42 pp. [material for hearing, 1946?], pp. 3–7, KAG Minden, file Lübeck.

75. Loerzer to Dibelius, 31 July 1948, p. 7, KAG Minden, file Loerzer.

76. Ibid.

77. Diehl, *Christ sein heißt Kämpfer sein*, pp. 274–75.

78. Meyer-Erlach, "Zum Muttertag," *Idsteiner Zeitung* (12–13 May 1962), clipping in LKA Bielefeld 5,1/288,1.

79. Hans Ködding to Wentz, 8 Oct. 1947, Bad Lippspringe, KAG Minden, no. 33.

80. "Urteilsbegründung," [Fiebig–Münster], 23 June 1948, Münster, signed Philippi, Brandes, and Franke, including testimony of superintendent, 15 Oct. 1945, p. 14, KAG Minden, file V Fiebig.

81. Otto Stockburger to Fiebig, 14 Aug. 1948, Michelbach a.d. Bilz, with copy of Stockburger's "Bescheinigung," dated 14 Aug. 1948, on behalf of Fiebig, KAG Minden, file V Fiebig.

82. Walther Schultz to Wentz, 12 Nov. 1956, Schnackenburg/Elbe über Lüchow, KAG Minden, file labeled May-KKampf-Walther Schultz.

83. Heinrich Stüven, circular, 2 Sept. 1946, p.1, KAG Minden, no. 9.

84. "Gedanken eines Deutschen Christen im Jahre 1951," pp. 1–2, KAG Minden, no. 17.

85. Flyer, Heinz Sting, *Was will die volkskirchenbewegung Freie Christen?*, 1952, Hanover, p. 2, KAG Minden, no. 49.

86. "Woran glauben die Angehörigen der Freien Christlichen Volkskirche?," in *Freie Christliche Volkskirche—Mitteilungsblatt für Freie Christen*, no. 1 (Mar. 1959): 1, KAG Minden, unlabeled folder.

87. "Rundbrief—Freie Christliche Volkskirche, Stuttgart," signed E. Tix, A. Schütz, K. Knabe, [date penciled on 6.5.1959], pp. 1–2, KAG Minden, folder

Tix. See also "Gemeinde Nachrichten für die Freie Christliche Kirche in Süd Deutschland–Stuttgart," Nov. 1958, no. 11, p. 2, for statistics.

88. Werner May to Wentz, 14 Jan. 1960, p. 1, KAG Minden, no. 1.

89. Handwritten account, Pastor Otto Koch, "Meine Erlebnisse als 'Deutscher Christ,'" [1954], p. 3, KAG Minden, no. 17.

90. Staedel to Heim, 17 June 1958, Holzhausen an der Porta (Westphalia), pp. 8–10, BA Koblenz, NL 252/13. The emphasis is Staedel's.

# Bibliography

## Archival Sources

Bensheim
  Evangelischer Bund, Konfessionskundliches Institut
    S.500          Akten des Evangelischen Bundes
Berlin
  Berlin Document Center
                  NSDAP Master File
                  Oberstes Parteigericht
                  Partei Kanzlei Correspondence
                  "Research"
    S I              Reichskulturkammer
    S II             Reichsschrifttumskammer
    SSO           SS Officers
  Evangelisches Zentralarchiv in Berlin
    Bestand 1    Deutsche Evangelische Kirche
    7            Evangelischer Oberkirchenrat
    50          Kirchenkampf (Archiv für die Geschichte des
                    Kirchenkampfes)
Bielefeld
  Archiv der Evangelischen Kirche in Westfalen
    Bestand 4,55  Kreissynode Soest
    5,1          Sammlung Wilhelm Niemöller—(Bielefelder Archiv des
                    Kirchenkampfes)
Bonn
  Politisches Archiv des Auswärtigen Amts
                  Abt. VI—Evangelische Angelegenheiten 2: Die
                    Verfassung der Evangelischen Kirche
                  Abt. Inland I-D: Kirche 2
                  Besetzte Gebiete: Saargebiet
                  Büro Reichsminister: Kirchenstreit, Saargebiet
                  Inland IIg: Kirchliche Angelegenheiten
                  Politische Abteilung, Pol. III, Heiliger Stuhl
Düsseldorf
  Archiv der Evangelischen Kirche im Rheinland
                  Archiv des Bevollmächtigteramtes der französischen
                    Zone

Nachlaß Superintendent Dr. Wilhelm Ewald Schmidt
Nachlaß Pfarrer Adolf Ernst Walter Wilm
Provinzialsynodalrat der Rheinprovinz

Freiburg im Breisgau

Bundesarchiv—Militärarchiv

| | |
|---|---|
| N 127 | Nachlaß Karl Marten, 1887–1958, Divisionspfarrer |
| N 282 | Nachlaß Franz Dohrmann |
| RH 14 | Der Chef der Heeresrüstung und Befehlshaber des Ersatzheeres |
| RH 15 | Oberkommando des Heeres |
| RH 53 | Wehrkreiskommando |
| RM 26 | Marinedekan |
| RW 12 I | Reichswehrminister: Evangelischer Feldbischof |

Koblenz

Bundesarchiv Koblenz

| | |
|---|---|
| NL 131 | Nachlaß Jakob Wilhelm Hauer |
| NL 252 | Nachlaß Bischof Wilhelm Staedel |
| NL 308 | Nachlaß Dietrich Bonhoeffer |
| NS 8 | Kanzlei Rosenberg |
| NS 10 | Persönliche Adjuntatur des Führers und Reichskanzlers |
| R 18 | Reichsministerium des Innern |
| R 22 | Reichsjustizministerium |
| R 43 | Reichskanzlei |
| R 58 | Reichssicherheitshauptamt |
| R 79 | Reichsministerium für die kirchlichen Angelegenheiten (Aktensplitter) |

Lübeck

Nordelbische Evangelisch-Lutherische Kirche, Nordelbisches Kirchenamt, Archiv Lübeck

| | |
|---|---|
| | Bestand Kirchenkampf Lübeck |
| KK 78 | Kirchenkampf in St. Gertrud II |
| KK 81 | Auseinandersetzung in der St. Matthai-Kirchengemeinde |
| | Bestand St. Lorenz—Travemünde |
| | Landeskirche Lübeck: Protokollbuch des Geistlichen Ministeriums zu Lübeck |
| | Protokollbuch des Kirchenrats Nr. 3 |

Minden

Kommunalarchiv

Kirchengeschichtliche Arbeitsgemeinschaft (uncataloged collection)

Munich

Bayerisches Hauptstaatsarchiv

MA          Akten der Bayerischen Staatskanzlei: Ministeramt

MK          Akten des Staatsministeriums für Unterricht und Kultus

RSth        Reichsstatthalter Epp, Reichsstatthalter in Bayern

Nuremberg

Evangelisch-Lutherische Kirche in Bayern, Landeskirchliches Archiv

KKU         Bestand Kirchenkampf

LKR         Akten des Evangelisch-Lutherischen Landeskirchenrats
            in München

KD Nbg      Kreisdekan Nürnberg

Potsdam

Bundesarchiv Potsdam (formerly Zentrales Staatsarchiv)

Files labeled "Deutsche Christen" and "Deutsche
Glaubensbewegung," containing materials from
Ministerium für Wissenschaft, Kunst und Volksbildung:
Geistliche Abteilung und Reichsministerium für die
kirchlichen Angelegenheiten

Deutsche Arbeitsfront—Zeitungsausschnitte

Reichslandbund—Pressearchiv

## Microfilmed Sources

Captured German Documents, National Archives Microfilm Publication.
Series T-175. Records of the Reich Leader SS and Chief of German Police.

## Newspapers

Individual copies and clippings from many daily, weekly, and monthly papers
appear in the archival files. The following list includes frequently encountered
papers that covered developments related to the German Christian
movement.

*Allgemeine Evangelisch-Lutherische Kirchenzeitung.*

*Blätter des Neuland-Bundes.* (Diehl) Eisenach.

*Briefe an den "Deutschen Christen."* (Leffler).

*Deutsche Christen Nationalkirchliche Einung—Informationsdienst.* (Dungs)
   Weimar.

*Des Deutschen Volkes Kirche.* (Hossenfelder) Berlin.

*Deutscher Sonntag.* (Schneider) Stuttgart.

*Deutsches Pfarrerblatt. Verbandsblatt der deutschen evangelischen
   Pfarrvereine und der Vereinigung preußischer Pfarrvereine.*

*Evangelische Nachrichten. Amtliches Organ der "Deutschen Christen" für die Provinz Westfalen.* (Lehbrink, Fiebig, Niemann) Münster.

*Evangelium im Dritten Reich. Kirchenzeitung für Christentum und Nationalsozialismus. Sonntagsblatt der Glaubensbewegung "Deutsche Christen."* Berlin. (also regional editions and supplements).

*Nachrichten-Blatt der Evangelischen Gemeinde Oberhausen I.* (Pack, Brökelschen) Oberhausen (Rhineland).

*Die Nationalkirche.* (Leutheuser, Dungs).

*Die Nationalkirche: Briefe an deutsche Christen.* (Leffler, Dungs) Weimar.

*Das Neulandblatt. Organ der Neulandbewegung für innere Erneuerung Deutschlands.* (Diehl) Eisenach.

*Positives Christentum. Wochenblatt für alle christlichen Aufbaukräfte im Dritten Reich.* (Wiedemann) Berlin.

*Theologischer Arbeitsbrief.* (Fiebig) Münster. (duplicated).

*Verbandsmitteilungen: Institut zur Erforschung des jüdischen Einflusses auf das deutsche kirchliche Leben.* (Hunger).

*Der Weckruf. Evangelisches Gemeindeblatt.* (Dungs) Mülheim-Ruhr. (with regional editions).

## Contemporary Publications, Including Pamphlet Literature

Angermann, August. *Was für Männer gab das evangelische Pfarrhaus dem deutschen Volke?* Essen: Lichtweg Verlag, 1940. Duke Divinity School.

Antonowitz. *Wir bekennen! Ein Wort über brennende Gegenwartsfragen der Evangelischen Reichskirche.* N.p., n.d. Concordia Theological Seminary Library.

Arendt, Paul, ed. *Deutschland erwache! Das kleine Nazi-Liederbuch.* Edition A. Sulzbach (Bavaria): self-publication, [1926?]. Private collection of Rudolf Fischer, Bielefeld.

Bauer, Wilhelm. *Feierstunden Deutscher Christen.* Weimar: Verlag Deutsche Christen, 1935. KAG Minden.

Bauer, Wilhelm, and Walter Grundmann. *Die Religionsunterricht in der deutschen Schule. Ausgeführte Lehrpläne für die Volks- Mittel- und höheren Schulen.* Frankfurt/Main: Moritz Diesterweg, [1940].

Baumgärtner, Hans, Dr. Gahr, Heinrich Kalb, Johannes Ruck, Christian Ruck, and Martin Weigel. *Deutsches Christentum dargestellt in Predigt und Vortrag.* Nuremberg: n.p., 1937. Private collection of Rudolf Fischer, Bielefeld.

Bergér, Wilhelm. *Der Evangelische Bund in Nassau und Hessen.* Berlin: Evangelischer Bund, 1937. EB Bensheim.

Beste, Axel. *Rasse und Religion: Gedanken zum völkischen Problem.* Göttingen: Geißel & Hohl, 1926. Rudolf Fischer collection.

Birnbaum, Walter. *Die neue Sprache in der Wortverkündigung.* Hamburg: Agentur des Rauhen Hauses, [1926]. Rudolf Fischer collection.

Bodelschwingh, Gustav von. *Unsere kleine Arbeit inmitten großen Geschehens.* Herford: Union Druckerei Bielefeld, 1935. KAG Minden, no. 28.

*Die Botschaft Gottes.* Edited by the Institut zur Erforschung des jüdischen Einflusses auf das deutsche kirchliche Leben. Weimar: Verlag Deutsche Christen, [1941]. KAG Minden.

Dannenmann, Arnold. *Kirche im Dritten Reich. Die Geschichte der Glaubensbewegung "Deutsche Christen."* Dresden: Oskar Günther, [1933].

*Deutsche Christen—Nationalkirchliche Einung, Liedblätter.* Weimar: Verlag Deutsche Christen, [1939?]. KAG Minden.

*Deutsche mit Gott. Ein deutsches Glaubensbuch.* Edited by the Institut zur Erforschung des jüdischen Einflusses auf das deutsche kirchliche Leben. Weimar: Verlag Deutsche Christen, [1941?]. KAG Minden.

*Die Deutschen Christen in Abwehr und Aufbau. Grundsätzliche Erklärungen zu den kirchlichen Aufgaben unserer Zeit, erarbeitet auf der ersten westfälischen Gautagung in Bochum am 31. März und 1. April 1936.* N.p., [1936]. KAG Minden.

Diehl, Guida, ed. *Deutsche Weihnacht in Not und Kampf.* Eisenach: Neulandverlag, [1941?].

Diem, Hermann. *Restauration oder Neuanfang in der Evangelischen Kirche?* Stuttgart: Franz Mittelbach, 1946.

Duhm, Andreas. *Der Kampf um die deutsche Kirche. Eine Kirchengeschichte des Jahres 1933–34.* Gotha: Leopold Klotz, [1934].

Duncan-Jones, Arthur S. *The Struggle for Religious Freedom in Germany.* London: Victor Gollancz, 1938.

Eisenhuth, Heinz Erich. *Christus unsere Kraft. Predigten und Betrachtungen.* Weimar: Verlag Deutsche Christen, [1936?]. Rudolf Fischer collection.

——. "Die Kirche der evangelischen Duldsamkeit." In pamphlet, *Um die Kirche der Gewissensfreiheit.* Weimar: Deutsche Pfarrergemeinde, Verlag Deutsche Christen, [1937?]. LKA Bielefeld 5,1/293.

Engelland, Hans. *Drei Wege zu Gott? Der völkische Glaube—Der katholische Glaube—Der biblisch-reformatorisch Glaube.* Furche Schriften, no. 15. Berlin: Furche, 1938. Rudolf Fischer collection.

*Evangelisches Feldgesangbuch.* Berlin: E. S. Mittler & Son, [1939]. BA-MA Freiburg.

*Das Evangelium Johannes deutsch.* Foreword by Heinz Weidemann. Bremen: H. M. Hauschild, 1936. KAG Minden.

Flemming, E. *Glaube und Christianisierung der Germanen.* Hannover: Evangelischer Preßverband für die Provinz Hannover, n.d. Rudolf Fischer collection.

Fliedner, Friedrich, ed. *Glaube und Tat. Religionsbuch für deutsche Jungen und Mädel.* Bielefeld and Leipzig: Velhagen & Klasing, 1940. KAG Minden.

Florin, Wilhelm. *Rosenbergs Mythus und evangelischer Glaube. Ein Gemeindevortrag.* Gütersloh: C. Bertelsmann, n.d. Rudolf Fischer collection.

Frick, Heinrich. *Christliche Verkündigung und vorchristliches Erbgut. Basler Missionsstudien,* no. 16. Stuttgart and Basel: Evangelischer Missionsverlag, 1938. Rudolf Fischer collection.

Frör, Kurt. *Die babylonische Gefangenschaft der Kirche.* Erlangen: Selbstverlag Pfarrerbruderschaft, [1937]. Rudolf Fischer collection.

Gebhardt, Hermann. *Das Buch von der deutsch-völkischen christlichen Religion.* Breslau: Ferdinand Hirt, 1934.

*Gesangbuch der Kommenden Kirche.* Foreword by Heinz Weidemann. Bremen: Verlag "Kommende Kirche," [1940?]. KAG Minden.

"Gnade und Männlichkeit." No author. *Rufende Kirche,* no. 3. Breslau: Geschäftsstelle des volksmissionarischen Amtes, Schlesien, n.d. LKA Bielefeld 5,1/289,2.

Goebel, Hans. *Dietrich Eckart und das Christentum.* Darmstadt: K. F. Bender, n.d. Rudolf Fischer collection.

*Die Gottesfeier. Entwürfe und Hilfen zur Feiergestaltung in den Gemeinden "Deutscher Christen, Nationalkirchliche Einung."* Weimar: Verlag Deutsche Christen, 1939 and 1940. KAG Minden.

*Großer Gott, wir loben Dich!* Weimar: Der Neue Dom, 1941. KAG Minden.

Grossmann, Constantin. *Deutsche Christen. Ein Volksbuch: Wegweiser durch die Glaubensbewegung unserer Zeit.* Dresden: E. am Ende, 1934.

Grundmann, Walter. *Gott und Nation. Ein evangelisches Wort zum Wollen des Nationalsozialismus und zu Rosenbergs Sinndeutung.* Berlin: Furche, [1933].

Handtmann-Kolberg, G. *Wir pilgern nach Wittenberg. Eine Antwort auf Alfred Rosenbergs "Protestantische Rompilger."* Stettin: Fischer and Schmidt, n.d. Rudolf Fischer collection.

Hartenstein, Karl. *Völkerentartung unter dem Kreuz? Mission und Gemeinde. Das Zeugnis der Mission in der heutigen Kirche,* edited by Erich Schick, no. 3. Stuttgart and Basel: Evangelischer Missionsverlag, n.d. Rudolf Fischer collection.

Hauer, Jakob Wilhelm. *Unser Kampf um einen freien Deutschen Glauben.* Flugschriften zum geistigen und religiösen Durchbruch der Deutschen Revolution, no. 3. Stuttgart: C. L. Hirschfeld, [1934]. LKA Bielefeld 5,1/296.

Haugg, Werner. *Das Reichsministerium für die kirchlichen Angelegenheiten.* Schriften zum Staatsaufbau, Neue Folge der Schriften der Hochschule für Politik, edited by Paul Meier-Benneckenstein. Berlin: Junker & Dünnhaupt, 1940.

Heger, Adolf. *Deutsches Wesen und Christentum.* Schriften der Glaubensbewegung "Deutsche Christen" in Niedersachsen, no. 2. Bordesholm in Holstein: Heliand-Verlag, n.d.

Hempel. *Die Aufgabe von Theologie und Kirche von der Front her gesehen.* Edited by the Institut zur Erforschung des jüdischen Einflusses auf das deutsche kirchliche Leben. Weimar: Der neue Dom, Verlag für deutsch-christliches Schrifttum, [1941?]. Rudolf Fischer collection.

Hertzberg, H. W. *Der Deutsche und das Alte Testament.* Gießen: Alfred Töpelmann, 1934. Rudolf Fischer collection.

Heydt, Fritz von der. *Die Kirche Luthers zwischen Rom und Mythus.* Berlin: Säemann Verlag, 1939. Rudolf Fischer collection.

Hirsch, Emanuel. *Das kirchliche Wollen der Deutschen Christen.* Berlin-Charlottenburg: Max Grevemeyer, 1933.

Homann, Rudolf. *Die Weltanschauung des Mythus und der christliche Glaube.* Witten: Westdeutscher Lutherverlag, 1936. Rudolf Fischer collection.

*Irrlehre? Unsere Antwort an den Reichskirchenausschuß.* Preface by Siegfried Leffler. Weimar: Verlag Deutsche Christen, 1936. LKA Bielefeld 5,1/291,1.

Kalle, Ernst. *Hat das Alte Testament noch Bedeutung für die Christen? Der Kampf-Bund,* edited by the Evangelisches Provinzialamt für Apologetik, no. 12. Gütersloh: C. Bertelsmann, 1932. Rudolf Fischer collection.

Kinder, Christian, ed. *Der Deutschen Christen Reichskalendar, 1935.* Meißen: Schlimpert & Püschel, [1935]. KAG Minden.

Klein, Werner. *Das Evangelium jenseits der Konfessionen.* Stuttgart: Tazzelwurm, 1939. KAG Minden.

Knak, Siegfried. *Kirchenstreit und Kirchenfriede beleuchtet von den Erfahrungen der Mission aus.* 2d ed. Berlin: Heimatdienst, 1934. Rudolf Fischer collection.

Koch, Georg. *Die bäuerliche Seele. Eine Einführung in die religiöse Volkskunde.* Berlin: Furche Verlag, 1935. KAG Minden.

Köberle, Adolf. *Von der Unterschätzung und Überschätzung des*

*Bekenntnisses in der theologisch-kirchlichen Lage der Gegenwart.* Vortrag
gehalten auf der 49. Mitgliederversammlung des Evangelischen
Pfarrvereins in Württemberg. Stuttgart: Quell-Verlag der Evangelischen
Gesellschaft, 1940. Rudolf Fischer collection.

Krause, Reinhold. *Rede des Gauobmannes der Glaubensbewegung "Deutsche
Christen" in Groß-Berlin. Dr. Krause. Gehalten im Sportpalast am 13.
November 1933.* [Berlin, 1933]. LKA Bielefeld 5,1/289,2.

Kremers, Hermann. *Nationalsozialismus und Protestantismus.* 2d ed.
Berlin: Volksschriften des Evangelischen Bundes, vol. 35, 1931.

Lamparter, Eduard. *Evangelische Kirche und Judentum. Ein Beitrag zu
christlichen Verständnis von Judentum und Antisemitismus.* Nowawes:
Dr. Brönner, 1928. Rudolf Fischer collection.

*Lehrplan für die weltanschauliche Erziehung in der SS und Polizei.*
Introduced and edited by SS Central Office, [1937?]. Duke Pamphlet
Collection, 14462.

Lieb, Fritz. *Christ und Antichrist im Dritten Reich. Der Kampf der
Deutschen Bekenntniskirche.* Paris: Editions du Carrefour, 1936.

Liebe-Harkort, Eleanor. *Frau und Kirche.* Series edited by Hans Hermenau,
no. 1. Potsdam: Frauendienst der DEK, 1935.

*Lieder der Kommenden Kirche.* Foreword by Heinz Weidemann. Bremen:
Verlag "Kommende Kirche," [1939]. KAG Minden.

Loewe, Busso. *Das A.B.C. des Deutschen Heiden!* Erfurt: Thiel and Böhm,
n.d. Rudolf Fischer collection.

Mahling, Friedrich. *Der Wille zur Volkskirche.* Sonderdruck aus der
Reinhold-Seeberg-Festschrift. Leipzig: A. Deichertsche Verlagsbuchhand-
lung, 1929. Duke Divinity School.

May, Gerhard. *Die volksdeutsche Sendung der Kirche.* Göttingen:
Vandenhoeck & Ruprecht, 1934.

Metzler, Thea. *"Flammen."* Nuremberg: W. Tümmels, 1931.

——. *"Heiliger Kampf für Gott und Volk. Ein Büchlein für die Deutschen
Christen."* Dresden: Verlag Deutsche Christen, n.d.

Meyer, G. A. Wilhelm. *Die deutsche Wende in neun Predigten.* Dresden and
Leipzig: C. Ludwig Ungelenk, 1933. Rudolf Fischer collection.

Meyer, Hugo. *Houston Stewart Chamberlain als völkischer Denker.* Munich:
F. Bruckmann, 1939.

Meyer-Erlach, Wolf. *"Das deutsche Leid"—Ein Schauspiel in vier Akten.*
Deutsche Bühnenbücherei, vol. 10. Munich: J. F. Lehmanns, 1923. BDC
Partei Kanzlei Correspondence, Wolf Meyer-Erlach materials.

——. *Glaubenstrotz. Acht Rundfunkreden.* Weimar: Verlag Deutsche
Christen, 1937. Rudolf Fischer collection.

Micklem, Nathaniel. *National Socialism and the Roman Catholic Church.* London: Oxford University Press, 1939.

*Mit brennender Sorge. Das päpstliche Rundschreiben gegen den Nationalsozialismus und seine Folgen in Deutschland.* Edited by Simon Hurt. Freiburg/Br.: Herder, 1946.

Moering, Ernst. *Gegen völkischen Wahn. Rede an Menschen guten Willens. Wege zur Verständigung,* no. 2. Berlin: Philo, 1924. Rudolf Fischer collection.

Müller, Adolf, and Alfred Stier, eds. *Deutsche Kirchenlieder zur Erneuerung des Gemeinde-Gesangs.* 7th printing. Dresden: Verlag Landesverein für Innere Mission, Abteilung Sächsische Posaunenmission, im Auftrag des Evangelisch-Lutherischen Landeskirchenamts Sachsens, 1936. KAG Minden.

Müller, Ludwig. *Deutsche Gottesworte aus der Bergpredigt verdeutscht.* Weimar: Verlag Deutsche Christen, 1936.

——. *Der deutsche Volkssoldat.* Berlin Tempelhof: Edwin Runge, 1939.

*Mutter betet. Frauendienst im Gebet.* Potsdam: Reichsstelle Frauendienst, 1937. KAG Minden.

*Nationalkirche?* Evangelischer Bund, no. 105, 1937. EB Bensheim S 500.9.136.

Neumann, Edwin, Richard Grohnert, and Richard Ulrich, eds. *Licht und Leben. Handbuch für den evangelischen Religionsunterricht an den Volksschulen Ostpreußens.* Edition A, part 2: Mittel- und Oberstufe. Halle/Saale: Pädogogischer Verlag von Hermann Schroedel, 1936. KAG Minden.

Pauli, Ernst. *Die Kirche im Dritten Reich.* Schriftenreihe des Eisenacher Arbeitsrings, no. 5. Eisenach: Neuland Verlag, n.d. Rudolf Fischer collection.

Paulsen, Adalbert. *Auf großer Fahrt. Silvesterpredigt 1933 von Landesbischof Adalbert Paulsen, Kiel—Übertragen von der Universitätskirche in Kiel auf den Deutschlandsender.* Bordesholm in Holstein: Heliand, n.d. Rudolf Fischer collection.

Petri, E. *Zu Jesu Füßen. Wegweiser für deutsche Christen.* Berlin: Verlag der Deutschkirche, im Auftrage des Bundes für deutsche Kirche, 1927. Rudolf Fischer collection.

Protz, Albert, ed. *So singen Deutsche Christen.* Foreword by Christian Kinder. Berlin: Gesellschaft für Zeitungsdienst, 1934. KAG Minden.

Rönck, Hugo. *Nationalkirchliche Einung Deutsche Christen?* Volksschriften der Nationalkirchlichen Einung Deutsche Christen, no. 2. Weimar: Verlag Deutsche Christen, 1939.

Rosenberg, Alfred. *Deutsche und Europäische Geistesfreiheit*. Munich: Zentralverlag der NSDAP, n.d. Duke Pamphlet Collection, 41125.

Schade, Gerhard. *Deutsche Art hört Christusbotschaft. Eine Handreichung für Laien*. Leipzig and Hamburg: Gustav Schloeßmann, 1935.

Scheuermann, Karl. *Aufruhr wider Gott! Der Deutschglaube und die Wahrheitsfrage*. Göttingen: Vandenhoeck & Ruprecht, 1935. Rudolf Fischer collection.

Schneider, Georg, ed. *Unser Glaube. Wegleite für Deutsche Christen*. Stuttgart: Döninghaus & Co., 1940. KAG Minden.

Schöttler, Hans. *Der deutsche Christ. Martin Luthers kleiner Katechismus in Erklärung und Nutzanwendung für heute*. Halle/Saale: Evangelisch-Sozialer Preßverband für die Provinz Sachsen, n.d.

——, ed. *Gottes Wort Deutsch. Aus Luthers Bibel, nach Luthers Regel, in Luthers Geist*. Wittenberg: Säemann-Verlag, 1934.

Schomerus, W. *Unsere Kirche im Geisteskampf der Gegenwart*. Aurich: Karl Meyer, n.d. Rudolf Fischer collection.

Schroth, Hansgeorg, ed. *Zeugnisse germanischer Religion*. Stoffsammlung für Schulungsarbeit, no. 42. Berlin-Spandau: Apologetischen Centrale, 1935. Rudolf Fischer collection.

Schwadtke, Paul, ed. *Lieder für Gottesfeiern*. Weimar: Verlag Deutsche Christen, 1938. LKA Bielefeld 5,1/293.

Schweinitz, Helmut von, ed. *"Mit Luther für Kirche und Volk." 50 Jahre Evangelischer Bund Sachsen-Anhalt*. [Halle/Saale: Evangelischer Bund, 1938]. EB Bensheim 3.05.20.

Slawinsky, Maz. *Blut und Rasse im Licht der Bibel*. Kassel: J. G. Oncken Nachf., 1936. Rudolf Fischer collection.

*Sonne und Kreuz. Ausgewählte Andachten von Lic. theol. Otto Waitkat, herausgegeben zu seinem zehnjährigen Todestag*. Weimar: Verlag Deutsche Christen, [1940?]. KAG Minden.

*Die Staatskirche ist da!* Foreword by Martin Niemöller. Berlin-Dahlem, 1936. KAG Minden, no. 26.

*Stärker als das Schicksal. Bestattungsfeiern*. Foreword by Hermann Ohland, Deutsche Christen Nationalkirchliche Einung, Fachabteilung Feiergestaltung. Weimar: Kommissions Verlag—Der neue Dom, Schneider & Co., n.d. KAG Minden.

Strathmann, ed. *Nationalsozialistische Weltanschauung? Christentum und Volkstum*, edited by Prof. Strathmann, no. 1. Nuremberg: Volksdienst, 1931. Rudolf Fischer collection.

Stroothenke, Wolfgang. *Erbpflege und Christentum: Fragen der Sterilisation, Aufnordung, Euthanasie, Ehe*. Leipzig: Leopold Klotz, 1940.

*Thüringer Kirchenordung vom 15. Juli 1944*. Introduction by Hugo Rönck. [Weimar]: n.p., [1944]. KAG Minden.

Tillenius, Josias. *Rassenseele und Christentum. Ein Versuch, die Erkenntnisse der Rassenforschung im religiösen Dienst am Volk zu verwerten*. Munich: J. F. Lehmanns, 1929. Rudolf Fischer collection.

Veigel, Fritz. *Deutsche Gebete*. Weimar: Verlag Deutsche Christen, n.d. KAG Minden.

Waitz, Hans. *Nationalkirche: Verschiedene Wege zu einem Ziel*. Special reprint from the monthly *Wartburg*, no. 4/5. Berlin: Evangelischer Bund, 1936. EB Bensheim.

*Vom Werden deutscher Volkskirche. Reden auf der 4. Reichstagung der Nationalkirchlichen Bewegung Deutsche Christen in Eisenach, 9. bis 11. Oktober, 1937*. Foreword by Heinz Dungs. Weimar: [Verlag Deutsche Christen, 1937?]. Rudolf Fischer collection.

Wiedenhöft, Bernhard. *Weib unterm Kreuz. Die Stellung der Frau im Christentum*. Durchbruch Schriftenreihe, no. 4. Stuttgart: Durchbruch Verlag Friedrich Bühler, [1936?].

Wieneke, Friedrich. *Die Glaubensbewegung "Deutsche Christen."* Schriftenreihe der "Deutschen Christen," edited by Joachim Hossenfelder, no. 2. Soldin: H. Madrasch, 1933.

———. *Die Kampf- und Glaubensbewegung "Deutsche Christen" (Hossenfelderbewegung)*. Soldin: H. Madrasch, 1936. EZA Berlin 1/A4/467.

Winkel, Erich. *Jesu ursprüngliche Verkündigung*. Kampen auf Sylt: Niets Kampmann, 1936.

Winter. *Der Gott der Schrift und die Rasse*. Münster: Balve, n.d. Concordia Theological Seminary Library.

*Wir sind tausend und sind eins. Eine Auslese Gedichte von Wilhelm Bauer, Hermann Ohland, Hans Paulin, Hans Robert Schröter*. Weimar: Verlag Deutsche Christen, 1938. KAG Minden.

Wobbermin, Georg. *Deutscher Staat und evangelische Kirche*. Göttingen: Vandenhoeck & Ruprecht, 1934.

Wohlert, Mathilde. *Frauendienst am deutschen Volke. Frau und Kirche*, edited by Hans Hermenau, no. 5. Freiburg/Br.: Bär & Bartosch, 1938. KAG Minden.

## Published Memoirs, Personal Papers, and Recollections

Alberti, Rüdiger. *Als Kriegspfarrer in Polen. Erlebnisse und Begegnungen in Kriegslazaretten*. Dresden: C. Ludwig Ungelenk, 1940.

*Anekdoten um Bischof Dibelius*. Munich: Bechtle, 1967.

Baedeker, Dietrich. *Das Volk, das im Finstern wandelt. Stationen eines Militärpfarrers, 1933–1946.* Hanover: Lutherisches Verlagshaus, 1987.

Beckmann, Joachim, ed. *Die Briefe des Coetus Reformierter Prediger, 1933–1937: Präses lic. Karl Immer zum 60. Geburtstag.* Neukirchen-Vluyn: Neukirchener, 1976.

Beschet, Paul. *Mission en Thuringe au temps du nazisme.* Paris: Editions Ouvrières, 1989.

Bonhoeffer, Dietrich. *Gesammelte Schriften.* 6 vols. Edited by Eberhard Bethge. Munich: Christian Kaiser, 1958.

Braun, Hannelore, and Carsten Nicolaisen, eds. *Verantwortung für die Kirche. Stenographische Aufzeichnungen und Mitschriften von Landesbischof Hans Meiser, 1933–1955.* Vol. 1. *Sommer 1933 bis Sommer 1935.* Arbeiten zur kirchlichen Zeitgeschichte, edited by Georg Kretschmar and Klaus Scholder, series A, vol. 1. Göttingen: Vandenhoeck & Ruprecht, 1985.

Conrad, Walter. *Der Kampf um die Kanzeln. Erinnerungen und Dokumente aus der Hitlerzeit.* Berlin: Alfred Töpelmann, 1957.

Diehl, Guida. *Christ sein heißt Kämpfer sein. Die Führung meines Lebens.* Giessen: Brunnen, [1959].

Fromm, Bella. *Blood and Banquets: A Berlin Social Diary.* New York: Harper & Bros., 1942.

Gülzow, Gerhard. *Kirchenkampf in Danzig, 1934–1945: Persönliche Erinnerungen.* Leer (Ostfriesland): Gerhard Rautenberg, 1968.

Kantzenbach, Friedrich Wilhelm, ed. *Widerstand und Solidarität der Christen in Deutschland, 1933–1945. Eine Dokumentation zum Kirchenkampf aus den Papieren des D. Wilhelm Freiherrn von Pechmann. Einzelarbeiten aus der Kirchengeschichte Bayerns,* vol. 51. Neustadt/Aisch: Degener & Co., 1971.

Kauffels, Susanna, ed. *Die Nationalsozialistische Zeit (1933–1945) in Neuss: Zeitzeugenberichte.* Neuss: Dokumentationen des Stadtarchivs Neuss 2, 1988.

Keding, Karl. *Feldgeistlicher bei Legion Condor. Spanisches Kriegstagebuch eines evangelischen Legionspfarrers.* Berlin: Ostwerk, [1937?].

Kinder, Christian. *Neue Beiträge zur Geschichte der evangelischen Kirche in Schleswig-Holstein und im Reich, 1924–1945.* 2d ed. Flensburg: Karfeld, 1966.

Loewenich, Walther von. *Erlebte Theologie. Begegnungen. Erfahrungen. Erwägungen.* Munich: Claudius, 1979.

Opitz, May, Katharina Oguntoye, and Dagmar Schultz. *Showing Our Colors: Afro-German Women Speak Out.* Translated by Anne V. Adams. Amherst: University of Massachusetts Press, 1992.

Perau, Josef. *Priester im Heere Hitlers. Erinnerungen, 1940–1945*. Essen: Ludgerus Verlag Hubert Wingen KG, 1962.

Schabel, Wilhelm, ed. *Herr, in Deine Hände. Seelsorge im Krieg. Dokumente der Menschlichkeit aus der ganzen Welt*. Bonn: Scherz, 1963.

Schleuning, Johannes. *Mein Leben hat ein Ziel. Lebenserinnerungen eines rußlanddeutschen Pfarrers*. Witten: Luther Verlag, 1964.

Solheim, Magne. *Im Schatten von Hakenkreuz, Hammer und Sichel. Judenmissionar in Rumänien, 1937–1948*. Translated by Cilgia Solheim. Erlangen: Verlag der Evangelisch-Lutherischen Mission, 1986.

Tügel, Franz. *Mein Weg. 1888–1946. Erinnerungen eines Hamburger Bischofs*. Edited by Carsten Nicolaisen. *Arbeiten zur Kirchengeschichte Hamburgs*, edited by Martin Elze, Georg Kretschmar, Helga-Maria Kühn, Bernhard Lohse, and Hans-Otto-Wölber, vol. 11. Hamburg: Friedrich Wittig, 1972.

## Published Documents and Collections

*Die Bekenntnisschriften der evangelisch-lutherischen Kirche*. 3d ed. Göttingen: Vandenhoeck & Ruprecht, [original 1930] 1956.

Boberach, Heinz, ed. *Meldungen aus dem Reich. Die geheimen Lageberichte des Sicherheitsdienstes der SS, 1938–1945*. 17 vols. Herrsching: Pawlak, 1984.

Buchheim, Hans, ed. "Ein NS-Funktionär zum Niemöller-Prozess." *Vierteljahreshefte für Zeitgeschichte*, no. 1 (Jan. 1956): 307–15.

Heidtmann, Günter, ed. *Kirche im Kampf der Zeit. Die Botschaften, Worte und Erklärungen der evangelischen Kirche in Deutschland und ihrer östlichen Gliedkirchen*. 2d ed. Berlin: Lettner, 1954.

Hermelink, Heinrich, ed. *Kirche im Kampf. Dokumente des Widerstands und des Aufbaus in der Evangelischen Kirche Deutschlands von 1933 bis 1945*. Tübingen: Rainer Wunderlich Verlag Hermann Leins, 1950.

Kupisch, Karl, ed. *Quellen zur Geschichte des deutschen Protestantismus (1871–1945)*. Göttingen: Musterschmidt, 1960.

——. *Quellen zur Geschichte des deutschen Protestantismus von 1945 bis zur Gegenwart*. 2 vols. Hamburg: Siebenstern, 1971.

Nicolaisen, Carsten, ed. *Dokumente zur Kirchenpolitik des Dritten Reiches*. 2 vols. Munich: Christian Kaiser, 1971 and 1975.

Noakes, Jeremy, and Geoffrey Pridham, eds. *Nazism: A History in Documents and Eyewitness Accounts, 1919–1945*. 2 vols. New York: Schocken, 1988.

*The Persecution of the Catholic Church in the Third Reich. Facts and Documents*. No editor or translator. New York: Longmans, Green, 1942.

Schäfer, Gerhard. *Die Evangelische Landeskirche in Württemberg und der Nationalsozialismus: Eine Dokumentation zum Kirchenkampf.* 5 vols. Stuttgart: Calwer Verlag, 1982.

Schmidt, Kurt Dietrich, ed. *Bekenntnisse und grundsätzliche Äußerungen zur Kirchenfrage, 1933–1935.* Göttingen: Vandenhoeck & Ruprecht, 1966.

Stasiewski, Bernhard, ed. *Akten Deutscher Bischöfe über die Lage der Kirche, 1933–1945.* Vol. 2: *1934–1935.* Veröffentlichungen der Kommission für Zeitgeschichte bei der katholischen Akademie in Bayern, edited by Konrad Repgen, series A: Sources, vol. 20. Mainz: Matthias Grünewald, 1970.

Volk, Ludwig, ed. *Akten deutscher Bischöfe über die Lage der Kirche, 1933–1945.* Vol. 4: *1936–1939.* Veröffentlichungen der Kommission für Zeitgeschichte, edited by Rudolf Morsey. Mainz: Matthias Grünewald, 1969.

Witetschek, Helmut. *Die kirchliche Lage in Bayern nach den Regierungspräsidentenberichten, 1933–1943.* Vol. 2: *Regierungsbezirk Ober- und Mittelfranken.* Veröffentlichungen der Kommission für Zeitgeschichte, edited by Konrad Repgen, series A: Sources, vol. 8. Mainz: Matthias Grünewald, 1967.

## General Reference Works

Bauks, Friedrich Wilhelm. *Die evangelischen Pfarrer in Westfalen von der Reformationszeit bis 1945. Beiträge zur Westfälischen Kirchengeschichte,* edited by Ernst Brinkmann, Wilhelm Kohl, Gerhard Ruhbach, Hans Steinberg, and Robert Stupperich, vol. 4. Bielefeld: Luther Verlag, 1980.

Ellinger, Walter, ed. *Evangelische Kirche der Union: Ihre Vorgeschichte und Geschichte.* Witten: Luther Verlag, 1967.

Friedmann, Wolfgang. *The Allied Military Government of Germany. Library of World Affairs,* edited by George W. Keeton and Georg Schwarzenberger, no. 8. London: Stevens & Sons, 1947.

Gausewitz, C., ed. *Doctor Martin Luther's Small Catechism.* Milwaukee: Northwestern, 1956.

Julian, John, ed. *A Dictionary of Hymnology.* 2d ed. London: John Murray, 1908.

Kupisch, Karl. *Die Deutschen Landeskirchen im 19. und 20. Jahrhundert.* Göttingen: Vandenhoeck & Ruprecht, 1966.

Rosenkranz, Albert, ed. *Das Evangelische Rheinland: Ein rheinisches Gemeinde- und Pfarrerbuch im Auftrag der Evangelischen Kirche im Rheinland. Die Pfarrer,* vol. 2. Düsseldorf: Presseverband der Evangelischen Kirche im Rheinland, 1958.

Routley, Erik. *A Panorama of Christian Hymnody*. Collegeville, Minn.: Liturgical Press, 1979.

Tappert, Theodore G., trans. and ed. *The Book of Concord: The Confessions of the Evangelical Lutheran Church*. Philadelphia: Fortress, 1959.

Winkworth, Catherine, trans. *Lyra Germanica: Hymns for the Sundays and Chief Festivals of the Christian Year*. London: Longman, Brown, Green, Longmans, and Roberts, 1858.

## Secondary Literature: Books and Articles

Abrams, Alan. *Mischlinge, Special Treatment: The Untold Story of Hitler's Third Race*. Secaucus, N.J.: Lyle Stuart, 1985.

Anderson, Benedict. *Imagined Communities: Reflections on the Origin and Spread of Nationalism*. London: Verso, 1983.

Atkinson, Clarissa W., Constance H. Buchanan, and Margaret R. Miles, eds. *Immaculate and Powerful: The Female in Sacred Image and Social Reality*. Boston: Beacon Press, 1985.

Bacharach, Walter Zwi. *Anti-Jewish Prejudices in German-Catholic Sermons*. Translated by Chaya Galai. Lewiston: Edwin Mellen, 1993.

Baeck, Leo. *Judaism and Christianity: Essays by Leo Baeck*. Translated by Walter Kaufmann. Philadelphia: Jewish Publication Society of America, 1958.

Baier, Helmut. *Die Deutschen Christen Bayerns im Rahmen des bayerischen Kirchenkampfes*. Nuremberg: Verein für bayerische Kirchengeschichte, 1968.

———, ed. *Kirche in Not. Die bayerische Landeskirche im Zweiten Weltkrieg*. Neustadt a.d. Aisch: Verein für bayerische Kirchengeschichte, 1979.

Baier, Helmut, and Ernst Henn. *Chronologie des bayerischen Kirchenkampfes, 1933–1945*. Nuremberg: Selbstverlag für bayerische Kirchengeschichte, 1969.

Baranowski, Shelley. *The Confessing Church, Conservative Elites, and the Nazi State*. Texts and Studies in Religion, vol. 28. New York: Edwin Mellen, 1986.

———. "Consent and Dissent: The Confessing Church and Conservative Opposition to National Socialism." *Journal of Modern History* 59, no. 1 (March 1987): 53–78.

———. "The German Protestant Church Elections: *Machtpolitik* or Accommodation?" *Church History* 49 (1980): 298–315.

Barnes, Kenneth C. *Nazism, Liberalism, and Christianity: Protestant Social Thought in Germany and Great Britain, 1925–1937*. Lexington: University Press of Kentucky, 1991.

Barnett, Victoria. *For the Soul of the People: Protestant Protest against Hitler*. New York: Oxford University Press, 1992.

Barth, Karl. *Die evangelische Kirche in Deutschland nach dem Zusammenbruch des Dritten Reiches*. Stuttgart: n.p., 1946.

——. *The Only Way: How Can the Germans Be Cured?* Translated by Marta K. Neufeld and Ronald Gregor Smith. New York: Philosophical Library, 1947.

*Karl Barth zum Kirchenkampf: Beteiligung—Mahnung—Zuspruch*. *Theologische Existenz Heute*, no. 49. Munich: Christian Kaiser, 1956.

Baum, Gregory, and John Coleman, eds. *The Church and Racism*. New York: Seabury Press, 1982.

Baumgärtel, Friedrich. *Wider die Kirchenkampf-Legenden*. Neudettelsau: Freimund, 1959.

Beckmann, Joachim. *Hoffnung für die Kirche in dieser Zeit. Beiträge zur kirchlichen Zeitgeschichte, 1946–1974*. Göttingen: Vandenhoeck & Ruprecht, 1981.

——. *Rheinische Bekenntnissynoden im Kirchenkampf. Eine Dokumenta-tion aus den Jahren 1933–1945*. Neukirchen-Vluyn: Neukirchener Verlag, 1978.

Berger, Teresa. "Liturgiewissenschaft und Frauenforschung: Getrennte Schwestern?" *Theologische Revue*, no. 5 (1989): 353–62.

Bergmann, Werner, and Rainer Erb, eds. *Antisemitismus in der politischen Kultur nach 1945*. Opladen: Westdeutscher Verlag, 1990.

Besier, Gerhard. *Krieg—Frieden—Abrüstung. Die Haltung der europäischen und amerikanischen Kirchen zur Frage der deutschen Kriegsschuld, 1914–1933*. Göttingen: Vandenhoeck & Ruprecht, 1982.

——. *Die protestantischen Kirchen Europas im Ersten Weltkrieg: Ein Quellen- und Arbeitsbuch*. Göttingen: Vandenhoeck & Ruprecht, 1984.

——. *"Selbstreinigung" unter britischer Besatzungsherrschaft. Die Evangelisch-Lutherische Landeskirche Hannovers und ihr Landesbischof Marahrens, 1945–1947*. Göttingen: Vandenhoeck & Ruprecht, 1986.

Besier, Gerhard, and Gerhard Ringshausen. *Bekenntnis, Widerstand, Martyrium. Von Barmen 1934 bis Plötzensee 1944*. Göttingen: Vandenhoeck & Ruprecht, 1986.

Besier, Gerhard, and Gerhard Sauter. *Wie Christen ihre Schuld bekennen. Die Stuttgarter Erklärung, 1945*. Göttingen: Vandenhoeck & Ruprecht, 1985.

Beste, Niklot. *Der Kirchenkampf in Mecklenburg, 1933–1945*. Göttingen: Vandenhoeck & Ruprecht, 1975.

Bethge, Eberhard. *Dietrich Bonhoeffer. Theologe. Christ. Zeitgenosse*. Munich: Christian Kaiser, 1967.

Bielfeldt, Johann. *Der Kirchenkampf in Schleswig-Holstein, 1933–1945.* Göttingen: Vandenhoeck & Ruprecht, 1964.

Binder, Ludwig. *Die Kirche der Siebenbürger Sachsen.* Erlangen: Martin Luther-Verlag, 1982.

Bock, Gisela. *Zwangssterilisation im Nationalsozialismus: Studien zur Rassenpolitik und Frauenpolitik.* Opladen: Westdeutscher Verlag, 1986.

Bohm, Hans. "Die kirchliche Neuordnung." *Die Kirche* 1/1945 and 2/1945.

Borg, Daniel R. *The Old Prussian Church and the Weimar Republic: A Study in Political Adjustment, 1917–1927.* Hanover, N.H.: University Press of New England, 1984.

Boyens, Armin. "Das Ende des Lutherischen Weltconvents: Die Krise des Weltluthertums während des Zweiten Weltkriegs und ihre Bewältigung." *Zeitschrift für Kirchengeschichte* 88, no. 2/3 (1977): 264–84.

——. *Kirchenkampf und Ökumene, 1933–1939: Darstellung und Dokumentation.* Munich: Christian Kaiser, 1969.

——. "Das Stuttgarter Schuldbekenntnis vom 19.10.1945. Entstehung und Bedeutung." *Vierteljahrshefte für Zeitgeschichte* 19, no. 4 (1971): 374–97.

——. "Treysa 1945—Die Evangelische Kirche nach dem Zusammenbruch des Dritten Reiches." *Zeitschrift für Kirchengeschichte* 82, no. 1 (1971): 29–53.

Boyens, Armin, Martin Greschat, Rudolf von Thadden, and Paolo Pombeni. *Kirchen in der Nachkriegszeit. Vier zeitgeschichtliche Beiträge.* Göttingen: Vandenhoeck & Ruprecht, 1979.

Brakelmann, Günter, ed. *Kirche im Krieg. Der deutsche Protestantismus am Beginn des Zweiten Weltkriegs.* Munich: Christian Kaiser, 1979.

Breitman, Richard. *Architect of Genocide: Heinrich Himmler and the Final Solution.* New York: Knopf, 1991.

Bridenthal, Renate, Atina Grossmann, and Marion Kaplan, eds. *When Biology Became Destiny: Women in Weimar and Nazi Germany.* New York: Monthly Review Press, 1984.

Brooten, Bernadette, and Norbert Greinacher. *Frauen in der Männerkirche. Gesellschaft und Theologie/Abteilung: Praxis der Kirche,* no. 40. Munich: Christian Kaiser; Mainz: Grünewald, 1982.

Brosseder, Johannes. "Kirche für die Menschen. Bemerkungen zum Problem der Akkommodation," *Begegnung: Beiträge zu einer Hermeneutik des theologischen Gesprächs,* edited by Max Seckler, Otto H. Pesch, Johannes Brosseder, and Wolfhart Pannenberg. Graz: Styria, 1972.

Browning, Christopher R. *Ordinary Men: Reserve Police Battalion 101 and the Final Solution in Poland.* New York: Harper Collins, 1992.

Brunotte, Heinz. *Die Evangelische Kirche in Deutschland: Geschichte, Organisation und Gestalt der EKD.* Gütersloh: Gütersloher Verlag, 1964.

——, ed. *Zur Geschichte des Kirchenkampfes*. Vol. 2, *Gesammelte Aufsätze*. Göttingen: Vandenhoeck & Ruprecht, 1971.

Buchheim, Hans. *Glaubenskrise im Dritten Reich: Drei Kapitel Nationalsozialistischer Religionspolitik*. Stuttgart: Deutsche Verlags-Anstalt, 1953.

Bühler, Anne Lore. *Der Kirchenkampf im Evangelischen München: Die Auseinandersetzung mit dem Nationalsozialismus und seinen Folgeerscheinungen im Bereich des Evang.-Luth. Dekanates München, 1923–1950*. Nuremberg: Selbstverlag des Vereins f. bayerische Kirchengeschichte, 1974.

Bühler, Karl-Werner. *Presse und Protestantismus in der Weimarer Republik. Kräfte und Krisen evangelischen Publizistik*. Witten: Luther Verlag, 1970.

Busch, Eberhard. *Juden und Christen im Schatten des Dritten Reiches. Ansätze zu einer Kritik des Antisemitismus in der Zeit der Bekennenden Kirche. Theologische Existenz Heute*, edited by Trutz Rendtorff and Karl Gerhard Steck, no. 205. Munich: Christian Kaiser, 1979.

——. *Karl Barths Lebenslauf. Nach seinen Briefen und autobiographischen Texten*. Munich: Christian Kaiser, 1975.

Bynum, Caroline Walker, Stevan Harrell, and Paula Richman. *Gender and Religion: On the Complexity of Symbols*. Boston: Beacon, 1986.

Cancik, Hubert, ed. *Religions- und Geistesgeschichte der Weimarer Republik*. Düsseldorf: Patmos, 1982.

Cochrane, Arthur C. *The Church's Confession under Hitler*. Philadelphia: Westminster, 1962.

Conway, John S. *The Nazi Persecution of the Churches, 1933–45*. New York: Basic Books, 1968.

——. "Die Rolle der Kirchen bei der 'Umerziehung' in Deutschland." *Das Unrechtsregime*, edited by U. Buttner, vol. 22. Hamburger Beiträge zur Sozial- und Zeitgeschichte. Hamburg: n.p., 1986.

Dahm, Karl-Wilhelm. "German Protestantism and Politics, 1918–39." *Journal of Contemporary History* 3 (Jan. 1968): 29–50.

——. *Pfarrer und Politik: Soziale Position und politische Mentalität des deutschen evangelischen Pfarrerstandes zwischen 1918 und 1933*. Dortmunder Schriften zur Sozialforschung, vol. 29. Cologne: Westdeutscher Verlag, 1965.

Delbanco, Hillard. *Kirchenkampf in Ostfriesland, 1933–1945. Die evangelisch-lutherischen Kirchengemeinden in den Auseinandersetzungen mit den Deutschen Christen und dem Nationalsozialismus*. Aurich: Verlag Ostfriesische Landschaft, 1989.

Delius, Walter. "Die Neuordnung der Evangelischen Kirche der altpreussischen Union." *Jahrbuch für Berlin-Brandenburgische Kirchengeschichte* 46 (1971): 131–46.

Denzler, Georg. *Widerstand oder Anpassung? Katholische Kirche und Drittes Reich*. Munich: Piper, 1984.

Denzler, Georg, and Volker Fabricius. *Die Kirchen im Dritten Reich. Christen und Nazis Hand in Hand?* Vol. 1: *Darstellung*. Frankfurt/Main: Fischer Taschenbuch, 1984.

Dickmann, Friedrich, and Hanno Schmitt. *Kirche und Schule im nationalsozialistischen Marburg*. Marburger Stadtschriften zur Geschichte und Kultur, vol. 18. Marburg: Presseamt der Stadt Marburg, 1985.

Diephouse, David J. *Pastors and Pluralism in Württemberg, 1918–1933*. Princeton: Princeton University Press, 1987.

Dierks, Margarete. *Jakob Wilhelm Hauer, 1881–1962: Leben, Werk, Wirkung*. Heidelberg: Lambert Schneider, 1986.

Dietrich, Donald. "Catholic Resistance in the Third Reich." *Holocaust and Genocide Studies* 3, no. 2 (1988): 171–86.

Elliger, Walter, ed. *Die Evangelische Kirche der Union. Ihre Vorgeschichte und Geschichte*. Witten: Luther Verlag, 1967.

Elling, Hanna. *Frauen im deutschen Widerstand, 1933–45*. Frankfurt/Main: Röderberg Bibliothek des Widerstandes, 1981.

Elshtain, Jean Bethke. *Women and War*. New York: Basic Books, 1987.

Elze, Martin. "Antisemitismus in der Evangelischen Kirche." *Geschichte und Kultur des Judentums*, edited by Karlheinz Müller and Klaus Wittstadt. Würzburg: Kommissionsverlag Ferdinand Schöningh, 1988.

Erbacher, Hermann, ed. *Beiträge zur kirchlichen Zeitgeschichte der Evangelischen Landeskirche in Baden. Preisarbeiten anläßlich des Barmenjubiläums 1984*. Karlsruhe: Verlag Evangelischer Presseverband für Baden, 1989.

Ericksen, Robert P. *Theologians under Hitler: Gerhard Kittel, Paul Althaus and Emanuel Hirsch*. New Haven: Yale University Press, 1985.

Feige, Franz G. M. *The Varieties of Protestantism in Nazi Germany: Five Theopolitical Positions*. Toronto Studies in Theology, vol. 50. Lewiston: Edwin Mellen, 1990.

Field, Geoffrey G. *Evangelist of Race: The Germanic Vision of Houston Stewart Chamberlain*. New York: Columbia University Press, 1981.

Fischel, Jack, and Sanford Pinsker, eds. *The Churches' Response to the Holocaust. Holocaust Studies Annual*, vol. 2. Greenwood, Fla.: Penkevill, 1986.

Fleischer, Manfred. "Lutheran and Catholic Reunionists in the Age of Bismarck." *Church History* 38 (1969): 43–66.

Fleischmann-Bisten, Walter, and Heiner Grote. *Protestanten auf dem Wege. Geschichte des Evangelischen Bundes.* Göttingen: Vandenhoeck & Ruprecht, 1986.

Frei, Norbert, and Hermann Kling, eds. *Der nationalsozialistische Krieg.* Frankfurt: Campus Verlag, 1990.

Friedländer, Saul. *Kurt Gerstein: The Ambiguity of Good.* New York: Knopf, 1969.

——. *Reflections on Nazism: An Essay on Kitsch and Death.* New York: Harper & Row, 1984.

Friedlander, Henry. "Step by Step: The Expansion of Murder, 1939–1941." *German Studies Review* 17, no. 3 (Oct. 1994): 495–507.

Fussell, Paul. "The Fate of Chivalry and the Assault upon Mother." In Paul Fussell, *Thank God for the Atom Bomb and Other Essays.* New York: Summit, 1988.

——. *Wartime: Understanding and Behavior in the Second World War.* New York: Viking, 1976.

Gerlach, Wolfgang. *Als die Zeugen Schwiegen. Bekennende Kirche und die Juden.* Berlin: Institut Kirche und Judentum, 1987.

Ginzel, Günther B., ed. *Auschwitz als Herausforderung für Juden und Christen.* Heidelberg: Lambert Schneider, 1980.

Gordis, Robert. "Politics and the Ethics of Judaism." *Judaism* 39, no. 1 (Winter 1990): 47–54.

Gordon, Sarah. *Hitler, Germans and the "Jewish Question."* Princeton: Princeton University Press, 1984.

Gotto, Klaus, and Konrad Repgen, eds. *Kirche, Katholiken und Nationalsozialismus.* Mainz: Matthias Grünewald, 1980.

Greschat, Martin, ed. *Die Schuld der Kirche. Dokumente und Reflexionen zur Stuttgarter Schulderklärung vom 18./19. Oktober 1945.* Munich: Christian Kaiser, 1982.

——. *Zwischen Widerspruch und Widerstand. Texte zur Denkschrift der Bekennenden Kirche an Hitler (1936).* Munich: Christian Kaiser, 1987.

Gurtler, P. *Nationalsozialismus und Evangelische Kirche im Warthegau.* Göttingen: Vandenhoeck & Ruprecht, 1958.

Gutteridge, Richard. *Open Thy Mouth for the Dumb! The German Evangelical Church and the Jews, 1879–1950.* Oxford: Basil Blackwell, 1976.

Haas, Peter J. *Morality after Auschwitz: The Radical Challenge of the Nazi Ethic.* Philadelphia: Fortress, 1988.

Hahn, Fred. *Lieber Stürmer. Leserbriefe an das NS-Kampfblatt 1924 bis 1945.* Stuttgart: Seewald, 1978.

Harder, Günther, and Wilhelm Niemöller. *Die Stunde der Versuchung. Gemeinden im Kirchenkampf, 1933–1945. Selbstzeugnisse.* Munich: Christian Kaiser, 1963.

Heinonen, Reijo E. *Anpassung und Identität. Theologie und Kirchenpolitik der Bremer Deutschen Christen, 1933–45.* Göttingen: Vandenhoeck & Ruprecht, 1978.

Helmreich, Ernst Christian. *The German Churches under Hitler: Background, Struggle, and Epilogue.* Detroit: Wayne State University Press, 1979.

Herbert, Karl. *Der Kirchenkampf—Historie oder bleibendes Erbe?* Frankfurt/Main: Evangelisches Verlagswerk, 1985.

Hering, Rainer. *Theologie im Spannungsfeld von Kirche und Staat.* Berlin: Dietrich Reimer, 1992.

——. *Theologische Wissenschaft und "Drittes Reich."* Pfaffenweiler: Centaurus, 1990.

Herlyn, O. *"Singen unter den Zweigen." Erwägungen zu einem theologisch verantworteten Umgang mit neuen und alten geistlichen Liedern.* Zurich: Theologischer Verlag, 1986.

Herman, Stewart W. *The Rebirth of the German Church.* New York: Harper & Brothers, 1946.

Hermand, Jost. *Der alte Traum vom neuen Reich: Völkische Utopien und Nationalsozialismus.* Frankfurt/Main: Athenäum, 1988.

Heschel, Susannah. "Nazifying Christian Theology: Walter Grundmann and the Institute for the Study and Eradication of Jewish Influence in German Church Life." *Church History* 63, no. 4 (Dec. 1994): 587–605.

Hetzer, Gerhard. *Kulturkampf in Augsburg, 1933–1945.* Augsburg: Hieronymus Mühlberger, 1982.

Hey, Bernd. "Die kirchenpolitische Arbeitsgemeinschaft: Ein Solidarisierungsversuch ehemaliger Deutscher Christen." *Jahrbuch für westfälische Kirchengeschichte* 80 (1987): 229–39.

——. *Die kirchenprovinz Westfalen, 1933–1945. Beiträge zur Westfälischen Kirchengeschichte,* edited by Gerhard Ruhbach, Hans Steinberg, and Robert Stupperich, vol. 2. Bielefeld: Luther Verlag, 1974.

Hilberg, Raul. *The Destruction of the European Jews.* 3 vols. Rev. ed. New York: Holmes and Meier, 1985.

——. *Perpetrators, Victims, Bystanders: The Jewish Catastrophe, 1933–1945.* New York: Harper Collins, 1992.

Jacke, Jochen. *Kirche zwischen Monarchie und Republik. Der preußische*

*Protestantismus nach dem Zusammenbruch von 1918*. Hamburg: Hans Christians, 1976.

Kaiser, Jochen-Christoph. *Frauen in der Kirche. Evangelische Frauenverbände im Spannungsfeld von Kirche und Gesellschaft 1890– 1945: Quellen und Materialien*. Düsseldorf: Schwann, 1985.

Katscher, Liselotte. *Krankenpflege und "Drittes Reich," 1933–1939. Der Weg der Schwesternschaft des Evangelischen Diakonie-Vereins*. Stuttgart: Verlagswerk der Diakonie, 1990.

Keegan, John. *The Face of Battle*. New York: Viking, 1976.

Kent, John. *The Unacceptable Face: The Modern Church in the Eyes of the Historian*. London: SCM, 1987.

King, Christine Elizabeth. *The Nazi State and the New Religions: Five Case Studies in Non-Conformity*. Toronto: Edwin Mellen, 1982.

Klee, Ernst. *"Euthanasie" im NS-Staat. Die "Vernichtung lebensunwerten Lebens."* Frankfurt/Main: Fischer, 1983.

——. *"Die SA Jesu Christi": Die Kirche im Banne Hitlers*. Frankfurt/Main: Fischer, 1989.

Klügel, Eberhard. *Die lutherische Landeskirche Hannovers und ihr Bischof*. 2 vols. Berlin: Lutherisches Verlagshaus, 1964–65.

Klüppel, Manfred. *"Euthanasie" und Lebensvernichtung am Beispiel der Landesheilanstalten Haina und Merxhausen*. Kassel: Gesamthochschule Kassel, 1985.

Klumpp, Martin, ed. *Wer ist unser Herr? Evangelische Christen und das Dritte Reich. Erfahrungen aus Stuttgart*. Stuttgart: Quell Verlag, 1982.

Koonz, Claudia. *Mothers in the Fatherland: Women, the Family, and Nazi Politics*. New York: St. Martin's, 1987.

Kremmel, Paul. *Pfarrer und Gemeinden im evangelischen Kirchenkampf in Bayern bis 1939, mit besonderer Berücksichtigung der Ereignisse im Bereich des Bezirksamts Weißenburg in Bayern*. Lichtenfels: Kommissionsverlag H. O. Schulze, 1987.

Krzesinski, Andrew John. *Religion of Nazi Germany*. Boston: B. Humphries, 1945.

Kuessner, Dietrich, "Die Braunschweigische evangelisch-lutherische Landeskirche und der Nationalsozialismus." In *Braunschweig unterm Hakenkreuz*, edited by Helmut Kramer. Braunschweig: Magni, 1981.

Kulka, Otto Dov, and Paul R. Mendes-Flohr, eds. *Judaism and Christianity under the Impact of National Socialism*. Jerusalem: Historical Society of Israel and Zalman Shazar Center for Jewish History, 1987.

Kunst, Hermann, ed. *Gott läßt sich nicht spotten. Franz Dohrmann, Feldbischof unter Hitler*. Hanover: Lutherisches Verlagshaus, 1983.

Lächele, Rainer. *Ein Volk, ein Reich, ein Glaube: Die "Deutschen Christen" in Württemberg, 1925–1960*. Stuttgart: Calwer Verlag, 1994.

Läpple, Alfred. *Kirche und Nationalsozialismus in Deutschland und Österreich*. Schaffenburg: Paul Pattloch, 1980.

Latzel, Klaus. *Vom Sterben im Krieg. Wandlungen in der Einstellung zum Soldatentod vom Siebenjährigen Krieg bis zum II. Weltkrieg*. Warendorf: Fahlbusch & Co., 1988.

Lewy, Guenter. *The Catholic Church and Nazi Germany*. New York: McGraw-Hill, 1964.

Libowitz, Richard, ed. *Faith and Freedom: A Tribute to Franklin H. Littell*. New York: Pergamon, 1987.

Littell, Franklin H. *The Crucifixion of the Jews*. New York: Harper & Row, 1975.

Littell, Franklin H., and Hubert G. Locke, eds. *The German Church Struggle and the Holocaust*. Detroit: Wayne State University Press, 1974.

Littell, Marcia, Richard Libowitz, and Evelyn Bodek Rosen, eds. *The Holocaust Forty Years After*. Symposium Studies, vol. 22. Lewiston: Edwin Mellen, 1989.

Lumans, Valdis O. *Himmler's Auxiliaries: The Volksdeutsche Mittelstelle and the German National Minorities of Europe, 1933–1945*. Chapel Hill: University of North Carolina Press, 1993.

McClaskey, Beryl R. *The History of U.S. Policy and Program in the Field of Religious Affairs under the Office of the U.S. High Commissioner for Germany*. N.p.: Historical Division, Office of the Executive Secretary, Office of the U.S. High Commissioner for Germany, 1951.

Marks, Sally. "Black Watch on the Rhine: A Study in Propaganda, Prejudice and Prurience." *European Studies Review* 13, no. 3 (1983): 297–334.

Maron, Gottfried, ed. *Evangelisch und Ökumenisch—Beiträge zum 100-jährigen Bestehen des Evangelischen Bundes*. Göttingen: Vandenhoeck & Ruprecht, 1986.

May, George. *Interkonfessionalismus in der Deutschen Militärseelsorge von 1933 bis 1945*. Amsterdam: B. R. Grüner, 1978.

Meier, Kurt. *Die Deutschen Christen: Das Bild einer Bewegung im Kirchenkampf des Dritten Reiches*. Göttingen: Vandenhoeck & Ruprecht, 1964.

——. *Der Evangelische Kirchenkampf*. 3 vols. Göttingen: Vandenhoeck & Ruprecht, 1976–84.

——. *Kirche und Judentum: Die Haltung der evangelischen Kirche zur Judenpolitik des Dritten Reiches*. Halle/Saale: VEB Max Niemeyer, 1968.

——. "Die Sportpalastkundgebung der 'Deutschen Christen' am 13. Nov. 1933:

Entgleisung oder Krise?" *Wissenschaftliche Zeitschrift der Karl-Marx Universität Leipzig*, Gesellschafts- und Sprachwissenschaftliche Reihe, no. 4 (1962): 771–78.

——. *Volkskirche, 1918–1945. Ekklesiologie und Zeitgeschichte. Theologische Existenz heute*, edited by Trutz Rendtorff and Karl Gerhard Steck, no. 213. Munich: Christian Kaiser, 1982.

Messerschmidt, Manfred. "Aspekte der Militärseelsorgepolitik in nationalsozialistischer Zeit." *Militärgeschichtliche Mitteilungen* 1 (1968): 63–105.

——. "Zur Militärseelsorgepolitik im zweiten Weltkrieg." *Militärgeschichtliche Mitteilungen* 1 (1969): 37–85.

Minkner, Detlef. *Christuskreuz und Hakenkreuz. Kirche in Wedding, 1933–1945. Studien zu jüdischem Volk und christlicher Gemeinde*, edited by Peter von der Osten-Sacken, vol. 9. Berlin: Institut Kirche und Judentum, 1986.

Missalla, Heinrich. *Für Volk und Vaterland. Die kirchliche Kriegshilfe im zweiten Weltkrieg*. Königstein: Athenäum, 1978.

Mohler, Armin. *Die konservative Revolution in Deutschland, 1918–1932: Ein Handbuch*. 3d ed. Darmstadt: Wissenschaftliche Buchgesellschaft, 1989.

Mybes, Fritz. *Der Evangelisch-kirchliche Hilfsverein und seine Frauenhilfe. Schriftenreihe des Vereins für Rheinische Kirchengeschichte*, edited by H. Faulenbach, D. Meyer, and R. Mohr, no. 92. Cologne: Rheinland Verlag, 1988.

Neuhäusler, Johann. *Kreuz und Hakenkreuz: Der Kampf des Nationalsozialismus gegen die katholische Kirche und der kirchliche Widerstand*. Munich: Katholische Kirche Bayerns, 1946.

Nicholls, David. *Deity and Domination: Images of God and the State in the Nineteenth and Twentieth Centuries*. London: Routledge, 1989.

Niemöller, Wilhelm. *Chronik des Kirchenkampfes in der Kirchenprovinz Westfalen*. Bielefeld: Ludwig Bechauf, 1962.

——. *Kampf und Zeugnis der Bekennenden Kirche*. Bielefeld: Ludwig Bechauf, 1948.

——. *Der Pfarrernotbund*. Hamburg: Friedrich Wittig, 1973.

——. *Wort und Tat im Kirchenkampf: Beiträge zur neuesten Kirchengeschichte*. Munich: Christian Kaiser, 1969.

Niesel, Wilhelm. *Kirche unter dem Wort. Der Kampf der Bekennenden Kirche der altpreussischen Union, 1933–1945*. Göttingen: Vandenhoeck & Ruprecht, 1978.

Norden, Günther van. *Der deutsche Protestantismus im Jahr der nationalsozialistischen Machtergreifung*. Gütersloh: Gütersloher Verlagshaus Gerd Mohn, 1979.

——, ed. *Kirchenkampf im Rheinland. Die Entstehung der Bekennenden Kirche und die Theologische Erklärung von Barmen, 1934.* Cologne: Rheinland Verlag, 1984.

Norden, Günther van, and Fritz Mybes. *Evangelische Frauen im Dritten Reich.* Düsseldorf: Presseverband der Evangelischen Kirche im Rheinland, 1979.

Nowak, Kurt. *"Euthanasie" und Sterilisierung im "Dritten Reich." Die Konfrontation der evangelischen und katholischen Kirchen mit dem "Gesetz zur Verhütung erbkranken Nachwuchses" und der "Euthanasie"-Aktion.* Göttingen: Vandenhoeck & Ruprecht, 1978.

Oberman, Heiko A. *The Roots of Anti-Semitism in the Age of Renaissance and Reformation.* Translated by James I. Porter. Philadelphia: Fortress, 1984.

Owings, Alison. *Frauen: German Women Recall the Third Reich.* New Brunswick: Rutgers University Press, 1993.

Phayer, Michael. *Protestant and Catholic Women in Nazi Germany.* Detroit: Wayne State University Press, 1990.

Philipps, Werner. *Wilhelm Zoellner—Mann der Kirche im Kaiserreich, Republik und Dritten Reich. Beiträge zur Westfälischen Kirchengeschichte,* edited by Ernst Brinkmann, Wilhelm Kohl, Gerhard Ruhbach, Hans Steinberg, and Robert Stupperich, vol. 6. Bielefeld: Luther Verlag, 1985.

Pois, Robert A. *National Socialism and the Religion of Nature.* New York: St. Martin's, 1986.

Prantl, Helmut, ed. *Die kirchliche Lage in Bayern nach den Regierungspräsidentenberichten, 1933–1943.* Vol. 5: *Regierungsbezirk Pfalz, 1933–1940. Veröffentlichungen der Kommission für Zeitgeschichte,* edited by Rudolf Morsey, series A: Sources, vol. 24. Mainz: Matthias Grünewald, 1978.

Prolingheuer, Hans. *Wir sind in die Irre gegangen. Die Schuld der Kirche unterm Hakenkreuz.* Cologne: Pahl-Rugenstein, 1987.

Rebentisch, Dieter. *Führerstaat und Verwaltung im Zweiten Weltkrieg. Verfassungsentwicklung und Verwaltungspolitik, 1939–1945.* Stuttgart: Franz Steiner, 1989.

Reimer, A. James. *The Emanuel Hirsch and Paul Tillich Debate: A Study in the Political Ramifications of Theology.* Lewiston: Edwin Mellen, 1989.

Reimers, Karl Friedrich. *Lübeck im Kirchenkampf des Dritten Reichs. Nationalsozialistisches Führerprinzip und evangelisch-lutherische Landeskirche von 1933 bis 1945.* Göttingen: Vandenhoeck & Ruprecht, 1965.

Rendtorff, Trutz. "Schuld und Verantwortung 1938/1988. Gedanken zum christlichen Umgang mit der Vergangenheit." *Zeitschrift für Theologie und Kirche*, no. 1 (Feb. 1989): 109–24.

Rhodes, James M. *The Hitler Movement: A Modern Millenarian Revolution.* Stanford: Stanford University Press, 1980.

Rieger, Paul, and Johannes Strauss. *Kirche und Nationalsozialismus. Zur Geschichte des Kirchenkampfes.* Munich: Claudius, 1969.

Rubenstein, Betty Rogers, and Michael Berenbaum, eds. *Reflections on the Thought of Richard L. Rubenstein: Triage, the Holocaust and Faith.* West Simsbury, Conn.: Hedgehog, 1993.

Rubenstein, Richard L. *After Auschwitz: History, Theology, and Contemporary Judaism.* 2d ed. Baltimore: Johns Hopkins University Press, 1992.

——. *The Cunning of History: Mass Death and the American Future.* New York: Harper & Row, 1975.

Ruhm von Oppen, Beate. "Nazis and Christians." *World Politics* 21, no. 3 (Apr. 1969): 392–424.

Rupp, Leila J. *Mobilizing Women for War: German and American Propaganda, 1939–1945.* Princeton: Princeton University Press, 1978.

Scheerer, Reinhard. *Evangelische Kirche und Politik 1945 bis 1949.* Cologne: Pahl-Rugenstein, 1981.

Scherffig, Wolfgang. *Junge Theologen im "Dritten Reich." Dokumente, Briefe, Erfahrungen.* Vol. 1: *Es begann mit einem Nein!* Neukirchen-Vluyn: Neukirchener Verlag, 1989.

Schleuning, Johannes, Eugen Bachmann, and Peter Schellenberg. *Und Siehe, Wir Leben! Der Weg der evangelisch-lutherischen Kirche in vier Jahrhunderten.* Erlangen: Martin Luther-Verlag, 1982.

Schmidt, Maruta, and Gabi Dietz, eds. *Frauen unterm Hakenkreuz.* Berlin: Elefanten Press, 1983.

Schmuhl, Hans-Walter. *Rassenhygiene, Nationalsozialismus, Euthanasie: Von der Verhütung zur Vernichtung "lebensunwerten Lebens," 1890–1945.* Göttingen: Vandenhoeck & Ruprecht, 1987.

Schneider, Thomas Martin. *Reichsbischof Ludwig Müller: Eine Untersuchung zu Leben, Werk und Persönlichkeit.* Göttingen: Vandenhoeck & Ruprecht, 1993.

Scholder, Klaus. *The Churches and the Third Reich.* Vol. 1: *Preliminary History and the Time of Illusions, 1918–1934.* Vol. 2: *The Year of Disillusionment: 1934. Barmen and Rome.* Translated by John Bowden. Philadelphia: Fortress, 1987–88.

——. "Die evangelische Kirche in der Sicht der nationalsozialistischen Führung." *Vierteljahrshefte für Zeitgeschichte* 16, no. 1 (Jan. 1968): 15–35.

Schübel, Albrecht. *300 Jahre Evangelischer Soldatenseelsorge.* Munich: Evangelischer Presseverband für Bayern, 1964.

Schwalbach, Bruno. *Erzbischof Conrad Gröber und die nationalsozialistische Diktatur.* Karlsruhe: Badenia, 1985.

Sereny, Gitta. *Into That Darkness: An Examination of Conscience.* New York: Vintage, 1974.

Siegele-Wenschkewitz, Leonore. "Geschichtsverständnis angesichts des Nationalsozialismus: Der Tübinger Kirchenhistoriker Hanns Rückert in der Auseinandersetzung mit Karl Barth." *Theologische Fakultäten im Nationalsozialismus,* ed. Siegele-Wenschkewitz and Carsten Nicolaisen (Göttingen: Vandenhoeck & Ruprecht, 1993), 18:113–44.

——. *Nationalsozialismus und Kirche: Religionspolitik von Partei und Staat bis 1935.* Düsseldorf: Droste, 1974.

——. *Neutestamentliche Wissenschaft vor der Judenfrage. Gerhard Kittels theologische Arbeit im Wandel deutscher Geschichte.* Munich: Christian Kaiser, 1980.

Siegele-Wenschkewitz, Leonore, and Gerda Stuchlik, eds. *Frauen und Faschismus in Europa.* Pfaffenweiler: Centaurus, 1990.

Sonne, Hans-Joachim. *Die politische Theologie der Deutschen Christen.* Göttingen: Vandenhoeck & Ruprecht, 1982.

Sontheimer, Kurt. *Antidemokratisches Denken in der Weimarer Republik: Die politischen Ideen des deutschen Nationalismus zwischen 1918 und 1933.* Munich: Deutsches Taschenbuch Verlag, 1978.

Spotts, Frederic. *The Churches and Politics in Germany.* Middletown, Conn.: Wesleyan University Press, 1973.

Stange, Jörg. *Zur Legitimation der Gewalt innerhalb der nationalsozialisti- schen Ideologie. Ein Beitrag zur Erklärung der Verfolgung und Vernicht- ung der Anderen im Nationalsozialismus.* Frankfurt/Main: R. G. Fischer Verlag, 1987.

Stegemann, Wolfgang, ed. *Kirche und Nationalsozialismus.* Stuttgart: W. Kohlhammer, 1992.

Stegmann, Erich. *Der Kirchenkampf in der Thüringer Evangelischen Kirche, 1933–1945.* Berlin: Evangelischer Verlagsanstalt, 1984.

Steinert, Marlis G. *Hitler's War and the Germans: Public Mood and Attitude during the Second World War.* Edited and translated by Thomas E. J. DeWitt. Athens, Ohio: Ohio University Press, 1977.

Stephenson, Jill. *The Nazi Organisation of Women.* London: Croom Helm, 1981.

Stöver, Rolf. *Protestantische Kultur zwischen Kaiserreich und Stalingrad: Porträt der Zeitschrift "Eckart," 1906–1943.* Munich: Christian Kaiser, 1982.

Stoevesandt, Karl. *Bekennende Gemeinden und deutschgläubige Bischofsdiktatur in Bremen, 1933–1945. Arbeiten zur Geschichte des Kirchenkampfes*, vol. 10. Göttingen: Vandenhoeck & Ruprecht, 1961.

Strohm, Theodor, and Jörg Thierfelder. *Diakonie im "Dritten Reich."* Heidelberg: Heidelberger Verlagsanstalt, 1990.

Tal, Uriel. *Christians and Jews in Germany: Religion, Politics, and Ideology in the Second Reich, 1870–1914*. Translated by Noah Jonathan Jacobs. Ithaca: Cornell University Press, 1975.

——. "On Modern Lutheranism and the Jews." *Leo Baeck Yearbook* 30 (1985): 203–14.

Thalmann, Rita. *Etre femme sous le III<sup>e</sup> Reich*. Paris: Editions Robert Laffont, 1982.

——. *Protestantisme et nationalisme en Allemagne de 1900 à 1945: D'aprés les itineraires spirituels de Gustav Frennsen (1863–1945), Walter Flex (1887–1917), Jochen Klepper (1903–1942), Dietrich Bonhoeffer (1906–1945)*. Paris: Klincksieck, 1976.

Theweleit, Klaus. *Male Fantasies*. 2 vols. Translated by Erica Carter and Chris Turner. Minneapolis: University of Minnesota Press, 1987.

Thomas, Charles S. *The German Navy in the Nazi Era*. Annapolis: Naval Institute Press, 1990.

Thornton, Larry. "The New Light: German Christians and Biblical Distortion during the Third Reich." *Fides et Historia* 18, no. 2 (1986): 32–43.

Tiefel, Hans. "The German Lutheran Church and the Rise of National Socialism." *Church History* 41 (Sept. 1972): 326–36.

Van Ingen, Ferdinand, and Gerd Labroisse, eds. *Luther-Bilder im 20. Jahrhundert*. Symposium an der Freien Universität Amsterdam. Amsterdam: Rodopi, 1984.

Vollnhalls, Clemens, ed. *Entnazifizierung und Selbstreinigung im Urteil der evangelischen Kirche. Dokumente und Reflexionen, 1945–1949*. Munich: Kaiser, 1989.

——. *Evangelische Kirche und Entnazifizierung, 1945–1949. Die Last der nationalsozialistischen Vergangenheit. Studien zur Zeitgeschichte*, vol. 36. Munich: R. Oldenbourg, 1989.

——, ed. *Die evangelische Kirche nach dem Zusammenbruch. Berichte ausländischer Beobachter aus dem Jahre 1945*. Göttingen: Vandenhoeck & Ruprecht, 1988.

Wilhelmi, Heinrich. *Die Hamburger Kirche in der nationalsozialistischen Zeit, 1933–45*. Göttingen: Vandenhoeck & Ruprecht, 1968.

Wirsching, Johannes. *Kirche und Pseudokirche. Konturen der Häresie*. Göttingen: Vandenhoeck & Ruprecht, 1990.

Wolf, Erik. *Ich bin der Weg, die Wahrheit und das Leben; Niemand kommt zum Vater denn durch mich. Der Kampf der Bekennenden Kirche wider das Neuheidentum.* Tübingen: Furche, 1947.

Wood, Diana, ed. *Christianity and Judaism: Papers Read at the 1991 Summer and the 1992 Winter Meeting of the Ecclesiastical History Society.* Oxford: Blackwell, 1992.

Wright, Jonathan R. C. *"Above Parties": The Political Attitudes of the German Protestant Church Leadership, 1918–1933.* London: Oxford University Press, 1974.

Zabel, James A. *Nazism and the Pastors: A Study of the Ideas of Three Deutsche Christen Groups.* American Academy of Religion dissertation series, edited by H. Ganse Little, no. 14. Missoula: Scholars Press for the American Academy of Religion, 1976.

Zahn, Gordon C. *German Catholics and Hitler's Wars: A Study in Social Control.* New York: Sheed and Ward, 1962.

Zipfel, Friedrich. *Kirchenkampf in Deutschland, 1933–1945.* Berlin: Walter de Gruyter & Co., 1965.

## Secondary Literature:
## Dissertations and Unpublished Manuscripts

Bleese, Jörn. "Die Militärseelsorge und die Trennung von Staat und Kirche." Ph.D. diss., Hamburg University, 1969.

Carter, Guy Christopher. "Confession at Bethel, August 1933—Enduring Witness: The Formation, Revision, and Significance of the First Full Theological Confession of the Evangelical Church Struggle in Nazi Germany." Ph.D. diss., Marquette University, 1987.

Dwyer, James Albert. "The Methodist Episcopal Church in Germany, 1933–1945: Development of Semi-Autonomy and Maintenance of International Ties in the Face of National Socialism and the German Church Struggle." Ph.D. diss., Northwestern University, 1978.

Eichenberg, Karl. "Sie waren anders als ihr Ruf. Die Deutschen Christen." Unpublished manuscript. [1970s]. KAG Minden, no. 6410.

Fleischmann-Bisten, Walter. "Der Evangelische Bund in der Weimarer Republik und im sogenannten Dritten Reich." Ph.D. diss., Kiel University, 1985.

Gailus, Manfred. "Protestantismus und Nationalsozialismus in der Spätphase der Weimarer Republik und im Nationalsozialismus (1930–1945)." Working paper presented at the Technical University of Berlin, 1989.

Gallin, Mother Mary Alice. "Ethical and Religious Factors in the German Resistance to Hitler." Ph.D. diss., Catholic University of America, 1955.

Götte, Karl-Heinz. "Die Propaganda der Glaubensbewegung 'Deutsche Christen' und ihre Beurteilung in der deutschen Tagespresse: Ein Beitrag zur Publizistik im Dritten Reich." Ph.D. diss., Westfälischen Wilhelms-Universität, Münster, 1957.

Gordon, Frank Joseph. "The Evangelical Churches and the Weimar Republic, 1931–1933." Ph.D. diss., University of Colorado at Boulder, 1977.

Laiser, Naaman. "The Communion of God and Man in the Holy Spirit: A Study of the Concept of the Holy Spirit in Contemporary Lutheran Theological Thinking." Ph.D. diss., Hamburg University, 1981.

Mellen, Peter J. "The Third Reich Examined as the Dramatic Illusion of Ritual Performance." Ph.D. diss., Bowling Green State University, 1988.

Miller, Eugene W., Jr. "National Socialism and the Glaubensbewegung 'Deutsche Christen,' 1932–1933: Analysis of a Political Relationship." Ph.D. diss., Pennsylvania State University, 1972.

Murphy, Frederick Ira. "The American Christian Press and Pre-War Hitler's Germany, 1933–1939." Ph.D. diss., University of Florida, 1970.

Nicolaisen, Carsten. "Die Auseinandersetzung um das Alte Testament im Kirchenkampf, 1933–1945." Ph.D. diss., Hamburg University, 1966.

Wall, Donald Dale. "National Socialist Policy and Attitudes toward the Churches in Germany, 1939–1945." Ph.D. diss., University of Colorado, 1969.

Wieneke, Friedrich. "Zehn Jahre Deutsche Christen." Unpublished manuscript. Berlin, 1942. KAG Minden, file V Fiebig.

# Index

Bormann, Martin: opposition to Christianity, 1, 60, 182; relations with German Christians, 137, 152, 153, 188; *See also* National Socialist German Workers' Party

Bornkamm, Heinrich, 174

*Die Botschaft Gottes*, 162, 280 (n. 101)

Brauchitsch, Walther von, 246 (n. 53)

Bremen: German Christian activity in, 98–99, 164. *See also* Weidemann, Heinz

Brökelschen, Otto, 37

Brombacher, Kuno, 262 (n. 35)

Browning, Christopher, 10

Brunotte, Heinz, 95

Buschtöns, Friedrich, 255 (n. 40); joins German Christians, 13; postwar resentments, 210, 211, 215, 216, 221, 296 (n. 43)

Calvinists. *See* Reformed churches

Cathari, 143, 273 (n. 2)

Catholic National Church Movement, 107, 108. *See also* Old Catholics

Catholics: in German Christian movement, 32, 101, 109–10, 135, 187; number in Germany, 101–2, 259 (n. 2); Protestant hostility toward, 114–16

Chamberlain, Houston Stewart, 155, 156, 157, 277 (n. 49)

Chaplains. *See* Military chaplaincy

Christian-German movement (Christlich-deutsche Bewegung), 34

*Christliche Welt*, 144

Christmas, 117, 118, 170; German Christian song, 50; revised account, 163

Church elections. *See* Protestant church elections

Church Foreign Office. *See* Protestant Foreign Office

Church membership, 183

Church music, 143; dejudaization of, 8, 164–71; manliness in, 79–81; motherhood in, 120–21; in church struggle, 140. *See also* Church musicians; Hymns

Church musicians: non-Aryan, 98–100, 259 (n. 89)

Church regulations: German Christian violation of, 183–91

Church struggle, 234 (n. 29); origins of, 8, 12; women's role in, 130, 141

Church taxes: German Christian protest, 55; non-Aryans and, 97; supraconfessionalism and, 110

Church-Theological Society (Kirchlich-theologische Sozietät), 211. *See also* Diem, Hermann

Church weddings, 184, 185; mass weddings, 132

Clarenbach, Adolf, 185, 186, 187, 189, 214

Clay, Lucius: on denazification of churches, 293 (n. 4)

Coch, Friedrich, 70

Communion, 159, 189, 195; Catholic teachings of, 115

Concentration camps, 217; pastors in, 33, 181, 189, 217; knowledge of denied by German Christians, 221. *See also* Dachau; Sachsenhausen

Confessing Church, 217, 241 (n. 73); relations with German Christians, 12, 36, 61–62, 107, 111, 138, 139, 140, 178, 188, 190, 215, 218; name, 13; missions and, 31; Jews, antisemitism, and, 35, 69, 95, 113; non-Aryan clergy in, 93; Catholics and anti-Catholicism, 112, 113, 139; women in, 129–30, 138; in theological faculties, 177

Confession of faith, 189. *See also* Apostles' Creed

Confirmation: German Christian version, 147, 148, 159, 222

Conway, John S., 12

Copenhagen: German Christians in, 53

Dachau (concentration camp), 180

Dannenmann, Arnold, 232 (n. 6)

Daum, Adolf, 251 (n. 64)

Dehls, Sophie, 268 (n. 17)

Denazification: of clergy, 208, 218, 222; German Christian resentment of, 221

Detel, Heinrich, 253 (n. 12)

Deutsche Christen. *See* German Christian movement

Deutsche Glaubensbewegung. *See* German Faith Movement

*Das deutsche Leid*, 30. *See also* Meyer-Erlach, Wolf

Dibelius, Otto, 55, 57, 233 (n. 12)

Diehl, Guida: endorses German Christians, 27; and Nazism, 119; and motherhood, 122; marginalized, 136, 140; and antisemitism, 144; and postwar period, 216, 219, 224

Diem, Hermann, 206, 211, 295 (n. 20)

Dinter, Artur, 14

Doehring, Bruno, 114

Dohrmann, Franz, 246 (n. 53)

Dresden: bombing of, 221

Dürer, Albrecht, 75

Dungs, Heinz, 59

Easter: German Christian version, 48, 163

Ehmann (vicar), 132. *See also* Women

Ehrenberg, Hans, 35, 93. *See also* Aryan Paragraph; Non-Aryan Christians

Elisabeth (mother of John the Baptist), 155

Engelke, Fritz: on church as feminine, 193, 194, 198

Epp, Franz Ritter von, 180

*Erbpflege und Christentum*, 41. *See also* Eugenics

Ericksen, Robert P., 13

Eschweiler, Carl, 116

Ethnic Germans (*Volksdeutsche*): idealized by German Christians, 51–54. *See also* Staedel, Wilhelm

Eucharist: debates about, 45. *See also* Communion

Eugenics: German Christian response to, 38–43, 196

Euthanasia program, 217; German Christian response to, 38–43

Evangelischer Bund. *See* Protestant League

*Evangelisches Feldgesangbuch*. *See* Protestant soldier's songbook

*Evangelium im Dritten Reich* (The gospel in the Third Reich), 174, 197; on race, 29; on manliness, 70, 75; on church music, 79, 166; woman editor of, 119

*Das Evangelium Johannes deutsch*, 161–62. *See also* Weidemann, Heinz

Fahrenhorst, Wilhelm: Protestant League and, 46, 114; German Christian sympathies, 115

Fellowship of Work for Religious Peace (Arbeitsgemeinschaft für den religiösen Frieden), 108

Fiebig, Walter, 237 (n. 9); wartime activities, 59; postwar, 208, 210, 215, 225; denies knowledge of concentration camps, 221, 297 (n. 63)

(n. 34); suspension of non-Aryan clergy, 90

John the Baptist, 155

Joseph (father of Jesus), 155, 163

Judaism: relationship to Christianity, 21, 142–43. *See also* Jews

Katz, Steven T., 9

Kerrl, Hanns: as minister of church affairs, 18, 47, 53, 95, 127; relations with German Christians, 19, 55; on Nazism, 44, 117; antisemitism, 159

Kessel, Friedrich, 51

Kinder, Christian: German Christian leader, 18, 130; hostility toward theology, 46, 174; leadership struggles, 119–20; on Old Testament, 145

Kirchengeschichtliche Arbeitsgemeinschaft Minden (Working Group for Church History), 14, 52, 136, 217. *See also* Wentz, Karl

*Kirchenkampf. See* Church struggle

Kisting, Dörthe, 137–38

Kittel, Gerhard, 174, 237 (n. 9)

Kleist, Paul, 297 (n. 64)

Knak, Siegfried, 31. *See also* Overseas missionaries

Koonz, Claudia, 121

Kotzde-Kottenrodt, Wilhelm, 260 (n. 22), 261 (n. 23)

Krause, Reinhold, 78, 156, 167, 254 (n. 24); role in Sports Palace rally, 17, 32, 103, 126, 166; and Aryan Paragraph, 89; and Jews, 142; on Old Testament, 145; on Paul, 158; and church music, 165; opposition to theology, 173

Kristallnacht pogrom, 26, 90, 97, 149, 219

Krummacher, Gottfried A., 129, 269 (n. 35)

Kube, Wilhelm, 5, 7, 31

Kwami (pastor from Togo), 29–30, 222

League for the Free People's Church (Bund Freier Volkskirche), 34

League of German Christians, 19

League of German Girls (Bund deutscher Mädel), 200; compared to neutrals in church, 272 (n. 91)

League of the Protestant People's Church, 225

Leffler, Siegfried, 5, 19, 117, 118, 137, 172, 181; and national church, 103, 106, 112; and anti-Jewish institute, 149; postwar recanting, 222

Leutheuser, Julius, 5, 19, 50, 137, 152; death, 49; national church and, 103, 104

*Lexikon der Juden in der Musik* (Encyclopedia of Jews in Music), 99. *See also* Church musicians

Liebe-Harkort, Eleanor, 128–29, 206; support of Aryan Paragraph, 90

*Lieder der kommenden Kirche*, 169. *See also* Weidemann, Heinz

*Lieder für Gottesfeiern*, 168

Lönnies, Klara. *See* Schlossmann-Lönnies, Klara

Loerzer, Fritz, 125

Lonicer, Heinrich, 58, 246 (nn. 52, 53, 55)

Lord's Prayer, 49, 216; as supra-confessional ritual, 104

Lord's Supper. *See* Communion

Ludendorff, Erich, 14

Ludendorff, Mathilde, 14

Ludwigsburg (internment camp), 222

Lübeck: German Christians in, 97. *See also* Balzer, Erwin

Luke: Gospel of, 155

Stab-in-the-back myth, 66, 176. *See also* World War I
Staedel, Wilhelm, 52, 53, 197, 214, 215, 216, 217, 221; and postwar racism, 227–28, 275 (n. 30). *See also* Siebenbürger Saxons
Stapel, Wilhelm, 68
Steinberg, Jonathan, 9
Sterilization Law, 40–41; Catholic response to, 116. *See also* Eugenics; Euthanasia program
Sting, Heinz, 226
Storm troopers, 65, 70, 132, 166, 180, 181, 195, 198, 201, 216; anti-Christian song, 241 (n. 73)
Strasser, Gregor, 271 (n. 73)
Streicher, Julius, 39, 128
Student Fighting League of German Christians, 67, 179
*Der Stürmer*, 39, 148, 199
Stuttgart Declaration of Guilt, 208–9
Supraconfessionalism. *See* Catholics; National church
Swastika, 117, 160

Tal, Uriel, 35
Talmud, 150
Tausch, Friedrich, 156, 182
Ten Commandments, 137, 147
Themel, Karl, 196
Theological faculties, 174; presence of German Christians in, 176–77
Thirty Years' War, 104
Thuringia: German Christians in, 102–3, 107, 118, 149, 161, 184, 210, 259 (n. 3). *See also* Leffler, Siegfried; National Church Union
Transylvania: ethnic Germans in, 52, 197, 214
Tügel, Franz, 249 (n. 26)

Ustasa movement, 9

Veigel, Fritz, 147
Versailles, Treaty of, 48, 65, 158, 209
*Völkisch* movement: as German Christian precursors, 28, 144, 234 (n. 40)
*Volksdeutsche. See* Ethnic Germans
*Volkskirche* (people's church), 4, 185; origins of idea, 10–11, 233 (n. 26); language of, 174
Volkskirchenbewegung Deutsche Christen (People's Church Movement of German Christians), 210
Volkskirchenbewegung Freier Christen, 226
*Das Volkstestament* (the people's testament), 162–63, 279 (n. 101)
*Volkstrauertag* (Day of Mourning), 78

Wagner, Richard, 155, 159
War: as source of religious unity, 106–7; opportunity for German Christian women, 135; fulfillment of German Christian goals, 192–93, 200–205
Wars of Liberation, 183
Weddings. *See* Church weddings
Weidemann, Heinz, 137; and anti-Jewish church, 26, 206; and non-Aryans, 98; version of Gospel of John, 161–62; building churches, 164, 280 (n. 111); purging hymns, 169, 171; anticlericalism, 180; denazification, 222
Wentz, Karl, 57, 59, 137, 201. *See also* Kirchengeschichtliche Arbeitsgemeinschaft; Schlachtensee Circle
Werdermann, Hermann, 149
Werner, Friedrich, 196; and non-Aryans, 91, 99

Wessel, Horst, 75; church named for, 164, 222

Wessel, Ingeborg, 75

Wessel, Ludwig, 75

Weyl, Josef, 166

Wiedemann, Miss (editor): invisibility as woman, 119–20

Wieneke, Friedrich: German Christian chronicler, 28–29, 136, 235 (n. 54); on race, 34, 86

Winkel, Erich, 177

Wohlert, Mathilde, 119

Woike, Fritz, 251 (n. 65)

Women: as German Christian mothers, 120–24; as wives, 124–25; corresponding with Reich bishop, 125–27; as religious conscience, 125–29; role in church struggle, 130–31, 141, 249 (n. 36); as German Christian office holders, 132–35; as secretaries, 134; viewed as liability, 135–41; church compared to, 193–94; Hitler's view of, 198–99; church membership of, 200; replacing men, 202; in postwar, 216. *See also* German Christian movement: women in

Women's Service (Frauendienst), 129

World War I, 63, 65, 158. *See also* Stab-in-the-back myth; Versailles, Treaty of

Württemberg: denazification of church, 210, 211, 294 (n. 11); response to Sports Palace rally, 235 (n. 49), 251 (n. 51)

Wurm, Theophil, 113, 208

Zöllner, Wilhelm, 172